# On Paper

# On Paper

*The Everything of Its
Two-Thousand-Year History*

Nicholas A. Basbanes

ALFRED A. KNOPF
*New York*
2013

THIS IS A BORZOI BOOK
PUBLISHED BY ALFRED A. KNOPF

Copyright © 2013 by Nicholas A. Basbanes

All rights reserved. Published in the United States by Alfred A. Knopf,
a division of Random House LLC, New York,
and in Canada by Random House of Canada Limited, Toronto,
Penguin Random House Companies.
www.aaknopf.com

Knopf, Borzoi Books, and the colophon are registered trademarks
of Random House LLC.

Library of Congress Cataloging-in-Publication Data
Basbanes, Nicholas A., [date]
On paper : the everything of its two-thousand-year history /
Nicholas A. Basbanes.
p.     cm.
Includes bibliographical references.
ISBN 978-0-307-26642-2
1. Paper—History. 2. Papermaking—History.
3. Paper industry—History. I. Title.
Z247.B34 2013
676.09—dc23
2012050267

Jacket design by Jason Booher
Book design by Cassandra J. Pappas

Manufactured in the United States of America
First Edition

**FOR CONNIE**

*My wife and companion on the paper trail,*
*With love and gratitude*

# Contents

# Illustrations

# *Preface*

As a writer of nonfiction, I have devoted a good deal of my life to the study of books in every conceivable context, so a work now on the stuff of transmission itself should come as no surprise to anyone. But in the end, these venerable containers of shared wisdom were merely the launching pad for what became a far wider and much deeper adventure of inquiry, one that still has me turning up stories and ideas that in a world without limits would demand inclusion in these pages—it is that compelling a subject.

Beyond paper's obvious utility as a writing surface, its invention in China during the early years of the modern era made possible the introduction of printing, with the first known devices being stamps made from carved wooden blocks, a process known today as xylography (literally, writing with wood). Not long after the Arab world learned to make paper from the Chinese in the eighth century, the Middle East became a center of intellectual energy, with paper providing the ideal means of recording the thoughts and calculations of Islamic scholars and mathematicians. Making its first toehold in Europe by way of Spain late in the eleventh century, the process moved in the thirteenth to Italy, which became, at about the same time, the cradle of what in later years would be known as the Renaissance. From Europe it made its way to North America and the rest of the inhabited world.

The inexorable spread of this versatile material has been told in bits and pieces by a number of paper specialists whose works are thoroughly referenced in my bibliography. While I am certainly mindful of the chronological sweep of this ubiquitous product, a conventional timeline of its discovery and adoption is not the central thrust of this book, even though one of the goals of Part I is nonetheless to provide a selective overview of its glorious history.

Instead, my driving interest points more to the *idea* of paper, one that certainly takes in the twin notions of medium and message but that also examines its indispensability as a tool of flexibility and function. The laser physicist and master origami folder Robert Lang, whom you will meet in Chapter 15, lives by the credo that "anything is possible in origami," which can pretty much be said about paper itself. Paper is light, absorbent, strong, plentiful, and portable; you can fold it, mail it, coat it with wax and waterproof it, wrap gunpowder or tobacco in it, boil tea in it. We have used paper in abundance to record our history, make our laws, conduct our business, correspond with our loved ones, decorate our walls, and establish our identities.

When it comes to pure utility, modern hygienic practice is unimaginable without paper; when used as currency, people will move heaven and earth to possess it. In realms of the intellect, every manner of scientific inquiry begins as a nonverbal spark in the mind, and more often than not that first burst of perception is visualized more fully on a sheet of paper. When it's used as an instrument of the generative process, innovators of every persuasion can sketch and tinker away on it at will, design buildings and machines on it, compose music and create poetry on it. As a "paper revolution" swept through Europe in the eighteenth century, architects and engineers transformed the manner and the means of the living landscape. The Industrial Revolution in particular is hard to conceive of without its precisely reproduced instruction sheets to guide assembly crews in their various assignments.

The word *virtual* has become, in the computer age, one way of describing a simulated reality that exists quite apart from the concrete world, an alternative existence that is not just a copy but a substitute for the real thing. In the expression of imagery, there is nothing at all new about the concept; people have endeavored to create likenesses of themselves and their surroundings for millennia, with examples to be found in cave paintings prepared thousands of years ago, during the last ice age, many of them impressive to this day for their artistry and execution. By no means unique in this regard, paper has nonetheless been around for centuries, nobly fulfilling that function.

When the seventeenth-century patron of the arts Cassiano dal Pozzo set out to assemble a comprehensive collection of visual knowledge, he commissioned a number of prominent artists to make what turned out to be seven thousand watercolors, drawings, and prints in fields that included botany, art, architecture, geology, zoology, and ornithology. Dispersed today among four major institutional collections, what was arguably the world's first virtual library is known now as the Paper Museum. In more recent times, lithography and photography—the words literally mean "writing with stone" and "writing with light"— used paper as the surface of choice to create and distribute surrogate images.

As a force in shaping historical events, paper rarely draws attention to itself, yet its role is evident to varying degrees in scenario after scenario. One telling case in point is the introduction of human flight during the eighteenth century in France, when the Montgolfier brothers used several layers of paper made in the family mill to line the inner skin of the world's first hot-air balloon. Another example is the American Revolution; historians generally agree that the run-up to the Battles of Lexington and Concord can be said to have begun with the Stamp Act of 1765, which was all about taxing the many ways colonists had come to rely on paper documents in their daily lives. A century later, the refusal of Hindu and Muslim mercenary soldiers in the employ of the British East India Company to bite open paper cartridges greased with animal fat sparked a bloody insurrection known variously today as the Sepoy Mutiny and the First War of Indian Independence.

A roll call of political scandals, international incidents, and sensational trials to have paper documents at some point play a crucial role in the unfolding of events would have to include the Dreyfus affair of the 1890s and early 1900s, involving a forged memorandum known as the *bordereau;* America's entry into World War I, with the Zimmermann Telegram; the Alger Hiss spy case of the late 1940s, which involved the damning testimony of Whittaker Chambers regarding the notorious Pumpkin Papers; the trial of Julius and Ethel Rosenberg in 1953, with its purloined sketch of a nuclear implosion device that was crucial in sending both off to the electric chair; and Watergate, precipitated by Daniel Ellsberg's brazen release in 1971 of the Pentagon Papers. And while the influence of computers is everywhere apparent, it is instructive to note that the earliest machines of any functional significance processed their data on punched paper cards, and that the progenitor of all electronic printing devices—the universal stock ticker—used narrow spools of newsprint to give real-time readouts of financial transactions, revolutionizing forever the way business would be conducted on Wall Street.

Not only are we awash in a world of paper; we are awash in a world of paper clichés. George W. Bush defeated Al Gore in 2000 by a "paper thin" margin, the deceit that surrounded the Enron fiasco was built on a "tissue of lies," and the fragile structure that subsequently collapsed was a "house of cards." To beat someone to a "pulp" is to inflict appalling injury. To "map out" a plan for something is to come up with a specific course of action. Day in and day out, we are mired in "red tape," a corollary of being "buried under a mountain of paper," while a "paper tiger" is either a wimp or a weakling or a fraud, take your pick. I readily admit to playing with a few of them in this book—something being "not worth the paper it is printed on" was irresistible, and it provided the premise for the chapter I call "Face Value."

At the very time I was completing the first draft of this manuscript, the Boston Red Sox—a team I have been following obsessively since my father took me to Fenway Park for the first time in 1953—finished the most spectacular flop in the history of Major League Baseball, squandering a seemingly insurmountable lead of nine games with less than a month to go in the 2011 season and finishing entirely out of the playoffs. Making their collapse doubly painful were predictions made at the start of the season that, with fifteen highly paid All-Stars in the lineup, Boston was by far the best team to take the field that year. *Sports Illustrated* had picked the Red Sox to win one hundred games and handily dispatch the San Francisco Giants in the World Series; even seasoned sportswriters in New York, home of the archrival Yankees, were impressed by their prospects for a championship.

"I can see why people are talking about our going back to the World Series," one of those highly paid Red Sox, J. D. Drew, had told Dan Shaughnessy, the estimable baseball columnist for the *Boston Globe,* as opening day drew near in April. "On paper, we have that kind of team." It was that blasé comment of presumed inevitability—all of it worked out abstractly on an imaginary notation pad—that gave Shaughnessy reason to pause and comment forebodingly, with uncanny prescience, "But it never plays out the way it does on paper, does it?"

At a meeting in Hanoi in June 2012, American secretary of defense Leon Panetta presented to Vietnamese minister of national defense Phung Quang Thanh a small maroon diary taken from a fallen North Vietnamese soldier by a U.S. Marine in 1966. In return, Thanh turned over to Panetta a passel of personal letters removed from the body of Army sergeant Steve Flaherty of the 101st Airborne Division after he was killed in action in 1969. The *Washington Post* summed up the artifact exchange by noting that these two relics, from a time when the two countries "were bitter enemies," had in an instant become "symbols of the evolving U.S.-Vietnamese relationship"—and each was recorded on otherwise unremarkable sheets of paper.

My research model for this book has been fairly straightforward, and should be apparent in each chapter. I traveled in China along the Burma Road, because Old China is where the story begins, and I proceeded in due course to Japan, because that was the only place where I could meet with a Living National Treasure papermaker. I spent seven months trying to get a tour of the National Security Agency, in Fort Meade, Maryland, because the cryptologists there pulp one hundred million ultrasecret documents a year (give or take) and send them off for recycled use as pizza boxes and egg cartons. I spent two days at the Crane Paper mill, in Western Massachusetts, because, as Willie Sutton is purported to have famously said, "that's where the money is"—or, more to the point, that is where all the paper for American currency is made. Since the idea of "disposability" is very much a paper theme, too, the same goes for a Kimberly-Clark mill in Connecticut, where close to a million boxes of Kleenex tissue, and as many rolls of Scott kitchen towels, are made every day. If there's a common thread to be discerned, it is what Graham Greene sagely called, in one of his novels, "the human factor."

A few years ago, the British Association of Paper Historians noted in a description of its activities that there are something on the order of twenty thousand commercial uses of paper in the world today, and that the organization's members are interested in each and every one of them. Rest easy, dear reader: I am not about to explore twenty thousand different uses of paper here. But if that claim is accurate—and one Pennsylvania company you will meet in Chapter 17 alone has a line of one thousand different products for its output—then the paper-less society we hear being bandied about so much today may not be as imminent as some people suggest. The words of the great Fats Waller seem especially relevant on this point: "One never knows, do one?"

# Part 1

*Statue of the poet Xue Tao (768–831), China's first female papermaker, in the city of Chengdu.*

# I

## Common Bond

The Emperor's Mint then is in this same City of Cambulac, and the way it is wrought is such that you might say he hath the Secret of Alchemy in perfection, and you would be right! For he makes his money after this fashion. He makes them take the bark of a certain tree, in fact of the Mulberry Tree, the leaves of which are the food of the silkworms—these trees being so numerous that whole districts are full of them. What they take is a certain fine white bast or skin which lies between the wood of the tree and the thick outer bark, and this they make into something resembling sheets of paper, but black. When these sheets have been prepared they are cut up into pieces of different sizes.
　　　　　　　　—Marco Polo, *The Travels of Marco Polo*, c. 1298

Paper is a tenacious substance, which can be cut and torn, so as to resemble, and almost rival the skin of any animal, or the leaf of vegetables, and the like works of nature; being neither brittle like glass, nor woven like cloth, but having fibres, and not distinct threads, just as natural substances, so that scarcely any thing similar can be found amongst artificial substances, and it is absolutely singular. And in artificial works we should certainly prefer those which approach the nearest to an imitation of nature, or, on the other hand, powerfully govern and change her course.
　　　　　　　　—Sir Francis Bacon, *Novum Organum Scientiarum*,
　　　　　　　　Book II (Aphorism 31), 1620

BEFORE EMBARKING on a relentless circumnavigation of the globe about fifteen hundred years ago, the technique for making paper was a carefully guarded proprietary craft, its applications so varied and so practical that the Chinese esteem it today as one of their four outstanding inventions of antiquity. In his *Novum Organum Scientiarum*

("The New Instrument of Science"), Sir Francis Bacon proposed that the three other technological milestones from that elite group—gunpowder, printing, and the magnetic compass—had "changed the whole face and state of things throughout the world" to the degree that "no empire, no sect, no star seems to have exerted greater power and influence in human affairs than these mechanical discoveries." While Sir Francis did not include paper in his short list of world-altering inventions, he did anoint it a "singular instance of art," another way of saying, essentially, that it was unique.

Bacon had no inkling, however, about how paper had first come into being, where it had originated, or how it had made its way from one country to another over the previous millennium; "merely by chance" is the neat phrase he used for the genesis of "all the most noble discoveries." What Bacon also failed to note—perhaps because it was as obvious in the seventeenth century as it is today—is that without paper, there would have been no printing, one of many instances in which scholars have lumped the pair together as allied technical advancements, with paper usually getting the shorter shrift of the two, especially in the impact they have had on the diffusion of culture.

The long list of writing surfaces used over the centuries includes stone, cured animal skins, woven cloth, flattened metal sheets, peeled tree bark, dried animal bones, seashells, and shards of pottery. In parts of India and Southeast Asia, entire libraries were incised on palm leaves and coconut husks; the Inca of Peru tied intricate knots in narrow cords known as *khipu* to keep track of their crops and record their mysterious calculations. In Egypt, scrolls fashioned from thinly sliced sections of a certain marsh reed were coveted throughout the Mediterranean for their lightness and flexibility, and for four thousand years that plant, papyrus, was the gold standard of recording surfaces. But in terms of longevity, pride of place belongs to clay, next to water the most productive natural resource in the region of the Middle East where writing was firmly established around 3000 B.C., and useful in ways that went well beyond the recording of information.

Named Mesopotamia by the ancient Greeks—the neologism translates as "Land Between the Rivers"—the flat terrain often called the "Cradle of Civilization" and the "Fertile Crescent" is bounded by the Tigris River to the east and the Euphrates to the west. It was home in ancient times to a succession of resourceful inhabitants that included

Sumerians, Assyrians, Akkadians, Hittites, Babylonians, Parthians, and Persians. In the absence of building stones and forests, the rich alluvial soil became vital to their quality of life. Though soft and pliable when wet, clay has elements that make it remarkably strong and resistant to deterioration when hardened by intense heat. Mixed with water and straw, the compound was formed into bricks that were used to build the world's first cities; turned by potters into containers, it was used for food storage and cooking. And with the development of writing, it was shaped into moist little mounds upon which scribes could record pictographs and letters with a reed stylus or sharp stick. Whether fired in kilns or baked beneath the scorching sun, these small tablets have proven remarkably durable; the first linguists to decipher them called the distinctive figures still visible on their surface "cuneiform," from the Latin for "wedge-shaped."

Despite their bulk, official correspondence was often relayed by courier in this manner, an example being an archive of diplomatic letters found at Tel el-Amarna, in Upper Egypt, in the nineteenth century, dating to about 1350 B.C. and mostly written in Akkadian cuneiform. The world's first recorded narrative poem, *The Epic of Gilgamesh,* written a thousand years before Homer composed the *Iliad,* comes to us entirely by way of these tablets, too, and suggests by its very premise the starkness of the Mesopotamian landscape and the reliance on clay. In their first adventure together, the Sumerian king Gilgamesh and his ferocious sidekick Enkidu travel north to the Cedar Forest of Lebanon to plunder precious trees and float them down the Euphrates River to Uruk, where the finest specimens could be used for a glorious gate. As a metaphor that spans the millennia, it seems doubly significant that the nuclear ingredient of the microchip—by common consent the recording medium of the foreseeable future—is metallurgical-grade silicon, an element derived from purified sand and, like its molecular cousin clay, a substance found thick on the ground throughout the world.

Several centuries before the invention of paper, the Chinese philosopher Mozi, also known as Mo Tzu (470–391 B.C.), wrote that the "sources of our knowledge lie in what is written on bamboo and silk, what is engraved on metal and stone, and what is cut on vessels to be handed down to posterity." A similar sentiment would be expressed five hundred years later by Gaius Plinius Secundus (A.D. 24–79), the Roman scholar known as Pliny the Elder, who included a lengthy discussion of papyrus in his monumental *Natural History*, the detailed commentary driven by his firm belief that "human civilization depends, at the most for its life, and certainly for its memory," on the versatile marsh reed.

Papyrus grew so plentifully along the Nile that it found a multitude of functions, with medicine, clothing, footwear, furniture, watercraft, nutrition, cordage, and sacred ornamentation among those at the forefront. In the Old Testament, strands of the plant (called the bulrush in the King James version of the Bible) are used to weave a getaway "ark" for the baby Moses; when the infant's improvised lifeboat comes to rest, it is a thicket of bulrushes that provides safe haven. Writing in the fifth century B.C., the Greek historian Herodotus mentioned the making of sails and rope from papyrus, and he reported that the lower parts of the plant not used for writing sheets could be roasted and consumed as food. Theophrastus, a successor of Aristotle at the Lyceum, reported how Egyptians "chew the papyrus stalk raw, boiled, or baked; they swallow its juice and spit out the pulp."

Given the close attention Pliny paid in his *Natural History* to agriculture and the bounties of systematic cultivation, there is little doubt that he would have been captivated by the whole concept of papermaking, if only for the ramifications it had for the propagation of human achievement. Ever the inquisitive thinker—and a voracious reader who never went anywhere without a wagonload of learned scrolls in tow, according to his nephew and biographer, Pliny the Younger—he was enticed, while sailing in the Bay of Naples with the Roman fleet in A.D. 79, to go ashore at Stabiae to see firsthand the chaos resulting from the volcanic eruption of Mount Vesuvius, and he died from what were believed at the time to be the effects of toxic fumes, but was more likely a heart attack.

By sheer coincidence, the most significant cache of papyrus scrolls to survive outside of Egypt comes from Herculaneum, not far from where Pliny drew his last breath—some seventeen hundred of them were discovered in the petrified ashes of a villa that had once been the summer retreat of Julius Caesar's father-in-law. When the library of Lucius Calpurnius Piso was excavated in the early eighteenth century—the opulent house where the carbonized scrolls were found is known today as the Villa dei Papiri—the once sacred reed had virtually disappeared from Egypt, no longer deemed of any practical use, no longer harvested for the making of writing sheets, nor for the many other functions it had once facilitated so nobly.

In its place was paper, which by the eighteenth century was being made in mills that had opened up throughout Europe and were just being established in North America. In contrast to the explosive manner in which the Internet has galloped its way from continent to continent over just a few recent decades, paper took root methodically, one country at a time. Yet, as "paradigm shifts" go, it was monumental, offering a medium of cultural transmission that was supple, convenient, inexpensive, highly mobile, simple to make once the rudiments were understood, and suited to hundreds of other applications, with writing being just the most far-reaching.

Unlike so many other landmark breakthroughs—be it the invention of the wheel, the methods for making glass, the smelting of bronze or iron—we know today with some degree of certainty when paper was first made, and where it emerged. The year traditionally given by the Chinese is A.D. 105, when an official in the Imperial Court of the emperor Ho Ti, responsible for making tools and weapons, a man named Cai Lun, announced the invention in a formal report and outlined specific instructions for its manufacture. Writing about this key achievement three hundred years later, the official historian of the Han Dynasty, Fan Ye, declared that Cai Lun (until recently spelled Tsai Lun in the West) had "initiated the idea of making paper from the bark of trees, hemp, old rags, and fishing nets," and that once perfected, the process was "in use everywhere."

Today, statues of Cai Lun are found in museums and public buildings throughout China, his image printed on postage stamps, his name revered by many millions of schoolchildren, even though archaeological finds from the past hundred years strongly suggest that papermaking was practiced several centuries before he introduced it at court. Some of the most persuasive evidence for an earlier provenance comes from excavations in the early years of the twentieth century by the British explorer Sir Aurel Stein along the Silk Road, the network of caravan routes that for close to two thousand years linked China and Europe. Stein is best known for the spectacular find of fifty thousand scrolls and artworks he recovered from the Caves of the Thousand Buddhas at the Dunhuang grottoes, also called the Mogao Caves and once a booming oasis in the Gobi Desert in Gansu Province.

*Detail of woodblock frontispiece, from* the Diamond Sutra, *A.D. 868, the world's earliest dated printed book, on handmade paper.*

Among the treasures Stein removed to England was a copy of the *Diamond Sutra* of the Chinese Tang Dynasty from A.D. 868, appearing more than five hundred years before Johannes Gutenberg introduced movable metal type in Europe, making it the earliest printed book on record to bear an identifiable date. A number of letters written on paper, which Stein found in the ruins of a watchtower in the Great Wall of China, have been dated more than seven hundred years earlier than that, to about A.D. 150. In an exhaustive history of Chinese paper published in 1985, the distinguished University of Chicago historian Tsien Tsuen-Hsuin suggested that the oldest paper specimens extant today are fragments discovered in 1957 in a tomb in Shaanxi Province, dating to about 140 B.C. Early examples from other locations have been identified as well, increasing the near certainty that the process evolved over several centuries.

Significantly, one of the first Chinese words for paper, *chih,* was defined in an early lexicon as "a mat of refuse fibers." While not correct in every respect, the description does provide a context for what paper is, and what it is not. Many manufacturers today certainly do mix discarded rags and "recovered" papers into their pulp, and paper may well be the first industrial product to include recycled materials on a significant level, but many other fiber sources often find their way into the final product, ones that are anything but disposable scraps. A more accurate definition might describe paper as a composite of water and pulverized cellulose fragments screened through a sieve and dried into a flat film. Using that description, there is a mat, and there are fibers—but there also is $H_2O$, which is vital to its composition.

Although the word *paper* derives from papyrus, the two materials have very little in common other than their pliable texture and their dependence on a vegetative source. The sixth-century Roman statesman and writer Cassiodorus praised papyrus for having been "a faithful witness of human deeds" and "the enemy of oblivion," but when viewed dispassionately as a material object, it remained, in his words, nothing more than "the snowy pith of a green plant." Phrased less elegantly, papyrus sheets were a lamination of strips sliced from the spongy stalk of a triangular-shaped marsh reed that sometimes grew to twenty feet in height or even more. Once cut and dried, the sections suitable for writing were placed in two layers, at right angles to each other. They were then moistened, flattened under pressure, and smoothed into sheets that were pasted end-to-end and spooled onto compact rolls.

Pliny suggested that it was the muddy properties of Nile River water that made the strips adhere to one another, but modern botanists believe it was chemicals released in the papyrus plant itself that enabled them to attach and form single sheets. Because the process worked only with freshly harvested stalks, production of papyrus rolls was limited to the few regions of the world where the plant grew—and more often than not by the very riverbanks where it was harvested—which is why the Egyptians were able to control its exportation for many hundreds of years, and even use it as an occasional bargaining chip in dealings with other nations. In one notorious embargo from antiquity, shipments were shut off to the city-state of Pergamum, in Asia Minor, home of a library that was regarded in Hellenistic times as a serious rival to the one in Alexandria, prompting the use of split sheepskin as an alternative resource. Thus was coined the word *parchment,* derived from the Latin for "from Pergamum."

The first Chinese papers, as Fen He had indicated, were made from a blend of bast—the soft, fibrous material scooped out of the inner bark of trees—and old fishnets, cloth scraps, and hemp gathered from frayed rope. According to Cai Lun's instructions, the combined ingredients were washed, soaked, beaten to a fine pulp with a wooden mallet, then placed in a vat of pure water and vigorously stirred, making sure that the filaments remained in a state of suspension. Next, a scoop of the slurry was ladled evenly over a screen of coarsely woven cloth that had been stretched taut within a four-sided bamboo frame—what we in the United States call a mold, or mould in British parlance—and suspended between a brace of poles.

As excess liquid drained out from below and the mat began to dry, mirabile dictu, each layer of interlocking fibers left behind in the mesh was transformed into a thin sheet of paper. Over time, spoons were abandoned and molds were dipped directly into the vats, and as the know-how spread throughout the world, and techniques were modified to suit individual needs, other types of vegetation were tried—everything from cooked straw and boiled banana peels to crushed walnut shells and mounds of dried seaweed. As demand for paper outpaced the capacity for supply, the quest for fiber focused more aggressively on mountains of cotton and linen rags, and in our own time on forests teeming with cellulose-rich trees. What has not changed at all over this span, however, are the three fundamentals of the process that were there at the very beginning and remain indispensable to it now: clean water, cellulose fiber, and a screen mold.

Whether the inspiration to make the first sheet came from careful experimentation or whether it was the result of a fortuitous fluke—some bright tinkerer, perhaps, perceiving possibilities in patches of disintegrating plant matter coagulating by the side of a stream—is anyone's guess. But what the Chinese had discovered—and on this point there is no ambiguity—was a type of molecular cohesion distinctive to all vegetative matter and known to modern chemists as hydrogen bonding. In the simplest of terms, hydrogen bonding is an oddity of nature that allows properly macerated and matted cellulose fibers to attach as if drawn to one another by a magnet, and this is fundamental to the formation of paper sheets. What makes this process possible is the presence in cellulose of individual chemical units known as hydroxyl groups, meaning that many of the hydrogen atoms and oxygen atoms are paired together structurally in a way that permits them to act as single entities.

When applied specifically to papermaking, some of the fiber-to-fiber hydrogen bonds take the additional step of replacing fiber-to-water hydrogen bonds as the pulp dries. One of many definitions put forth by chemists is that paper is a "sheet-like material that is formed from individualized fibers by the removal of water." Hydrogen bonding was not fully articulated until the twentieth century, but its characteristics were evident enough to the Chinese, who initiated a period of human dependence that has continued well into the third millennium.

As a writing surface, paper arrived at a moment in time when a new medium was urgently required by a people who for many centuries had scrupulously recorded every manner of religious, literary, artistic, social, bureaucratic, and business detail on a variety of materials, each of which had the drawback of being either too cumbersome to handle or, in the instance of silk, much too expensive to produce in great quantity. To fashion a book from bamboo, a worker would slice narrow strips from the skin of the plant and fastened them together with twine. The convention of writing Chinese characters vertically—top to bottom, not side to side—developed from restrictions imposed by the dimensions of these strips, known as "slips" to scholars. To inscribe characters on solid surfaces, knives, sticks, and chisels were employed, but it was the introduction of the animal-hair brush in around 250 B.C. that allowed for the direct application of ink and paint to flat surfaces, and the brush was the writing instrument of choice when paper arrived.

Bamboo documents were stored in spacious warehouses that were crammed to bursting, prompting Mozi to complain that, while certainly essential—and he was writing less than a hundred years after Confucius—the "books that belong to the scholars of the world of the present day are too many to be conveyed." Qin Shi Huang, the emperor who undertook the building of the Great Wall in the third century B.C. and is credited with unifying China, is said to have read through 120 pounds of governmental reports each day, all of them routinely hauled before him for executive action.

One of the most unusual libraries ever constructed—it is known today as the Mountain of Stone Scriptures—is a repository of seven thousand granite stelae carved on Fangshan Mountain, outside Beijing. Begun in 605, during the Sui Dynasty—fully five hundred years *after* the formal announcement of paper—it was maintained through 1091, well into the Ming Dynasty, a span of more than five centuries. As a body of work, the stones contain 105 Buddhist scriptures, known as sutras—more than four million words, all told—making it the only complete set of texts of the Buddhist canon carved on stone to survive in China. A full set of paper rubbings taken of the inscriptions is preserved today in the Guangji Temple, in Beijing.

The earliest known essay to consider the technology of papermaking is to be found in *Wen Fang Ssu Phu,* a general discussion of calligraphy compiled in the tenth century by Su I-Chien, a scholar from the first Sung Dynasty. Known today as the Four Treasures of the Scholar's Study—the four treasures being brush, ink, inkstone, and paper—the treatise included a section on paper that is enlivened by anecdotes and literary references from earlier periods. Su told of one ambitious project in which the hold of a ship was converted into a massive vat to make premium-quality sheets for use as panoramic paintings, some of them fifty feet in length. Coordinating their movements to the rhythmic beat of a drum, fifty workers lifted and agitated a giant mold in unison. To achieve a smooth consistency, the team did not brush the wet mat on the side of a heated wall to dry, as would otherwise have been customary, but gently moved the freshly formed sheets over the embers of an open fire while they were still in the frame.

The low cost and flexibility of paper made it ideally suited to the making of fans, umbrellas, lanterns, and kites, and its usefulness in maintaining personal hygiene—disposable toilet paper made from low-grade straw was another Chinese idea—quickly gained in popularity. In mountainous terrain, warriors from the ninth century on wore a form of body armor made of layered paper that had the advantage of being light and resistant to rust. The Venetian merchant Marco Polo told how the Chinese fabricated "very fine summer clothing" from "stuffs of the bark of certain trees." He also described the burning of paper effigies at funerals and reported how the bereaved would "take representations of things cut out of cotton-paper"—images of horses, servants, camels, armor, even fake money—"and these things they put on the fire along with the corpse so that they are all burnt with it."

In the fall of 2007, I joined a small group of paper historians from the United States, Britain, and Denmark as they traveled through remote sections of southwestern China, eager to see for myself how this phenomenon of human resourcefulness that had begun in that part of the world continues to be made in much the same way as when it was first developed, two thousand years ago. We started out along the old Burma Road in Yunnan Province, an agricultural region that provides food for the nation's 1.3 billion people and minerals for its factories. Situated in the foothills of the Himalayas, Kunming, the provincial capital, was the destination during World War II of American pilots "flying the hump" over the treacherous mountains, from bases in India, with supplies for Chiang Kai-shek's nationalist troops. Today a subtropical metropolis of 6.2 million people, the city's downtown streets and avenues are lined with willow trees, camellias, azaleas, and magnolias. Bright neon signs and honking horns greet throngs of people eager to enjoy the bounties of an emerging superpower, many of them spending money freely at Walmart superstores, others waiting in long lines for hamburgers at McDonald's and fried chicken at KFC restaurants.

But outside the municipal limits, the landscape changes dramatically, and the clogged air of inner-city pollution gives way to azure skies and breathtaking vistas. One historian of China's "urban revolution" has called the nation's industrial boom "an age of unprecedented growth and societal transformation," but many of the old ways still predominate in the mountains of Yunnan, where twisting roads make their way through a rugged countryside of terraced hillsides, and where carefully manicured fields are worked by teams of water buffalo.

As in the United States, where economic development started on the Atlantic seaboard and spread inward, industrialization in China has been following a similar "go west" pattern, beginning along the coastal provinces of the Pacific and moving steadily toward the borders in Central Asia. In ancient times, Yunnan was an important gateway on the southern leg of the legendary Silk Road; aptly, the most evident sign of change out there these days is a modern highway being carved through the mountains, one section of a massive network of road construction that soon will allow convoys of semitrucks to travel nonstop from Beijing to Mumbai on an expressway of three thousand miles.

During the 1920s and '30s, the Austrian-born botanist Joseph Rock wrote a series of essays for *National Geographic* magazine about life in southwest China, taking special note of the flora, native tribes, and languages of the region. Based in the ancient city of Lijiang, Rock set down descriptions of the idyllic landscape that are said to have inspired

James Hilton's 1933 novel *Lost Horizon*, which was set in the fictional Himalayan paradise of Shangri-la. Given its location at the crossroads of so many cultures, Yunnan is the most diverse province in China, with twenty-six ethnic groups—Naxi, Yi, Bai, Miao, Dai, and Hani are some of their exotic names—constituting almost half of the fifty-five minority peoples recognized by the central government.

Viewed on a map, the province occupies a dangling pocket of territory about the size of France, sharing borders with Laos and Vietnam to the south and southeast, with Myanmar, the country historically known as Burma, taking up its entire western flank; a tip of Tibet lies to the northwest, with the provinces of Sichuan, Guizhou, and Guangxi to the north and east. The high terrain of the fertile Yungui Plateau on which most of the province lies is crossed by three major river systems—the Yangtze, the Mekong, and the Salween—each running through deep gorges that in places are several thousand feet below the nearby peaks. With an abundance of limestone-filtered mountain water, the region is ideally suited to the making of paper; the other core ingredient, cellulose fiber, is provided by a cornucopia of vegetation.

Of thirty thousand species of higher plants known to grow in all of China, about seventeen thousand can be found in Yunnan. Of these, some ten thousand are tropical and subtropical species, a number of which, such as Yunnan nutmeg and the Yunnan camphor tree, are unique to the province. According to Ministry of Commerce figures, there are close to five thousand species of herbal plants—more than two thousand of them classified as medicinal—and some four hundred different spices cultivated in Yunnan. No surprise, either, that Yunnan is the principal tea producer in all of China; other cash crops include rice, rubber, sugar, soybeans, corn, tobacco, and arabica coffee. The official flower of the province is the camellia, examples of which are cultivated at the Kunming Botanical Garden, a sprawling arboretum where four thousand varieties of tropical and subtropical plants are grown—and which was the first place our group visited before setting off in search of hand papermakers.

Our host for the visit there, and for the overland tour through Yunnan Province that followed, was Guan Kaiyun, a professor at the Kunming Institute of Botany, a senior member of the Chinese Academy of Sciences, and, from 1999 to 2006, director of the Botanical Garden. The author of many monographs and technical papers, Guan is a working botanist who has obtained numerous patents for his work and has been designated an Outstanding Scientist by the Chinese government. He is regarded as one the world's foremost authorities on the begonia, which grows in more than 150 varieties in Yunnan. A stated goal of the Botanic Garden where he works is to study "economically valuable" vegetation of all kinds.

"We are always interested in the various plants that are being used out here," he told me in perfect English during one of our long drives through the countryside, a proficiency acquired while earning his doctorate in botany at the University of New Zealand and during extended research visits to the United States. "In theory, any plant can be used for making paper, but the difference is the quality and the quantity of the fibers." An added incentive for Guan on this trip was to see for himself undocumented examples of what he considers a vanishing skill in his own country. "This is a disappearing way of life. The big factories have taken over the making of paper, and in one generation, two at the most, these family workshops will be gone forever."

The person who organized the excursion for us was Elaine Koretsky, an independent scholar from Brookline, Massachusetts, who at the time had already spent more than thirty-five years traveling throughout China, Japan, Korea, Southeast Asia, Indonesia, the Philippines, Africa, and Europe—forty expeditions in all, to forty-three countries, since 1976, the goal in each instance to document hand-papermaking techniques distinctive to each region of the world. In the course of this ongoing research, always made with her husband, Dr. Sidney Koretsky, a Boston physician now retired and a paper enthusiast in his own right, who has served admirably as her photographer, Elaine has produced twelve documentary videos and written eight monographic works. In 1995, she established the Research Institute of Paper History and Technology in a restored carriage house that adjoins her home. To display the hundreds of artifacts, paper samples, and tools acquired in her travels, she also founded the International Paper Museum, a small but comprehensive gallery open to visitors by appointment.

A few days into the journey, Christine Harrison, a paper conservator from England, joked that our group of eight adventurers was embarked on a kind of *Canterbury Tales* pilgrimage, each of us with stories to share during our long drives through the countryside on why we had chosen to make such an unusual trip to the other side of the globe.

Harrison told me she'd chosen to come along as a way of celebrating the recent completion of her doctoral dissertation on the pioneering work of Jacob Christian Schäffer, the brilliant eighteenth-century German scientist whose experiments with plants and wasp nests contributed to the use of wood pulp in the manufacture of modern paper. But she was motivated most of all by the prospect of going on a paper odyssey with Elaine Koretsky.

"Elaine is a dear friend of mine, and in my humble opinion she is the Dard Hunter of our generation," Harrison explained simply, a reference to the American author and fine-press printer of the early twentieth century, credited with reviving interest in what had become an abandoned craft in the United States and for energizing what is known as the book arts movement. Hunter's authority in the field derived in large measure from the numerous trips he made to distant lands in search of his material, and from being an eloquent champion of craftsmanship in all its forms. In 2001, Koretsky was presented with a Lifetime Achievement Award from the Friends of Dard Hunter, an international organization dedicated to paper history, papermaking, paper art, paper conservation, and paper science.

A 1953 Phi Beta Kappa graduate of Cornell University with a degree in linguistics—I was envious beyond words when she told me she had taken Vladimir Nabokov's famous course on European literature—Koretsky came to the study of paper by happenstance. "It was a project I took on in the 1970s as something I could do with my daughter when she was in junior high school, something we could enjoy together," she said during our first meeting in Brookline, which included a tour of an indoor garden maintained in her house, every plant one that can be used in papermaking, including a ten-foot-tall papyrus.

"We were making paper by hand, and the whole idea of it, the process, just sort of took me over," she said. Her passion for the subject was shared by Donna Koretsky, her daughter, who today owns and operates Carriage House Paper, in Brooklyn, New York, a company that makes handmade paper for artists and offers a wide range of papermaking equipment designed and manufactured by her husband, David Reina. Donna Koretsky also worked on organizing her mother's research trips to the Far East and arranged for others, such as our group, to tag along.

Our first day out of Kunming was spent almost entirely on the road, headed for the city of Tengchong, about five hundred miles due

*Duan Win Mao, proprietor of the paper mill at Yùquán (Jade Spring), outside Tengchong.*

west, deep in jade country and famous for the geothermal springs that abound in the nearby Gaoligong Mountains. We spent a night along the way in Dali, an ancient walled city noted for its tie-dyed indigo cotton fabrics, which a number of us purchased as souvenirs; a member of our group, Anna-Grethe Rischel, formerly head of the paper-textile-and-leather section of the National Museum of Denmark and in 2009 elected president of the International Association of Paper Historians, suggested we wash the fabric in a mixture of cold water and vinegar when we got home, to fix the colors.

We finally got down to business in a village outside Tengchong called Yùquán, or Jade Spring, where a steady source of pure groundwater had proven ideal for the making of paper over many generations. Until just a few years prior to our visit, several dozen families operated small mills there, but when we arrived, only one was still operating. The fiber they used was prepared from a combination of wood pulp and the inner bark of the paper mulberry tree, which had been cooked in lime and bleached. An additive—a "formation aid," in papermaking jargon—made from the prickly pear cactus was part of the shop's formula.

The proprietor was a man named Duan Win Mao, and other than

*Wife of Duan Win Mao*

a tour of duty many years earlier in the People's Liberation Army, the
boundaries of his eighty-five years on earth had pretty much been
defined by the time he spent as a maker of paper in this tiny hamlet.
Duan spoke no English at all, not even a phrase or two, and our words
were translated by Guan, who soon told us that paper had been made
on this site by successive members of the same family for six centuries.
The papermaker's eighty-two-year-old wife prepared tea for our group
as their fifty-six-year-old son went about the task of bundling up the
samples we had just purchased to take with us. Goodwill flowed back
and forth, yet there was a bittersweet undercurrent of finality when we
learned that the following month the operation would close forever
and that the family would entertain offers to sell the property to land
speculators, who probably would build new apartments for the growing numbers of workers moving constantly into Tengchong.

The operation was not closing for lack of business, we were told, since there remained a steady market for the "spirit paper" they made among the millions of Chinese who still pay their respects to deceased ancestors by burning small offerings according to time-honored traditions. It was more a matter of changing times and lifestyles. A grandson who under normal circumstances would have been next in line to take over was not at all interested in carrying on the family trade and was not even on the premises the day of our visit—he was out in the mountains, working for good pay on the new highway we had seen being built during our drive in.

Inside the vat room, two female employees toiled alongside each other at a pair of upright tubs filled with prepared pulp, known universally among papermakers as "stuff," each woman producing, on average, three sheets a minute—up to one hundred and eighty sheets an hour, eighteen hundred sheets per day. Their wooden-frame molds were counterbalanced by ropes strung from the ceiling, with a bamboo screen held in place by two hinged sticks, known as deckles. There was a gentle sound of swirling water as they went about the task, a finely executed motion mastered by many thousands of papermakers before them: one thrust forward, one pull back, one even shake side to side, followed by a lateral move to a stack known as a post, where the newly formed sheets were couched—pronounced *cooched*—and allowed to accumulate. Excess water would be squeezed out later with a screw press, and the moist sheets would be flattened onto vertical heated plates with a brush for drying.

From Jade Spring, we headed northeast for Lijiang, a majestic old city in the mountains and the jumping-off point to a remote village in Heqing County called Junying that Elaine had first visited in 1994 and was eager to see again. The five-mile ride up a steep, winding slope was a challenge for our driver, Sun (pronounced *Soon*), who was hampered by a heavy rainfall that had left the rutted road thick with mud, and little room to maneuver around the sharp turns that hugged the edges. We were rewarded finally by the sight of a massive cauldron just above a busy mountain stream, fully involved in a rolling boil that filled the air with steam. "They're cooking," Elaine shouted, excited by what she immediately recognized as a thick stew of mulberry bast fiber bubbling away in the pot, a sight that she later told me was a first for her on these

*Papermaking in the village of Longzhu in Yunnan Province*

trips. "Usually when they cook the fiber, it's only for a couple of days every month or so, and being there to see it is pretty much a matter of blind luck. Today we hit the jackpot."

Shortly after we made our way up to the mill, two women in traditional native dress arrived, bearing bundles of paper mulberry branches on their backs, hauled down from a storage barn farther up the hill. They deposited their cargo in a large pool of creek water near the cauldron, where it would soak and soften before going on to the next step in the process. Guan told us that a number of people from the same family worked in the seasonal operation, all supplementing their income by farming vegetables. Their practice was to sell their finely textured paper in bulk to itinerant brokers, who in turn sold it as fancy wrapping for blocks of Pu-erh tea, a large-leaf variety of the plant *Camellia sinensis,* named for the county in Yunnan where it is grown.

A long drive through tobacco fields and rice paddies next took us to a cluster of papermakers in Suojia, in the Gaoligong Mountains.

Satellite dishes were on the roofs of the houses; cell phones and brightly painted motorbikes were popular among the youngsters. About forty-five families in the village made paper, we learned, all of it also from mulberry fiber and in a variety of bright colors for use primarily in ceremonial burning rituals and for the making of decorative objects. The finished sheets were smoothed onto brick walls and allowed to dry naturally in the sun. All of the fibers were processed in an antiquated Hollander beater (see Chapter 3) jury-rigged for power to a heavily rusted gasoline engine.

On our final day in Lijiang—the name, meaning "Beautiful River," was coined by Kublai Khan in 1254—we were introduced to Dongba paper, an exceedingly sturdy and quite beautiful sheet that is made from the skin of the *Stellera chamaejasme,* a herbaceous relative of daphne (*Thymelaeaceae*), a plant that has proven resistant over the centuries to insects, making it useful as an archival medium for official documents. According to Guan, the plant also has properties that make it poisonous to humans, and it is still used in veterinary medicine to purge livestock of worms and other intestinal parasites. It was first used to make paper around the seventh century, by the Naxi people, an ethnic group native to this region that is said to maintain the only pictographic writing system still in use anywhere in the world.

Many of the individual symbols of their language, totaling 276 sound complexes, are compounds, and are read as a phrase in which verbs and other parts of speech are supplied from memory. A superb collection of Naxi manuscripts collected by Joseph Rock, numbering 3,342 documents written on this remarkably durable paper, is now in the Library of Congress and is the largest collection in the world outside of China. Local artisans who make Dongba paper described the process for us as a kind of "living fossil," in that their techniques and tools have not changed appreciably in more than a thousand years; the demonstration we saw used a ladle to pour the pulp onto a primitive screen held up by a kind of tripod device.

Why so many family paper mills are to be found high on mountainsides, reachable only by twisting pathways that frequently jut out over sloping landscapes or down steep hills to the banks of fresh running streams, has been determined over time by a simple circumstance. "The purity of the water always comes first," Anna-Grethe Rischel told me during one of our extended conversations. Rischel is an authority in paper analysis, including the forensic study of documents to determine whether they are authentic or clever forgeries, and has written numerous articles based on her research, which includes the study of papers gathered along the Silk Road. Everywhere we went, she asked questions about the various formation aids being used to regulate the flow of water through the mesh, either to slow it down, and thus make a thicker sheet, or to speed it up, for one that is thinner; two of the more memorable additives we were told about were made of pulverized pomegranates and a wild grass called dragon's breath.

The second phase of the trip began in Chengdu, to the north, in the heart of Sichuan Province, another good-sized city of four million people, not quite as bustling as Kunming but busy all the same, and struggling with a choking veneer of air pollution that made us eager to hit the road and get out in the countryside. Before leaving, we stopped by an urban park on the south side of the Jiang River devoted entirely to the memory of Xue Tao (768–831), one of the outstanding poets of the Tang Dynasty and China's first female papermaker. Visitors are able to enjoy tea brewed with water from the well Xue Tao used to make her paper, which was distinctively pink, suggesting the red hibiscus flowers she used in her pulp.

Once we were in the countryside, it quickly became apparent why Sichuan is the natural home of the panda bear, with one sprawling bamboo forest after another filling the landscape. In Changning County we stayed one night at a nicely appointed hotel on the grounds of a massive preserve named the Shunan Bamboo Sea. Out in the villages, it was part of an unspoken protocol that wherever we went, Elaine Koretsky led the way. During this segment of the trip—now well into our third week—we heard about a village called Renhe, in Jiang'an County, where thirty families were said to be involved in bamboo papermaking. After a number of false leads, we made our way to the side of a heavily pitted dirt road about a hundred feet above a tributary of the Yangtze River and were told that the people we wanted to see had their workshop down below by the water.

The path was steep, and the rich red clay underfoot was sodden from a heavy rain that had fallen throughout the morning, making the trek through a dense cluster of bamboo treacherous. About halfway down, the trail of flat stones that served as markers ended abruptly. At the head of the pack as always, Elaine stopped, unsure of where to proceed. Noticing her predicament, one of the men waiting for us at the bottom scooted up and carried her down piggyback, beckoning for the rest of us to follow one by one. Elaine described what happened next in an article she later wrote for a newsletter published by an organization of hand-papermaking enthusiasts. "Directly behind me was Nick Basbanes," she recalled. "First he photographed me on the back of the papermaker, then started down himself, immediately landing on his backside, and sliding right down to the river, though luckily not into it." This was accurate in every respect, as I wrote in a piece of my own for *Fine Books & Collections* magazine, adding that the only bruises I had suffered in the muddy mishap—all of it preserved amusingly on my digital voice recorder, which had been running throughout the descent—were to my ego, not my rear end.

Once we were on the riverbank among the workers, it was all business. The bamboo used here for fiber, Elaine learned, was harvested after five months of growth and cut into lengths of 1.5 meters, then softened for four months in a lime pool. She was surprised to learn that no cooking was done by these papermakers to soften the stalks; the next step in their process went directly from the pit to beating, which until just recently had been done with a stone wheel turned by a cow, but these days with an agricultural grinder powered by a gasoline engine. Elaine wrote down dimensions of the different molds, noting how one formed two pieces of paper at a time, each measuring 15 inches by 11.5 inches. She counted the number of immersions into the vat—two quick dips, with the excess pulp thrown off to the right—and examined the hand-operated screw press used to squeeze excess water from the posts of paper. Sheets were then hung out to dry on lines strung between poles. Elaine inquired whether the formula there involved any formation aid. At Renhe, she was told, a powder obtained from the root of *Abelmoschus manihot*—a flowering plant often added to soups for flavoring—worked perfectly for their purposes, which is the making of paper to be used as burnt offerings in burial ceremonies and for "sanitary purposes." The papermakers worked ten-hour days and produced up to 2,400 sheets apiece during each shift. "I ask a million questions," Elaine confided to me later. "I drive guides crazy."

We spent the next day high on the side of a mountain near the northern arm of the Yangtze River, visiting with Shi Fuli, a master artist and fifth-generation papermaker whom Elaine had met in 1985

*Papermaking in the village of Ma in Yunnan Province*

in Atlanta, at a cultural exhibition put on by the High Museum of Art. Because Elaine and Sidney had visited him in 1987, we knew in advance to prepare for a steep walk up to his property, where he supervised the work of six families. Location, once again, was determined by a single factor, in this instance a spring of pure mountain water—"and also soft," Anna-Grethe Rischel said approvingly after we got there.

When we arrived, two men were working a large screen mold to produce what we were told were examples of China's highest-quality paper, called *xuanzhi* for the region of Xuan, in Anhui Province, where it was first perfected, and made for calligraphy and painting. (*Zhi* is the Chinese word for "paper.") The bamboo used for these luxurious sheets—the richly textured samples I acquired were snow white, and each six feet long—had been boiled before pulping, and lime, not bleach, was used as an additive for whitening. Shi Fuli haltingly allowed that a formation aid of birch leaves ground into a powder was occasionally added to the mix, but he insisted there were "no secrets" to his recipes, "just good technique."

At that point, we had already seen more types of papermaking than any of us, I am quite certain, had ever expected. But we pressed on, and the next day we found, entirely by chance, a cluster of papermakers while driving up a narrow road in a vehicle that was much too large for the hilly surroundings, and shouted for the driver to stop. We were headed to another mill we knew about farther up, but the discovery of these two shops—one of them staffed by three teams of muscular papermakers working two-man molds in unison, the other with an automated machine that looked like it belonged in a museum—seemed somewhat miraculous to me, and I said as much afterward, but Elaine would have none of my ebullience.

"It really isn't luck, Nick," she said reproachfully, reminding me with a stern look that she had spent a good deal of her adult life seeking out workshops precisely like the ones we had just found and that locating them by whatever means possible is what the exercise had been all about. "This place is very special to me," she told me when we were back on the bus, making our way back finally to Chengdu and to flights out of the country the following day. "This is where I saw the entire process of papermaking for the first time—from start to finish."

# 2

## Goddess by the Stream

This village has such small fields, it must be difficult to make a living cultivating rice. However, this land has beautiful clear water; I will teach you to make paper so that you and the generations following you can make a living.

> —The Goddess Kawakami Gozen,
> to the villagers of Echizen, c. A.D. 500

Papermaking in Japan is prospering greatly even today. Of course, even now exquisite handmade paper is made. There is probably no other country where the usage of paper is more extensive than Japan. Paper is used for printing and writing but besides that, it is used for window glass, handkerchiefs, clothing, lamp wicks, cords and in many other items and among them, that outward appearance and color tone compare favorably with natural leather. Moreover, even an imitation which could be mistaken for French leather wallpaper is carried out.

> —Count Friedrich Albrecht zu Eulenburg,
> *Report on the Eulenburg Expedition to Japan,* 1860

DURING THE MIDDLE of what is known in Japan as the Meiji Restoration of 1868 to 1912, a government survey determined that there were 68,562 workshops actively making paper in various reaches of the island nation, all of it produced manually with fiber coming principally from the inner bark of three trees known as kozo, gampi, and mitsumata. A good number of these enterprises were seasonal occupations pursued on farms by extended families during the winter months, after the rice crops were in and when conditions were optimal for harvesting shoots from the paper mulberry trees. Skills, ingredients, and techniques for preparation varied from region to region, with subtleties perfected over the generations painstakingly passed on from masters to apprentices, which more often than not meant parents to their children.

Today, with the overwhelming preponderance of commercial paper for everyday needs being made mechanically in Japan by industrial giants such as Nippon Paper Industries, Oji Paper Company, and Mitsubishi Paper Mills Ltd., and with massive supplies of wood pulp imported from abroad on cavernous container ships, that number is down to fewer than three hundred, with long-term prospects for survival uncertain at best. The graceful practice of making paper according to time-honored methods is so threatened with extinction, in fact, that some traditionally made papers have been designated by the government as a "cultural property" urgently in need of preservation and protection.

*The Japanese technique of making paper, as illustrated by the eighteenth-century artist Tachibana Minko in a series of color-printed studies of artisans at work, of which the first printed edition appeared in Japan in 1770.*

In its purest form—and purity is an image that resonates among the Japanese—*washi*, the word used to identify handmade paper, is as much an expression of the human spirit as it is of craftsmanship. Another Japanese word, the verb *migaku*, for "polish," "master," or "improve," is used often to describe the knack these people have to take a product, idea, or skill introduced somewhere else and make it distinctively their own, with language and writing systems adapted from the Chinese centuries ago being two compelling examples, and cameras, electronic devices, and automobiles among the more recent. Papermaking did not originate in Japan, either, but once it was established there during the seventh century, it took on a life and a context of its own.

In a land where order and cleanliness are virtues to be prized, pristine paper that has not been treated with chemicals is an expression of goodness and reverence, and the wholesome color of the material itself—white—is a sign that represents the natural rhythms of birth and death. The entryways to shrines and sacred places—the concept of a threshold separating the temporal world from the spiritual has been explored at length by Dorothy Field, a Canadian papermaker and poet who has traveled extensively throughout Asia—are typically marked with streams of washi that have been cut and suspended from lintels by ropes made of rice straw; trees and rocks deemed holy are set apart in a similar fashion.

"The Japanese have found in their paper a vehicle for the entire range of human expression, from the most noble, religious, and artistic manifestations to the most common, everyday thought," the American author Sukey Hughes wrote in *Washi*, a highly respected book published in 1978, on the "evolution" of the material as a cultural concept. For her material—which included dozens of samples produced by a wide variety of studios tipped into a limited edition of the book—Hughes drew on several years she spent in Japan working as an apprentice with a master papermaker. One of her central points was that in Japan, washi goes beyond functionality to a point where it becomes "an expression in itself," a productive process of affirmation steeped in long tradition, and cultivated with reverence "as if it was a product of nature." The word *kami* has several meanings in Japanese; one is to identify the Shinto spirits and deities that govern the natural world—phenomena like wind, rain, and lightning, and objects such as rivers and trees—while a second meaning is "paper." Whether this is coinci-

dental or deliberate is unclear, but the pronunciation is similar, and the use of paper charms, amulets, and folded shapes at shrines as expressions of divine nature to ward off evil influences has been in practice for many centuries.

A research trip I made to Japan a year after my visit to China began on the main island, Honshu, at a holy place dedicated to a woman revered locally as the goddess of paper. Located four hours west of Tokyo in the papermaking city of Echizen, Okamoto Otaki Shrine stands at the foot of a mountain where it is said, among the residents, that a charismatic woman arrived at a time when their ancestors were desperate for guidance. Although the rice of the region is esteemed today to be among the best in Japan, the terrain is nonetheless high and rough and difficult to manage throughout the year, and an alternative source of occupation was needed.

When I visited this pristine community, a papermaker who makes stock for postcards in a studio not far from the shrine told my companions in Japanese that we were standing on the very ground where the goddess is reputed to have met with the villagers and changed their lives for centuries to come. The time generally given for her arrival is

*Okamoto Otaki is the Shinto shrine of Kawakami Gozen, the goddess of papermaking, in Echizen, Japan.*

around A.D. 500, when it is said that a young prince—who was to become the emperor Keitai—was living in Imadate, a village that's now part of Echizen City. Tradition holds also that, when asked to identify herself, the spirit replied simply, "I am merely someone who lives above the stream." Kawakami Gozen—the name given to her from then on—means "the Goddess Who Lives above the Stream."

Though revered today as a local deity, Kawakami Gozen is not worshipped as a personification of faith, but exalted as a harbinger of good fortune and the bearer of an enduring gift. Every spring, in May, a likeness of the goddess is placed in an ornately decorated litter and carried down from the summit of Mount Omine, also known as Mount Gongen, where it resides the rest of the year. Supplicants dressed in white carry the effigy about the various papermaking districts of Echizen during the three-day celebration, a hopeful occasion known as the *Kami no Matsuri*—the Festival of God and Paper. Some fifty washi studios employing about three hundred craftspeople still operate in Echizen, a number of which I would see over the next few days, but only after paying my respects at the shrine, set sublimely among sacred stones and a towering stand of Japanese cypress trees.

From the time of its invention in China, two millennia ago, knowledge of the papermaker's craft traveled in two directions: westward along the Silk Road through Central Asia toward Europe, and east to Korea and Japan. In both movements, the earliest purveyors were Buddhist monks, who used the material to propagate sacred sutras. The first region outside of China to begin making paper on its own is believed to have been Korea, during the four-hundred-year period (108 B.C. to A.D. 313) when China occupied its next-door neighbor. The Koreans also adopted Chinese religious precepts and assimilated Chinese art and customs, most notably a writing system that was formed in the fifth century, based on Chinese characters. By the sixth century, Korean monks and scholars studying in China had brought back numerous aspects of Chinese material life, including the manufacture of brushes, ink, and high-quality paper. Sheets made in Korea became so highly regarded that a substantial percentage of the output was turned over each year to their Chinese overlords as "tribute paper."

In 610, two Korean Buddhist priests are known to have taught the fundamentals to the Japanese in Fukui Prefecture, on the Sea of Japan. Within a century, paper was being made throughout the country, primarily as a luxury item for the nobility and the military elite (samurai) but also for use by monks in the widening transmission of Buddhism. Its popularity grew sufficiently that in 764 the empress Shotoku, who ruled Japan intermittently from 748 to 769, was able to make a gesture of thanksgiving that could only have been facilitated by a ready abundance of paper. Relieved, apparently, that an eight-year rebellion mounted against her rule had been suppressed, and grateful that she had been spared from the contagion of smallpox that had gripped so much of Japan a few years earlier, Shotoku ordered that one million Buddhist prayers, or "charms," known as *dharani,* be made and distributed among ten temples throughout the empire, each one to be encased in a tiny wooden replica of a three-tiered pagoda.

The enormous number of texts the empress required was consistent with the Buddhist practice of repeating the same prayers over and over again, a reflection of just how powerful the religion had become in Japanese life. "He who repeats it with all his heart shall have his sins forgiven," reads one of the lines in the prayer, a Buddhist classic that was written originally in Sanskrit as the *Vimala Nirbhasa Sutra* and translated into Chinese in 705. Another line quoted the Buddha: "Whoever wishes to gain power from the *dharani* must write seventy-seven copies and place them in a pagoda." One historian speculates that "the empress evidently tried to be on the safe side and ensure long life by ordering a million copies of the charm."

Since writing one million mini-scrolls by hand was not an expeditious option, each was printed on strips of washi eighteen inches long by two inches wide, the characters either cut on woodblocks or etched on copper plates or perhaps, as some scholars suggest, a combination of both, since at least six different *dharani* were produced as part of the project, each containing about thirty columns of five characters each and each spooled into compact coils that fit perfectly in the pagodas. Two different kinds of paper were used as well, one thick and of a woolly texture, the other thinner and firmer, with a smooth surface.

Completed within six years, the *dharani* are recognized today as the earliest dated printed documents in existence, ninety-eight years older even than the *Diamond Sutra* removed from Dunhuang, China, by Sir Aurel Stein; several hundred are known to survive, most in deteriorated condition, but many are intact and still in their tiny wooden pagodas; I handled one of these at the rare books library of the University of California at Los Angeles. Copies periodically appear on the antiquarian market; a lovely specimen was sold to a Florida collector of miniature books at a 2008 Bloomsbury auction for $32,000.

Part of the evolving use of paper soon extended to domestic architecture, earning equal rank with wood, earth, and reeds as essential to the design of a traditional Japanese house. Conspicuously absent from that list, it is worth noting, is clear plate glass for windows, which did not become popular in Japan until the twentieth century, and then only selectively. Indeed, one of the enduring enigmas in the history of technology was the failure of flat glass to establish much of a foothold anywhere in China, Japan, or India until well after its introduction in Europe, between the tenth and sixteenth centuries.

In the absence of glass, shoji screens, made with thin layers of washi, served as windows in Japanese houses, and in a society where imagery matters, paper as a source of refracted light became an obvious metaphor. The natural strength of kozo made it suitable for casements on the sides of buildings, and it also provided excellent insulation. Inside the houses, *byobu* screens and *fusuma* doors, made of opaque paper with vertical panels that slide from side to side, were used as partitions for bedrooms. (The meaning of *byobu* is "wind wall," and *fusu* is a word for "lying down.") For added versatility, screens were made with overlapping paper hinges that allowed panels to fold back and forth in either direction, thus the name *chotsugai,* which translates as "butterfly pair hinge." Among accessories and appliances, paper was the principal material in lanterns, lamps, parasols, and folding fans, and its use in making kites, dolls, and kimonos is legendary.

Over the long term, one of the horrifying consequences of this reliance on wood, grass, and paper for housing materials was how susceptible they made Japanese cities to the incendiary bombs dropped by American aircraft during the waning weeks of World War II, accounting for more civilian deaths by conventional ordnance in Tokyo alone than resulted from either of the nuclear strikes on Hiroshima and Nagasaki. The most devastating firebomb attack to take advantage of this glaring vulnerability came on the night and early morning of March 9–10, 1945, when more than three hundred B-29 Superfortresses flying at low altitude released nearly half a million M-69 cluster bombs, each ignited by fused napalm fillers, setting off a series of blasts that merged into one mass of flame known as a firestorm. Fed by gale-force winds that sucked the oxygen out of the air, the raging inferno consumed everything flammable in its path, incinerating sixteen square miles of the city and killing as many as one hundred thousand people in a single night.

While it is a papermaking fiber of uncommon strength and resilience, the distinctive characteristics of kozo were also a factor in another military initiative involving aerial bombardment, this one undertaken by the Japanese army against the United States under a shroud of secrecy. In this instance—the design and fabrication of ten thousand transoceanic balloons—paper provided the airframe for the weapons deployed.

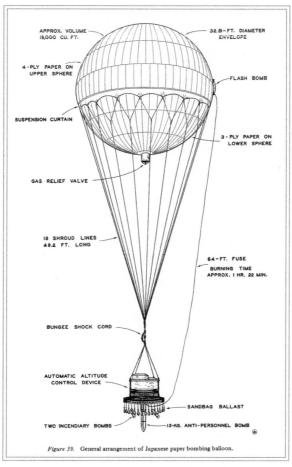

APPROX. VOLUME 19,000 CU. FT.

32.81-FT. DIAMETER ENVELOPE

4-PLY PAPER ON UPPER SPHERE

FLASH BOMB

SUSPENSION CURTAIN

3-PLY PAPER ON LOWER SPHERE

GAS RELIEF VALVE

19 SHROUD LINES 49.2 FT. LONG

64-FT. FUSE BURNING TIME APPROX. 1 HR. 22 MIN.

BUNGEE SHOCK CORD

AUTOMATIC ALTITUDE CONTROL DEVICE

SANDBAG BALLAST

TWO INCENDIARY BOMBS

15-KG. ANTI-PERSONNEL BOMB

*Figure 39.* General arrangement of Japanese paper bombing balloon.

*Schematic drawing of paper-bomb design, from* Japan's World War II Balloon Bomb Attacks.

*A Japanese mulberry paper balloon,
reinflated at NAS Moffett Field,
California, following its downing by
a Navy aircraft in January 1945.*

The genesis of the operation, according to a report prepared for the Smithsonian Institution and published by the U.S. Government Printing Office in 1973, was retaliation for the high-profile attack on Tokyo in 1942 by U.S. Army general James "Jimmy" Doolittle and sixteen B-25 bombers, a raid that did minimal physical damage to the Japanese capital but was an unqualified propaganda triumph for Americans still reeling from the surprise attack on Pearl Harbor, four months earlier. "In a desperate attempt to find a means of reprisal, the Japanese conceived a method that would allow them to strike directly at the American continent," Robert C. Mikesh, author of the Smithsonian report, wrote. "Their plan was simple; launch balloons with incendiary and anti-personnel bombs attached, let them travel across the Pacific with the prevailing winds, and drop on American cities, forests, and farmlands."

Though preposterous on its face, and imprecise even to its proponents, the ambitious offensive was deemed feasible on the strength of meteorological research conducted in the 1930s that had discovered "rivers of fast moving air" flowing in the upper atmosphere toward North America, wind patterns that we know today as jet streams. To facilitate the five-thousand-mile flights across the Pacific, sophisticated control mechanisms and gas-relief valves were developed to operate up to 38,000 feet, with variations in altitude to be controlled by clusters of sandbags that would be released at timed intervals, each one triggered by fuses attached to a wet-cell battery.

Seven manufacturing centers were set up around Tokyo to assemble what was code-named the Fu-Go Weapon (the first character of the word for balloon is *fu*), with handmade paper selected for the skin of the thirty-two-foot-diameter balloons, six hundred individual sheets required for each one, all glued together in a lamination that made no allowance for gas leakage. "The strength of the paper was dependent chiefly upon the fiber which had to be uniform, yet it was necessary to have it be very light." Kozo was the obvious choice. For close to two years, hundreds of papermakers were enlisted to the task, and with 13,500 workshops operating in Japan when the war broke out, there were plenty to choose from.

It is believed that nine thousand balloon bombs were launched from three coastal locations in Japan between November 3, 1944, and April 5, 1945, each inflated with nineteen thousand cubic feet of hydrogen. About a thousand are thought to have reached North America; about three hundred were confirmed visually—a few were shot down off the coast—and others by debris that was recovered. Sightings were confirmed in locations that ranged from Alaska, British Columbia, and Manitoba, in the extreme north, to Oregon, Washington, California, Montana, Colorado, Wyoming, and Nebraska in the lower forty-eight, and Sonora, Mexico, south of the border. One traveled as far east as Grand Rapids, Michigan, and another made its way to Ashley, North Dakota. Wreckage from others turns up from time to time in densely wooded areas, one as recently as 1992. The National Air and Space Museum has in its collection a balloon that landed intact in Echo, Oregon, on March 13, 1945, after its bomb had failed to detonate. Assuming it took seventy-two hours to cross the ocean—a three-day passage was the typical time of transit—the launch would have happened on March 9 or 10, precisely when the apocalyptic attack on Tokyo was taking place.

Unwilling to give the Japanese any information they could use to fine-tune their assaults, American censors placed a strict embargo on all details of the raids. When the episode finally was reported at war's end, it generated very little attention, and it is scarcely remembered even today. The Japanese aerial assault was not without its victims, however. On May 5, 1945, a woman and five children on an outing near the Gearhart Mountains, northeast of Klamath Falls, Oregon, came across a strange object lying on the ground; all six were killed when one of them apparently tugged on a dangling line, triggering a bomb. A memorial plaque erected after the war identifies the location as the "only place on the American continent where death resulted from enemy action during World War II."


IN 2009, Timothy D. Barrett, senior research scientist and adjunct professor of papermaking at the University of Iowa, was singled out by the John D. and Catherine T. MacArthur Foundation for his efforts over three decades to document and preserve "centuries of old hand-papermaking practices that may otherwise be lost," and awarded a $500,000 fellowship. When notified of the award, Barrett was already conducting scientific analysis of European papers produced by hand between the fourteenth and the nineteenth centuries before the introduction of mechanical processes.

While Barrett was equally proficient in Asian and Western techniques, it was his efforts as a hands-on scholar in the Japanese tradition that drove his earliest work and was the subject of his first two books, *Nagashizuki: The Japanese Craft of Hand Papermaking* (Bird & Bull Press, 1979) and *Japanese Papermaking: Traditions, Tools, and Techniques* (John Weatherhill, 1983), both the fruit of two years spent in Japan between 1975 and 1977. In 1986, he was the founding director of a papermaking studio at the University of Iowa Center for the Book, the only academic program in the United States that focuses on producing both traditional Western and Japanese-style papers. The unit not only makes its own paper; it also grows its own paper mulberry trees and processes the bark according to methods that Barrett mastered while studying in Japan in the 1970s.

In 2001, Barrett and his colleagues were commissioned to make the paper used to rehouse the Declaration of Independence, the Bill of

Rights, and the Constitution, which annually draw more than a million visitors to National Archives headquarters in Washington, where they are displayed in the Rotunda for the Charters of Freedom. The following year, he invited me out to Iowa City to give a talk at the Iowa Center for the Book, and it was during my visit there that the seed for what became this book was planted.

Seeing paper made by hand for the first time, I began to appreciate just how luxurious a sheet of this material could be. When Barrett talked about Japanese paper, he used such words as "warmth" and "character" to describe its qualities, and he enthused about how it always feels "so alive" in his hands. His 1983 book had been dedicated "to early unknown craftspeople, Eastern and Western, who left behind paper that speaks for itself," reinforcing a conviction of his that the end product often stands quite apart from the function it serves. "Paper is not silent," he explained when I asked him to elaborate on what he meant by that. "On its most essential level, good paper makes manifest the interaction between nature and human beings—between natural fiber, water, and the artisans. Somehow it's all present in the finished sheet. It is that essence I find most powerful in handmade paper."

When he went to Japan in 1975, Barrett admitted to having been drawn at first by the sheer beauty of the product. "Japanese papers to me are mystifyingly attractive, and I didn't understand where that came from. There were some technical things I wanted to learn, too, like why can the Japanese make such thin sheets and stack them up one on top of the next while still wet, press them, and get them apart without using a felt between each sheet—that was a big mystery to me—but it was mainly the aesthetic qualities that brought me there in the first place. It's an oversimplification, of course, to say I'm interested only in beautiful papers. Materials and workmanship, regardless of where they are, whether Japanese papermaking or fifteenth-century Italian papermaking, fascinate me just as much. But I was drawn first by the beauty, and a need to know where it all comes from."

Barrett was not a novice when he went to Japan, having already spent several years working as an apprentice at Twinrocker Handmade Paper, a pioneering enterprise established in 1972 in Brookston, Indiana, by Howard and Kathryn Clark, a visionary couple committed to reviving a moribund tradition in the United States (see Chapter 16), and he was fully proficient in Western papermaking. He was awarded grants by the National Endowment for the Arts and the Fulbright Program, sponsored by the U.S. Department of State, to study *nagashizuki*—the word combines two verbs, one meaning "to flow" or "to slosh," the other "to make paper"—and to document what he found. "I can't say I perceived who my audience was going to be at first," he told me, "but I felt obligated to share what I learned. There are a few other books that discussed Japanese papermaking, but none of the ones that were out there really tell you how to actually do it. Where do you start, how do you harvest, how do you cook, that sort of thing. I had gone to Japan with those questions in mind, so sharing the answers I found seemed like an obvious thing for me to do."

Eastern and Western traditions of hand papermaking are similar in that both form layers of cellulose fiber on porous flat surfaces, with the fundamental differences coming in the initial preparation. "Rags have to be beaten more aggressively than tree barks, but the biggest difference is the use of formation aid in the vat that allows the Japanese to make very thin tissues," Barrett said. "There's nothing like that added to the European vat. The European sheets are couched, or stacked, using interleaving felts, and the Japanese sheets are stacked one on top of the next, so that's another difference. Interleaving felts in the European process allow you to squeeze the pile pretty quickly; Japanese and most Asian sheets, by contrast, are pressed slowly."

Every other year, Barrett teaches a one-week course during the summer at Rare Book School, at the University of Virginia, on the history of paper and papermaking with John Bidwell, curator of printed books and bindings at the Morgan Library, in New York. Barrett concentrates on the hands-on details and the aesthetics—students get to make their own washi—while Bidwell handles the historical overview. Once I knew I would be writing a book about paper, it made sense for me to take the course, and when I decided I needed to visit Japan, I turned once again to Barrett, who gave me the names of two people, Paul Denhoed and Richard Flavin, who would turn out to be excellent guides in the Land of the Rising Sun.

IT IS CUSTOMARY in Japan for visitors to offer small gifts when calling on people, a tradition that expresses gratitude, respect, and friendship. While preparing for my research trip, I thought long and hard about what kind of token I could present to the papermakers I would be meeting that might be useful and unusual at the same time. Since Japanese are said to enjoy sweets with their afternoon tea—and because I'm a lifelong New Englander—I settled finally on bottles of premium maple syrup from Vermont, offered in fancy paper bags I bought in Tokyo, since presentation, I was told, means as much in Japan as the gift itself. Syrup being a renewable resource collected naturally from adult trees, there was additionally, I thought, a resonance that might be appreciated by the papermakers, though their collective weight—I brought a dozen of the bottles along—prompted me to reconsider more than once the wisdom of the choice.

But when we arrived at the studio of Ichibei Iwano IX in Imadate, I was rewarded with a knowing smile and a word of appreciation passed on through Paul Denhoed, a Canadian papermaker and former student of Tim Barrett's who moved to Japan in 2002 and who coordinated the arrangements for my trip. Denhoed's fluency in the language—coupled with his ongoing research of compiling what he calls a "process database" of several dozen Japanese hand papermakers—proved useful in situations where nuance meant as much to me as a literal translation. "What I make is entirely organic," Iwano said, "just like your syrup." It was a thoughtful touch, entirely in character for a man renowned

*Living National Treasure papermaker Ichibei Iwano IX, in his Echizen studio.*

for spreading the gospel of his craft with grace and goodwill. He went on to explain how the bast for his fiber is harvested each winter from the inner bark of new shoots without destroying the trees that produce them, and that all of the ingredients he uses are "entirely from nature" as well.

Ichibei Iwano IX was sixty-seven years old in 2000, when he was designated a Living National Treasure by the Ministry of Education, Culture, Sports, Science and Technology, following by thirty-two years the selection of his father, Ichibei Iwano VIII, as the first papermaker in Japan to be chosen for the honor. In the Iwano family, the name Ichibei is not passed on automatically, and not necessarily to a firstborn son. "It can even go to a nephew, if necessary," Denhoed told me, the single criterion being a demonstrated willingness to learn papermaking under the guidance of the patriarch and to carry the skills forward into the next generation. Ichibei IX's son Junichi was forty-three years old at the time of my visit in 2008, and his father told us the reason he had accepted the Living National Treasure honor was his son had assured him he would follow in his footsteps, and at his passing be designated Ichibei X. When we arrived at their hillside studio, Junichi was working alongside his father preparing fiber, the phase in the process Barrett said he regards as most essential of all. They were in a building known informally as the washing shed, picking the tiniest flecks of bark from the prepared kozo, kneeling side by side before a trough of mountain water so cold that their hands were beet red when they got up to exchange pleasantries.

Nothing was rushed in this workshop, and through Rina Aoki, an Echizen artist and papermaker who learned English while living abroad in the 1990s and joined us for the visit, Iwano told me the single most important lesson he learned from his father was that there are no shortcuts. "He says actually that he has to calm himself down to make good paper—there can be no anger, and no irritation while he is working." From the washing shed, Iwano led the way to the studio where his wife, Takako, a papermaker herself for close to half a century, was forming sheets at the vat. Iwano put his finger in the pulp, declared the temperature too high, and said that it needed to be colder. Denhoed indicated a plastic pail full of pulp that had been brought over to the vat. "He says he is aiming for seven sheets from that bucket," Denhoed said.

"He knows exactly what they should get out of that pulp. He wants thick paper to be used for printing out of this batch, bigger than the traditional size; he says he has an order for it. If you put more fiber into the vat, the ratio of the fiber is higher, the sheets will be thicker. If the bucket makes six sheets, then it's too thick. If it's eight, it's too thin. The more you shake, the more fiber collects on the surface, the thicker the paper. The more formation aid you add, the more you slow the drainage. Everything has to be the exact amount." Almost on cue, Iwano's wife added more *neri,* a formation aid made from the root of the hibiscus plant called *tororo-aoi.*

A type of washi the Iwanos make, known as Echizen *hosho,* is of the highest quality, labor intensive to the extreme, and favored by calligraphers, woodblock carvers, relief printers, artists, and makers of collage for its uncommon strength, fluffiness, absorbency, and creamy white texture. It does not tear easily or shrink, either, making it desirable when precise registration of images is demanded. When first introduced, many centuries ago, *hosho* was used by the ruling shogun for official pronouncements. Iwano's fiber of choice is grown in Nasu, a hilly area north of Tokyo, in Tochigi Prefecture, that has been supplying his family for three generations. Other Japanese papermakers use bast from the *mitsumata* and *gampi* trees, some use bark imported from other Asian countries, but Iwano insists on using kozo grown in Japan.

As with all traditional Japanese papers, there is no bleaching with chemicals, and any additional whitening that might be needed is done by exposing the pulp to sunlight. Iwano has a mechanical beater known as a *naginata,* which is similar to the machine developed by the Dutch in the seventeenth century to prepare pulp from rags. The Japanese machine is distinguished by a set of long, curved blades (*naginata* is also a word for sword) designed to retain maximum length of the fibers by "teasing" them apart from one another, as Barrett put it in his book, not mincing them. Denhoed said that while Iwano does use the machine to some extent, he prefers to beat his raw materials with a wooden mallet. It is a time-consuming technique, but one that allows him to exert maximum control over the process, or, in his words, as passed on to me, "preserve its original state as much as I can."

Iwano usually cooks the kozo in a large stainless-steel drum, in a solution made from relatively mild caustic soda ash, otherwise known as sodium carbonate. When the situation demands something different, he will prepare an alkaline solution with the ashes of buckwheat husks, an additive derived from the same agricultural plant, called soba, that is milled to make noodles. Cedar needles picked by his son from trees in the back of the property are used in the straining phase of the lye-making process. The entire procedure is extraordinarily detailed, and while Timothy Barrett wrote as good an explanation as is likely to be found anywhere on the precise steps and sequences to be followed, the only reliable way to learn *nagashizuki* at the highest levels of performance is at the side of a master, over a sustained period of time.

From the vat room, Iwano led the way to where finished sheets are brushed onto special boards made of ginkgo wood and left to dry in a heated space, one of the few tweaks he allows to the process, which historically was done outside in the sunlight. "The room here will get up to about forty-three degrees Celsius," or about 110 degrees Fahrenheit, Denhoed said. "If you keep the temperature too low, and do it slowly, then it won't dry properly." Iwano showed me one of the well-worn brushes he uses for this phase of the process, and said the biggest problem he was having these days was not insufficient orders— the Canadian-born woodblock printer David Bull, whose studio is in Japan, acclaims Iwano's washi as the world standard—but finding a reliable source for the right tools. "He doesn't have anyone to make these brushes for him anymore," Denhoed said. "He likes them because they are easier to use with one hundred percent kozo. He says it is the same with screens, frames, and boards—the people who make them are disappearing, too."

But Iwano had not taken me into the drying room to complain about changing times. He pulled a sheet from a shelf where finished inventory was kept and invited me to tear it. I did not want to do such a disrespectful thing to such a magnificent specimen, and said as much through Denhoed, but he insisted I give it a try. It was remarkably resistant—perhaps I was being too gentle—prompting Iwano to finish the job himself, though not without considerable exertion. I took some close-up photos of the long strands of luxurious white kozo fiber that had been exposed by the tear. "This paper will last a thousand years," he said, and from there we went into the living quarters to continue our discussion in a book-lined study known as the *shosai*, sitting cross-legged on tatami mats of woven grass.

Certain phrases kept repeating themselves, and among the more relevant were Iwano's continued insistence that the length of the fiber is of crucial importance, that the mountain water of the region is among the very best in the world, that "original papermaking is superior by far" to all others, and that "new things are not good"—and by "new things" I was led to understand that he meant any variation from routines and techniques that had been handed down for several hundred years. The meeting had the aura of an audience, and I felt genuinely privileged to have been with this gentle man who embodied such a clear sense of mission, purpose, and place in life.

"My paper is closest to the paper that was taught by the goddess," he said toward the end of our conversation, and beamed when it was clear to him that I understood the translation. "From simple paper such as this, all other papers have come. Before I could start with my father, I had to believe absolutely in my paper—and in my ability to make it as he taught me." He gave me a business card made on his paper, and a bookmark bearing several Japanese characters that he wrote down as I watched. Their meaning, according to Rina Aoki, is "the joy of living with paper." The sentiments of his late father, expressed in a brief statement written for a federation of Japanese papermakers forty years earlier, were words that Ichibei ix said he himself has always lived by. "Never be in a hurry—and never skip regular steps."

*"The Joy of Living with Paper," a gift to the author from Ichibei Iwano ix.*

EVERY YEAR in late January or early February, well after the leaves have fallen to the ground and the crisp winter months have arrived, a group of volunteers gather in a western suburb of Tokyo and harvest shoots from a cluster of kozo trees planted by an American artist and papermaker who took up permanent residence in Japan in the 1970s and is committed to reviving a tradition that has largely been ignored by his Japanese colleagues. At a time when many makers of washi import most of their kozo from other Asian countries, Richard Flavin is one of the very few craftsmen in Japan who makes paper by hand from the bast fiber of his own kozo trees, supervising every step of the process from start to finish. His one-man effort to "reseed" interest in the ancient tradition began in 1990, on a piece of land loaned to him by a local environmentalist. One Tokyo colleague who was prominent in the arts scene was quoted in the *Japan Times* as saying that Flavin's commitment to the project reflected "a mind that is more Japanese-like than a Japanese."

Timothy Barrett and Richard Flavin had first met when both were learning the finer points of *nagashizuki* at the Saitama Prefecture Paper Industry Research Station in the early 1970s. As the only two Americans enrolled in the program, they struck up a friendship that has remained strong ever since. When Barrett returned to the United States and began writing about his experiences, it was Flavin who contributed the illustrations for *Nagashizuki,* which the Bird & Bull Press published in a fine-press edition in 1979 and Weatherhill later expanded into *Japanese Papermaking* for the general trade.

In addition to wood engravings and prints, Flavin creates and exhibits collages from his own washi and makes paper for various artists, calligraphers, and commercial clients. His wife, Ryoko Haraguchi, is a Tokyo textile designer of some note who was profiled in an Indian newspaper in 2009 on the opening of an exhibition of her fabrics as a person for whom "creativity knows no limits." Drawing close attention was the line of garments and handbags she introduced, combining papers crafted by her husband with luxurious silks she buys in India. The paper is dyed using what is known as the *kakishibu* method, a process that uses the fermented juice of unripe persimmons for waterproofing; the fruit has been used in Japan for centuries to seal canvas bags, fishing nets, boats, and wood.

A native of Boston, Flavin studied graphic arts, design, etching, woodblock carving, and fine printing in the United States before serving a tour in Korea with the U.S. Army in the late 1960s. While on leave in 1968, he visited Kamakura, in Japan, and made the decision fairly straightaway that he liked the lifestyle and admired the Japanese approach to creative expression. Following his discharge from military service, he studied for two years at Tokyo National University of Fine Arts and Music, with the idea of learning more about making woodblock prints. "I try very hard to do everything," he told me with a shrug when we met at his studio in Ogose, so it was only a matter of time before he decided that in order to excel at making Japanese prints, he should learn how to make washi. "I had a teacher tell me that artists don't make washi; artists *use* washi," he said. "That was all fine and good, but I still wanted to know more about it. I have always believed very deeply in learning from the materials at hand."

The traditional Japanese aesthetic that drives this conviction, known as *wabi-sabi,* is rooted in austerity, quiet elegance, simplicity, and being one with nature, ideals that Flavin came to assimilate once he moved to Japan. A practicing Buddhist, he served as the part-time caretaker of a Zen temple in Ogawamachi, at Jionji, and for a time had his own publishing imprint there, which he called Jionji Press. Ogawamachi is located about forty miles west of Tokyo in the prefecture of Saitama, the same prefecture where Barrett and Flavin attended the paper research institute in the 1970s. In 2005, Flavin moved into a house in the village of Ogose and set up a shop in a building next to the living quarters. Once a working orchard growing Japanese plums, the fertile land provides numerous plants that are useful to Flavin's various projects, and a stream that runs through the property supplies the water for what he calls his "annual bark-off," a festive event in which the kozo harvested in Ogawamachi is transformed into bast fiber by the forty or so volunteers who support his homegrown effort.

"When I was living in Ogawamachi, the papermakers told me that if it weren't for imported kozo from Thailand, we would all *banzai*—give up. I always thought this town was a traditional Japanese papermaking town. I said, 'What's the future of papermaking if we don't raise our own kozo?' So I decided to try it. I thought the Japanese papermakers would be inspired if an American started something like this. At that time I was deeply involved in the environment; the surrounding hills were being turned into golf courses. One of the members of this environmental awareness group owned this field, a silk mulberry field, for raising silkworms—that is a different tree, by the way, it is not the paper mulberry tree—and it was overgrown, and he told me I could use it. I came in with a backhoe and pulled out the stumps and bought a hundred saplings in Tochigi, and then reality set in. So, okay, I just planted some trees, now what? The problem is that I like to do so many things. I couldn't take care of this all by myself, so that first year it got overgrown and didn't produce very much."

But as he became more attuned to the natural rhythms of the land, and as others applauded his effort by offering to help, careful routines were put in place, and today it is an orderly field with five hundred trees that produce sufficient kozo for Flavin's needs; in 2010, the figure was sixty kilograms—more than 130 pounds—of clean white bark from the harvest. "I have about an acre, and it supplies me for a full year," he said. "We cut the shoots down, bundle them up and bring them over here and steam them, and another team will peel the bark. We usually do this in the winter. If you cut the trees in summer, you will damage them, because the sap is still flowing. When the sap stops, the trees are basically sleeping, and you cut them at the stump. You can cut anytime after the leaves drop, from sometime in November until March, but we usually do it in January."

Flavin said he prefers earth-toned colors for his papers, and for pigments he uses such materials as indigo, clay, persimmon, and pine soot, the latter material being precisely what its name implies: a powder produced from the burning of pinewood. When there was a break in the rain that had fallen on the day of my visit, we walked outside on the grounds so he could show me the stream where the kozo is washed and the stove where it is cooked. There was vegetation everywhere, much of it useful to his work.

From Ogose, we took the short drive to see the kozo trees in Ogawamachi, visited a few other papermakers in the region, and continued on into Tokyo, where Flavin introduced me to his wife, Ryoko, at Gallery Sind, her office and studio. I gave him a bottle of the maple syrup and several of my books, and he, in turn, had a few things for me, including half a dozen sheets of washi pulled from a bundle of old materials he had bought a few months earlier at a country auction and marked as having been made in 1944—which left me speechless. Each one was a perfect square, twenty-four inches by twenty-four inches.

"All this paper came from an old washi shop in Ogawamachi, and the interesting thing about this is that it is square—not *cut* square, *formed* square—and the dimensions are precise. I did some research, and it's exactly the size of the sheets they made for the balloon bombs— and it's dated 1944." Because papermakers all over Japan were involved in the bomb effort, Flavin said he had no doubt about what he had come across. "I showed some samples to an old papermaker in Oga-wamachi, and there was no doubt in his mind what it was, either."

Flavin also had some "frames and folding screens" he had picked up at one of the auctions, which he wanted to show me as well. "These are all old ledger books from offices and shops, and when they were no longer useful, they were used to line these screens. It's all good kozo, of excellent quality. I remove that paper, put it in hot water, run it through my beater, and get paper that turns out like this—and then I make an artistic construction out of it. It doesn't totally dissolve, so as you can see there are characters that remain. So nothing is wasted— not even old kozo."

# 3

## Road Trip

By the production of a cheap writing material, and its supply to markets both east and west, the Arabs made learning accessible to all. It ceased to be the privilege of only one class, initiating that blossoming of mental activity which burst the chains of fanaticism, superstition and despotism. So started a new era of civilization. The one we live in now.
—Alfred von Kremer,
*Kulturgeschichte des Orients unter den Chalifen,* 1877

It is scarcely too much to say that paper made the revival of Europe possible.
—H. G. Wells, *The Outline of History,* 1920

RENOWNED FOR CENTURIES as a key stop on the Silk Road trade routes between China and Europe, the fabled city of Samarkand, in the heart of Central Asia, is where mastery of the papermaker's craft passed from one mighty culture to another—possibly, according to several early accounts, as a spoil of war, though just as likely an evolutionary consequence of overland commerce. Forced to choose between the two, I would admit a preference for the venerable tale of skilled Chinese craftsmen being captured during the territorial war between the Arab Abbasid Caliphate and the Chinese Tang Dynasty at the Battle of Talas, in 751, and turning over details of the prized formula, if only because it is a splendid example of fruitful serendipity.

What is certain, though, is that by the middle of the eighth century, two essential pieces of the papermaking puzzle—a watery pulp laden with cellulose fiber and the screen mold—had been taught to the Arabs, and it was the Arabs who introduced the process to present-day

Iraq, Syria, Egypt and North Africa, and Spain, where Muslims controlled part of Europe for nine hundred years. As workshops opened up one after the other throughout the Islamic world, paper rapidly became essential to multiple forms of creative expression, allowing for an entirely new means of assisted thought—notation—that did not rely on memory alone and was portable enough to always be within arm's reach. In the realm of intellectual inquiry, Muslim scholars used paper during the Islamic Golden Age to record in their own language knowledge received from the Greeks, Central Asians, and Indians. The most famous institution devoted to this pursuit, Bayt al-Hikma, or House of Wisdom, was established in Baghdad by the caliph Abu Ja'far al-Mansur, the first person, according to the tenth-century historian al-Mas'udi, "to have books translated from foreign languages into Arabic."

To obtain original texts, the caliph dispatched emissaries to the Byzantine Empire to buy whatever was available. In addition to renderings of such classic works as Euclid's *Elements* and Aristotle's *Poetics,* transcriptions of original works such as the tales we know as *The Thousand and One Nights* were made in multiple editions by a corps of professional copyists and sold at bookshops known as *warraqs,* or "paper bazaars." The Umayyad caliph al-Hakam II of Córdoba is said to have amassed an astounding library of 400,000 volumes, undoubtedly an exaggeration, but a considerable accumulation certainly, and nourished by a bountiful supply of paper. The one manuscript from his collection known to survive bears a note indicating that it was copied in 970. The oldest manuscript written on Arabic paper to have been preserved anywhere is a Greek text containing miscellaneous teachings of the Christian church fathers, probably copied at Damascus around 800 and now in the Vatican Library. On more subtle levels, paper expanded the modes of common discourse and helped transform the exercise of governmental activity; the sprawling Ottoman Empire made it an essential tool in managing civilization's first modern bureaucracy.

Paper was introduced to the Arab world a little more than a century after the death, in 632, of the Prophet Muhammad, a time when the divine tenets of the Holy Koran were being recited aloud to the newly converted. According to sacred tradition, the revelations, which Muslims regard as the actual Word of God, were passed on to Muhammad through the Archangel Gabriel in the Arabic language over twenty-two years and were committed to memory by the first believers. To pre-

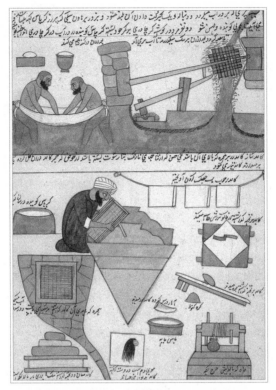

*A papermaker and his tools. From a Kashmiri
manuscript, c. 1850–1860, illustrating traditional
crafts and trades, original in the British Library.*

vent the transmission of profane versions, the first Muslim caliph, Abu
Bakr, decreed soon after the prophet's death that the Koran be written
down as it had been received, and he appointed a committee of "memo-
rizers" to prepare a comprehensive version. Their first compilation was
made primarily from oral recollections but also from fragments that
had been recorded on papyrus, palm leaves, thin white stones, leather,
and the bones of camels, sheep, and asses; the earliest surviving copies
are on parchment.

But as Islamic faith spread beyond the Arabian Peninsula, it became
necessary to establish a text that would be the same for everyone,
including non-Arab Muslims, since Arabic, according to Islamic belief,
is the only language spoken in Paradise. With this in mind, the third
Caliph, 'Uthman ibn 'Affan, under whose leadership Islam had reached
present-day Iran, Afghanistan, and Armenia, ordered that a definitive

Koran be codified in Arabic script and distributed to every province, along with orders that all other versions be destroyed. Since it was the *words* of the prophet, and not images, that were revered above all else, one consequence of this was that calligraphy emerged as the most venerated form of Islamic art.

Samarkand, as it has been known since the Arab takeover of 712 (the name translates as "Strewer of Gold"), was settled by indigenous Sogdians in about 1500 B.C., near an oasis fed by two converging tributaries of the Zarafshan River, a fertile and productive region that proved attractive to the Persian king Cyrus the Great, who conquered it in 550 B.C. While on his way to India in 327 B.C., Alexander the Great married the teenage daughter of a Sogdian nobleman there, with the hope of forming closer ties with his newly subdued subjects; the Greek name for the outpost was Maracanda.

Today, Samarkand is the second-largest city in Uzbekistan, a land-locked nation about the size of California that lies one hundred miles west of the western edge of China and just north of Afghanistan. The network of ancient trade routes the German geographer Baron Ferdinand von Richthofen later christened *Seidenstrasse,* or Silk Road, split, to the west of Samarkand, into several branches, allowing camel caravans to carry their wares southwest to Arabia or northwest to the Black Sea, creating an ideal way station for merchants traveling thousands of miles with their goods between China and the West. In the fourteenth century, the Mongol conqueror Timur—known to fearful Europeans as Tamerlane—made Samarkand his home base and initiated an architectural expansion of such grandeur that the city became known to some as the Heavenly City and the Fourth Paradise.

Irrigated by a network of canals fed by crisp glacial waters from the nearby mountains, the area's hemp, flax, and cotton crops supported a prosperous textile industry, which enabled the city to become Islam's first center of papermaking. Three centuries after its introduction there, the prolific eleventh-century historian 'Abd al-Malik al-Tha'alibi would write that "paper is among the specialties of Samarkand, and it looks better and is more supple, more easily handled, and more convenient for writing than papyrus and parchment." From Samarkand, knowledge of the craft spread rapidly. In what is now Iraq, a paper mill was established at Baghdad, the new Abbasid capital, in 794, to compensate for a shortage of parchment. "Thus paper came to be used for government documents and diplomas," the fourteenth-century North African historian and philosopher Ibn Khaldun wrote, and the demand for the product was so great that it "reached a considerable degree of excellence."

In Syria, the paper made in Damascus was referred to by Europeans as *charta Damascena;* Egypt, in turn, became a producer of such consequence that in 986, the Palestinian geographer Muhammad ibn Ahmad Shams al-Din al-Muqaddasi wrote that paper was one of the country's principal exports, more important by then than papyrus. Fifty years later, Nasiri Khusrau, a Persian visitor to Cairo, would report that street vendors of vegetables, spices, and hardware provided individual sheets "in which all they sold was immediately wrapped up," persuasive evidence of the material's widening versatility. About the same time that Moors from North Africa were introducing the techniques to Spain, toward the end of the eleventh century, some 472 mills were said to be making paper at Fez, a major trading post on the Moroccan coast.

Although the magnitude of the migration itself is well documented, Arab sources are extraordinarily mum about the techniques and equipment their papermakers used and the precise fibers that went into their pulp, a void that has allowed for considerable misinterpretation over the centuries. Because the know-how came from China, and because Chinese papermakers relied preponderantly on plants, not cloth remnants, for their fiber, the widely held assumption in the West for decades had been that raw cotton was the principal ingredient used by the Arabs and that the use of rags was a European improvisation. As an added complication, watermarks—which would be introduced in Italy in the thirteenth century and prove of inestimable assistance to paper historians seeking to identify manufacturers—were used by neither Arab nor Chinese papermakers, making determinations of origin more problematic.

A typical view was expressed in the 1888 *Encyclopaedia Britannica,* which stated categorically that paper made throughout the Islamic world and at Arab settlements in Spain was "in the first instance cotton paper." To support that view, the lengthy essay cited just one piece of evidence, a code of laws established in Spain in 1263 in which paper "is referred to as cloth parchment, a term which well describes the thick material made from cotton." Linen paper, it was further presumed, did not appear in the Islamic world until the fourteenth century, and only then in areas where no cotton was grown, in which case "woolen fabrics" were thought to have been included in the pulp as well—or so it was then believed.

Around the same time that this explanation was being asserted in the *Britannica,* two Austrian academics—one a history professor with a specialty in papyrology and Islamic art, the other a plant physiologist schooled in the use of laboratory microscopes—were coming to another conclusion entirely. Their pathbreaking research was made possible by an enormous discovery of ancient materials unearthed between 1877 and 1880 from several desert dumping grounds south of Cairo in a region of the Fayoum oasis where stone had been quarried in pharaonic times. By far the most spectacular component of the find were 100,000 or so papyrus documents, written in ten languages, ranging from the fourteenth century B.C. to the fourteenth century A.D. and offering an unprecedented opportunity to study the use of the marsh reed as a writing surface over a 2,700-year period. Purchased en bloc by Archduke Rainer Ferdinand of Austria, the materials were given as a birthday present in 1889 to the emperor Franz Joseph I, who made them a centerpiece holding of what is today the Austrian National Library.

While papyrus was the marquee attraction of the discovery, there was a respectable assortment of paper recovered as well, about twelve thousand sheets, a collateral windfall that intrigued Professor Joseph von Karabacek at the University of Vienna. "The collection, unique in its unity and importance, contains an enormous number of documents on paper from the start of papermaking up to the late Middle Ages, showing the development of this writing material over a period of 600 years," he declared of his findings. On the basis of his observations, Karabacek was able to determine when papyrus manufacture had ended in Egypt and when paper became preeminent. He was able also to postulate that water-powered mills were "definitely an Arab invention," a technological breakthrough that "Europe must concede to the Arabs although they claimed it for themselves."

And while Karabacek was conducting that research, a younger colleague of his, Dr. Jerome Wiesner, was subjecting a selection of the same documents to microscopic and chemical analysis, with results that would lead an eminent Oxford University scholar to conclude in 1903 that "some of the hitherto most unquestioned opinions regarding the material and the history of paper" had been dramatically upended by the Austrians. In an essay coyly titled "Who Was the Inventor of Rag Paper?" Dr. A. F. Rudolf Hoernle unhesitatingly affirmed Wiesner's conclusion that "all the papers" in the Vienna collection were made of rags and that "practically all those rags have been found to be linen."

Wiesner further determined that every piece of paper he examined—the earliest dated examples were a letter from A.D. 874, a contract from A.D. 900, and a receipt from A.D. 909—had been "sized" with starch paste and "loaded" with starch flour. "The object of sizing, at that time as in the present day, was to render the paper capable of being written on, and that of loading, to improve its quality," Hoernle wrote. "It is thus shown that in the ninth and tenth centuries, and probably as early as the end of the eighth century, the Arabs were acquainted with the art of making paper from linen rags in network moulds, and sizing and loading it with starch, that is, in fact, substantially with the whole method of paper-making as practiced in Europe till the invention of the paper-machines in modern times."

With such persuasive evidence laid before them, paper historians in the West grudgingly came to reconsider their theories, though, given the dearth of Arab accounts, their approach for the most part was to ignore that phase of the transmission entirely. In an attempt to fill the void, one American scholar who is not a professional paper historian but is an authority on Islamic art, architecture, and calligraphy has approached the subject from two parallel directions: one based on what can be deduced from evidence available in related areas, the other from the application of basic common sense. Jonathan M. Bloom's day job is teaching Islamic and Asian art at Boston College, a full-time chair he has shared with his wife, Sheila S. Blair, since 2000. The unusual convention of a joint professorship allows the couple to alternate teaching in the classroom with pursuing their own projects as independent researchers and writers, a partnership that began in the 1970s, when both were pursuing doctorates at Harvard University in fine arts and Middle Eastern studies. They have written books individually and together and have served as consultants to a three-part television documentary aired by the Public Broadcasting Service in 2001, entitled *Islam: Empire of Faith.*

"Sheila and I were working very hard on Islamic art and the history of Islamic architecture, which inevitably led to my interest in the question of how people knew things," Bloom told me during an interview at the couple's home in southern New Hampshire. "People are always talking about influence—like it's a disease or something, something that you catch, you catch a bit of influence—and so I grew very curious about the practical aspects of how people learn. And people are always talking, too, about plans—except that in this instance, no plans survive at all. So that inevitably led me to consider the remarkable influence of paper, and how essential it had to have been in the face of so much extraordinary accomplishment."

Bloom cited, as one telling example, the Taj Mahal, in India, built over twenty years in the middle of the seventeenth century and widely recognized as one of the most beautiful buildings ever constructed, certainly one of the most metaphoric and allegorical in spirit and execution, and by no means ordinary or unimaginative. Yet nothing survives of the detailed planning certain to have occupied the team of architects, artists, and calligraphers assembled by the Mughal emperor Shah Jahan to honor his departed wife, Mumtaz Mahal. "To me, what they did there is inconceivable without paper," Bloom said. "You have to look behind the work and realize that it was planned out in such a meticulous way that demands the use of paper. Designers encoded their thoughts on paper, and then gave paper drawings to builders to use in the construction. I can't conceive of it happening any other way."

The deeper Bloom got into the history of the region, the more convinced he was that virtually every one of the other art forms he and his wife had studied had developed in ways that required a stage of planning that could not have been done without paper, either. And there was nothing at all to document what he further concluded was an essential step in the creative process: notation, which was taken up in earnest in the West in later centuries. The next step, he decided, was to gather information from existing sources, which gave him the framework of a narrative. "I am not an intellectual historian, but it seemed odd to me that nobody else had thought of this already. It's that obvious." Bloom's book *Paper Before Print: The History and Impact of Paper in the Islamic World* was published in 2001 by Yale University Press.

Sheila Blair, whose specialties also include calligraphy and epigraphy—the writing of inscriptions on stone—noted at this juncture of our discussion that "everything in the Muslim world—certainly in the East after the twelfth century, and the West after the fourteenth—is on paper," at which point Bloom continued along on that line of thought. "A major misconception people have is that the Islamic world took to paper because of religious needs. But this is the time when the Abbasid Empire had expanded—this is the empire that made Baghdad its capital. It was ruled from Iraq and stretched to the shores of the Atlantic and into Central Asia. So when you're administering an empire of that size, you have endless kinds of documents that you need. And paper was the perfect material for that as well."

To that, Blair, who has also written incisively on the Silk Road, added that paper was "much lighter" than any other recording medium and much easier to transport on long overland trips. "And furthermore, the one thing you cannot do on paper that you can do on parchment is change the writing. If you've got a tax document written on parchment, for example, you can scrape the ink off and change the letters. But ink soaks into paper, and you can't remove it. We think about erasable paper today and pencils, but that is today; paper was adopted by the Ottoman bureaucracy for exactly the opposite reason." Bloom said he finds it curious that the only term from Arab papermaking that has made its way to the West is the word *ream,* a unit of measurement that can vary but is generally taken to be five hundred sheets. "It comes from the Arabic *risma,* meaning 'bundle,' and it came to English through the Spanish word *resma* and the old French *reyme.* But that's it—no other Arabic words. The record is pretty much silent on the whole papermaking tradition from that part of the world."

But what most energized Bloom to take up the study of paper was the twin concepts of memory and notation. "In the Islamic lands," he wrote in his monograph, "the great time lapse between the introduction of paper and the introduction of printing reveals for the first time how important the medium of paper itself was in this giant step of human history." Unlike the Europeans, who very quickly seized on the availability of paper to develop mechanical printing, Islam openly scorned the press as a means of textual replication and aggressively hindered its use for several hundred years. Why the Arab world failed to keep technological pace with Europe as it emerged from the Middle Ages is a question historians have pondered for centuries. Also never far from the center of such discussions is how important a part the Arabic resistance to printing might have played in the reversal of roles.

The Golden Age of Islam is commonly dated from the eighth to the thirteenth century, beginning with the establishment of Baghdad as the capital of the Abbasid Caliphate and reaching a climax during the reign of the Mongol conqueror Genghis Khan and the ascendancy of the Ottoman Turks that followed. Movable metal type was introduced in Europe in the 1450s, at the very time that Constantinople was falling to the Turks. At this time, Byzantine Christian scholars were also streaming into Italy with their precious collections of manuscripts, many of them going to Venice, where the printing press of Aldus Manutius, established there toward the end of the century, would provide a lifeline for Greek learning. Arriving at the peak of the Renaissance, printing accelerated the dissemination of knowledge in ways that have been richly articulated by Elizabeth Eisenstein in her magisterial work *The Printing Press as an Agent of Change* and played a central role in allowing Europe to surpass the Ottoman Empire as a world force.

Bloom cited two reasons why he believes the Muslim power structure resisted printing for so long. "Most importantly, there is deep respect and devotion to the act of writing and copying in Muslim society, and it's related to the role of the Koran," he told me. "It meant, as the revealed word of God, that Muslims revered the actual act of writing. Writing was a gift to mankind from God, and thus it became a blessed act to actually *copy* the text, and therefore all writing becomes a blessed act—and making writing beautiful is just as important. It's not that you just write it any which way; you write it beautifully. And so the importance given to calligraphy and beautiful writing in Islam is enormous, far more than in the West. People appreciated it as the one art form that was universally appreciated. Printing was like applying a kind of mechanical intrusion to a blessed process—and that was unacceptable to them." Printing was deemed so offensive to Islamic sensibilities, in fact, that the sultans Bayezid II and Selim I, successive rulers of the Ottoman Empire from 1481 to 1520, issued edicts that outlawed all printing in Arabic and Turkic, bans that held force for three hundred years.

Paper, meanwhile, trickled into Europe at the height of the Crusades, its first points of entry coming by way of Muslim settlements in Spain and Sicily. Tensions ran strong on both sides at this time, and resistance to anything that even hinted of "heathen" influence was widespread. The oldest recorded document on paper is a deed of King Roger II of Sicily, dated 1102, so the new material certainly found some official function on that island. But a provision inserted in the Constitutions of Melfi by Frederick II of Sicily in 1231 decreed that all official documents—*instrumenta publica*—be written thenceforward on parchment, presumably because animal skin was believed to be more durable. The edict nonetheless suggests that paper was being used for official documents at this time, if only to a limited degree. Not nearly as dismissive of paper as Frederick, but equally contemptuous, was Frederick's Spanish contemporary Alfonso X of Castile, known in his lifetime as "the Wise" or "the Learned," who limited its use to lesser categories of record.

Every paper museum I visited for this book featured somewhere among its exhibits a chart depicting the spread of papermaking throughout the world, a kind of cross-cultural road map that begins in China and moves in two directions: east to Korea and Japan, and west to Samarkand, Baghdad, Damascus, Cairo, and Fez and across the Mediterranean into Europe, where the trail becomes quite specific, with fairly well established dates for most of them, though recent scholarship has modified a few. Beginning in Spain in 1056—a full century earlier than was suggested by Dard Hunter—the trail moves to Italy in 1235, possibly even earlier in the thirteenth century; France in 1348; Austria in 1356; Germany in 1391; Switzerland in 1411; Flanders in 1405; Poland in 1491; England in 1494; Bohemia in 1499; Hungary in 1546; Russia in 1576; Holland in 1586; Scotland in 1591; Denmark in 1635; Norway and North America in 1690, Australia in 1818. One country after another took it up, the technology being handed over city by city, workshop by workshop, a classic case of what in other historical contexts has been described as a "domino effect."

The first specific mention of a paper mill on the Iberian Peninsula dates from 1056, near the city of Xàtiva, southwest of Valencia, famous for its fine linens woven from locally grown flax. Precisely how the first papers were made there remains pure speculation, but given the analysis of surviving examples, we know that the fiber was rags and that the pulping, as Joseph von Karabacek had speculated, was probably done in stone troughs with water-driven pistons, or with trip-hammers known as stampers, though there is no definitive evidence to support either view.

One fanciful tale of transmission to the West tells how a French soldier taken prisoner during the Second Crusade and forced to work in a Damascus paper mill set up an otherwise unrecorded papermaking establishment in France upon his safe return home in 1157. Charming as it may be, the only reason the story enjoys any longevity at all is that the man's supposed name was Jean Montgolfier, linking him to later generations of Montgolfiers, who would indeed distinguish themselves not only as papermakers but also as pioneers in the development of human flight. Of relevance in this context is that the brothers Joseph-Michel Montgolfier and Jacques-Étienne Montgolfier, builders in 1783 of the world's first manned hot-air balloon, lined the inside of the sack-cloth envelope they assembled with three layers of laminated paper made in the family factory at Vidalon. But that mill did not begin operations until 1348; its successor, Canson & Montgolfier, remains a maker of fine papers in France and has, as its company logo, the styl-ized outline of a hot-air balloon.

That curiosity aside, what the Montgolfier tale does reinforce is a detail that is undeniably certain: the fact that people did cross cultural and geographic lines repeatedly to learn the skill from others. The Chi-nese, as we have seen, taught papermaking to Koreans, Japanese, and Arabs; Arabs, in turn, brought the know-how into Spain and Italy; and it was in Italy that the German entrepreneur Ulman Stromer recruited two brothers, Marco and Francisco di Marchia, to set up the first mill north of the Alps, at Nuremberg, in 1390. A contemporary image of Stromer's mill survives to this day, shown in a famous double-page woodcut of the city of Nuremberg first published in Hartmann Sche-del's *Nuremberg Chronicle* (*Liber Chronicarum*) of 1493, with the mill pictured outside the walls of the medieval city, below a stream that rushes down to drive the waterwheels.

Quite apart from that image—but giving it an expanded context—is the lucky circumstance that Stromer's careful notes of his papermak-ing activities have survived, including a business journal that offers a unique anecdotal glimpse into the daily workings of a medieval paper mill. Among the details Stromer discussed were the technical tasks involved in building the necessary equipment, negotiating water rights, securing raw materials, and, of particular interest, how he handled an often recalcitrant labor force. The Italians proved especially trouble-some and before long sought concessions from Stromer that would

*The city of Nuremberg, with the paper mill of Ulman Stromer pictured at lower right.
From the* Nuremberg Chronicle, *1493.*

have made them responsible to him only for rent, and free to bring in
workers of their own choosing.

Stromer countered by invoking the terms of legal declarations he
had required all his workers to make before he hired them: each Italian had "sworn a holy oath to the Saints" that he "shall in all of Germany here on this side of the Lombard Mountains not make paper
for anybody except myself and my heirs" and that he "shall not teach
anybody how to make paper, nor instruct anybody in any way, nor
advise, counsel, help, or guide anybody to come from Italy to make
paper in Germany." Stromer related further how "in the very first year"
of their employment, the Italians proved to be "quite disobedient," and
had "hampered" his work by refusing to install a third waterwheel to
complement the first two, which were operating eighteen stampers at
full capacity. "It was their intention to force me to import more skilled
workmen from Lombardy, but I did not wish to do that." Failing to
reach an agreement, Stromer had the men arrested and locked "in a
small room" for four days, whereupon they acceded to his demands.

The critical point of leverage in the dispute centered around the expert preparation of a suitable pulp, which required a constant supply of fiber, and it was this element more than any other that preoccupied papermakers for another five hundred years. There were trade secrets to protect in these preindustrial days, as Stromer's diary emphasizes, but over time the basic process of manufacture differed only by degrees of sophistication and advancing ingenuity. The earliest Arab papermakers probably prepared their rags for pulping by fermenting them first in water, followed by cycles of boiling in wood ash and rinsing. Pounding was almost surely done manually with stones, wooden mallets, and mortar and pestles—the way the Chinese who taught them had prepared it themselves—and later by foot-driven trip-hammers.

By the time the Arabs brought papermaking to Spain and Italy, water-powered stamping mills might have already been in use, as Karabacek suggested, but that is only conjecture. In some areas, grindstones were powered by teams of animals, while the Dutch used windmills. The introduction, at Fabriano in the thirteenth century, of protein-rich gelatin sizing—an additive derived from animal hides, horns, hooves, and bones, probably furnished by local tanneries—gave paper a hard, opaque surface that was nicely suited to quill pens.

In the late seventeenth century, the ever practical Dutch developed a mechanical processor that expedited the refinement of fiber by a factor of ten. Known to this day as the Hollander beater, the ingenious device had a rotating axle fitted with rectangular metal blades that circulated the softened rags against the bottom of an oval tank—grinding them to a pulp in much the same way that old manual lawn mowers cut grass. A hundred years later, the English papermaker James Whatman developed a mold with a woven brass wire-cloth cover that eliminated the furrows left on wet sheets by laid chain links, producing a far smoother surface that quickly gained favor with printers, cartographers, and artists.

Although the *Nuremberg Chronicle* image of Stromer's mill shows only the outside of the building, the interior layout would not have differed substantially from the one pictured in a woodcut made by Jost Amman, a Nuremberg artist who was noted for a series of images that celebrated various trades of the day. His depiction of papermaking offers a comprehensive view of the process as it would have been done in the sixteenth century. Outside two rear windows, a wooden waterwheel can be seen driving a wooden stamper, while inside, a vat-man deftly dips a mold and a layboy carries off a stack of sheets to be dried in another room; in the background is a screw-powered press to squeeze out excess water. The only step missing is the couching of wet sheets onto felt mats. Until the introduction of papermaking machines in the early nineteenth century, this remained the basic process.

Through it all, the quest for fiber was competitive and often contentious. Whether the Europeans picked up on the idea of recycling discarded textiles from the Arabs or came upon it independently is quite irrelevant when considered in terms of the "big picture," as postulated in 1974 by Lynn White Jr., a recognized authority on medieval technology, in an essay on the subject of "unforeseen consequences." The introduction of the spinning wheel in Europe during the fourteenth century accounted for an immense increase in the production of linen shirts, underwear, bed linen, and towels, White pointed out. This was a predictable development of the innovation; what was not anticipated was a sudden glut of linen rags, which enabled the newly estab-

*An early German paper mill, illustrated by Jost Amman in* The Book of Trades, *1568.*

lished paper industry to expand production, lower prices, and increase consumption. "We know that in 1280 at Bologna paper was already six times cheaper than parchment," a circumstance that undoubtedly gave the German goldsmith Johannes Gutenberg all the incentive he needed to "experiment with mechanical means of writing and, when a method was found, to make the considerable capital investment needed to operate it. This was Gutenberg's accomplishment. Its presumption was the spinning wheel."

Introduced in the 1450s, printing consumed Europe in a matter of fifty years, producing, according to some estimates, twenty million volumes through 1500, and with it came an unprecedented demand for paper, which in turn produced an unquenchable need for rags. Stories of peddlers traveling about in wagons making deals for discarded fabrics are numerous, and their quests continued well into the twentieth century. Though dominant as a producer of woolen textiles, England was not a major producer of linen cloth in these embryonic years of European papermaking—one of many reasons why a paper mill was not successfully established there until the later decades of the sixteenth century and why, through the end of the seventeenth century, printers in England, Scotland, Wales, and Ireland relied on imports from Italy, France, Germany, and Holland. England's first long-term success came in 1588—the year Sir Francis Drake's intrepid fleet crushed the Spanish Armada—when John Spilman, jeweler to Queen Elizabeth I, converted a Dartford corn mill to the making of fine white paper and staffed it with workers brought over from his native Germany.

The search for fiber, meanwhile, continued without any form of regulation or code of standards. A plague that swept through much of England in 1636–38 was rumored to have been caused by infected rags imported from the continent. As a partial response to the dwindling supplies, Parliament passed several laws between 1666 and 1680 known collectively as the Burial in Woollen Acts, that required every citizen to ensure that all of their dead relatives—with the notable exception of plague victims—be interred in pure English woolen shrouds. Oaths had to be sworn before justices of the peace that the provisions were met, with noncompliance punishable by £5 fines. The language of the measure approved in 1666 was quite specific, stating that "no person or persons whatsoever shall be buried in any shirt, shift or sheet, made of, or mingled with, flax, hemp, silk, hair, gold or silver, or other than

CARTIERA OVERO PISTOGIO CHE
PESTA LE STRAZZE PER FAR LA CARTA.

*The earliest known illustration*
*of a stamping mill for preparing*
*paper pulp, published in* Novo
Teatro di Machine et Edificii,
*by Vittorio Zonca, 1607.*

what shall be made of wool only," the justification being to lessen "the importation of linen from beyond the seas, and the encouragement of the woollen and paper manufacturers of this kingdom." Though largely unenforced, the prohibitions remained in effect until 1815, when they were formally rescinded.

A few seventeenth-century literary references to the rag trade are worth mentioning. In a nondramatic essay published in 1607, the playwrights Thomas Dekker and George Wilkins belittled the work of a writer they reviled as being so consumed with anger and hate that it deserved to be printed on paper "made of the filthy linen rags that had beene wrapt about the infected and vicerous bodyes of beggars, that had dyed in a ditch of the pestilence." In *The Guardian,* a play performed before a royal audience in 1641, the poet Abraham Cowley has one character say of another that the "breeches he weares, and his hat, I gave him: till then, he went like a Paper-mill all in rags."

In 1873, Carl Hofmann, a onetime papermaking executive in Germany and the United States and the author of a widely referenced "practical treatise on the manufacture of paper," prefaced his nuts-and-bolts treatment of the subject by noting that the product, "at the present day, is made from such an infinite number of materials that it would hardly be possible to enumerate them all." But to make the very best sheets, there was still just one superior ingredient, which he expressed colorfully in four words: "Rags are yet King!"

These sentiments were echoed in a sweeping history of American wealth and influence by the nineteenth-century educator Henry Barnard. Despite measured advancements in technology, he wrote, the paper industry still relied overwhelmingly for its finer products on linen remnants, with a good deal of the supply often provided by a rugged corps of gritty opportunists. "The industrious, but not particularly aesthetic or cleanly, *chiffoniers* gather from every ash barrel and from all the gutters and street sweepings every bit of rag or waste paper, and carefully sort these and sell them to the dealers in paper stock," he wrote. The word *chiffoniers,* French for "rag pickers" and a euphemism for "scavengers," has disappeared from American usage since the practice was abandoned but was once very much a rude reality of urban life.

In an 1887 magazine piece, Richard Rogers Bowker, founder of the publishing firm R. R. Bowker Company and for some years editor of *Harper's New Monthly Magazine,* described a visit he had recently made to a "modern mill" in the United States, with the idea of following "a sheet of paper from its beginning to its end." The process of making pulp from logs was well on its way to transforming the industry by then, but old habits, it appeared, died hard. "If it is to be of the best quality, such as is used for printing this Magazine," Bowker wrote— and *Harper's* was one of the outstanding periodicals of the age—"it begins where other things end, in rags."

Given the unusual nature of a supply chain that relied on the detritus of another manufactured product, the dependence in Europe and North America on a steady source of rags was always uncertain, and the hunt for alternative fibers unending. One of the most important books in the literature of papermaking is Jacob Christian Schäffer's eighteenth-century account of his experiments with vegetable fibers not normally used in the process. Lauded by Dard Hunter for its unprecedented attempt to expand the search, the landmark effort was published in six volumes, between 1765 and 1771, with a long title that loosely translates from German as "experiments in the making of paper without rags."

Even though the text is in German, Schäffer dedicated the book, in English, to King George III, a lifelong supporter of scientific inquiry and patron of the Royal Society of Britain, which had elected Schäffer to membership the year before. Important as the text may be—and Hunter found it significant enough to include a lengthy excerpt translated from the original in his book—it is Schäffer's precise illustrations, and the gorgeous paper samples that were bound into each volume, that make them such a tour de force. Among the eighty-seven fibers represented are cotton grass, black poplar down, tree moss, hop tendrils, grapevine bark, aloe leaves, stinging nettle, cabbage stalks, water moss, lily of the valley leaves, mallow, orache, pinecones, walnuts, tulips, cattail, thistles, Indian corn husks, genista, and potato skins, all either grown in Schäffer's own garden, in the Bavarian city of Regensburg, or gathered from nearby fields.

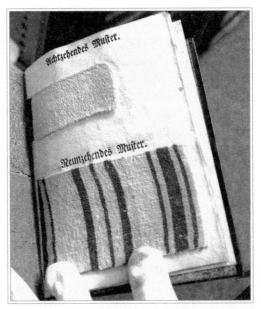

*One of Dard Hunter's personal copies of Jacob Christian Schäffer's eighteenth-century account of experiments with various papermaking fibers, opened to a page containing several handmade samples.*

Because he made the papers without benefit of bleach, which would not be invented until 1774, each specimen bears a tint of its original color. By also including a swatch made from wasps' nests he had gathered, Schäffer recognized the pioneering observations of the French physicist, entomologist, and naturalist René-Antoine Ferchault de Réaumur, whose 1719 study of the flying insect's nesting behavior led ultimately to the making of paper from ground wood pulp. To prepare his experimental papers, Schäffer first chopped the vegetable matter he had collected with a knife, then macerated the fragments to a consistent pulp in a set of miniature stampers, pictured in a fanciful vignette on the frontispiece and again in a full-page illustration.

"I decided myself to make all the experiments, from beginning to end, in my own home," Schäffer wrote, an activity he found so pleasurable that he made it his "regular winter occupation" over a period of years. "And what sweet satisfaction did I feel when I saw that everything came out better than I had imagined! In a short time I was able to produce a reliable new sort of paper." As pleasing as the results were, Schäffer was dabbling as an amateur, and had no interest in applying the knowledge he had acquired to a commercial enterprise; like Réaumur before him, he was content to show the way, allowing others to follow his example.

Another experimenter determined to do exactly that was Matthias Koops, an entrepreneur originally from Pomerania whose early life was spent in military service on the Continent. Naturalized as an English citizen in 1790, he saw potential in producing a commercial-grade paper that did not rely on linen or cotton rags. His first efforts were rewarded in 1800 with publication of a ninety-two-page book titled *Historical Account of the Substances Which Have Been Used to Describe Events, and to Convey Ideas, from the Earliest Date to the Invention of Paper,* on its face an overview of writing surfaces through history, but in reality a sales pitch to prospective investors. Like Schäffer, he also included an effusive dedication to George III, then forty years into what would be the third-longest reign of an English monarch, 1760 to 1820.

In his remarks to the king, Koops expressed gratitude for the royal patents he had already received, one of them for a process to extract ink from wastepaper and convert it into white paper "fit" for writing and printing, and two others "for manufacturing paper from straw, hay, thistles, waste and refuse of hemp and flax, and different kinds of wood and bark." A single line of type on the title page made clear that Koops was by no means discussing a concept and that what he needed was sufficient backing to expand on a papermaking enterprise he had already begun in earnest at a mill in the village of Neckinger, at Bermondsey. The very book lying open in the reader's hands, he wrote, was "printed on the first useful paper manufactured solely from straw." Further on in the text, Koops justified the enterprise by pointing out the alarming shortage of rags then hindering the production of paper. "All Europe has of late years experienced an extraordinary scarcity of this article, but no country has been so much injured by it as England." The "evil consequences of not having a due supply of rags," he continued, "has been the stoppage of a number of paper-mills."

Staked to £70,000 in seed money from new investors, he promptly opened another factory, the Straw Paper Manufactory, at Millbank in Westminster. For a second edition of his book, published just a year later, Koops printed the text on paper made from recycled waste, an initiative recognized today as a first of its kind. But having spent all the money he'd raised on buildings and machinery, the company quickly went bankrupt, and the effort to find a lasting alternative to rags would remain for others to accomplish later in the century.

Like the Schäffer book, the Koops title is also a great rarity, and while I was more than happy to read the text in what we have all learned to call a PDF—or portable document format—file, it was a special thrill for me to handle the Houghton Library's original copy. Yellow, with the texture of fine sand, the pages are unmistakably suggestive of straw, yet it was the agreeable aroma—of fresh-cut grass, I thought—that left the strongest impression on me, unmistakable after the passage of more than two hundred years. I mentioned as much in an e-mail to Christine Harrison, in England, one of my traveling companions on the trip to China and the author of a doctoral dissertation on Jacob Christian Schäffer. A papermaker in her own right, Harrison wrote in reply that she was about "to stir up my daffodil leaves, which will be paper by this evening; the last effort was seaweed paper—very pretty, and still smelling of the sea!"

While deemed a failure in the short run, the Koops effort did demonstrate that alternative processes were feasible, and it was very much a precursor to the Industrial Revolution, then about to reach full flower in England. Other innovative papermaking efforts would have their ups and downs as well. Indeed, a machine conceived in France that proved as revolutionary to the making of paper sheets as the Hollander beater had been to mass-producing pulp would also suffer the ignominy of bankruptcy before achieving widespread acceptance.

The continuous papermaking machine known today as the Fourdrinier—so named for the two wealthy English stationers who invested heavily in its development, the brothers Sealy and Henry Fourdrinier—was based on a design patented in France in 1799 by the inventor Louis-Nicolas Robert. The most obvious application was the potential for making spools of wallpaper, which had become fashionable in France with the introduction of decorative colored papers from China. The principle, as explained by Dard Hunter—"and the same principle holds with all modern papermaking machines"—was to form paper on an "endless woven-wire cloth" that retained the bonded fibers on top while allowing water to be pulled out by suction from below.

Failing to get the project off the ground in France, Robert's financial backer, an entrepreneur named Saint-Léger Didot, had brought the idea to England, where it was taken up by the Fourdriniers, who invested £60,000 in building a prototype. Their machine made decent enough paper, but endless litigation with creditors and assignees ultimately brought the operation down, enabling other engineers to design improved versions without paying royalties on any existing patents. The ability to form spools of uncut paper, meanwhile, led directly to the development of the rotary press, which in short order would revolutionize the newspaper industry.

With the increased use of machines, chemicals, ground wood pulp, and bleaching agents, papermaking became less of a craft and more of an assembly-line industry, and the quality of the product itself suffered a significant decline. Only in recent years has the effort to produce better paper staged something of a comeback, with the increased production of higher-grade archival stock intended to stand the test of time. For John Bidwell, a librarian and historian of book culture who has spent more than thirty years studying papermaking, the focus is on that key period, which had very little to do with the romance of paper and more with the fundamentals of its transformation into a dominant industry.

"In theory, you're not supposed to notice paper, and if you're noticing paper, that probably means there's something wrong with it," Bidwell

told me during an interview in his office at the Morgan Library &
Museum, in New York, where he is the Astor curator of printed books
and bindings. "I readily acknowledge that there's a great irony in this.
In the world of fine printing, you do notice texture, color, substance,
the famous crackle of the well-sized sheet, but when you're dealing
with commercial publishing, if you're noticing the paper, that usually
means there's a problem that has to be fixed." Bidwell also teaches, with
Timothy Barrett, a course at Rare Book School, at the University of
Virginia, in Charlottesville—an intensive weeklong program of classes
and hands-on instruction that I took during the early stages of my
research for this book. As the course is structured, Barrett concentrates
on what might well be called the aesthetics of the process, Bidwell on
the history. "One of the reasons Tim and I make such a good team is
because we look at paper from completely different directions," Bidwell
told me.

"He is, as you point out, very interested in craft, and he is very
much involved in the fine-printing world, and interested in superb luxury paper. I, on the other hand, am interested in the industrialization
of the paper trade, so my period of interest begins in the 1790s and
ranges up to about the 1860s. Paper has always been essential to the
book trade, but before industrialization it was expensive. This is the
great transition period in the book trade in general, with all sorts of
things going on. You've got the steam press, you've got stereotyping,
you've got lithography—all these new technologies coming on at the
same time—and then you have all these great changes in the paper
trade itself. If you're a publisher, an author, or a printer, one of your
major concerns is going to be the expense of paper. So when I say that
Tim Barrett looks for good paper and I look for bad paper, what I am
saying is that I look for the papers that indicate cost-cutting measures
of the industrial period. I've been very interested, for example, in the
first paper that had bleach in it, which is pretty dismal stuff. That is
very bad paper—but of great interest to me."

Bidwell said that being a historian of paper demands that he be
something of a purist in the approach he takes to the medium, especially since it begins with a blank sheet. "A person who is interested
in prints, or a person who is interested in type history—they all have
visual information to work with. But if you're a paper historian, your
response to the object is on a much more subtle plane, and maybe

that explains some of the missionary zeal of people like Dard Hunter. They really needed to go the extra mile to get people excited about something, which after all was just supposed to be a medium; paper is supposed to be a vehicle for information—not a mode of information in and of itself."

Given that his professed specialty was "bad" paper, Bidwell—a past president of the Bibliographical Society of America who, when we spoke, was working on a project to identify and describe paper mills operating in America between 1690 and 1832—did more or less break his own rules when he agreed to look at a large aggregation of paper acquired in 1986 by the English fine-press publisher John Randle, from Oxford University Press. The paper became surplus when the press discontinued its printing operations and began jobbing the work out to subcontractors. "Valuable artifacts were practically put out on the street," Bidwell said, including a warehouseful of handmade paper left over from books published between 1900 and 1970. Randle, owner of the Whittington Press, suggested that Bidwell "write a few lines about each sample" for a portfolio he was going to issue in a limited letter-press edition.

"Typical librarian that I am, I got totally drawn into the project, because it turned out these were blank sheets of paper, and the challenge for me was to identify which books they were used in. This is one of the party tricks librarians can do when there are watermarks. You are able to take caliper measurements, look at a whole bunch of books, and say, 'Yes, that's the paper.' I'm quite proud of some of my discoveries for this book. What was going to be a few lines per sheet turned out to be a couple hundred pages long." Published in 1998, *Fine Papers at the Oxford University Press* served, in Bidwell's view, "as a kind of valedictory to the end of hand papermaking in England, and the fun thing about the book is that people generally jump to the conclusion that when the papermaking machine came in, this spelled the end of the old ways. Well, that wasn't always the case, as we found out in these few examples."

Having said that, he quickly added his view that "most of the handmade paper today is paper artistry" not suitable for printing on a large production basis. "Not even Tim Barrett makes paper suitable for printing on a production basis. A lot of the hand papermakers you are talking with will probably disagree with me about some of this, but they are making objects in which paper is to be viewed as *paper*. After the Second World War, when the English mills closed down, production of hand papermaking as a regular economic basis was no longer feasible. And that's why I say it's a lost art. One reason I got involved with the Oxford papers was because this was a way to chronicle the very end. So when I told you that Tim does the good paper and I do the bad paper—this is the exception. I couldn't resist the opportunity."

# 4

## Rags to Riches

Rags are as beauties, which concealed lie,
But when in paper, how it charms the eye;
Pray save your rags, new beauties it discover,
For paper truly, every one's a lover:
By the pen and press such knowledge is displayed,
As wouldn't exist if paper was not made.
Wisdom of things, mysterious, divine,
Illustriously doth on paper shine.
—*The Boston News-Letter,* a public plea for rags,
   March 6 and 23, 1769

We are sorry we cannot oblige our customers with more than half a sheet this week owing to the want of paper. The present scarcity throughout this county will certainly continue unless a paper-mill is established in this neighborhood.
—Isaiah Thomas, *The Massachusetts Spy,* February 7, 1776

In a little more than a quarter of a century, the machines have entirely superseded the diminutive hand-mills which sparsely dotted the country, and gigantic establishments have risen up in their places. Paper-mill villages, and banking institutions even, have grown out of this flourishing branch of industrial art, and we behold with satisfaction and amazement, what has been brought about by the aid of a commodity so insignificant in the eyes of the world as linen and cotton rags.
—Joel Munsell, *Chronology of Paper and Paper-Making,* 1864

PRINTING WITH METAL TYPE developed in Europe in direct response to a profusion of paper, which would seem to be the natural scheme of

things, but the order of battle was reversed, as it were, by more than
half a century in British North America, where presses led the way
and where several generations passed before domestic supply was in
a position to satisfy constantly growing local needs. To manufacture
paper according to traditional Western methods, a sufficient quantity
of rags and an abundant supply of pure water were merely the first
requirements; the process also involved such steps as shredding, pulping, rolling, molding, sizing, and drying, not to mention the purchase
of expensive equipment, the mobilization of a skilled labor force, and
harnessing a source of power to run the beaters. Shipping a press, fonts
of metal type, and bundles of handmade paper on a long sea voyage
was no simple task in the seventeenth century, either, but once a printing shop was up and running, the logistics were manageable, so long as
the needs were modest.

That was the rationale, presumably, that justified the opening of the
continent's first English-language printing press, at Cambridge, Massachusetts, in 1639. The initial expectation for Stephen Daye, the printer
brought over on the same ship that carried the equipment, was that he
produce legal documents for the colonial government and theological
tracts for the English settlers. The following year, Daye used 115 reams
of French paper to produce 1,700 copies of *The Whole Booke of Psalmes
Faithfully Translated into English Metre,* a hymnal commonly called the
Bay Psalm Book and considered to be the Gutenberg Bible of the New
World; only eleven copies are known to survive.

By the time William Rittenhouse began making paper outside
Philadelphia fifty years later, a handful of other printers were at work
in Massachusetts, Pennsylvania, and Virginia, the bulk of their activity
also being job orders for provincial offices and the clergy. Their work
was both tedious and pedestrian, summarized by no less an authority
than Isaiah Thomas, the proprietor of sixteen printing presses during
the early federal period, an esteemed historian of his craft, and the
founder, in 1812, of the American Antiquarian Society. The role of the
earliest colonial printers, he wrote in *History of Printing in America,*
was to serve as "fellow laborers in the great work of settling a dreary
country and civilizing the children of the wilderness."

It was that latter pursuit in particular—"civilizing the children of
the wilderness"—that persuaded the Puritan missionary John Eliot, in
1659, to begin compiling a remarkably audacious edition of the Holy

Scriptures with the assistance of a Nipmuc tribesman who had been allowed to take courses at Harvard College. Using the Roman alphabet to spell words out phonetically, Eliot translated both testaments of the Bible into the Natick dialect of the Algonquin tribes then living in eastern New England. One thousand copies were authorized by the Society for the Propagation of the Gospel in New England, an undertaking of such complexity that a second press was sent over from England, along with a special order of Dutch paper and an apprentice to assist Samuel Green, the new manager of the Cambridge press, on the job.

When they finished in 1663, several copies of *Mamusse Wunneet-upanatamwe Up-Biblum God*—the formal title of what we today call the Eliot Indian Bible—were sent to London, where they were regarded immediately as true oddities, since nobody in Europe could comprehend a word of the printed text. Indeed, it was this circumstance above all others that argued for producing the Bible in Massachusetts in the first place—though the job would have been managed far more efficiently in England, there were no people available who understood the words being set into type.

While it made perfect sense to produce texts written in an alien tongue in situ, the early colonists still relied overwhelmingly for their own reading on books brought over from the Old Country, a reality emphasized by the paucity of other materials printed in North America during these formative decades. Between 1639 and 1700, a period of sixty-one years, fewer than one thousand books and pamphlets were published in the colonies, all of them issued in modest print runs. "Those who lov'd Reading," Benjamin Franklin wrote in his *Autobiography*—and the great Founding Father was speaking of himself in the 1720s, as a young man with a voracious appetite for intellectual stimulation—"were oblig'd to send for their Books from England."

What changed the dynamic exponentially and accelerated the demand for paper from then on was the introduction of newspapers toward the end of the seventeenth century, a phenomenon of social networking that had taken hold in England just a few decades earlier. The news was crossing the Atlantic with each shipload of new settlers as an evocative reminder of the homeland left behind. The first effort to publish a continuing chronicle of current events in the colonies was undertaken by Benjamin Harris, a radical pamphleteer who had left

England in 1686 after being imprisoned repeatedly for issuing tracts deemed distasteful to the Crown. Resettled in Boston, Harris introduced *Publick Occurrences Both Forreign and Domestick,* a lively periodical of news and chitchat modeled on the *London Gazette.* Intended to appear monthly, the initiative was limited to the September 25, 1690, debut issue. Offended by Harris's impudent opinions on how to govern a colony and his crass suggestions of rampant infidelity in the French royal family, the austere Puritans who controlled the Massachusetts Bay Colony ordered the operation shut down and the entire printing confiscated. Ironically enough, the only copy that survives—a single sheet of twelve-by-twenty-inch paper folded once to produce four pages—was the one sent to London to document the offense.

A far more stable enterprise turned out to be the *Boston News-Letter,* a weekly that opened for business in 1704, committed to reprinting articles published in "the Public Prints of London, besides those of this and the Neighboring Provinces." Among its notable "scoops" was a riveting account of the death, in 1718, of Edward Teach, the brigand better known as Blackbeard the Pirate, at the Battle of Ocracoke Inlet, off the coast of North Carolina. By taking care to ruffle few feathers, the *News-Letter* published without interruption for seventy-two years.

Farther south, Pennsylvania was emerging as a dominant center of printing, pioneered there by William Bradford, a colorful entrepreneur who had immigrated to America in 1685 at the invitation of William Penn, founder and "absolute proprietor" of the province, to introduce the "art and mystery" of printing to the Middle Colonies. His first effort was an all-purpose almanac filled with miscellaneous pieces of practical information. Required to submit the journal to local authorities for prior review, Bradford was told to delete a phrase judged offensive to Lord Penn and ordered in the future "not to print anything but what shall have lycense from ye council," a caveat he ignored in 1692 with the issuance of a tract deemed critical of the governing Quakers.

Arrested and charged with seditious libel, Bradford defended himself successfully at trial but decided the following year that the time was ripe to accept an invitation to become the royal printer in New York. Not long after establishing himself there, he took on the same duties in New Jersey, and did other job work, too, all the while building a modest printing-and-publishing empire that operated in three colonies. To manage the Pennsylvania operation in his absence, Bradford had brought in an experienced Dutch printer, an arrangement that proved beneficial for both until Andrew Bradford, William's son, was old enough to take charge in 1712. Andrew's publishing credits would include establishment of Philadelphia's first newspaper, the *American Weekly Mercury,* in 1719; six years later, his father launched the *New-York Gazette,* that province's first newspaper, leading Lyman Horace Weeks to muse in 1916 that, had William Bradford "been of 1900 instead of 1700, he would have shone pre-eminently as one of our modern hustlers."

Bradford may well have been a "hustler" in that he was highly competitive and shamelessly ambitious, but he was also a pragmatist possessed of a knack for staying one step ahead of the competition, a trait no better evidenced than in how he went about securing a domestic paper supply that was not reliant on foreign imports. Before leaving Philadelphia for New York, Bradford had persuaded William Rittenhouse, a forty-two-year-old German immigrant who had learned papermaking in Holland, to set up a mill on a twenty-acre site they leased in 1690 with two other investors. It was built in the suburban village of Germantown, on the banks of a stream that flows into Wissahickon Creek, a tributary that in time would be known as Paper Mill Run.

By 1706 Rittenhouse had acquired total ownership of the mill, though in return for his share of the business Bradford had made sure that his printing operations would be fully supplied, and at very favorable rates. Stipulated precisely in the sales agreement were assurances that the Bradfords would have first refusal of "all ye printing paper" that Rittenhouse made, an arrangement that gave them a stranglehold on the local supply. When a second mill opened, on the west side of Paper Mill Run in 1710, it was under the ownership of William Dewees, a native of Holland who had married into the Rittenhouse family. The Rittenhouse mill remained in business through four generations, its closing, in the years leading up to the Civil War, consummated without fanfare. The original site is now a national historic landmark within Fairmount Park known as Rittenhouse Town, and it includes a small museum housed in one of several restored buildings.

As media moguls of their time, the Bradfords were able to retain their edge for two full decades, their grip on the paper supply challenged finally by an ambitious young man from Boston who would distinguish himself in a variety of dazzling ways. Among the minor ironies attending Benjamin Franklin's initiation into the cozy world of colonial publishing was that before moving on to Philadelphia in 1723, he had sought employment in New York with none other than William Bradford. Turned away there, Franklin was advised to try his luck in Philadelphia, with son Andrew.

Though just seventeen at the time, Franklin was already a capable printer, trained from the age of twelve by his older brother James, who in 1721 had begun the *New-England Courant,* the second successful newspaper to be established in Boston. Failing to get regular work with the Bradfords, he was taken on by Samuel Keimer, a recently established competitor in need of able assistance. Disdainful in his autobiography of Keimer's skills—"a mere Compositor, knowing nothing of Presswork"—Franklin quickly emerged as a force to be reckoned with, not only for his expertise with type and ink but for his shrewd ability to play by other people's rules and continually emerge victorious.

In 1729—the same year that Franklin purchased the failing *Pennsylvania Gazette* from Keimer "for a Trifle"—the colony's third paper mill was opened, twenty miles southwest of Philadelphia, by Thomas Willcox. Over time, Franklin and Willcox would become close friends and associates, with Willcox providing a good deal of the newsprint for Franklin's various enterprises; his company, known as Ivy Mills, furnished the paper on which the continental government printed currency notes and, until it was outbid by Crane and Company in 1879, supplied high-quality paper for the nation's first "greenbacks." To assure additional supplies for his burgeoning empire, Franklin took his cue from the Bradfords and became actively involved in the paper trade. By his own count, he financed no fewer than eighteen paper mills during his years as a printer, and went a step further by effectively cornering the market in rags. He offhandedly mentioned this strategy in his autobiography while crediting his common-law wife, Deborah, for having "assisted me cheerfully in my Business, folding & stitching pamphlets, tending Shop, purchasing old Linen Rags for the Paper-makers."

A number of Franklin's account books documenting various details of his business activities through 1747 are preserved in the library of the American Philosophical Society, in Philadelphia. The volume known as Ledger D records sales of rags between 1739 and 1747 to seven Pennsylvania papermakers totaling 166,000 pounds; Franklin's purchases of paper in various grades from these mills over the same period came to just under three thousand reams. These figures are strictly for credit sales and represent just a fraction of the business he is known to have conducted during those years, but they are substantial enough to suggest that his involvement was anything but casual. "There seems no reason to doubt," James Green and Peter Stallybrass concluded in a study of Franklin's career as writer and printer, "that Franklin became the largest paper merchant in the colonies."

The accelerating need for paper was such that colonial governments came to regard the supply as something of a public utility deserving of special status. Not one to miss out on a target of opportunity, William Bradford unsuccessfully petitioned the New York General Assembly in 1724 to pass a bill that would have given him exclusive authority to make paper in the colony and "prohibit all other persons from making the same in the Province during the space of fifteen years." Turned down there, Bradford invested in a new mill in Elizabethtown, New Jersey.

In 1728, an Act for the Encouragement of Making Paper, passed by the colonial legislature in Massachusetts, granted a consortium of Boston merchants "the sole Privilege and Benefit of making Paper within this Province" for a period of ten years. Within two years the group was producing paper seven miles south of Boston on the Neponset River. Similar initiatives were undertaken elsewhere, but as Lyman Horace Weeks pointed out in his chronological survey of the industry, "papermaking did not keep pace with paper-using." Much of the imbalance, he added, was due to the "studied and persistent opposition of the mother country" to permit any kind of industry that might jeopardize the lucrative markets it controlled in the colonies.

Beyond the obvious economics of supply and demand, what the frenetic scramble for paper also suggests is how essential the product had become in America, so much so that when officials in London began thinking of creative ways to raise revenue, they came up with a strategy that took dead aim at this new dependence. The sweeping measure they proposed in 1764, a notorious bill we know today as the Stamp Act, was made especially urgent by the recently concluded French and Indian War and was loosely modeled on a similar plan implemented in England in 1694. England's national debt had almost doubled, to £130 million, during the long battle with France and Spain for dominance

*A selection of embossed duty stamps produced in England in accordance with the*
*Stamp Act of 1765, in the collections of the Massachusetts Historical Society.*

in North America, conducted between 1756 and 1763. With the acquisition of Canada and Florida as fruits of victory, the prospect of posting ten thousand soldiers along the Mississippi and Ohio River valleys
threatened to swell the deficits by an additional £220,000 a year.

Having failed to collect levies on the importation of sugar, molasses,
indigo, coffee, linen, and Madeira wine, Parliament proposed an alternative approach of internal taxation that would assess fees on a wide
spectrum of social, domestic, business, legal, and regulatory exchanges.
The one feature they all had in common was that each was validated
by a paper document. Under legislation approved on March 22, 1765,
it was also decided that newspapers—and many historians came to
regard this provision as the fatal flaw of the act—would have to be
printed on embossed paper purchased from the government. Liquor
and wine licenses would be subject to duties, too, as would the purchase
of playing cards and dice. But it was duties on all the paperwork—the
more "red tape," the better, apparently—that were going to fatten the
royal coffers.

The genius of Prime Minister George Grenville's plan—and it does
have a degree of spiteful brilliance to it—was that by controlling all
governmental business, the Crown could legitimize any activity that
required the force of law, and it cut across all sectors of society. By long

tradition and custom, for example, a sale of real estate could not be consummated until an agreement was signed, witnessed, and recorded in a registry of deeds; under the new rules, the property could not legally change hands until stamps certifying that a revenue tax had been paid were affixed to the instrument. Anticipating the likelihood of Yankee chicanery (agreements concealing the actual figures could easily be finagled sub rosa), property taxes were to be assessed according to the amount of acreage involved, not by the purchase price.

The inclusiveness of the act was expressed in provision after provision, more than fifty of them all told, none more sweepingly than in a clause citing the various transactions that would require a duty of two shillings and sixpence each: "any indenture, lease, conveyance, contract, stipulation, bill of sale, charter party, protest, articles of apprenticeship, or covenant." The honor of receiving "any degree taken in any university, academy, college, or seminary of learning" would require a payment of £2; the filing of "any declaration, plea, replication, rejoinder, demurrer, or other pleading" imposed a burden of threepence. For the privilege of practicing law in any manner—and the edict pointedly included every "counsellor, solicitor, attorney, advocate, or proctor" within "the said colonies and plantations"—a whopping payment of £10 had to be forked over first. And death itself offered no relief; before a will bequeathing an estate could be probated, a fee of sixpence would have to be paid to the Crown by the survivors.

Lord Grenville estimated that the levies would realize £60,000 the first year alone, and since the code would "remain a perpetual resource," it would increase as the colonies grew and prospered. Because the duties prescribed for legal documents varied, stamps would be impressed in colorless relief on official papers and distributed by royal agents who were responsible for collecting the fees. Acts of forgery and counterfeiting were declared to be capital offenses punishable by death. Since newspapers were mass produced and of an ephemeral nature that existed outside the jurisdiction of bureaucratic control, publishers would be required to buy prestamped paper manufactured in England before they would be allowed to print.

For every copy of a newspaper published on what was called a "half-sheet" of paper, a fee of a halfpenny was to be levied; the next largest and more common size would require a full penny. Every advertisement sold would trigger an additional duty of two shillings, and there was a sliding upward scale for outside job work on almanacs and pamphlets. All materials printed in any language other than English—an especially onerous sanction for the German-language publications of Pennsylvania, which were considerable—were subject to double fees. Publishers failing to comply with any of these regulations were threatened with severe fines, which would be imposed by British vice-admiralty courts, not locally administered jurisdictions, and without benefit of a jury, as was the case in England's common law courts.

Recently returned from a five-year mission to England, where he was widely known and respected, Benjamin Franklin was asked by the Pennsylvania House of Representatives to voice the province's concerns before Parliament. He agreed to do so but sailed for Europe in 1764 resigned to the inevitability of some sort of tax burden, a concern he confided to several close acquaintances. Once arrived in London, he guardedly ordered one hundred reams of "half-sheet" newsprint for the *Pennsylvania Gazette,* then being managed by his business partner, David Hall.

In what would prove to be a rare tactical error on his part, Franklin recommended the appointment of his friend John Hughes for the position of Pennsylvania tax collector and stamp distributor, a blunder that would incite a mob of angry citizens to gather outside his house in Philadelphia, terrifying his wife, Deborah, who had remained behind in America. Alerted by Hall of mounting displeasure, Franklin wrote a series of eloquent essays critical of the Stamp Act and remained a strong advocate of colonial rights through the remainder of his stay in England—which ended ten years later, on the eve of revolution.

With the new levies set to go into effect on November 1, 1765, pockets of protest solidified throughout the colonies, none more defiant than among the Sons of Liberty, a loose coalition of merchants and landowners that extended from New England to Georgia. As the general population became increasingly engaged, demonstrations turned violent and destructive. In fear for their lives, many stamp distributors resigned their commissions, offering no resistance to the seizure and destruction of their consignments. Responding warily at first, newspapers soon became organs of indignant energy, astutely sensing the mood of an outraged citizenry and spurring it into a chorus of unified opposition.

Writing twenty-five years after the fact, David Ramsay, a South

Carolina delegate to the Continental Congress and the first historian of the Revolution, noted how fortunate it had been "for the liberties of America" that newspapers "were the subject of a heavy stamp duty." Printers, he explained—and by that he meant the publishers, editors, and writers of the various journals, who very often were one and the same individuals—"when uninfluenced by government, have generally arranged themselves on the side of liberty, nor are they less remarkable for attention to the profits of their profession. A stamp duty, which openly invaded the first, and threatened a great diminution of the last, provoked their zealous opposition." In a trenchant monograph on the decisive events leading up to July 4, 1776, the historian Arthur M. Schlesinger Sr. would call the decade that followed the Stamp Act travesty "the newspaper war on Britain" and credit it with successfully "fueling the discontents that flamed into Independence."

In New Haven, the *Connecticut Gazette* proclaimed on July 5, 1765, that those "who would give up Essential Liberty, to purchase a little Temporal Safety, deserve neither Liberty nor Safety." In Rhode Island, a paper called the *Providence Gazette, Extraordinary,* appeared on August 25 in a single issue asserting boldly the credo "VOX POPULI, VOX DEI" ("The voice of the people is the voice of God"), accompanied by the biblical injunction from Corinthians: "Where the Spirit of the Lord is, there is Liberty." On October 10, as zero hour drew near, an Annapolis printer changed the name of his newspaper to the *Maryland Gazette, Expiring,* with the motto "In uncertain Hopes of a Resurrection to Life again."

One of the prize holdings of the Library Company of Philadelphia is a remarkably well-preserved copy of the *Pennsylvania Journal and Weekly Advertiser* of October 31, 1765—Halloween—which also happened to be the day before the Stamp Act was scheduled to go into effect. Bold black lines run up and down the front page, between the columns, to form the outline of a gravestone, with a skull and cross-bones inserted in the masthead. The publisher, William Bradford—namesake of his grandfather, William Bradford, and the nephew of Andrew Bradford—vowed to suspend publication until the duties were lifted. Bradford bade his readers "Adieu, Adieu," and when war broke out ten years later, he joined the Pennsylvania militia, fought bravely in the Battles of Trenton and Princeton, and achieved the rank of colonel.

On November 1, courts throughout the colonies refused to con-

*William Bradford's* Pennsylvania Journal *of October 31, 1765—the day before the Stamp Act was set to take effect—at the Library Company of Philadelphia.*

vene, and administrative offices remained closed. In New York, a mob threatened to hang the governor if he enforced the act. One observer of the mayhem wrote, "the Tempers of the people are so alter'd by the frightful Stamp Act, tis beyond Conception, so violent & so universal." The *Boston Gazette* published the names of stamp agents, calling them "mean mercenary Hirelings or Parricides among ourselves." The first issue of the *New-York Gazette: or, the Weekly Post Boy,* to appear after the act took effect defiantly proclaimed itself dedicated to "LIBERTY and PROSPERITY, and no STAMPS." Within a matter of months, the act had been recognized in London for what it was—an utter disaster—and Parliament repealed the measure on February 21, 1766. Most of the stamped paper sent to America was either destroyed by angry colonists or repurposed when returned to England, with the result that very few examples in original condition survive. A few specimens are preserved in the collections of the Massachusetts Historical Society and the Library Company of Philadelphia, and some are on file in the National Archives in London.

In the decade that followed the Stamp Act, demand for paper remained steady in the colonies, and to meet the growing need new mills were established in Connecticut, New York, Maryland, North

Carolina, and South Carolina with the acquiescence of royal officials. But once hostilities began at Lexington and Concord, on April 19, 1775, paper imports from England were cut off, and domestic production was totally inadequate to meet everyday needs. Writing to General George Washington on August 27, 1775, from Albany, New York, General Philip Schuyler apologized for the "scraps of paper" he was forced to use for his reports, explaining that "necessity obliges me to use them, having no other fit to write on." Writing from Philadelphia on April 15, 1776, John Adams advised his wife, Abigail, that he was forwarding to her copies of "every newspaper that comes out, and I send you, now and then, a few sheets of paper [for personal use], but this article is as scarce here, as with you. I would send a quire, if I could get a conveyance." On August 20, 1776, a consortium of Pennsylvania papermakers petitioned Congress to discharge from army service a man named Nathan Sellers, claiming he was the only person in the colony able "to make and prepare suitable moulds for carrying on the paper manufactory." The petition was granted, and one of Sellers's first tasks was to make molds fitted with specially designed watermarks used by Ivy Mills for continental currency paper.

Paper shortages were made all the more critical by the growing need to produce musket cartridges, a function of paper I will discuss more broadly in Chapter 7. Nowhere was this shortage more evident than in the fate of a book known today as the Gun Wad Bible, so named because several thousand unbound copies were repurposed as munitions casings during a key phase of the war. Printed in 1776, the book was the third edition of the first Bible to be printed in America in a European language, preceding Robert Aitken's first edition in English by six years. The publisher was Christopher Sower, a second-generation printer whose father, also named Christopher Sower, had produced the first edition of the book in 1743. A prosperous man who also owned a small paper mill in Germantown, the younger Sower brought out a second edition in 1763, and this was the first book to be printed on paper made in America. The third edition followed thirteen years later, with sheets sufficient to produce three thousand copies.

How many copies circulated is not known, but as with its predecessors, the print run of the 1776 edition was intended to accommodate demand over a lengthy period of time. Conventional practice then was to fold the finished pages into quires—twenty of which make up a ream—and store them unbound until sold. Where these third-edition copies were warehoused is not entirely clear, but some of the sheets, it was later asserted, were kept in the loft of the town meetinghouse, where they supposedly had been hung and left to dry many months earlier. It was further suggested that following the Battle of Germantown, on October 4, 1777—more than a year after the third printing— occupying British troops used the sheets stored there for a variety of purposes: as litter for their horses and kindling for their campfires, but mostly as casings for their musket cartridges.

Details published by the American Antiquarian Society in 1921, based on more thorough research, determined that unbound Bibles probably were used to make munitions, but more likely by General Washington's Continental Army and not General William Howe's redcoats. Giving further weight to that argument is the undisputed fact that the devoutly religious Christopher Sower was what we today would call a conscientious objector, and that his failure to support the rebel cause with sufficient enthusiasm led, in 1778, to the seizure of his property and its sale at public auction. All of the printing equipment and all of the unbound books still tied in bundles went to John Dunlap, a Philadelphia printer who produced the first copies of the Declaration of Independence, and whom we shall meet again in Chapter 11.

Having little use for paper sheets bearing words in the German language, Dunlap may well have found a more practical use for them on the field of battle. Writing thirty-five years after the war had ended, Isaiah Thomas chose to cast responsibility for the episode on both armies. "Some copies of them had been before, and others of them were now, converted into cartridges, and thus used, not for the salvation of men's souls but for the destruction of their bodies," he wrote vaguely of the incident, and diplomatically left it there. Today, the Gun Wad copies that did survive—including the one I examined at the Library Company of Philadelphia—are prized for their relative scarcity; a census published in 1940 documented the existence of 195 copies, most of them now in institutions.

Regardless of which side sent the Bibles up in smoke, the incident was hardly unique. In a memoir of his wartime experiences, Richard Peters Jr., a jurist and politician from Pennsylvania, recalled how he had dealt with one battlefield shortage during his tenure as secretary of the Continental Board of War. "On our entering Philadelphia in

June 1778, after the evacuation of the British troops, we were hard pressed for ammunition. We caused the whole city to be ransacked for cartridge paper." These determined efforts, he continued, led to the discovery—in a "garret" storeroom once occupied by the printing interests of Benjamin Franklin—of "more than a cart body load of *Sermons on Defensive War,* preached by a famous Gilbert Tenant" during the years of the French and Indian War, gathering dust after so many years because they had never been paid for. "These appropriate manifestoes were instantly employed as cases for musket cartridges," Judge Peters was pleased to report, "and were fired away at the Battle of Monmouth against our retiring foe."

Before the Revolution began, Isaiah Thomas had operated his printing business in Boston, on the southeast corner of Marshall Lane and Union Street, a building now occupied by Ye Olde Union Oyster House, the oldest continuously operating restaurant in the United States. Marked for arrest by the British as a troublemaker, Thomas fled Boston on the eve of the Battles of Lexington and Concord, his printing press disassembled and safely in tow. Relocated in Worcester, he resumed publication of his influential newspaper, *The Massachusetts Spy,* on May 3, 1775, with the first eyewitness accounts of the shot heard round the world.

After the war, Thomas expanded his interests to include bookbinding, papermaking, and retail sales. Benjamin Franklin would call him "the American Baskerville," a flattering reference to John Baskerville of Birmingham, England, the outstanding type designer and printer of his generation. Using Worcester as his base, Thomas developed his publishing enterprise into the largest in the fledgling nation, and likely used more paper than any other single consumer. In his history of printing in North America, Thomas calculated that by 1810 there were 195 paper mills operating in the United States and its territories, sixty of them in Pennsylvania, forty in Massachusetts.

In 1843, some two million pounds of rags were imported into the United States; seven years later, the number had reached twenty-one million. By 1857—the year France and Italy prohibited the export of rags—the total had reached 44,582,080 pounds. The need for fiber was so acute that several entrepreneurs arranged for the importation of linen wrappings stripped from mummies freshly exhumed in Egypt. Though the crude practice is doubted by some historians, recent research has documented several instances in Maine, New York, and Connecticut during the 1850s of the ancient swaths being used to produce lower grades of wrapping paper, and they were blamed in one instance for an outbreak of cholera.

When the Civil War broke out, in 1861, there were 550 paper manufacturers in the United States, only fifteen of them located in the eleven states that just seceded from the Union, none at all in Mississippi. The disparity was severe enough that the *New-Orleans Commercial Bulletin* warned early on that the South would do well to "temper its opinions on secession until it became independent of Northern ink, type, presses, and paper." The burning by Union troops of the largest Southern plant, in Augusta, Georgia, in 1863, made shortages that were already serious especially grave. To provide paper for Confederate currency—which became more and more worthless as the conflict wore on—a mill outside Manchester, Tennessee, that remained active for most of the war worked without interruption on nothing else, pausing only to clean the boilers.

As part of his strategy for a northern campaign in 1863, Confederate general Robert E. Lee sent a detachment into Cumberland Valley, Maryland, for the express purpose of foraging for needed supplies, with paper ranking high on his want list. In the run-up to the Battle of Gettysburg, soldiers under the command of General Richard S. Ewell filled six wagons with paper removed from three mills operating in a southern Pennsylvania village known as Papertown, today located in the borough of Mount Holly Springs. For the few manufacturers able to make paper in the South, there was, as usual, an insufficient inventory of rags. As early as June 1861, the *Richmond Whig* cautioned that, without rags, newspaper publishers—whose output was always in great demand during anxious times—would be unable to operate, and urged citizens to conserve their tattered garments. By 1863, rags that could be spared for papermaking—most were being diverted for conversion into bandages—were selling for eight cents a pound.

The printing stock that was sold to newspapers was of the most common grades, oftentimes coarse wrapping paper made from processed straw. From October 1862 to November 1863, the Houston *Tri-Weekly Telegraph* was printed on papers that were brown, pink, orange, blue, yellow, and various shades of green. Some intrepid publishers made their deadlines with editions printed on the blank side of wallpaper, most famously the Vicksburg *Daily Citizen* of July 2, 1863, issued two days before the city's surrender to General Ulysses S. Grant.

Writing paper and stationery were in great demand as well, with ledger sheets, printed business forms, medical prescriptions, and blank flyleaves ripped from books often filling in as substitutes. Envelopes refolded for multiple use became known as "adversity covers." Personal journals—including the famous Civil War diary kept in forty-eight volumes by Mary Boykin Chesnut of South Carolina—were recorded on a shabby stock referred to as "Confederate paper," made with rice straw that gave it a brown tinge.

An unpublished manuscript containing improvised recipes for various food items and soaps was written anonymously over four months in 1864 on the blank sides of Confederate bonds, used envelopes, and old letters and discovered at war's end stitched inside the binding of a ledger book bearing the name of a South Carolina bank. That effort may well have been inspired by the publication, in 1863, of the *Confederate Receipt Book,* a compilation of one hundred recipes—or receipts, as they were then known—for such items as "apple pie without apples," "artificial oysters," and "bread without yeast." A "substitute for coffee" called for roasting "sound ripe acorns" with "a little bacon fat." The original edition was bound in yellow polka-dotted wallpaper; only five copies are known to survive.

With the Union restored in 1865, the United States entered a determined phase of national development, its march toward industrial dominance about to continue in earnest. What amounted to a paradigm shift in papermaking was becoming apparent, too, as machinery pioneered in Europe came increasingly to America, where the technology was advanced considerably by homegrown engineers. Still lacking was a sufficient source of fiber, though that would soon become a part of the new calculus as well.

The task of the papermaker has always been to isolate cellulose fibers from the raw material. Higher-quality papers have fewer impurities, which is why cotton is superior to all other plants: fibers from the seed hair of the plant are the purest form of cellulose. Nobody has ever disputed that rags make the best paper, but once mass production, not perfection, became the driving impulse, concessions on quality were not difficult decisions for the captains of commerce to make when a feasible alternative finally presented itself. The demand had encouraged experiments with every manner of vegetative source, all yielding uneven results. The "vast majority of the so-called fibers fail," the leading trade publication of the day, *Paper Trade Journal,* observed dourly in 1876, "and people who are experimenting today with such materials will only have their labor for their pains."

Boiled straw had been attempted in America as early as 1829, but the results there were mixed as well, and the efforts largely abandoned. Beginning around 1850, a tall grass from northwest Africa known as esparto was used productively in England to make a surprisingly good-quality paper, often used for printing, but the cost of transportation made its use in the United States prohibitive. The potential for ground wood had been recognized in 1719 by Réaumur's studies of wasps, but it took more than a century before a practical application of the concept would enjoy any kind of sustained success. The first viable plan for the production of mechanical wood pulp was patented in 1845 by Friedrich Gottlob Keller, a German machinist whose failure to renew his share of the license seven years later allowed his financial partner in the hopeful undertaking, the papermaker Heinrich Voelter, to begin production on his own and prosper mightily in the years that followed.

Making ground wood pulp involves little more than cutting logs of equal length from freshly harvested trees, peeling off the bark, and grinding the stripped bolts that remain against a rotating stone under a stream of water. Once it's reduced to finely shredded bundles of fiber, more water is added to produce a pulp; as the technology advanced, a disk-type mill was adapted to hasten the task. Cellulose fiber obtained in this manner is adequate for most applications, but the downside is the presence of a brown-colored chemical compound commonly found in trees known as lignin, from the Latin word for "wood." Lignin's natural function is to cement tree fibers together by filling the spaces within the cell walls between the ropelike cellulose bundles. Durable and useful for many applications, highly lignified wood yields more energy when burned and is an excellent source of fuel. But when allowed to remain in pulp, it is unstable, and its brittle nature makes for a frail sheet of paper that yellows over time when exposed to air and sunlight.

When it was introduced commercially in the 1860s, the mechanical process simply yielded paper with the impurities left in; it was fast, easy, and useful for products such as wrapping paper that were never intended to last long in the first place. The reason newspapers printed on wood pulp turn yellow with age—and indeed why the phrase "pulp fiction" entered the language to identify inexpensive books of little literary merit printed on cheap paper that rapidly deteriorates—can be credited to lignin. The strength of ground wood pulp is so low that higher-grade fibers often had to be blended in to hold the paper together; more often than not, that other fiber was rags—the greater the concentration, the better the grade.

The first wood-grinding plant was established in 1867, in Western Massachusetts, near Stockbridge, by Albrecht and Rudolph Pagenstecher, prosperous cousins who opened a much larger facility on the Hudson River in upstate New York two years later, transforming the industrial climate of the region. The *New York Times* converted over to newsprint made entirely from wood pulp in 1873, and by 1882 "nearly every paper in the United States with a large circulation had changed over," according to figures compiled by David C. Smith, a historian of American forestry. By that time, chemical processes were being developed with an eye toward removing the lignin and preserving longer fibers, but there were trade-offs.

The chief advantage of chemical pulping is that it degrades lignin into molecules that can be washed away from the cellulose. The first process to be employed, called the soda process, called for cooking the wood chips in a solution of sodium hydroxide—caustic soda—producing a bulky pulp with good opacity, which appealed to book manufacturers who needed to print text on both sides of the page. The disadvantage to this was that the paper was not very strong, and because effective bleaching systems had not yet been developed, the pulp had low brightness. Much better brightness could be achieved by using an alternative method called sulfite pulping, though a major downside to using sulfites was that the chemicals ended up as pollutants in the waterways where the effluents were discharged.

The sulfate, or kraft, chemical process was developed toward the end of the nineteenth century by the German chemist Carl F. Dahl. With this method, the cooking "liquor," as it is called, also uses caustic soda but adds sodium sulfide, which breaks the bonds linking the lignin to the cellulose. Introduced in Sweden, the kraft process—the word comes from the German word for "strength"—was notable for producing a sturdier paper that resists tearing. Another key advancement came in the early 1930s with the invention of the recovery boiler, enabling kraft mills to recycle almost all of their pulping chemicals; this innovation, along with the ability to accept a wider variety of woods, helped make it the dominant procedure for producing pulp.

In 1880, Clark W. Bryan, a publisher from Springfield, Massachusetts, introduced *Paper World,* a trade journal devoted entirely to papermaking. Best known professionally for his periodical *Good Housekeeping,* Bryan was responding to what had rapidly become a booming industry in the years following the Civil War, particularly along the Connecticut and Housatonic rivers in New England, where his own business interests were located. "Over one-third of all the paper now made in the world is manufactured in the United States," he reported in the premier issue. "The annual product amounts to about 640,000 tons—about 1,830 tons daily. It is estimated that of wood pulp paper alone 52,000 tons per year are made."

The numbers were robust enough for the time—American papermakers had assumed control of the world market—but wood pulp still represented only about 20 percent of total production. *Paper World* occasionally published articles on numerous kinds of fibers still being tried out in the industry—experiments undertaken with corn, for instance, or attempts in Florida to capitalize on the ready availability of palmetto trees—but the industrial might of the United States was finding ground wood to be a panacea, at first in the Northeast, where timberlands dotted the landscapes of New York, the northern New England states, and Canada.

In timber-rich Maine, mills began to spring up along a number of waterways during the 1860s, most notably the Androscoggin, Kennebec, Penobscot, Presumpscot, and St. Croix rivers. Most were small operations, few producing more than three hundred pounds of pulp a day, but as demand accelerated, they became larger and more sophisticated. Most of the pulpwood during the pioneer days of the industry in northern New England was poplar and willow, supplied by farmers who cut the wood, peeled it, and hauled it by wagon to the nearest railroad station, sometimes directly to the buyers. "It was not until mills began to take 2,000 to 3,000 cords a year (roughly 1 million to 1.5 million board feet) that more formal methods of procurement had to be found," according to David Smith. Those methods inevitably led to the companies buying up vast tracts of land to supply their individual needs. In 1890, a Lewiston, Maine, firm drove thirty-six million board feet of timber down the Androscoggin River.

Propelling production to these prodigious heights, of course, was the unprecedented growth of the newspaper industry. The volume of newsprint used by American newspapers rose from 106.8 million pounds to 670.9 million pounds between 1880 and 1890, while the total daily circulation during that same period, according to U.S. Census figures, went from 31.8 million to 69.2 million copies a day. By 1900 the total circulation of American newspapers was 114.3 million copies a day. The robust demand led to the 1898 merger of eighteen paper manufacturers operating twenty mills in Maine, New Hampshire, Massachusetts, Vermont, and New York, and with it the founding of the International Paper Company, which quickly secured a monopoly in the making of newsprint.

In an in-house history of its first quarter-century, the company trumpeted figures that would make environmentally sensitive executives of today cringe with their candor. "In round numbers, the mills of the International Paper Company convert into paper 700,000 cords of pulp-wood annually," W. W. Haskell wrote in the aptly titled *News Print.* "As pulp wood averages about five cords to the acre it is obvious that each year there is consumed the available wood on 140,000 acres, or nearly 220 square miles. In order, therefore, to maintain its leading world position in the paper industry, the International Paper Company has purchased and now holds a total of 4,460,080 acres in the United States and Canada. Of this total, 1,589,840 acres are owned in fee, while 2,879,240 acres are so-called Crown lands in Canada held by virtually perpetual leases." One photograph in the book folds out to picture what the caption identifies as "46,000 cords of wood" lying outside the company's Hudson River Mill, dwarfing a row of boxcars lined up on the rails nearby.

On the occasion of its fiftieth anniversary, International Paper reported that the annual consumption of paper in the United States for all uses had reached twenty-five million tons annually, a twelve-fold increase over 1898, a span in which the population of the country had only doubled. The average American in 1948 was using an estimated 340 pounds of paper products a year, and five million cords of wood—more than seven times the volume reported twenty-seven years earlier—were being used to make pulp. Along with newsprint, linerboard, containerboard, and food container papers—most notably brown grocery bags and milk cartons—were being produced in great volume, too.

A forestry report prepared in 1937 for the Weyerhaeuser Timber Company noted a similar statistic, and added this: "In fact, people of the United States use as much paper as is consumed by the rest of the world combined." The disparity would modify over time, but the American appetite for the product remained rapacious, with the realization finally dawning that long-range prospects depend on careful management of resources. "Eventually, our paper and pulp industries will have to depend upon sustained yield units for their supply of wood fiber," the company acknowledged. "In order to assure the operation of our forests on a sustained yield basis, there must be an adequate forestry program, which in turn depends upon stable industries to utilize forest products."

By the time that report was written, paper was being made from wood harvested throughout the United States, with pulp produced from every manner of tree, and for a multitude of commercial uses. The first paper mill west of the Rocky Mountains was built on a creek near Salt Lake City in 1852, a handmade operation established to support the Mormon settlement of Brigham Young. The first papermaker on the Pacific coast opened in 1856 near San Rafael, California—a rag mill that made less than a ton of newsprint a day. Papermaking in the Pacific Northwest got under way in 1866 on the banks of the Willamette River in Oregon City, Oregon, producing brown straw wrapping paper for $1.50 a ream. The first mill in Washington Territory opened for business in Camas in 1883, equipped with an eighty-four-inch Fourdrinier machine, five eight-hundred-pound rag engines—and a German-born expert papermaker imported from the East Coast to run it. When the building was leveled by fire, a larger mill was built on the same site and five years later began using white fir, spruce, and hemlock to make eight tons of newsprint a day.

When Canada restricted its exports of wood to the United States in the 1920s, a paper industry began to develop in the South, where development had been hindered previously by fears that southern pines contained excessive pitch that would foul machines and make newsprint too dark, though technologies were adapted to counteract that impediment. Founded in 1927, Georgia-Pacific has become one of the world's leading manufacturers and marketers of tissue, pulp, paper, and packaging. Other regions of the country assumed expanded roles too, nowhere more evident than Wisconsin, which in 1951 laid claim to being the new center of papermaking in the United States, a distinction it still maintains.

"Perhaps no other industry has utilized the natural resources of the Pacific Northwest and developed them to such an extent as has the paper industry," W. Claude Adams wrote in a detailed history of papermaking in that region of the country. "It has used tule and wood, native to the region, its water for power, its lava rock for beater rolls, its limestone for the sulphite process, and its clay for filler and finish in the manufacture of paper products and has developed various skills and processes to build up one of the most extensive and indispensable industrial concerns to be found in the Pacific Northwest, in the country at large, or, as some claim, in the world." It is an assessment that could easily be applied in principle to other areas of the continent where the pulp and paper industries took root and prospered, a case study of an enterprise going, quite literally, from rags to riches.

# 5

The Sound of Money

It is this tendency on the part of paper to take the place of everything else, to become a universal substitute, so to speak, which leads to the conclusion that the future has a grand development in store for it, and that in the years to come its manufacture will hold a magnificent position among the great industrial interests of the world.

—Editorial in support of free tariffs, *Paper World,* 1881

IN 1799, a twenty-two-year-old papermaker steeped in the family trade set out by horseback for the foothills of Western Massachusetts to what was still a rural outpost of the new republic. After much casting about, the young man found what he was looking for on the banks of the Housatonic River: a fourteen-acre wedge of prime farmland that he bought for $194. With the financial backing of two investors, Zenas Crane opened the first paper mill in the United States west of the Connecticut River, a one-vat operation in the village of Dalton that relied in the beginning on his own manual labor for success. Within twenty years the business had grown sufficiently that the thrifty Yankee assumed sole control of a company that is now in its seventh generation of family ownership, and renowned as the dean of American papermakers.

Best known for the currency notes it has produced exclusively for the United States Treasury Department since 1879, Crane and Company is admired also for a line of 100 percent cotton stationery that has been used approvingly by numerous American presidents and successive members of the British royal family and made as branded products for such elite clients as Tiffany and Cartier. As other papermakers have

*A fanciful depiction of Zenas Crane testing the waters of the Housatonic River in Dalton, Massachusetts, by the commercial artist Nat White.*

come and gone, Crane has remained viable primarily by remaining nimble, but also because the founder's well-documented insistence on producing a quality product has never been compromised.

Zenas Crane was born in 1777, seven years after his uncle Thomas Crane and two partners assumed control of a mill on the Neponset River, the same one that two decades earlier had been authorized by the Massachusetts legislature. Ardent patriots to a man, the trio had brazenly called their business the Liberty Paper mill and had done their part to further the cause of independence. The old mill's business ledger, today a prized possession of the Crane Museum of Papermaking, in Dalton, lists among its clients the *Boston Gazette, and Country Journal,* an anti-British newspaper published by Benjamin Edes and John Gill, as well as Isaiah Thomas, who used Liberty paper for the May 3, 1775, edition of the *Massachusetts Spy,* which reported the first accounts of the Battles of Lexington and Concord.

Just four days before the onset of hostilities, the Committee of Safety of the Province of Massachusetts recorded in its journal that "four reams of paper be immediately ordered to Worcester for the use of Mr. Thomas, Printer," and approved an additional shipment immediately following the battles. Another Liberty entry records the sale, on January 4, 1776, of thirteen reams of "money paper" to the silversmith and engraver Paul Revere, for a run of provincial currency known as "Sword in Hand" notes issued to cover debts incurred during the Siege of Boston; the consignment was picked up at the mill and delivered to Revere under armed guard. It is further recorded that Revere drew on his friendship with Thomas Crane in other ways, receiving permission from him the following year to graze forty-six warhorses on the Liberty Mill property, in Milton.

At war's end, Stephen Crane Jr., who had learned the papermaking craft at his uncle's mill in Milton, opened his own business along a vigorous stretch of the Charles River near Newton Lower Falls, in Needham, a busy community of iron makers, weavers, millers, and tanners, and taught the fundamentals to his younger brother Zenas, who before long was apprenticing in Worcester for Isaiah Thomas at a paper mill set up for him by the Crane brothers. When Thomas sold that operation to Major General Caleb Burbank, another wartime colleague, who already owned several other mills in central Massachusetts, Zenas decided it was time to strike out on his own. Located 140 miles west of Boston and 150 miles northeast of New York City, Dalton was within striking distance of both urban centers yet far enough removed that there was space to grow. To power his beaters, there was the Housatonic River, a robust waterway that rises in the Berkshire Hills and flows 180 miles south through Connecticut into Long Island Sound, and to prepare the pulp he had an artesian well on the property to furnish water of uncommon purity.

Zenas's goals initially were modest—six reams of paper a day, twenty tons a year, all of it made by hand in the classic manner, with labor supplied by what has proven, over more than two centuries, to be a highly devoted and reliable workforce. Significantly, the first public announcement for the enterprise, published on February 8, 1801, in the *Pittsfield Sun,* targeted a key segment of the local citizenry for support. "Ladies," the notice implored, "save your RAGS," and offered a "generous price" in return for their cooperation.

> ## Americans !
> *Encourage your own Manufactories,*
> *and they will Improve.*
>
> LADIES, fave your RAGS.
>
> AS the Subfcribers have it in contemplation to erect a PA-PER-MILL in *Dalton*, the enfuing fpring ; and the bufinefs being very beneficial to the community at large, they flatter themfelves that they fhall meet with due encouragement. And that every woman, who has the good of her country, and the intereft of her own family at heart, will patronize them, by faving her rags, and fending them to their Manufactory, or to the neareft Storekeeper—for which the Subfcribers will give a generous price.
>
>                      HENRY WISWALL,
>                      ZENAS CRANE,
>                      JOHN WILLARD.
> *Worcefter*. Feb. 8, 1801.

*A public appeal for rags, 1801*

Within five years, Crane was counting among his customers bankers who issued their own currency, and printers who specialized in engraving stock and bond certificates. The word "bond" as a term to identify a certain grade of paper suitable for printing archival documents came into use by way of this context. As his business grew, Zenas expanded his search for fiber, forging deals with tin peddlers and postal carriers to haul cloth in from other areas and buying linen remnants from European textile mills that were shipped to him by packet boat up the Hudson River from New York. "Our wagons arrived late last night from Troy with eleven bales of rags consigned to us by the sloop *John Hancock*," Crane wrote a colleague in June 1811. "Upon examination, the contents met with our approval, and they promise ready conversion into our paper." In 1831, he purchased a cylinder machine developed in nearby Springfield, and on his own he invented a mechanical layboy that removed the paper from the device; to expedite drying, he also installed steam-heated tubes of his own design. Other improvements included an automated trimming knife, a pulp dresser, and a cutting machine.

A few months before Zenas's death, in 1844, the company's first
Fourdrinier machine went online, a move that strengthened its position in the face of growing competition along the Housatonic and
Connecticut rivers. By the early 1890s, Berkshire and Hampden counties would become one of the most prosperous papermaking regions in
the world, with much of the new blood drawn to Western Massachusetts, as Zenas Crane had been, by the proximity to major seaports, an
inducement made all the more attractive with the opening of the Erie
Canal, in 1825.

To exploit the full potential of a natural waterfall that drops fifty-
eight feet within a fifth of a mile on the Connecticut River, nineteenth-
century engineers built the industrial city of Holyoke around three
circular canals that generated sufficient power to operate a cluster of
twenty-eight mills, which at their peak accounted for nearly 90 percent
of the paper produced in the United States. Though every one of these
mills would close in the years following World War II, the economically stressed community still calls itself "Paper City." One nostalgic
reminder of past glory is a full-bodied line of boutique ales and pilsners
produced on the fifth floor of one of the old buildings by the Paper City
Brewery Co. Inc.

One company that claims to have invented the oversize yellow
legal pad, American Pad and Paper Company, now based in Texas and
known as Ampad, moved its Holyoke operation to Mexico in 2005.
The departure for more profitable pastures and cheaper labor south of
the border signaled the end of a local institution that had begun in 1888
with a clever idea to buy rejected remnants from nearby mills, known
as "sortings," and transform them into distinctively lined writing tablets that became indispensable among attorneys, judges, clerks, and law
students. Why the extra length of the pad, why the double vertical line
in red along the left margin, and why the color yellow remain anyone's
guesses, since no patents were ever filed.

The grim distinction of being Holyoke's last paper manufacturer
to expire, however, goes not to Ampad but to Frank Parsons Paper
Company, which had been the first mill to set up shop in the city and
was by common consent the most distinguished of them all. Founded
in 1853, Parsons at one time was the largest manufacturer of premium
stationery and office ledgers in the United States, and specialized in
making cotton rag document paper for many cultural institutions and

museums. Like Crane, Parsons was family-owned through several generations, but its sale to National Vulcanized Fiber of New Jersey, in
1958, marked the beginning of a long decline that ended in 2005, when
the corporation declared bankruptcy and abandoned the massive brick
mill that occupied four and a half acres of downtown real estate to
the elements. The unshuttered and unsecured building was reduced to
rubble in 2008 by a spectacular nine-alarm fire that burned for three
days, the victim of an arsonist's match.

How Crane and Company has managed to survive as an industrial
force in New England when so much of its competition has come and
gone is a topic worthy of a doctoral dissertation, which some young
candidate may well consider as the privately held company continues
to prosper well into the twenty-first century, with annual sales estimated at more than $500 million. It has helped, certainly, to have had
a recession-proof government contract for more than 130 years making banknote paper for the United States Treasury, but the contract
still goes out to competitive bid every four years and is contingent on
delivering a high-quality specialty paper that is essentially all rag, making American currency the most versatile and resilient banknote in the
world.

Unlike the mills that began using ground wood pulp in the 1860s,
Crane has remained a "tree free" operation that uses cotton and linen
fibers exclusively. The realization, too, that paper has multiple applications has allowed the company to embrace new opportunities as they
have arisen. For instance, with the introduction, in 1847, of adhesive
postage stamps in the United States, Crane was among the first to enter
the market with a viable surface developed for that purpose; with the
introduction of the mechanically folded envelope in the 1850s, the line
was expanded further to feature stationery that in time would find
favor with such customers as Queen Victoria and President Theodore
Roosevelt. Among high points in the Crane Museum, in Dalton, is an
1886 request to attend the dedication of the Statue of Liberty; another,
from 1937, invites special guests to the formal opening of the Golden
Gate Bridge.

During the Civil War, the company manufactured cartridge paper
for the Union army. In 1873, Winthrop Murray Crane, a grandson of
the founder and, from 1904 to 1913, a United States senator from Massachusetts, won a major contract to make what were known as bullet

patches for a new repeating rifle produced by the Winchester Repeating Arms Company of New Haven, Connecticut, a weapon that would earn fame as "the gun that won the West." The design involved making thin linen bonds that served as a kind of gasket for rounds that were assembled in two parts, the chief advantage being that they burned cleanly and left little ash. That contract—and the manufacture of disposable paper collars by the millions for the men's fashion industry—helped the company weather the long economic depression precipitated by the Panic of 1873. In 1903, Crane technicians developed a transparent tracing paper with sufficient strength that it quickly found favor among architects and engineers as a durable drawing medium. During the Great Depression, the company made cigarette paper for the tobacco industry, and it augmented its stationery division with a line of carbon paper that remained a staple in its inventory until the advent of xerographic copying machines and computer-generated copies eliminated the demand.

What would prove most consequential of all, though, certainly in terms of the long run, was an innovation Zenas Marshall Crane, a son of the founder, had introduced in 1844 as a deterrent to counterfeiting. His process of inserting parallel silk strands into the "wet end" of the papermaking machine during the formation stage—one thread for $1 bills, two for $2 bills, and three for the $3 denominations that were then in vogue among many of the issuing banks—got the company seriously involved in the making of security papers. This technology proved especially useful thirty-five years later when Crane decided to bid on a contract to supply paper for United States currency, then being made for the federal government exclusively by J. M. Willcox & Co. of Philadelphia. A last-minute offer of thirty-eight and nine-tenths cents per pound, submitted by the future Senator Crane, was significantly below the seventy cents a pound then being paid to Willcox, and it began a relationship with the Bureau of Engraving and Printing that has continued ever since.

In more recent years, a subsidiary operation located just outside Stockholm, acquired from the Central Bank of Sweden in 2002, supplies currency paper to other countries that have included Mexico, Egypt, Canada, India, Saudi Arabia, South Korea, Tanzania, and Thailand, making Crane one of the world's largest manufacturers of banknote paper, accounting for 60 percent of its world production.

According to the Bureau of Engraving and Printing, some thirty-five million bills, with a face value of $635 million, are run off each day. The life expectancy of a $1 bill, according to the Federal Reserve, is forty-one months, and it is designed to be folded back and forth a minimum of eight thousand times—or four thousand "double folds"—before tearing.

In Dalton, the making of paper for American currency is done in three sprawling brick buildings situated within a mile of one another. Teams of workers in one of them prepare the pulp, called half-stock, according to precise government specifications, while the paper itself is made in the two others. The finished product is produced on a proprietary Fourdrinier machine that runs continuously under security restrictions monitored by the U.S. Secret Service.

Located nearby is the Crane Museum of Papermaking, housed in a restored one-story gray fieldstone building built in 1844 by Zenas Crane to receive rags brought in for sorting; next door are the executive offices, where my wife, Connie, and I met one summer morning with Douglas A. Crane, a company vice president and manager of U.S. government products, including security features for American currency.

*Douglas A. Crane, a seventh-generation American papermaker.*

Given that he's a seventh-generation papermaker—and one of four family members currently holding a senior position in the company—it is irresistible to assume that paper, in a sense, runs in his veins. "Pulp is more likely," he replied at the suggestion; "it flows a lot easier." Crane's earliest memories as a child growing up in Dalton include making frequent trips through the various plants with his father, Christopher Crane. "I was always aware that papermaking was right around the corner," he recalled. "I lived on a hill above the mills, and looked out over them as a kid. Whenever my father took me through, I was fascinated by the activity that was going on."

A 1982 graduate of Brown University, Crane worked briefly in the biomedical industry before taking a position in the family business. "I went to work in the engineering department, where I started designing these neat little fixtures and systems for inserting security features into paper," he said, and invited us to examine a few of the materials he had with him that incorporated the latest security devices being developed by his division. "As I got into the practical side of the business and began to understand the processes, it struck me as to just how complex this system of making paper really is. There's a lot of physics involved. But the true beauty is that there's also a fair amount of art as well."

Crane said that once he was on the payroll, he quickly immersed himself in the lore and techniques of the craft. "I became intrigued with handmade paper and the history of papermaking, and actually, after I was back here working for a period of time, I started dabbling around with the idea of our producing a line of handmade papers—in a sense returning to our roots—and we actually got a few things up and running. It was motivated more through passion than by any business impulse, I suppose, because it didn't take long for the economics to kick in, which was really too bad, because we made some absolutely beautiful paper."

But making paper by hand did give Douglas Crane a feel for the product that goes well beyond the sense of touch, and it was no surprise for me to learn that one of his favorite exhibits in the museum next door is a functional model of Zenas Crane's first vat room, a handsome display commissioned by the company in 1929 and assembled to scale by Dard Hunter, who at the time had just established a handmade paper operation a few hours south of Dalton in Lime Rock, Connecticut.

"I love the way paper feels, and the way it handles, I love the rattle when you shake it—I just love being around it," Crane said. "And I also love being in the mills where we make it, and when you see the finished product, whether it's a box of stationery or a ream of currency paper, you realize that you've just taken all of these fibers from the raw state and pulled them together and ended up with this miraculous product. The absolutely amazing thing about paper is that cellulose fibers are the only fibers in nature that are self-adhering. If you want to make felt or something out of protein-based fibers, you've got to really work them and get them all mechanically entangled. But with cellulose, as you start removing the water, they've got all these hydrogen-bonding sites on the surface of the cellulose chains, and when they dry, they end up getting closer and closer together, and then they just bond to each other. So a dry sheet of paper is good, strong stuff, all on its own. The issue, then, of course, especially with things like currency paper, becomes, if you get it wet—you don't want it to fall apart in the washing machine—you have to add in additional wet-strength chemicals for added performance. But on a very basic level, paper is an incredibly strong and durable substance."

Among the items Crane had brought along for us to see that morning was a prototype of a newly designed bill to serve as a sample for foreign governments in need of special security paper for their own currency. Looking exactly like a typical banknote, but with markings identifying it as a product of the Crane company, the bill included sophisticated features incorporating the most current technological developments designed to outwit potential counterfeiters. Certainly the most impressive was the engraved image of a dragonfly that gives off a variety of colors when tilted to the light and has eyes that appear to follow the viewer around the room as he moves.

"You're looking at a new security device; we call it motion—a thread that gets woven in and out of the banknote that has tiny images printed on it that slide around on the surface when you move it. If you tilt that thread back and forth, those images will slide right and left. If you tilt it right to left, the images will slide up and down. It's a highly complex optical system on a microscopic scale; there are about fifty thousand individual lenses working together to make that one eyeball image that you see on the thread. We used the dragonfly for the sample because the compound eye of that insect actually has much of the same structure."

The filament that weaves its way within and along the surface of the paper is a strip of plastic, and it varies by color for currency from denomination to denomination. "We produce these films in a web form, then we slit them down into the security threads and incorporate them into the sheets during the papermaking process. This, right here, is the ultimate in technology when it comes to papermaking." When Douglas Crane demonstrated these features to us, they had been approved for use in only a handful of currencies; they were later incorporated into the newly designed $100 bill originally announced by the Bureau of Engraving and Printing to be in circulation in 2011, but delayed to the autumn of 2013 by what were reported by the government to have been "creasing problems" encountered during the initial printing phases. Among the new security features installed are the combination of microprinting techniques, multiple watermarks, and tiny lenses—nearly a million of them—on each bill.

The next note Crane produced for our examination was a crisp $100 bill that he allowed me to rub between my fingers, but not photograph, since it was on loan to him from the Secret Service. "What do you think?" he asked, and I replied that the paper felt "pretty good" to my touch. "It *is* pretty good," he said, "but it's a phony all the same." What I was holding, he explained, was what has been called a "supernote" by the U.S. Treasury and the Secret Service, alleged by some government officials, including former president George W. Bush, to have been produced with the complicity of an unfriendly foreign country, most likely North Korea, though Iran was also mentioned as a distinct possibility.

"This is not a typical case of counterfeiting," Crane said. "As a matter of fact, this is an extremely rare example in which someone has very cleverly gone to considerable lengths to counterfeit the paper itself. Other counterfeiters sometimes will take authentic banknotes and remove the ink to get a substrate to print on—they'll take a five-dollar bill, let's say, and try to turn it into a hundred." But in this instance, the notes had been printed on high-quality paper made with the proper balance of ingredients—75 percent cotton, 25 percent flax—and included various security features and watermarks common to United States currency.

"Whoever is doing this has counterfeited the security thread itself and embedded that in the note, too, and no single individual is capable of doing that." The printing, moreover, had been done with the intaglio process, producing an exceedingly professional-looking note, though not one without its imperfections—precisely what, Crane would not say, but they were sufficient to identify it as a counterfeit to the knowing eye. "I can tell you that what actually drew attention to these notes, initially, was the feel—something didn't seem just right to the touch," Crane said.

"The challenge to me, then—from our government in particular—is how do I raise the bar in such a way that someone with all the wherewithal is still unable to do this sort of thing and get away with it? That's why we're doing analysis on some of these notes for the Secret Service. When you are dealing with an individual who is at this level—someone who is well funded and has all the basic equipment—you develop things like this motion thread you see there. That is certainly one response. But when it's another government—a government, perhaps, that's also building up a nuclear arsenal—it brings another dimension to what you're doing altogether."

In the years before the American Civil War, when the United States did not have a national currency, paper money was issued in a multitude of denominations and designs—more than ten thousand variations by 1860—creating conditions that were ripe for abuse. Counterfeiting was so commonplace that Herman Melville used it as a narrative device in *The Confidence-Man: His Masquerade,* an 1857 satire set on a riverboat that plies the Mississippi River, with all of the action taking place on April Fool's Day.

One of the most aggressive efforts to undermine a nation's paper currency was carried out in Sachsenhausen concentration camp outside Berlin by Jewish prisoners who had agreed to create bogus British pounds for their Nazi captors as a way to avoid the gas chambers. The counterfeit bills they produced were of such sophistication that sample notes deposited in a Swiss bank by German agents were declared authentic by Bank of England examiners. Like the American superbills believed to have been made in North Korea, the German effort was carried out by a team of experts skilled in every aspect of graphic production and used paper that had the texture, feel, look, and "crinkle" of actual British currency. To determine the precise identity of fibers and the exact proportions, a German paper company was directed to conduct a painstaking process of laboratory analysis. The scientists determined that the British formulation was a combination of Turkish linen and an Asian nettle called ramie. They were able to get the right flax locally in Germany; the ramie plant they brought in from Hungary.

To form the sheets, a Dutch machine was adapted and configured to include watermarks. To replicate as closely as possible the color of the British stock when examined under a quartz lamp, a special water was prepared to mimic as closely as possible the kind used by the company in England that had been manufacturing royal currency paper since 1725. For the watermark, more than a hundred trials were conducted before a satisfactory image was produced. The project was foiled only by the end of hostilities in 1945, and even then the counterfeits were persuasive enough that the Bank of England withdrew from circulation the entire series that had been compromised and discreetly introduced a new five-pound note with a different design and composition.

It should come as no surprise that when the topic of conversation turns to whether or not a paperless society is in the offing, Douglas Crane is bullish on the subject of conventional currency. "I'm not sure why anyone would want a paperless society anyway," he said. "What's the benefit there? The truth is that we're using more paper now than ever before. So where's the paperless society? When you think about it, paper is such an effective way of delivering information. Readers get to read it when they want to, they don't have to turn on a power button, it's very portable, it's extraordinarily convenient. I acknowledge that as transactions increase, currency's percentage declines, but currency is still growing."

The number of notes is increasing across the world, too, he continued, an observation borne out by statistics that indicate 60 percent of the approximately twenty-five billion American currency notes in circulation at any given time are outside the United States. "People hoard U.S. currency overseas, they stuff it under their mattresses, because their local currencies might have an inflation issue or merely may be weak," he said. "Beyond that, currency is a means of stored value, as well as a means of effecting a transaction. Something like 20 percent of households in the United States don't have a bank account. And then you have a large immigrant population in the United States—a lot of these folks don't have bank accounts, either. They do everything in currency." Although Crane and Company manufactures many kinds of paper products—and the next day we would see a number of them being made at various other plants it operates in Western

Massachusetts—Douglas Crane is responsible in his job for assuring the satisfaction of a single client, which he constantly referred to in our conversation as "our customer," that customer being the U.S. Bureau of Engraving and Printing.

"My principal accountability is to make sure that our customer is happy, and I'm in charge of our contract with the government, which really is the lifeblood of the business. I end up spending a whole lot of my time going down to Washington, which is something that I know is necessary. But if I were given the choice of where I'd like to go first thing in the morning, it would be the paper mill." And the first thing he does on those occasions, he said, is to "go right up to the wet end of the machine to check things out and see what's happening." I wondered if that sort of hands-on spot-checking is akin to the interest a master chef might take in overseeing the operation of a five-star kitchen.

"I could tell you all kinds of stories about people who do weird stuff," he said. "We don't run beaters anymore, but we used to batch-refine the fibers in beaters, because you just couldn't get enough energy into it otherwise. And so the beater engineers would be involved in the art of papermaking. They'd sit there and they'd run their beater, but instead of just running it for a certain amount of time with a certain amount of pressure to it, they'd dip their hands in it every once in a while—they'd take a good look at it—and some would even chew it to see if it was just right." That sort of attention to detail reflects a form of connoisseurship that can come only from years of experience, he suggested—the kind that we would see in the two paper mills that Connie and I were about to visit.

The Byron Weston Building is named for a former competitor in the Housatonic River region, a company that was absorbed by Crane and Company during its most dynamic years of growth. This is the unit where the many components required by the "customer" are combined in precisely stipulated proportions to form the "half-stock" for currency, and is then sent off to the other buildings where the paper is made. In this preliminary phase, the person in charge is Jonathan R. Drosehn (pronounced *Dro-seen*), a Crane employee since 1979 and one of more than 120 members of his family to have worked for the company over the past four generations, including his father and three brothers, one of whom we would meet later. A lifelong Dalton resident, Drosehn has the title of raw materials operations manager, and though we did not expect to have a tutorial in the finer points of industrial papermaking, our tour of the Byron Weston plant became exactly that. We started in the receiving area, where bales of flax and cotton are trucked in from warehouses in Pittsfield and the surrounding region.

"We're actually recycling the waste from other industries," Drosehn said as we got started, beginning with the bundles of flax that originate in the linen-spinning industry. "It comes to us rolled up in bales like you might see for hay. After they've taken what they need for their cloth, they lay what is left down in the field for a while to ret. What retting of the fiber does is break down some of the unnecessary organics in the outer shell. If you get the proper amount of retting, it lends itself to a better fiber. So then they roll the bales, chop the roots off, and then the stalk itself goes through a combing process. It goes in looking like a plant and comes out looking like a wig of light brown hair." He picked up a handful of the flax and invited us to feel how soft it was, then moved on to the other essential fiber in the process.

"This cotton we use is fiber recovered from the cotton gin," he said. "When cotton is picked in the field, you get three basic products. You get the seed, you get spinnable cotton, and you get the waste, which they call motes. What we have here is the molt, and what you see over here is a bale from the combing-and-cleaning process that takes out the sticks and the twigs and the leaves. It's almost eighty percent secondhand recovered cellulose. When we blend these materials together, we maintain precise amounts of the sources."

In addition to cleaning, combing, spinning, and screening phases that remove "dirt and organics," every bale has to be passed under black light "to make sure we pick up any fluorescent fiber that might be in there, which would indicate synthetic contamination—the shreds of a plastic bag, for instance, something that is pretty common out on the prairies, where a lot of this stuff comes from." This step is necessary, because one characteristic that sets currency paper apart from so many other papers is that it does not fluoresce. "You put it under a black light, the only thing that should fluoresce is the security threads, or whatever else that is in there that might have a fluorescent component. If we put something into the pulp that competes with that, then we're compromising the integrity of the paper. Counterfeit currency will usually fluoresce. That is often why a little black light is all you need to provide counterfeit recognition."

Although the production process is continuous, it takes about two and a half hours for the raw materials to go from the intake stage to where it is ready to be shipped to the finishing mill. Another step involves immersion in a solution of sodium hydroxide, a chemical also known as lye, and cooking in a huge cylindrical piece of equipment called a digester boiler. An advanced phase of refinement is performed in what is called a pulper tank; more washing and rinsing is done in what is called a gyro cleaner—another name for a rotating disk in which dirty water is expelled through a screen and fresh water is added.

Drosehn pointed out a mechanical process in which "we are delivering a certain amount of horsepower to shorten and fibrillate" the fiber. "What we want to do is spread it out into all these fine fibrils so they can intertwine and get more physical." Bleach is added to achieve a desired standard of brightness, and by the end of the run about half of the water that had been introduced along the way has been removed. The material is then cut into rectangular sections, which to the uneducated eye appear for all the world to be thick pieces of coarse paper. "What you have here is an entire manufacturing process before it even starts to become U.S. currency paper," he said, and described half-stock as being "almost structural" in strength. "It's in a form now that they can continue to manipulate to get the proper consistency. They'll shorten this fiber even more, they'll fibrillate it even more—there's still a lot of work left in it—but this is my finished product. From here it's going down there to my brother."

Our guide "down there," in the building known as the Currency Mill, was Jonathan's older brother Donald J. Drosehn, who began working for Crane in 1969 as a summer intern in the research laboratory and whose title at the time of our visit was manager of manufacturing for United States currency. "My grandmother Nettie walked me into Bruce Crane's office one day and she said, 'Mr. Crane, Donnie here is eighteen years old, he's going to be a chemist, and he needs a summer job,'" he told us. "I worked twelve hours a day, and I made twenty-three hundred dollars my first summer here. Grandma Nettie was a farmer in Berkshire County, and she basically provided kids for Crane and Company's workforce. Every one of the kids at some point has worked here. I have to say that the Cranes always cared about family. When my grandmother died, there was Bruce Crane, the president of the company, in the back of the funeral home."

In order for him to proceed into the final phase of the papermaking process, Donald Drosehn said, the half-stock "has to be a specific fiber length, freeness, and color so we can make sure that when we mix it in the pulpers and the blend tanks, we get the proper degree of strength, durability, formation, and quality necessary to satisfy the Bureau of Engraving and Printing. All of the cooking was done up at Jonathan's place; what we do here is refine it and make it into paper."

I shot photos of several large vats at the beginning of this sequence, each containing about 2,700 pounds of pulp, and it became quickly apparent to me why the making of the half-stock at the other mill is not considered the "wet" phase, even though it involves plenty of water. "This is now about five percent fiber and ninety-five percent water, and from this point on we're going to dilute it with millions of gallons of water to get it down to a solution that ends up at being .6 percent fiber, and 99.4 percent water when it enters the papermaking machine."

The only phase of the procedure we were not allowed to see was the "wet end," where properly diluted pulp is fed into a roaring complex of rollers and moving screens that transform it all into currency paper. It is there that distinctive strands of the plastic security threads developed for each denomination, and produced at a subsidiary of Crane in New Hampshire, are inserted, a proprietary process that is off-limits even

*U.S. currency paper at the Crane and Company mill, in Dalton, Massachusetts.*

to most company employees. It is tempting to compare the rumbling energy of this inexhaustible complex of machinery that we saw to that of a giant locomotive roaring through the countryside, with wheels spinning at high, rhythmic speeds, a web of creamy white paper whizzing by in an endless sheet that is rolled onto enormous spools at the end of the run, each one sufficient to make fifty thousand currency notes.

When Donald Drosehn called the American greenback the "strongest and most durable currency in the world," he was speaking in a literal sense about the composition of a product he manufactures on a daily basis. The British five-pound note, he said, will last less than twelve months in circulation; the American dollar, up to three and a half years. "When you hold up a British five-pound note, you see a beautiful picture of the queen. Our currency is cotton-and-linen fiber and doesn't lend itself quite so easily to making perfect watermarks, but it makes a very durable banknote. So we've kind of found the trade-off."

As a lifelong papermaker, Drosehn said he considers what he does as much of an art as a science, an observation he made while demonstrating the unmistakable rattle of a sheet of currency paper in one of the testing labs where samples are constantly being examined for quality control. "That's the sound of money," he said. "And the Bureau of Engraving and Printing does not want that changed. So one of my jobs is to make sure it keeps its snap. But there is no specification written down for sound—or for feel, either, for that matter, which the government also insists we keep, since that is still the number-one way that counterfeit money is detected. So the only tests we have for snap and feel are what your fingers tell you is there. As much science and engineering that goes into getting the thread and the watermark in the right place, there's still that extra level that you get only after doing this all of your life."

I asked Drosehn if he had any thoughts on why Crane has managed to thrive as a New England papermaker when so many competitors have gone by the wayside, victims of declining demand, changing economics, and the new awareness so many government agencies and interest groups have for the environment. "First of all, we have never used trees for our paper; all of our fibers come from yearly renewable resources," he said. "Here at Crane, we actually dry our paper with steam made from the garbage burned in the Energy Answers plant

down the road, so there's that, too. And we began treating our water in
the 1950s, well before it became fashionable. So we are a very environmentally conscious company."

As to the "other part of your question," he concluded: "It is true,
too, that the papermaking business is shrinking, and the specialty
papermakers are the ones that probably will survive. You could check
this out, but I believe cotton-based paper represents maybe two or three
percent of the industry in the world. I like to brag about currency not
really being a sheet of paper—I call it a sheet of cloth, because it is cotton and linen. We make such a special product, and we ought to be able
to avoid the extinction that's happening in lots of areas with paper. You
can say it's paper, but to my mind we're weaving a sheet of the strongest
durable banknote in the world, and we've been doing it a long time. It's
a complex paper made out of cotton and linen, cellulose, so technically
it is paper—but I still call it cloth."

# 6

One and Done

The American wasps form very fine paper, like ours; they extract the fibers
of common wood of the countries where they live. They teach us that
paper can be made from the fibers of plants without the use of rags and
linen, and seem to invite us to try whether we cannot make fine and good
paper from the use of certain woods.

—René-Antoine Ferchault de Réaumur,
*A History of Wasps,* 1719

ZENAS CRANE MAY WELL have been the first papermaker to set up
shop along the Housatonic River, but he was by no means the last,
as sixty-five other mills followed his example in succeeding years, all
churning out tons of product for every manner of commercial use.
In 1958, an established powerhouse in the industry, Kimberly-Clark,
opened a one-million-square-foot tissue-and-towel factory eighty miles
downstream in New Milford, Connecticut, as part of a global strategy to serve targeted geographical areas—in this instance the heavily populated cities and towns of the Northeast—with a steady supply
of personal products that had become essential domestic accessories
within a very short period. The word "disposable" does not appear
in the company's mission statement—employees prefer to describe the
nondurable products they make as "health and hygiene" necessities—
but everything manufactured in the Connecticut plant, as throughout
much of the huge company itself, is an item intended for single use, a
life span, by design, of "one and done."

  Chief among Kimberly-Clark's trademarked consumer products
are Kleenex and Kotex, brand names for facial tissues and sanitary

napkins that have become as synonymous for those personal articles as Band-Aid, Xerox, and Google are for adhesive bandages, photocopiers, and computer searches, and as another signature product made from cellulose, the 3M Company's Scotch-brand transparent tape, has been since its introduction, in 1930. Other Kimberly-Clark staples that enjoy strong brand identity include Scott kitchen towels, Huggies diapers, Depend incontinence pads for adults, and Cottonelle quilted toilet paper.

When people boldly predict the obsolescence of paper, they are generally talking about tools in the modern office or how reading and writing habits are being redefined by e-books and computers. In matters of personal hygiene, the question is rarely whether consumers will continue to buy bathroom tissue, but whether fiber from virgin wood should be used, to produce the levels of softness they have come to expect, or be replaced by a coarser product made from "post-consumer recycled waste."

In 2004, the international environmental advocacy organization Greenpeace made the "tissue issue" a front-list item on its agenda of political activism, singling out Kimberly-Clark as its top target. Tauntingly code-named Kleercut, the aggressive campaign was aimed at forcing the company it called the "world's largest tissue-product manufacturer" to substantially reduce the volume of virgin hardwood fiber it uses to make its top-earning products, the very fibers that give its brands their softness. In 2009, the five-year effort, which included customer boycotts, came to a halt when the two sides reached an understanding that Greenpeace declared to be an unqualified victory in the cause of environmental protection.

"The Kleercut campaign is over," Greenpeace announced on its website, ebullient over the news that Kimberly-Clark had signed "an historic agreement that will ensure greater protection and sustainable management of Canada's Boreal Forest and other ancient forests around the world." The rapprochement, Greenpeace further asserted, represented a "new collaborative relationship to further promote forest conservation, responsible forest management, and the use of recycled fiber for the manufacture of tissue products." Kimberly-Clark, in turn, committed itself to buying forest products only from sources with certified sustainability programs in place. In 2012, the company went even further, with the announcement of long-term plans to reduce its "forest fiber footprint" in the manufacture of tissue products by up to 50 percent, using, among other alternative sources, bamboo, which can be farmed and harvested far more quickly than wood. "In 2011, the company used nearly 750 thousand metric tons of primary wood fiber sourced from natural forests," K-C said in its announcement. "With this new commitment, Kimberly-Clark pledges to cut the amount sourced from natural forests in half by 2025, an amount equivalent to the fiber used to manufacture over three and a half billion rolls of toilet paper."

Word choice is a delicate business when describing exactly what it is that Kimberly-Clark does so well as a company, one that was singled out in a 2001 study of American businesses that exemplify corporate excellence. "We are not papermakers," I was told repeatedly by media relations specialists at corporate headquarters in Dallas, who arranged for me a tour of the New Milford plant, and again by the people I met on-site there, even though the centerpiece attractions of my visit were by far two of the largest and noisiest papermaking machines I have ever seen anywhere. One of them occupied an area I estimated to be more than six hundred feet long and four stories high, and it was producing enough tissue to manufacture close to a million boxes of Kleenex a day. In a separate area, another marvel of modern engineering was spooling roll after roll of Scott paper towels, a superstar brand acquired by Kimberly-Clark in 1995 in a $9.4 billion merger that pooled the strengths of two companies into one multinational dynamo.

Yet none of this world-renowned product I was about to see being made, these officials assured me, was paper per se—certainly not the kind of paper the company had produced over the first hundred years of its history—but rather "paper-based consumer products." While promising to note the nicety in these pages, I made clear to my hosts that "paper-based" is very much a part of the "paper story" and that any of the many uses of the material are totally relevant to the discourse. Trading under the ticker symbol KMB, Kimberly-Clark has been listed on the New York Stock Exchange since 1929 and is ranked by brokerage houses as a top performer that unfailingly pays dividends to its stockholders, dubbed "huggable shares" by some Wall Street admirers.

Long before the company began to concentrate on innovative products, however, it produced one basic commodity, and one alone: newsprint, tons and tons of it, for a voracious communications industry transformed almost overnight by what at times seemed to be a limitless supply of paper to feed its printing presses. Kimberly, Clark & Co. was established in 1872 in Neenah, Wisconsin, by a partnership of four businessmen brought together by John Alfred Kimberly, the respected proprietor of a general goods store, and Charles B. Clark, a Civil War veteran and part owner of a hardware emporium. None of the principals was a papermaker by trade, but each was a seasoned judge of economic trends, and what they saw was a publishing industry that was just beginning to boom in nearby Chicago, Milwaukee, and Detroit, but that was wholly dependent on East Coast suppliers for stock.

Pooling $30,000 in start-up money, they converted an old furniture factory on the Fox River into their first mill, and, to secure a high-end niche for themselves, they catered to clients willing to pay a premium for a superior product. For six years, the Neenah plant relied on cotton and linen rags for fiber, but when it became apparent where the future of the industry lay, they were quick to adapt, equipping all of their new mills to use wood pulp exclusively. By 1899, Kimberly, Clark & Co. was producing fifty-five tons of newsprint a day, acquiring 85 percent of its timber on the open market and harvesting the remainder from forests it had acquired in Wisconsin and northern Michigan.

While certainly a player in this emerging new field, the company was by no means dominant, that distinction belonging to the International Paper Company, which had been created in 1898 with the merger of eighteen Northeastern companies into one monolith under the dynamic leadership of Hugh Chisholm, a Canadian-born entrepreneur who owned several mills in Maine and had a knack for high-stakes financial maneuvering. Producing fifteen hundred tons of newsprint a day, the new company he had shaped quickly secured 60 percent of the market. With passage of the Underwood-Simmons Tariff Act, three years later, restrictive duties on the importation of timber were removed, clearing the way for increased competition from Canadian suppliers.

Faced with these various market forces, Kimberly, Clark & Co. (the name would get hyphenated in 1928) began to consider creative ways to exit the newsprint business altogether, and a measured restructuring allowed it to achieve that goal by 1916. Ten years later, a joint ownership with the *New York Times* of a mill in northern Ontario brought the company back into making newsprint, but only as a sideline and only for a few select clients. When that partnership ended, in 1991, Kimberly-Clark had already reinvented itself, and the key to the transformation had been the establishment, several decades earlier, of what today would be called a "research and development" unit charged with creating new products.

The prime mover in this course correction, according to various company histories, was Kimberly-Clark general manager Frank J. Sensenbrenner, by all accounts an energetic man who had the foresight, in April 1914, to hire a twenty-seven-year-old chemist from Austria named Ernst Mahler and to give him the authority to make fruitful use of his imagination. The son of a papermaker himself, Mahler set up a laboratory across the street from the company's executive offices, in Neenah, and within a matter of weeks was visiting paper mills in Europe with James Kimberly, a company vice president and son of one of the founders.

The ostensible goal of the trip was to get ideas for how Kimberly-Clark could adapt printing papers for the new rotogravure rotary presses then gaining favor among publishers of books, magazines, newspapers, and mail-order catalogs. For Mahler, the immediate challenge was to develop a printing stock that would accept additional colors without running or smudging, and resolving this dilemma became his first priority when he returned to Wisconsin. His solution was to introduce a bleaching phase that eliminated the lignin and whitened the stock, which nicely suited the paper, trademarked Roto-Plate, to rotogravure printing. The product paved the way for the introduction of magazine supplements by major newspapers—the *New York Times* became a customer in 1915—and remained a stock item for decades.

Of secondary interest to Mahler on his trip to Germany, Austria, and Scandinavia that summer was to pay a visit to his alma mater, the Darmstadt University of Technology, and meet with scientists who specialized in papermaking and cellulose chemistry. Among the topics they discussed was a new material that could absorb liquids without disintegrating; they called it a "creped cellulose wadding," and it was initially made from bagasse, a pulp by-product of processed sugarcane. Driving the effort to perfect an alternative absorbent was the skyrocketing price of cotton, which in the five years leading up to the war in Europe had increased by 30 percent, a victim of the boll weevil infestation that had afflicted the American Southwest.

Mahler's trip to the Continent was cut short in August by the outbreak of World War I, but within months of his return to Neenah, he
had developed another process that chemically removed lignin and res-
inous impurities from spruce pulp without affecting the length of the
fiber, an essential element in assuring absorbency. Promptly securing a
patent for a product trademarked Cellucotton, Kimberly-Clark set up
an experimental mill to produce an ultrathin film of paper that was
encased in gauze wrappers, and tested it for use as a surgical dressing
in a Chicago hospital. By 1917, orders were coming in from medical
centers throughout the country, and when the United States entered
the war, later that year, the company offered the wadding at cost to the
United States Army and the Red Cross as a substitute for cotton bandages. A thinner version of the same material was used to make filters
for gas masks.

At the height of production, wadded cellulose was being produced
by the truckload, averaging eighty-eight tons a month by the time the
Armistice was signed, in November 1918. As a result, a huge surplus
remained unused at war's end. Facing massive cutbacks, the company
began to explore ways to find new customers and expand its inventory. Orders for rotogravure paper continued to be filled, and a mill in
New Jersey was retooled to produce wallpaper, but another strategy was
being considered that would use the leftover bandages for a bold new
product, and this time it would take the additional step of appealing
directly to consumers.

In what would prove to be another inspired move, Sensenbrenner
hired Walter W. Luecke, a marketing specialist from Chicago who had
bought vast quantities of Kimberly-Clark paper to produce mail-order
catalogs for Sears, Roebuck, in order to work his magic in Wisconsin. His first order of business was to find a viable market for the surplus Cellucotton, which had become a distraction once the war ended.
Many company executives, in fact, were recommending that it be discontinued outright, as Scott Paper Company had done with its line of
cotton substitute, a laminated cellulose material brand-named Zorbik.

But while poking through company files—the story has been thoroughly documented by two Ohio State University economists in a
scholarly study of Kimberly-Clark's business practices, cleverly titled
*Kotex, Kleenex, Huggies*—Luecke ran across some intriguing letters
from a number of Army nurses who had recalled using the surgical

dressings for their own needs while caring for wounded soldiers in Europe. In their correspondence, the women wondered why such a material could not be made available commercially for consumers like themselves everywhere. The proverbial lightbulb flashed in Luecke's head, and a euphemism for a feminine hygiene product—the sanitary napkin—would enter the language in due course. The name initially chosen for the product, Cellu-Naps, went nowhere, and the product was slow to catch on. An advertising consultant brought in to toss ideas around came up with a hybrid word that played off the product's "cottonlike texture" but was constructed in a way that would avoid mispronunciation; thus Kotex was born, and a trademark obtained in 1920.

While fully half of the adult population was viewed as potential customers, coming up with an inoffensive way to promote the product raised questions of propriety not unlike those faced several decades earlier, when rolled toilet paper was being introduced to American consumers by the Scott Paper Company. Although sensibilities had tempered considerably since Victorian times, menstruation was not by any means a topic suited to genteel conversation. The Woolworth's in Chicago agreed to sell the first cartons—Luecke had called in a number of markers from his old stomping grounds in the Windy City—but did so with the explicit understanding that no packages would be displayed openly in the store.

Manufacture, meanwhile, was assigned to Cellucotton Products Company, a wholly owned Kimberly-Clark subsidiary established for the single purpose of making Kotex. Promotion was discreet to a fault, with a heavy emphasis on medical science. The most effective strategy, it soon developed, was to feature the wholesome image of a nurse outfitted in a crisp linen uniform, set off smartly by a white cross printed on a green background, with the slogan "inexpensive, comfortable, hygienic and safe," at the top.

The public was slow to catch on at first, but sales picked up in 1926 when Montgomery Ward began offering the product in its mail-order catalogs, with social consequences that had an impact on much more than the K-C bottom line, as asserted by a Wellesley College professor in a monograph titled *The Modern Period: Menstruation in Twentieth-Century America*. For the first time in history, Laura Freidenfelds wrote, women were finally able to "manage" their natural rhythms in ways that allowed them to pursue roles in society that previously had been "inhibited." With this new option available to them, women could replace cloth napkins, which they had to launder, with disposable pads, and move away from "old concerns about keeping unmarried girls innocent about sexuality and reproduction in favor of early menstrual education." By the 1940s, "clear class lines would be drawn between the mass of women who enjoyed the middle-class comfort of Kotex and the truly poor women who could not afford them and continued to use cloth pads."

In 1924, K-C transformed the ultrathin Cellucotton linings that had been made for gas masks during the war into an absorbent facial tissue that catered to the rapidly expanding cosmetics industry, replacing almost overnight the cotton balls most women had been using to remove cold cream. When consumers began reporting that the tissue was a splendid replacement for the cloth handkerchief—chief among them Ernst Mahler, who suffered from hay fever—marketing strategies were modified accordingly. The pop-up box was introduced in 1929, and it remains a popular feature of the Kleenex brand.

While stories of paper-based innovations like these are commonplace in paper-company histories—the introduction of single-use Dixie Cups as an antiseptic response to the spread of contagious disease, the superiority of the paper towel over rolled cloth in public restrooms, the invention of the Post-it notepad—only a select few inventions ever rise to the level of indispensability. I am not aware of any statistical surveys that have been conducted on this topic—and I have done my due diligence searches—but I believe I am on safe ground when I suggest that toilet paper would probably top such a poll if one were to be conducted. It is an everyday essential so taken for granted that even the merest hint of a shortage can cause spasms of uneasiness.

The most celebrated instance of toilet paper panic was precipitated by the television host Johnny Carson on December 19, 1973, during one of his top-rated *Tonight Show* broadcasts. "You know, we've got all sorts of shortages these days," he said in his opening monologue, a reality not lost on a national audience that just a few months earlier had endured exasperatingly long lines at gasoline pumps after Arab countries instituted an oil embargo. "But have you heard the latest? I'm not kidding. I saw it in the paper. There's a shortage of toilet paper."

What Carson had read was a wire-service story that reported a Wisconsin congressman's warning of a possible shortage in government procurements of bathroom tissue, a topic of some concern in a state that had become a leading producer of paper products. The fears were proven to be without merit, but not in time to stop a buying frenzy that depleted supplies throughout the country and occasioned a front-page story in the *New York Times* about a new wave of "shortage anxiety" gripping the nation, with the Carson episode being a prime example.

In one of his dispatches from North Africa, the legendary World War II correspondent Ernie Pyle reported how a chaplain who had gone through the pockets of ten Americans killed in battle had found more packets of toilet paper than of any other item. "Careless soldiers who were caught without such preparedness have to use twenty-franc notes," he glibly added. The attitude of American commanders when it came to providing this most basic of personal accessories was similar to their stance toward assuring a steady supply of cigarettes, a luxury evident even to their closest allies. "The British army stocked toilet paper on the assumption that the soldier would use three sheets a day; the American ration was twenty-two and a half sheets," according to Lee B. Kennett, in *G.I.: The American Soldier in World War II.*

Beyond the desire to maintain high morale, there were sound hygienic reasons to keep the soldiers amply provisioned, as Dr. Walter T. Hughes, the former chairman of the Department of Infectious Diseases at St. Jude Children's Research Hospital, in Memphis, Tennessee, and a recognized authority in the field, documented in a 1988 journal article. "The value of modern sewage systems, waste disposal, water purification, and personal hygiene practices is well known in the prevention of infectious disease," he began. "Antibiotics and vaccines are lauded as miracles of modern medicine. Skilled epidemiologic studies, case-reporting systems, computerized data handling, and sophisticated biostatistical methods have played significant roles in providing us with a reasonably safe environment. But what about toilet paper?"

In the centuries before bathroom tissue was introduced, Dr. Hughes continued, "plagues of dysentery, typhoid, and cholera scourged the world." He asked his colleagues to consider how something as simple as "highly standardized, readily available, cleansing, absorbable, and disposable tissue paper" had contributed to reducing such horrific pandemics. To support his thesis, he cited official statistics kept during successive American conflicts that reported the frequency of typhoid fever among the troops, beginning with the Civil War, when eighty cases per year were documented for every thousand soldiers. The frequency figures doubled during the Spanish-American War, and it was only when the military began issuing toilet paper to troops, in the early years of the twentieth century, that the upward trend was reversed. During World War I, the incidence was down to three cases per thousand soldiers a year; in World War II, it was 0.1 per thousand; during the Korean War, even lower; and today it is statistically nonexistent. By providing "a physical barrier between fecal excretion and the hand," Dr. Hughes concluded, the evidence proved that toilet paper prevents "infectious diseases that are transmitted by the fecal-oral route."

While the sudden availability of inexpensive wood pulp during the nineteenth century had made the proliferation of toilet paper possible, accounts of widespread use much earlier than that have been documented. An eighteenth-century mention of the practice, in makeshift fashion, comes in one of the letters Philip Dormer Stanhope, the fourth Earl of Chesterfield, famously wrote to his illegitimate son, also named Philip, amid a general discussion urging the lad to avoid idleness and to use every minute of his time productively.

"I knew a gentleman who was so good a manager of his time that he would not even lose that small portion of it which the call of nature obliged him to pass," Lord Chesterfield wrote in the 1747 letter, noting that whenever his acquaintance found himself so indisposed, he seized the opportunity to read through all the Latin poets. "He bought, for example, a common edition of Horace, of which he tore off gradually a couple of pages, carried them with him to that necessary place, read them first and then sent them down as a sacrifice to Cloacina," a reference to the goddess in Roman mythology who presided over the Cloaca Maxima, or "Great Drain," which served as the main trunk of the sewer system in Rome. "I recommend you to follow his example. It is better than only doing what you cannot help doing at those moments and it will make any book which you shall read in that manner, very present to your mind."

Credit for producing the first commercial toilet paper in the United States goes to Joseph C. Gayetty, a New Jersey inventor who in 1857 introduced a line of Medicated Paper treated with aloe, which he claimed had "perfectly pure" and "therapeutic" qualities that were ideal "for the toilet and for the prevention of piles," a condition more com-

monly known today as hemorrhoids. The paper was sold in flat packages of five hundred sheets—each with Gayetty's name watermarked
on it—and the wrapper identified the ingredients as "unbleached pearl-
colored pure manila hemp paper." The trend toward general acceptance
began in 1871, when the first American patent for rolled perforated
paper was granted to Seth Wheeler, of Albany, New York, an innovation that led to the establishment, in 1879, of the Scott Paper Company,
in Philadelphia, by the brothers E. Irvin and Clarence Scott. Their
Waldorf brand quickly became the standard and was a considerable
upgrade for people living in rural communities who, until now, had
kept the Sears, Roebuck catalog (affectionately remembered by some
as "Rears and Sorebutts") in outhouses for this purpose. Others had
favored the *Old Farmer's Almanac* (which had a hole punched in the
upper-left corner to hang on a nail in the privy) and pages ripped from
outdated telephone books. Because one of its physical attributes is that
it dissolves readily in water, professionally manufactured toilet paper

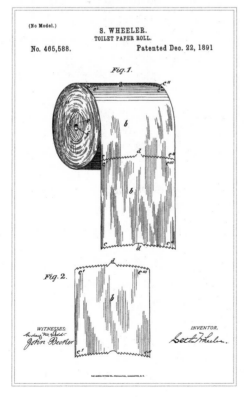

*Seth Wheeler's 1891 patent (number
465,588) for rolled toilet paper.*

proliferated as indoor plumbing streamlined methods of disposal in urban areas, and also solved the problem of clogged drains that resulted from use of thicker papers in the new systems.

According to industry figures, American companies produce more than seven billion rolls of toilet paper annually, or 22.3 rolls per person. The average consumer, according to Procter & Gamble, the manufacturer of Charmin, uses fifty-seven sheets a day, or just under twenty-one thousand a year. The standard sheet is 4.5 by 4.5 inches square, with one thousand of them usually spooled on one single-ply roll, five hundred on a double-ply. "What American does not have access to it?" Dr. Hughes had asked in wonder. "It's found in homes, offices, hospitals, churches, gas stations, factories, roadside parks, trains, buses, airplanes, ships, submarines, and outer-space transports."

PARLAYING THE SUCCESSES it had begun to rack up into sustained profits, Kimberly-Clark emerged as a classic example of entrepreneurial opportunism, with smart economic decisions leading ultimately to expansions, mergers, and acquisitions, which were combined with prescient technological advancements and the skillful marketing of new products. In 2011, the company reported net sales of $20.8 billion (12 percent of which were to one customer, Walmart Stores Inc.) and that it was operating plants in thirty-six countries, in a variety of clearly defined specialties, with a combined workforce of fifty-seven thousand employees, accommodating, by its reckoning, the personal needs of 1.3 billion people a day throughout the world.

Dan Lachmann, manager of the New Milford mill at the time of my visit, in 2009, explained that his plant concentrates on making just two products: Kleenex tissue and Scott towels, which are both part of a dedicated segment of the company's operation known as "family care," so called because they are "generally shared in the household by the whole family." A line of "personal care" products made at other company mills are "single person, single use items," such as Kotex, Huggies, and Depends; a "business to business" division makes single-use products for the service industry, and a "health care" division manufactures disposable surgical room apparel. The company's annual report for 2010 reported that it was operating sixty-nine "tissue facilities" worldwide. It stated further that "most" of the cellulose it uses, be it kraft pulp derived from virgin wood and wood products or fiber recycled from recovered wastepaper—now constituting 20 percent of the supply—is bought from third parties.

Because toilet paper, facial tissue, and kitchen towels tend to be bulky, they can be costly to ship, which encourages manufacturers to reduce transportation costs by operating plants in strategic geographic locations. Bill Welsh, the engineering director of the New Milford plant, who accompanied us on our tour, noted that because Kleenex and Scott towels are made with "two different technology bases," only the base paper for the tissue is produced from scratch in New Milford; the base material for Scott towels is shipped in from another mill already prepared for final production. The mill runs three full shifts every day, with a combined labor force of 350 workers, well short of the twelve hundred people employed in earlier years, when the division also manufactured Kotex and Huggies.

Water for the New Milford mill is drawn from the Housatonic River at the rate of three and a half to four million gallons a day. After going through an extensive filtration process involving several pieces of equipment known as clarifiers, about 90 percent of the treated water is returned to the river. Before we went into the mill, Welsh explained that Kleenex tissue is a blend of "two different fiber mixes": one that uses what is called "softwood kraft" to furnish strength, and another derived from hardwood pulp that accounts (counterintuitively) for softness. Softwood trees include pine, spruce, fir, and hemlock, and their fibers are strong and durable, by virtue of their length. Hardwood trees, such as birch, aspen, and eucalyptus, have smaller fibers, accounting for more fibers per gram. "That gives you the bulk and the softness of the tissue."

A sense of how much fiber is shipped into New Milford on a regular basis was apparent at the rear of the plant, where seven railroad cars that had been backed inside off a nearby spur were being unloaded. Some of the bales bore the name Suzano, a Brazilian company that cultivates eucalyptus trees for the pulp-and-paper industry. Nearby stood three high-capacity hydro-pulpers, equipment that Welsh described as "industrial-sized blenders." Though proportions for bathroom tissue and facial tissue vary, the approximate balance, according to industry sources, is about 70 percent hardwood fiber to 30 percent softwood.

To begin the papermaking process, a "fiberized slurry" is sprayed

onto the moving screen at the wet end of the machine. Unlike a traditional Fourdrinier, this piece of equipment, known in the industry as
a "twin wire former," uses two wire-mesh belts instead of one, a variation in design that allows excess water to be removed from the tops
and bottoms of the moving screens at the same time, producing an
extremely thin paper that has the same texture on both sides. Drying
is accomplished with gas-generated heat, and this also helps fluff the
paper, which is spooled onto rolls wide enough across to make a line of
ten 8.4-inch facial tissues. "Each roll is ten miles long," Lachmann said.
"That works out to one hundred miles of tissue per roll."

Because Kleenex is made with two kinds of fiber bases—one ply
of paper is formulated for softness, the other for strength—the procedure begins with the making of separate rolls that are just as quickly
unwound so that some can be treated with aloe lotion or stamped with
various words or logos. Once that is done, the two components are
joined in another stage called "crimping," then slit so they can easily
be sectioned into individual sheets, and then spooled again into "hard"
rolls ready for transformation into finished boxes of multi-ply facial tissue. For that to happen, the rolls are sent along by forklift to another
complex of machines, where "conversion" and packaging take place.
"If everything's going right, it takes about two and a half minutes to
go from a hard roll to a pallet on the dock ready to be shipped out,"
Lachmann said.

This final phase begins with several webs of tissue scooting along
at breakneck speed through an intricate suppression process that constantly combines, funnels, and folds it all down into a single tube of
layered tissue, known as the "sausage." Moving along constantly, the
streaking column is fed finally into a howling chamber, where it is
cut—by an upright saw revolving at speeds so fast that it was impossible to distinguish anything other than a whirling blur—into precisely
measured units ready for packaging. "It's got two dual spinning blades,
and it sharpens between each stroke," Lachmann said. Visible behind
a plastic sheath, the saw was carving up the sausage at a savage rate of
460 boxes a minute and, if the demand had called for more, could have
been pushed to 600 a minute. That's ten boxes of facial tissue every
second. "Do the math," Lachmann said. "This machine has the capacity to turn out close to a million boxes of Kleenex a day."

# Part II

# 7

Fiery Consequences

The mighty English who boast of having vanquished Russia and Persia, have been overthrown in Hindustan by a single cartridge.
—Bahadur Shah II,
the last Mughal emperor of India, 1857

The injurious agent in cigarettes comes principally from the burning paper wrapper. The substance thereby formed is called *acrolein*. It has a violent action on the nerve centers, producing degeneration of the cells of the brain, which is quite rapid among boys. Unlike most narcotics this degeneration is permanent and uncontrollable. I employ no person who smokes cigarettes.
—Thomas A. Edison,
letter to Henry Ford, April 26, 1914

HISTORIANS CITE numerous technological breakthroughs over the decades that have fundamentally changed the nature of armed warfare, though few have proven more enduring than the systematic deployment in the seventeenth century of the paper cartridge. Introduced at a time when paper mills were beginning to flourish throughout Europe, the new casings were light and supple and allowed for the wrapping of a metal projectile and a charge of gunpowder within a single tube. Of arresting simplicity, the innovation enabled the unwieldy musket to be deployed more efficiently on an enemy force; by one calculation, the number of separate actions required of an infantryman to reload a weapon was trimmed from forty-two steps to twenty-six.

Like paper, gunpowder—"that capricious compound," according to the nineteenth-century munitions expert Arthur B. Hawes—originated in China, and like paper it followed a path of sustained migration about the globe, traveling through the Middle East by way of the Silk Road trade routes to Europe, where the light and flexible qualities of one material would in time be used to facilitate the highly volatile nature of the other. The handheld firearm was introduced in the fourteenth century, about four hundred years after Chinese alchemists recognized the combustible nature of sulfur and charcoal when combined with potassium nitrate, also known as saltpeter, and ground into a granular mixture. What those ancient scientists were looking for in their experiments is uncertain—some say an elixir for immortality—though warnings of caution about the concoction's properties were circulated to the unwary.

Gunpowder's earliest documented uses were for primitive rockets fashioned out of bamboo casings and incendiary devices thrown by catapult, and, later, as fireworks to illuminate the night sky. The first producers sagely recognized that it could be used as a low-grade explosive, or even more suitably as a propellant to launch lethal objects at an adversary. Though highly volatile, the mixture does not explode or create thrust unless it's confined in a closed space, a property that influenced the development of early gun design, the central considerations being barrel size, tensile strength, and how powder was encased in the firing chamber.

Within two hundred years of gunpowder's arrival in Europe, sufficient advancements had been made so that, in addition to the much larger artillery pieces that had already achieved widespread deployment on land and sea, commanders were arming their infantry with the harquebus, a primitive firearm fitted with a matchlock for ignition, a wooden stock for a frame, and a metal barrel that was loaded compactly at the muzzle, or mouth, of the piece, with the help of a tamping rod. (From these came the phrase "lock, stock, and barrel.")

Because of its smooth bore and modest length, the harquebus— from the Dutch word *haakbus,* meaning "hook gun"—was accurate only to about fifty yards, and because it took several minutes to reload after every shot, it did not by any means render obsolete the role of archers and pikemen on the field of battle. The next advancement was the musket, a Spanish adaptation that, at twenty pounds, was twice as heavy and more cumbersome to carry than the harquebus but had a longer barrel, to provide additional power and greater range. For ammunition, the earliest musketeers carried individual charges of gunpowder in small leather pouches that they attached to belts slung across their chests—an accessory known as the bandolier. These tiny canisters, sometimes called the "twelve apostles" for the number of packets that typically dangled from each strap, freed the soldiers from having to measure out firing loads between salvos, eliminating one essential step, at least, in the loading process.

The invention, by German clockmakers in the sixteenth century, of the spring-loaded wheel lock dispensed with the necessity of using smoldering wicks or flaming candles for ignition—it employed the same striking concept, flint on steel, that sparks the modern cigarette lighter—and was followed a hundred years later by the flintlock, a French improvement that remained popular well into the 1700s. In a parallel development, the eighteenth-century British mathematician and scientist Benjamin Robins determined that elongated projectiles fired with spin have lower air resistance than spherical objects—a majestically thrown spiral pass in American football is a graceful example of the principle—leading gunsmiths to cut helical grooves inside the barrels of muskets and artillery pieces; the process, called rifling (from the French verb *rifler,* "to scratch, graze, or groove") gave rise to the era of the marksman and the sharpshooter and introduced a term for a type of firearm that is still used universally today, the rifle.

While the reliability of these weapons steadily improved, the rate of fire in combat still remained one shot at a time, a circumstance that did not change until the arrival of the repeating rifle, in the nineteenth century. Thus, for four hundred years—from the 1400s to the late 1800s, from the time of the conquistadores to the limited use by cavalry of bolt-action carbines during the American Civil War—soldiers could only fire single volleys. Given that limitation, the challenge for field commanders was to speed up the turnaround time between salvos, and the most efficient solution, by far, to accomplish that was the paper cartridge. The person frequently credited with standardizing the practice is King Gustavus II Adolphus of Sweden, a brilliant military strategist and innovator who is often called the "father of modern warfare," though the concept had been around well before he adopted it during the Thirty Years' War (1618–48).

In 1590, the English military historian and diplomat Sir John Smythe, a strident advocate of the longbow on the battlefield—he claimed that the traditional stringed weapon was lighter, shot faster, was more accurate, and was not incapacitated by rain—made reference to musketeers who used paper "cartages, with the which they doo charge their peeces both with powder and bullet all at one time," unambiguous evidence that the concept was being applied selectively several decades before Gustavus Adolphus standardized it among his infantry. Smythe's derisive comments on musketeers and what he called "harquebusiers" included this: "Their bullets doo worke as much effect against the Moone, as against the Enemie that they shoote at."

Equally injurious, Smythe felt, was that the bulk of the larger firearm left infantrymen "lame in their armes, shoulders, and backes." To consider the cranky old knight's complaints today is not unlike reading the fifteenth-century German abbot Johannes Trithemius grumble over why he preferred the tried-and-true scribe to the upstart printing press. In both instances, technology prevailed, and in the case of the firearm, the paper cartridge became the preferred casing, supplanted finally in the late nineteenth century by shells made entirely of copper and brass, but before that not disrupted even by the invention, in 1807, of the percussion cap, the successor to the flintlock. In its earliest form, a cartridge was no more than a paper cylinder rolled to contain a bullet and a precisely measured portion of gunpowder, with the wrapper itself serving as a wad for the charge. The word *cartridge* derives from several roots, the most common being *cartouche,* French for "roll of paper," and *cartoccio,* Italian for a cone-shaped container that translates as "paper comet," with "carton" being another derivative.

A field manual written in 1644 by John Vernon, a cavalry officer for the parliamentary army during the English Civil War, instructed mounted soldiers on the proper way to make "cartrages" for carbines and pistols, and specified procedures for the loading of their weapons. Using a standard-issue "turned wooden pin," or dowel, as a measuring stick, the troops were taught to cut strips of paper to a width "something broader than the pin is in length," and then use the same tool to shape the individual tubes. After closing off one end with a simple twist, they would then load each cartridge "almost full" with powder, taking care to leave room for a musket ball on top, and then tie that end securely. To prepare for firing, the soldiers were required to "bite off that end of the paper" containing the powder, pour the compound in the muzzle, and insert the bullet, along with some of the paper on

*Group of sepoys at Lucknow, India, at the height of the insurrection. From the* Illustrated London News, *October 1857.*

top for wadding. To "make ready" for shooting, they would then cram everything "home" with a ramrod and cock the lock. Skilled musketeers could discharge four rounds a minute in this manner, and maintain such a pace for up to four minutes before needing a brief break to clean the weapons of residue.

Over time, soldiers were issued cartridges that were assembled in munitions factories, but with their hands otherwise occupied, the requirement that they tear the paper pouches open with their teeth remained in force, and this was largely responsible for triggering, in 1857, one of the bloodiest episodes in the annals of British colonialism. Known variously today as the Indian Mutiny, the Sepoy Rebellion, the Indian Uprising, the Great Mutiny, the Bengal Mutiny, the First War of Indian Independence, the Great Rebellion, or simply the Sepoy War—points of view and national sympathies still determine what the episode is called—the brutal confrontation flared as the culmination of cultural differences that had been simmering for decades, worsened by a class divide that grew wider and more insensitive over time.

While by no means the root cause of the violence that erupted, the refusal by Hindu and Muslim soldiers employed by the British East India Company to put substances forbidden by their religious convictions into their mouths was nevertheless the flash point that set off the mayhem. The greater irony is that the impasse was foreseeable and could have been avoided easily by the application of simple common sense, but British officials blithely ignored the matter until it was far too late to resolve.

The East India Company had been trading in India since the early 1600s, gradually securing political and economic control of such magnitude that by the 1750s it had raised, with the full blessing of the British government, local armies commanded by English officers to protect its vast interests, which included monopolies on the export of cotton, silk, tea, indigo dye, spices, and opium. At the time of the bloody flare-up, there were 257,000 sepoys (from *sepâh*, Persian for "army") divided among four district forces known individually as the Madras, Calcutta, Bombay, and Bengal armies, the last one being, by far, the largest. As members of the ruling elite, English officers posted to India were denied none of life's comforts, while the enlisted natives who outnumbered them six to one remained mired in squalor and virtual servitude. "Sepoys had three advantages," the military historian G. J. Bryant explained of the arrangement, which could be viewed as an early example of the economic outsourcing that is so prevalent in today's global economy: "They were on the spot, cheap, and acclimatized."

For years, the standard-issue weapon in India had been the smoothbore musket, but in January of 1857 the British government announced it would begin to equip the Bengal army with a firearm designed at the Royal Small Arms Factory, in Enfield, England, that was based on an 1849 French piece known as the Minié rifle, named for French army captain Claude-Étienne Minié, who had helped develop it. Combining the barrel length of a musket with the grooves of a rifle, the Enfield Pattern 1853 rifle musket, with a reported range of nine hundred yards, had been used effectively against Russia in the Crimean War of 1854–56 and was regarded as a considerable upgrade over the older weapons then in service.

Because the bore of the Enfield barrel was scored with helical grooves—and because rifles require tightly fitted bullets in order to maximize the explosive power of the expanding gases—it became necessary to add lubricants that would facilitate loading. For the new weapons, ready-to-use cartridges were manufactured with various concoctions of beeswax and animal fat already applied in the factories.

Though the composition would be changed once the greased cartridge became a cause célèbre, the animal fats used at first were either tallow, which is derived from cows, or lard, which is rendered from pigs. Given that cows are sacred to Hindus, who made up three-quarters of the Bengal army, and that pigs are repugnant to Muslims, who composed the remainder, resentment against the practice was assured. A few British officers cautioned that the cartridges might cause grave problems, and early warnings were sounded. "We have at Barrackport been dwelling upon a mine ready for explosion," Major General J. B. Hearsey wrote to his superior in Calcutta as the leadership began, finally, to take the growing discontent seriously. He even convened a special court of inquiry in which the sepoys were invited to express "the cause of their continued objection to the paper of which the new rifle cartridges were composed."

Other attempts at damage control included assurances that the lubricants were not, in fact, derived from animal fat, though it was hard to disclaim the language printed in the standard instruction manual for infantrymen prepared by the Adjutant General's Office in 1854, which included this final step for the making of ammunition: "When completed, the base of the cartridge must be dipped up to the shoulder of the bullet in a pot of grease, consisting of six parts tallow to one of bee's wax." And there was no leeway, either, in how soldiers were to load their new rifles, beginning with this basic rule: "Bring the cartridge to the mouth, holding it between the forefinger and thumb, with the ball in the hand, and bite off the top, elbow close to the body." It was only when the grievance began to escalate out of control that the sepoys were told they could tear open the cartridges with their fingers and that they could grease their own casings with pure beeswax—but by then it was far too late to put the genie back in the bottle.

The response in England to reports of mounting unease was one of shock and astonishment, the prevailing assumption being that contentment and compliance prevailed among their subjects. Though unrelated to the cartridge brouhaha directly, another "paper factor" at play in the rapidly deteriorating crisis was that the East India Company, to all intents and purposes, was controlled by absentee landlords who had rarely, if ever, been to the subcontinent. A hierarchical order had developed over many decades, according to which few key decisions of any sort were made on the scene. Instead, written dispatches issued thousands of miles away in London had to be carried out precisely by subordinates and recorded in such painstaking detail that red tape became entrenched in a civil service bureaucracy that to this day is mired in a quagmire of paperwork. A guiding premise of the book *Indian Ink,* a scholarly examination of how the East India Company used both printed regulations and handwritten instructions to build and manage its sprawling economic empire, is that the firm's tightly controlled world of long-distance governance "was one made on paper as well as on land and sea."

By the time the British discontinued the use of animal fat, the grievance had gained such traction that repeated calls for calm went unheeded. Before long, rumors were circulating that the paper itself might be tainted, a fear given credence by the fact that a local manufacturer hired to make cartridges for the Enfields at the Dum Dum Arsenal produced a much coarser product than the ammunition cartridges made in England, raising concerns about its composition.

The first overt expression of defiance came on March 29, 1857, when three sepoy regiments refused outright to take possession of the new weapons and were summarily disbanded. When eighty-five soldiers stationed at the cantonment town of Meerut were publicly stripped of their uniforms and marched off in shackles, the assembled troops mutinied and marched southwest to Delhi, where, on May 11, they proclaimed the royal prince Bahadur Shah II to be their ceremonial leader. The governor-general of India, Lord Canning, would later describe the "riveting of the men's fetters" on the parade grounds and marching them off "to the gaol" in front of their countrymen to have been "a folly that is inconceivable."

Known familiarly by the pen name Zafar, Bahadur Shah II, eighty-two at the time of his unexpected rise to short-lived political prominence, was an accomplished poet, calligrapher, theologian, and creator of beautiful gardens. A direct descendant of Genghis Khan and Timur, he held court in the besieged city for two months, earning him the distinction of being the last Mughal emperor of India. By early June, all but three of the fifty-seven regiments in the Bengal army—nearly ninety thousand men, or 70 percent of the 150,000-soldier force—had joined the mutiny, which remained confined to the northern territories. The three smaller mercenary armies did not rebel, but with their loyalties nonetheless suspect, they could not be relied upon to oppose their own countrymen, so the British brought in troops from Burma and other postings. After major setbacks at the Kanpur garrison and Lucknow, they were finally able to quell the mutiny. Estimates of casualties are imprecise but suggest that about two thousand Britons and ten thousand Indians died in the conflict, at a cost of £36 million.

Quickly following the cessation of hostilities, in 1858, imperial rule was transferred to the Crown, marking the abrupt termination of British East India Company control and commencing the period of colonial rule known as the British Raj (meaning, in Hindi, "to rule," or "kingdom"). England was able to maintain political and military control well into the twentieth century, but the groundwork for independence had been established, and it would triumph finally in 1947, by way of a nonviolent version of civil disobedience embraced by Mahatma Gandhi and his many millions of followers. The defiant couplet penned by Bahadur Shah II at the height of the Delhi siege, nine decades earlier—quoted in full at the beginning of this chapter—proved prophetic. "The mighty English," the last Mughal monarch had trumpeted boldly, "have been overthrown in Hindustan by a single cartridge."

As for the Enfield rifle, it remained in service through the end of the 1860s and was manufactured by several companies licensed by the British government for sale abroad. Some 900,000 of the pieces are believed to have made their way to North America during the Civil War, and they were used by combatants on both sides of the Mason-Dixon Line, surpassed in the North only by the Springfield Model 1861 rifle musket, which also used paper cartridges. At Gettysburg, it was used by the Twentieth Maine Infantry Regiment, under the heroic command of Colonel Joshua Lawrence Chamberlain during the famous bayonet charge at Little Round Top.

The introduction of a shorter-barreled field weapon, the Spencer Repeating Carbine—which could fire seven bullets from a magazine and was used primarily by mounted cavalrymen—did not do away with the single-shot rifles, mainly because of inadequate supplies of the all-brass cartridges it required. A summary report issued at war's end by United States secretary of war Edwin M. Stanton, itemizing military purchases made between 1861 and 1865, suggests with uncanny precision just how much paper would have been required to arm the Union troops. In a line for "cartridges for muskets, cal. .577 and

.58"—ammunition for both the Enfield and the Springfield—a total of 470,851,079 charges were acquired; rounds for all other muskets, carbines, and pistols came to 557,326,395. This amounted to more than a billion cartridges altogether.

Figures of such specificity are not available for the Confederacy—indeed, several studies have been written that detail the improvised, seat-of-the-pants approach adopted by the rebellious alliance to supply itself with various necessities and munitions—but the South usually gave as good as it got on the battlefield, and the number of cartridges expended by its forces undoubtedly numbered well into the hundreds of millions as well, though there were always severe shortages, not only of paper but of every imaginable necessity for home and commerce, including food, clothing, and medicine.

In a technical report prepared while assigned to the Royal Arsenal, Woolwich, Arthur B. Hawes, a former infantry officer who saw duty in India, explained the process for making Enfield cartridges. The pamphlet, titled *Rifle Ammunition,* was published a year after the Sepoy

*The noted combat artist Alfred R. Waud, who drew numerous front-line sketches throughout the Civil War for* Harper's Weekly *and other publications, here pictured a soldier taking paper cartridges from a dead comrade during the heat of an unidentified battle, 1864.*

Mutiny had been quelled and two years before the first shots in the American Civil War were fired, on Fort Sumter, in South Carolina. Hawes cited a number of requisites that were paramount for achieving high-quality paper, a few of which explain why, in succeeding years, custom-made cartridge paper would gain favor among many artists as a preferred medium: "regularity of texture, evenness of surface, a certain amount of tenacity, and freedom from spots." Random samples from every ream were tested "by stretching or pulling" and by holding up to the light. "For all paper used in making ball ammunition, care must be taken that such paper is selected as will not increase the diameter of the bullet, when rolled tightly round it, more than .009 of an inch, and the paper should not be highly sized."

Gone, obviously, were the days when soldiers fashioned their own cartridges in the field. Precision and uniformity were essential for use with rifled weapons, and these could be guaranteed only with the assistance of machines. Once every step on the manufacturing checklist had been completed, the "cartridge has then only to be filled, twisted, and greased, or lubricated," and as Hawes pointed out, the best lubrication—or "anti-fouling agent," as he called it—was beeswax. He acknowledged that tallow had been used in India, and subsequent tests in the Woolwich laboratory, he wrote with understated delicacy, had determined it to be un unstable lubricant that "will not remain permanent, but will gradually pass away into the paper of the cartridge; and, in cases where the tallow preponderates in a large degree over the beeswax, a portion of the tallow will remain on the cartridge, in the form of a dry powder."

By the time of the Hawes report, paper was also being used with great success to pack explosive loads for artillery pieces. For those weapons, the pressing need had been to ensure a cleaner bore after a barrage had been fired, but other than introducing the use of linen bags to keep powder dry, artillery procedures during the fifteenth, sixteenth, and seventeenth centuries "had not emerged from the womb of time," according to O. F. G. Hogg, author of a definitive history of the Royal Arsenal, where weapons for the British military were perfected and manufactured for more than three hundred years. During those embryonic phases of artillery design, the most widely employed method of loading a cannon was simply to insert the powder into the bore with a ladle and position the projectile on top.

Taking their cue, finally, from the infantry, artillery crews began to prepare bagloads of powder in advance, with casement materials fashioned from parchment, boar skin, canvas, linen, merino wool, and bombazet, a kind of thin wool, as well as various grades of paper. Fabrics made from cotton and linen were prone to incomplete ignition, however, while parchment tended to shrivel and choke off adequate venting under the heat of combustion. After much trial and error, paper was found to be the most efficient alternative, even though, as manufactured through the end of the eighteenth century, it lacked sufficient strength and discharged unevenly, often leaving a residue of unexpended powder that blew up during reloading.

"Naval and military history is replete with instances of the destruction of ships of war, and of military magazines, by accidents arising from the exposed and defective manner in which gun powder is kept," an American munitions designer wrote a year before the outbreak of the War of 1812, in a report that advocated the introduction of "leaden cartridges" as a replacement for paper. The lead cartridge he proposed "may be perforated with as much ease as paper; and as it is not necessary to ram home the charge, or prime the gun, until intended to be used, it may remain at all times in the gun, ready for service, without injury from wet or damp."

Several decades passed before that approach was implemented; until then, paper bags remained the material of choice, in large part by virtue of a patent filed on November 12, 1807, for a "cannon cartridge paper, manufactured on an improved principle," by John Dickinson, an innovative nineteenth-century British papermaker who was at the forefront of many advancements. "My invention," he wrote in his application,

> consists in the addition of a certain proportion of wool or woolen rags to the linen rags or other materials, consisting of hemp or flax, that have hitherto been made use of for manufacturing this kind of paper; by means of which, in consequence of the intermixture of the woolen fibres with those of the hemp or flax, when the paper is lighted by the explosion of the powder in the gun, it is prevented from retaining sparks of fire after the flame goes out.

Dickinson gave a detailed formula for preparing the mixture and for the proportions to be used. "The linen should be very strong and sound, and beat as wet, and at the same time as long as possible, otherwise with the proportions mentioned above, the paper will not be sufficiently strong." So, with one bold tweak to the process, Dickinson had removed the two most challenging stumbling blocks—insufficient strength and uneven combustion—in the making of paper for artillery use. Five months earlier, he had secured a patent for a mechanical design that included significant modifications to the Fourdrinier machine, and in January 1809 he was awarded yet another, for a machine that would manufacture paper mechanically by his own design.

Dickinson opened his first mill twenty-five miles northwest of London at Hemel Hempstead, a town on the Gade and Bulbourne rivers, and began to manufacture his paper for cannon cartridges. The Board of Ordnance's adoption of paper for use by the Royal Army and Navy has been credited with playing a vital role in the resounding victories over Napoleon in the Peninsular War and at the decisive battle of Waterloo, in 1815. The texture was ideal for rifle cartridges, too, and with the entry of England into the Crimean War, there came "a fresh demand for Minié paper," Joan Evans, daughter of the founder's nephew, wrote in a history of the family business. Then, in 1857, she continued, "came the Indian Mutiny," and the company's workers "were busier than they had ever been." As the rebellion wore on into 1858, a government contract for thirteen thousand reams of the paper—"always called the Minnie in the mills"—was secured.

Though lucrative, the making of cartridge paper was never regarded by John Dickinson & Company as anything more than a sideline for what had become a variety of highly desirable products. In 1812, Dickinson introduced a thin, tough, opaque paper that was used in the publication of Samuel Bagster's *Pocket Reference Bible,* a best seller that attracted effusive praise for the texture and color of the stock from the Reverend Thomas Frognall Dibdin, in his *Bibliographical Decameron.* In 1823, Dickinson registered a process that made possible the insertion of various threads—cotton, linen, silk, lace—into the fabric of paper, a feature that proved most attractive as a foil to counterfeiters in the manufacture of currency. In 1850, he introduced the manufacture of gummed envelopes, at the same time pioneering the use of matching stationery, which to this day remains a company specialty. Other products—and, along with them, many new uses—included what was called duplex paper, or what we now know as cardboard.

A quite unexpected use for paper—certainly one that was not planned in any systematic way—began to emerge around the middle of the nineteenth century, and may well have had as its genesis the ready availability of cartridge paper to soldiers serving in various conflicts, and the affection so many of them already had for the "evil weed," as tobacco was called by the Puritan settlers of Massachusetts who encountered its use among the native Indians. Until then, tobacco was consumed in a variety of ways, either by smoking, chewing, or inhaling through the nostrils as snuff. Those who preferred to smoke the plant did so either from the bowl of a pipe or as cigars (from *sikar,* the Yucatec Mayan word for smoking), which were compact bundles of dried tobacco wrapped in a reed or leaf and shaped in the form of a narrow cylinder.

Introduced to Europeans in the sixteenth century by explorers returning from the New World, tobacco rapidly developed a passionate following, so much so that by the mid-1700s it was the principal agricultural crop in Virginia and the Carolinas, exchangeable by those who grew it for European products. Tobacco proved useful during the Revolution as a source of funds for the war effort and as a soothing palliative for the weary troops. "If you can't send money," a desperate George Washington wrote the Continental Congress in 1776, "send tobacco." A similar sentiment would be expressed 142 years later, during World War I, by General John J. "Blackjack" Pershing. "You ask what we need to win this war," he wrote in a letter to the secretary of war, in Washington, from the front in Europe. "I will tell you, we need tobacco, more tobacco—even more than food."

As to who, exactly, came up with the idea to wrap the shredded leaves of the plant in a sheath of paper remains a matter of debate, though there is evidence to support the belief that Spain—with its lucrative tobacco plantations in the West Indies and an active paper industry at home—was the originator. The idea is believed to have been inspired by a crude practice mastered by resourceful vagabonds who gathered half-smoked cigar butts from the streets of Seville, shredded the unused tobacco portions, and layered them inside pieces of scrap paper, which was readily available. It was only a matter of time before someone saw a clever way to make profitable use of trimmings left behind in the warehouses where cigars were rolled from prime tobacco leaves.

Known variously as *papeletes* and *cigaritos,* this cheap alternative to cigars quickly found favor among Spanish and Portuguese sailors, who spread the practice to Russia and the Levant, where the Ottoman Turks had established a reputation for growing flavorful tobaccos of their own. The development of luxury cigarettes in Egypt did not go unappreciated; the first brand offered to American consumers by the R. J. Reynolds Tobacco Company in 1913 was called Camel, and it featured on its package art images of pyramids, palm trees, and Islamic architecture.

A variant version of the genesis story, offered up in corporate histories of both the American Tobacco Company and P. Lorillard & Co., gives 1832 as a critical year in the evolution of the modern cigarette. Each of these accounts cites a probably apocryphal event that is said to have taken place during a siege of the Turkish city of Acre by Egyptian forces under the direction of Ibrahim Pasha, and each makes a strong connection with cartridge paper. According to this story, a crew of Egyptian artillerymen improved their rate of fire during the six-month operation by packing gunpowder in improvised paper tubes—the practice was being used widely by other armies at the time, so this part of the story is certainly credible enough. As a token of gratitude for their resourcefulness, an admiring commander is said to have given the soldiers a generous ration of tobacco. Because the clay bowl they normally used to smoke had been shattered, they used artillery paper instead.

Another, almost identical version of this story comes from the makers of Zig-Zag cigarette papers, a French company that has as a logo on all of its products a caricature of a nineteenth-century infantryman known as a Zouave. As the company's official history tells it, a French soldier fighting at the Siege of Sebastopol, in 1854, during the Crimean War, had "the brilliant idea of rolling his tobacco in a piece of paper torn from a bag of gunpowder" after his clay pipe had been destroyed. Twenty-three years later—apparently using the soldier's heady improvisation as their inspiration—two French entrepreneurs, Maurice and Jacques Braunstein, established a papermaking concern in Paris, and in 1882 they opened the Papeterie de Gassicourt (often called Papeterie Braunstein de Gassicourt), a production plant near the town of Mantes-la-Jolie. A packaging process they later perfected, in which thin sheets of the wrappers were interleaved in a crisscross manner, led to the introduction, in 1894, of little booklets of the wrappers sold under the name Zig-Zag, a product marketed for roll-your-own enthusiasts that became commonplace during the 1960s and '70s, when marijuana use was rampant among a generation caught up in the upheavals of the day.

Whether actual or invented, the Zouave incident followed by a dozen years the documented production of twenty thousand cigarettes for a charity bazaar in Paris organized by Marie-Amélie de Bourbon, widow of King Louis XVIII, the constitutional monarch who ruled for ten years after the fall of Napoleon. By that time, tobacco had become a critical source of revenue for the French government, a development tacitly acknowledged in 1810, when Napoleon took control of the industry to help support his military operations.

Regardless of who was first to wrap tobacco in paper, few dispute the importance of the Crimean War in spreading its popularity. While not global by twentieth-century standards, the conflict did pitch the combined forces of England, France, Turkey, and Sardinia against the Russian Empire in a protracted contest to secure control of the Holy Land, and resulted in the exchange of numerous cultural practices among the combatants. British soldiers returning home after the war brought the cigarette—the word is a French coinage—with them. Because cigarettes lacked the panache and richness of cigars, men who smoked them were considered in some eyes to be weak and effeminate, and were often the objects of ridicule.

Still, cigarettes were cheap, convenient, and sufficiently popular that by the late 1850s, Philip Morris, a London tobacconist, was making them domestically for a higher-class clientele. What quickly developed from there—the transformation of a quaint vice into a monster industry, with ramifications that have influenced the world economy in multiple ways, as well as the growth of a legally manufactured product whose impact on public health is unparalleled—happened as the result of several converging developments. But all were made possible by a ready supply of inexpensive paper.

By the 1880s, cigarettes were being made in England, France, Turkey, Egypt, and the United States, all of them using tissue-thin paper produced by machine in a number of factories but assembled by hand, and thus labor intensive—a trained worker could roll up to four cigarettes a minute. There was a market for them, but cigars, chews, and snuff still dominated, and given that production was limited by the size and skill of the workforce—and the fact that labor accounted for 90 percent of the manufacturing cost—sales remained moderate. In an attempt to invigorate the business, Lewis Ginter, a founder of the Richmond cigarette manufacturing firm Allen & Ginter, offered a $75,000 prize to anyone who could come up with a machine to automate the process.

A quick response came from James A. Bonsack, the son of a Virginia tobacco grower, who had been tinkering with just such a contraption for years and had obtained a patent in 1880. Allen & Ginter tried a prototype but, for reasons never fully explained, rejected the design, and withheld the reward. Quick to step in and secure immediate use for his growing operation was James Buchanan "Buck" Duke, the twenty-four-year-old son of a Confederate gunnery officer from Durham, North Carolina, and a shrewd businessman just beginning to build a combine of manufacturers that in 1890 would become the American Tobacco Company. Duke cut costs by offering the Bull Durham brand of tobacco in loose packages, along with slips of paper—together they

*A roll-your-own enthusiast pictured in a 1904
cover illustration for* Sunset *magazine.*

were called "the makings"—giving customers the wherewithal to roll their own smokes.

The demand for Duke's products was nudged along by a mounting taste for cigarettes, but it also benefited from his brilliant use of advertising—almost all of it by way of paper. In addition to chic newspaper ads and attractive logos with catchy taglines—"Your nose knows," for the Tuxedo brand; "Ask Dad, he knows," for Sweet Caporal; "It's toasted," for Lucky Strike; "Outstanding, and they are mild!" for Pall Mall—came an onslaught of ephemeral materials, not least among them coupons that could be redeemed for glitzy gifts, lithographed picture cards aimed at collectors, handbills inserted into programs at plays and sporting events, billboard and poster displays, and every other manner of printed inducement. More than a quarter-million of these objects, pertaining to every conceivable aspect of tobacco, were collected by George Arents—an inventor and younger colleague of Duke's who came up with improved designs for the cigarette rolling machine—and presented in 1944 to the New York Public Library, where they reside today in a third-floor suite of rooms provided by his bequest.

In human terms, the impact of cigarettes on society was summed up best, perhaps, by Richard Kluger in *Ashes to Ashes,* a Pulitzer Prize–winning account of America's economic "cigarette war" of the 1900s, in which Duke was a very active principal. "No one can make more than an informed guess at the total loss of life" caused by cigarettes in the twentieth century, he wrote, "but those decrying it most urgently assert that the mortality figure from smoking for the century as a whole rivals the multimillions who have fallen in all its wars." The American Cancer Society has reported that cigarette smoking causes 87 percent of lung cancer deaths and is responsible for most cancers of the larynx, oral cavity and pharynx, esophagus, and bladder. According to figures compiled by the National Fire Protection Association, cigarettes have been the leading cause of fire fatalities for decades, responsible for seven hundred to nine hundred deaths a year in the United States, many of them caused by people smoking in bed. And beyond the loss of human life is the destruction of woodlands caused by careless drivers who discard smoldering butts out the windows of their trucks and automobiles.

While medical science firmly holds that it is the carcinogenic properties of tobacco, and not the cellulose wrappers, that put cigarette smokers at grave risk, one of the earliest alarms voiced against their use nonetheless centered on the paper. In 1914, the automobile magnate Henry Ford privately published and distributed nationwide a pamphlet provocatively titled *The Case Against the Little White Slaver.* A letter Ford had solicited earlier that year from Thomas A. Edison, reproduced in its entirety at the beginning of this chapter, appeared in facsimile. In his preface, Ford wrote about how Edison's experiments to find a "suitable filament for use in incandescent lamps" had involved "combustion of various substances," including paper, which produces a pulmonary irritant gas known as acrolein when burned. An appreciative cigar smoker in his own right, Edison believed it was the acrolein, not nicotine, that posed the far greater health hazard, and it was this conviction that persuaded Ford to launch his short-lived crusade.

People who smoke cigarettes, of course, have always done so because of the tobacco, but the composition of the paper is critical nonetheless. A report prepared in 1975 by British American Tobacco—one of more than eleven million documents now on deposit in the Legacy Tobacco Documents Library, maintained at the University of California, San Francisco—makes the point in a single sentence: "Cigarette paper must be tasteless and odourless, must possess a high degree of whiteness, opacity, strength and elasticity, must not cling to the lips when moist and must burn at the same rate as the tobacco."

Cigarette makers, as a rule, do not produce their own paper; they buy it from companies that specialize in its manufacture, though the tobacco industry has been known to subsidize paper mills to ensure a steady supply. This kind of arrangement proved especially perceptive during World War II, when France—until then the dominant supplier of cigarette paper to America—fell under Nazi occupation, and shipments to the United States were curtailed. In the months leading up to the onset of hostilities, American cigarette makers had committed their combined support to a company hastily established in North Carolina by Harry H. Straus, a Jewish immigrant from France who set up a plant thirty miles southwest of Asheville, North Carolina, in the heavily wooded Blue Ridge Mountains, deep in the heart of tobacco country.

Part of the capital to underwrite the operation had come from guaranteed orders paid up front by Liggett & Myers, R. J. Reynolds, Lorillard, and Philip Morris. On September 2, 1939, Ecusta Corporation spooled out its first bobbin of cigarette paper. Within three months, the company was operating non-stop, around the clock, and was already meeting 50 percent of all domestic needs. Prior to World War II, the principal fiber used to make cigarette paper was rags, but under Straus's direction the formula changed so that it consisted largely of cellulose derived from flax and hemp, in combination with precipitated calcium carbonate—chalk—along with a few other additives to control what is called the "burn rate." In the United States, flax straw—a waste product from the growing of linseed flax—is also used, along with high-grade chemical wood pulp. A twenty-thousand-foot bobbin will spool enough paper to make eighty-five thousand cigarettes, at a rate sufficient for two hundred million per week.

Within a year, the Ecusta mill employed nine hundred people; when the war ended, in 1945, that number had grown to two thousand, having reached at its height nearly three thousand employees. Straus was a benevolent owner who paid the best wages in the region, opened a medical clinic for workers, established a summer camp for the children of his employees, and sponsored Fourth of July parades and Christmas parties. In 1951, the company was acquired by the Olin Mathieson Chemical Corporation, a major manufacturer of ammunition that two years earlier had entered the cellophane-making business. Olin operated the company for thirty-five years, selling it finally to P. H. Glatfelter, of Spring Grove, Pennsylvania, in 1987, for $220 million. Glatfelter suffered a major setback in 1992, when Philip Morris Co. announced that it would buy all of its domestic cigarette paper from Kimberly-Clark, depriving the mill of its largest customer. Glatfelter attempted to sell Ecusta through the rest of the decade, finally closing it for good in 2002, a move I discuss further in Chapter 17.

The leading manufacturer of cigarette paper today is Schweitzer-Mauduit International Inc., a Georgia-based conglomerate that describes itself as "the world's largest supplier of fine papers to the tobacco industry" and is traded on the New York Stock Exchange under the symbol SWM. A 1995 spin-off from the same Kimberly-Clark division that had effectively put Ecusta out of business, the company operates eleven production plants on four continents, three of which are "fiber-pulping operations." In its 2011 annual report, the company asserted that it is the "sole domestic producer of Cigarette Papers in North America" and that wood pulp is the primary fiber, with 83,000 metric tons purchased in 2011. "Our operations also use other cellulose fibers, the most significant of which are in the form of flax fiber and tobacco leaf by-products." Net sales for the year were $816.2 million, up $72 million from 2010.

Given the negative attitude regarding tobacco use that now prevails in America, it is little surprise that a manufacturer whose principal product is the paper used to make cigarettes would choose to lay low. The company maintains a basic website for the benefit of investors and prospective clients but has ignored repeated attempts, on my part at least, to visit any of its plants or to speak with company officials. My e-mails are not answered, my telephone calls are never returned. An announcement on its website reporting first-quarter figures for 2010 offered what could well be a reason for such wariness: "The company's sales are concentrated to a limited number of customers. In 2009, 56% of its sales were to its four largest customers. The loss of one or more of these customers, or a significant reduction in one or more of these customers' purchases, could have a material adverse effect on the company's results of operations." Interestingly, the report for the same period in 2009 noted that 60 percent of the company's sales were to its *five* largest customers, suggesting that a major client had indeed left the fold. That same year, the Commonwealth of Virginia, home to what Schweitzer-Mauduit identified in its annual report to be its largest customer, Philip Morris USA, banned smoking in all public places. In this kind of hostile environment, it is easy to see why a low profile may well be the most desirable; even better, perhaps, is no profile at all.

# 8

---

# Papers, Please

This passport you must have renewed once a year, unless you are a noble
or an honorary citizen, and the process is as tedious and painful as moult-
ing is to a fish. A voluminous correspondence, and a pile of documents
with copies, petitions, and fifteen supplements, was the result of a man
named Dudinsky in the Government of Smolensk, to renew his passport
two years ago. And yet his papers were in order, his conduct irreproach-
able, and his right to have his passport renewed was not even called in
question. These obstacles and irritations make one's soul weary of life;
and explain why it is that in the course of one year in St. Petersburg alone
14,799 persons were arrested and imprisoned for not having complied
with the passport laws. Many of these wretched creatures may be now on
their way to Siberia.

—E. B. Lanin, "Russian Characteristics,"
in *Fortnightly Review,* 1889

WHO WE SAY WE ARE—and whether or not we can prove it—has
been a social and legal obligation for centuries, and more often than
not the first step in the validation process is to furnish supporting credentials that back up our claims. On an intellectual level, *identity* is
a concept that takes on philosophical, moral, theological, sociologi-
cal, cultural, ethnic, and even cosmic considerations. In cognitive psy-
chology, having an identity suggests a capacity for reflection and an
awareness of self. On a far more elemental level, it is a confirmation
of uniqueness that in recent times can be nailed down definitively by
fingerprints, dental records, iris scans, voice recognition, and DNA—
what people in the forensics business call biometric indicators—but on

a daily basis very much relies on tried-and-true standbys such as driver's licenses, voting records, Social Security cards, and passports.

Even today, with electronic documents becoming more and more acceptable as legal instruments, hard copies are still preferred for birth certificates, quitclaim deeds, and the issuance of a legal summons. Traditionally, a request—or a demand, as the case may be—to "show your papers" is an order to present unimpeachable documentation that corroborates who you purport yourself to be. Put another way, identity "constitutes the attempt to control how others define us—as anyone who has ever lost their papers in an unfriendly environment knows all too well," Valentin Groebner, author of a penetrating study of identification, deception, and surveillance in early modern Europe, has pointed out.

In the years before paper established a foothold in Europe, people with means often commissioned artistic depictions of themselves to function as portable likenesses they could furnish as necessary, while others of lesser station oftentimes had distinctive markings tattooed on their skin; in some societies, the branding of slaves, criminals, and vagrants was compulsory. Many people displayed familial coats of arms or wore specific insignia on their outer clothing in much the same way that members of urban street gangs of today defiantly wear their "colors" and exchange secret handshakes as signs of recognition. Over the centuries, public officials have been issued distinctive badges made of tin, leather, cloth, and fabric to confirm their legal authority, a medieval custom that continues to this day among law enforcement personnel around the world. In the years before identity documents became commonplace, people were distinguished by attire that was representative of their social class or occupation, and individually by physical attributes such as scars, birthmarks, complexion, height, and hair color. While military garments are apparel that by definition is "uniform"—they are identical, in other words, throughout a given branch of service—each has specific insignia to denote the rank of the soldier, sailor, or aviator, and in modern times they also have surnames sewn or pinned on the breast.

Using documents to establish identity ushered in an entirely new standard, and paper was the ideal medium with which to achieve consistency. The material was cheap, light, produced in abundance, and, because of its flexibility, portable—meaning it could be folded and carried about with ease. Unlike parchment and vellum, ink could not be scraped or washed away from the surface, which discouraged tampering. With this feature, officials quickly realized that a person's signature, unique to each hand, could function as an additional safeguard. The introduction in the late eleventh century of the seal—a stamping device embossed with a symbol, phrase, or design that could be embossed in hot wax—gained popularity as a means of verifying legal and theological documents that might otherwise be subject to forgery.

From the twelfth century on, merchants and diplomats traveling about Europe carried beautifully calligraphed letters of safe conduct—frequently referred to as *salvus conductus, salvacondotto,* or *sauf-conduit*—and to this day ambassadors arriving at new postings in foreign countries must still "present credentials" to the host nation in order to receive formal recognition of their standing. Diplomatic communiqués carried by emissaries abroad have traditionally followed careful protocols as well, including the use of high-quality paper and intricate calligraphy that "carried important messages to the recipients," which were evident simply by their appearance, according to the British historian Miles Ogborn, whose specialty is an emerging field of scholarly inquiry known as cultural geography. "Such letters were a crucial part of the exchanges of ambassadors and envoys that structured the politics of early modern Asia, and were also the mechanism for making agreements between empires and the smaller states of maritime southeast Asia, which were themselves undergoing processes of centralization and scribalization in the seventeenth century."

One of Benjamin Franklin's very first acts as minister plenipotentiary at the court of France during the American Revolution was to issue, on March 10, 1779, a circular letter addressed to commanders of all armed ships in the service of the recently declared United States, ordering them to treat the English explorer Captain James Cook, then embarked on a historic voyage of exploration around the earth, with "Civility and Kindness" should they encounter his naval detachment on the high seas, and to render "all the Assistance in your Power" to their expedition, which he regarded as "no more than a Duty to Mankind." Franklin was unaware that Cook had died in the Hawaiian Islands the month before he issued the declaration of safe conduct, but his gesture did not go unnoticed and was recognized by the British after the war.

What has been, arguably, the most consequential personal identification document of the past five centuries, though, is the passport, a word that claims a fairly straightforward provenance from French, for centuries the international language of diplomacy, to identify a permit that allows citizens from one country to pass freely across the borders of another. As a screening device, the passport has been used to oversee trade and travel between nations with roots that can be traced back to ancient times in a multitude of forms. A drawing found in an Egyptian tomb dating from about 1600 B.C. depicts a magistrate issuing identity tablets to a waiting line of temporary workers. Further evidence is provided in the Old Testament, where the Hebrew prophet Nehemiah recalled obtaining written permission from the Persian king to travel from Susa (now Shush) to Jerusalem, a journey that in today's world would require a 450-mile trip from Iran to Israel. "I came to the Governors of the province Beyond the River," he wrote, "and gave them the King's letter."

With the arrival of paper, passports began to be standardized and more widely recognized. A variation of the word itself first appears in English law in 1498, its stated purpose to "gif the said Inglismen sauffconductis or pasportis for thare factouris, servandis." By the eighteenth century, a British passport consisted of a single sheet of paper emblazoned with a coat of arms, and bore a formal statement, in script, requesting freedom of movement for the bearer. Other variations have controlled maritime commerce and, in the form of visas, have been used to regulate passage across national boundaries. In pre-revolutionary France, peasants could not migrate from town to town without papers identifying who they were; in the People's Republic of China today, citizens wishing to move from one province to another are required to furnish travel documents.

Not surprisingly, traffic in bogus travel documents has been brisk over the centuries, and, when recognized, their misuse can have dire consequences. One of the most notorious examples involved King Louis XVI, who was arrested in 1791 while trying to flee France with the aid of a spurious letter that identified him as a valet, and his wife, Marie Antoinette, as a maid. Fifteen miles from the border with Belgium at the village of Varennes, the local postmaster recognized the fugitive monarch from the engraved portrait of him that appeared on official coins of the realm. The king's use of false documents was included in the list of his alleged transgressions, which together sent him off to the guillotine.

Even today, having the right papers is essential for those wishing to move from place to place, as the arrest on June 22, 2011, of the notorious Boston gangster James "Whitey" Bulger made embarrassingly clear for authorities who had ranked him second only to Osama bin Laden on the FBI's list of the Ten Most Wanted Fugitives. In addition to plenty of cash and firepower—$822,000 and thirty fully loaded automatic weapons were found stashed in the Santa Monica, California, apartment where he had hidden in "plain sight" for at least thirteen years—they found an assortment of papers for fifteen different identities for him, and ten for Catherine Greig, his girlfriend. Also recovered was a well-thumbed copy of *Secrets of a Back Alley ID Man,* a how-to manual for the making of fake identification papers.

The indictment issued against Bulger alleged that the aliases belonged to people from four different states. Among documents released by the U.S. attorney in Boston were New York resident cards issued in 1996, a New York employee ID, a medical alert card indicating that Bulger was diabetic, a Social Security card, and two AARP membership cards. Most persuasive was an authentic California driver's license Bulger had obtained in the name of a down-and-out Army veteran he had helped out financially.

The first American passports were designed and printed in 1783 by Benjamin Franklin, at a small printing shop he had set up for his personal amusement in France, his home for nine years during the Revolution. Franklin printed a number of other interesting documents as well, some of them on behalf of the new republic he had helped create, others for a series of witty offprints, which he called "Bagatelles," produced for his friends, one of the more entertaining being "Dialogue with the Gout." In 1856, responsibility for American passports was assigned exclusively to the Department of State; the booklet-style documents used today became standardized throughout the world in 1926, on the strength of guidelines issued by the League of Nations.

In the chaotic aftermath of World War I, millions of people displaced by the global conflict, who were known as refugees—by definition, anyone living unwillingly outside the borders of their own nation or, even worse, anyone who through persecution, discrimination, or natural calamity no longer has any nationality at all—were in desperate need of finding places where they could get legal employment but were unable to move about for lack of documentation. Given the horrific losses suffered among all of the combatant nations, jobs were available to those able to fill the void, but no countries would allow anyone to cross their borders without passports.

A temporary solution was provided by the League of Nations, which in 1922 issued an international document that came to be called the Nansen passport, in honor of Fridtjof Nansen, the Norwegian explorer and statesman who developed its use. Valid for a year—but with options available for renewal—the documents were recognized by fifty-two countries, with France alone taking in 450,000 workers under the program. In 1938, the Nansen International Office for Refugees was awarded the Nobel Peace Prize for its efforts to establish a unique system of international documentation; since 1954, the United Nations has presented a medal named for Nansen that recognizes outstanding service to the cause of helping the displaced.

During World War II, the possession of a passport often meant the difference between life and death for innocent people trapped within the turmoil. "No document confers as much awesome power," Karl E. Meyer, editor emeritus of *World Policy Journal* and a noted historian of the modern Middle East, asserted in a searching essay devoted to the "curious life of the lowly passport." The document, he explained, has the power to "save or claim lives, liberate or incarcerate, speed or derail passage through ports of entry." One long-term consequence is that most countries today use passports to regulate the flow of immigrants into their countries, a policy that has created awkward situations in nations that do not have secure borders across their entire length, such as the United States, where many millions of undocumented foreigners work illegally without having obtained a Permanent Resident Card, known more familiarly as a "green card."

To monitor and account for the internal activities and movements of their own citizens, many governments issue identity cards, which became commonplace in the age of paper. But attempts to introduce a federally issued national identity card in the United States for all residents—aliens and citizens alike—have been unsuccessful, opponents of the ongoing initiative maintaining that it would be a first step toward a more totalitarian government and a further infringement on individual privacy. What suffices, in the meantime, as an "official government identity card"—and, since the terrorist attacks of September 11, 2001, is closely scrutinized at airports by agents of the Transportation Security Administration—is the motor vehicle driver's license, issued by individual states.

In an eerie foretelling of things to come, the German philosopher and historian Johann Gottlieb Fichte—sometimes called the father of German nationalism—wrote in 1796 that the chief responsibility of a "well-regulated police state" was to ensure that every citizen—at "all times and places"—be manifestly "recognized as this or that particular person." The salient imperative of this aim, he emphasized, was to assure that no one "remain unknown to the police," and the only way to guarantee that was to require that everyone "carry a pass with him, signed by his immediate government official, in which his person is accurately described."

A person's paperwork, in other words, must always be "in order," a situation that would reach nightmarish extremes during the frightful years of World War II, as dramatized in a number of critically acclaimed films based on actual events. In *The Great Escape* (1963), forged documents are essential to the plan of Allied soldiers to break out en masse from a Nazi prison camp; in *Schindler's List* (1993), eleven hundred Jews are spared from certain death at Auschwitz by spurious documents that declare their skills, ones that are vital to the Third Reich, and by the determination of an enlightened German businessman to use bribery as a means of including their names on a manifest of essential personnel—namely, the "list" of the title. "The list is life," the Ben Kingsley character, Itzhak Stern, says reverentially as the last name is typed. "All around its margins lies the gulf."

As pieces of paper, identification cards have come a long way over the past 150 years or so, with holograms, security threads, anti-tampering devices, and electronic scans being just a few of the security measures developed, making the task of the forger that much more difficult. The ingenious utensils of espionage in general have been the stuff of awe and amazement—the glitzier and the slicker the doodads, the better, as the long-running success of numerous James Bond films over the past five decades has suggested. And while some of the deadly toys used to such great effect by the fictional Agent 007 might seem preposterous, they are not entirely the product of an imaginative scriptwriter's fancy, as the displays at a museum maintained by the Central Intelligence Agency at its Langley, Virginia, headquarters bear out quite persuasively. Unfortunately, the galleries there are not open to the public, and permission to see them does not come without some effort, as I learned when I was allowed to view—but not photograph—what General Michael Hayden, the director of the CIA from 2006 to 2009, described on *Meet the Press* as "the best museum you'll probably never see."

As grateful as I was to view some of the more imaginative tools of this highly specialized trade—matchbox cameras, "dead-drop" spikes, intricate cipher machines, hollowed-out coins, microscopic listening devices, miniature weapons, multipurpose umbrellas, and the like— what I found informative was evidence indicating how so much of what has been done to support various clandestine operations over the years has relied on paper. Predictably, some of the most fundamental applications have been for identification documents and what are known as "one-time" pads, which are used in exchanging encrypted messages. But on a far more sophisticated level are special papers that have been formulated to dissolve in the stomach when swallowed, and others that are made with fibers distinctive to the region of the world being targeted. In a whole category of their own are documents conceived with the explicit purpose of creating cover for agents in the field, in some cases to fashion "legends" for operatives that are unique unto themselves.

In the very first gallery of the museum is an alcove devoted to the Office of Strategic Services, the wartime unit that was the forerunner to what in 1947 became the CIA. On one wall is a tribute to Stanley P. Lovell, a Boston research chemist who was recruited by General William J. "Wild Bill" Donovan during World War II to be what was euphemistically called the director of research and development. Given a free hand to tinker with such outlandish devices as bat bombs, exploding cookie dough, booby-trapped camel feces—even a dose of female hormones designed to give Adolf Hitler a falsetto voice and make his mustache fall off—he chose to begin by concentrating on the basics. "I decided," he wrote in a 1963 memoir, "that the very first job to be done was the organization of a plant for documentation—a fascinating, meticulous, deadly business, indeed. It was obvious that any spies or saboteurs O.S.S. placed behind enemy lines would have short shrift unless they had perfect passports, workers' identification papers, ration books, money, letters and the myriad little documents which served to confirm their assumed status. These are the light things upon which the very life of the agent depends."

It was an assortment of carefully contrived papers, in fact—the "light things," as Lovell so playfully called them—that made possible one of the most dramatic covert schemes to be hatched by the Allies in World War II: a British undertaking, known as Operation Mincemeat, that involved the creation of a credible identity for a dead man whose body was set adrift from a submarine off the Spanish coast, under darkness, with hopes it would float into unfriendly hands. The point of the operation was to convince the German High Command that the first Allied landings in Europe would take place not in Sicily, as everyone expected, but farther east in Greece. The clever deception, cobbled together in June 1943 by a British counterintelligence unit known as Twenty, or XX (for Double-Cross), was "swallowed whole" by the Nazis, according to Ewen Montagu, the person charged with planning and executing the scheme, and its success depended almost entirely on an array of persuasive documents prepared specifically for the purpose and placed in a briefcase that was handcuffed to the dead man's wrist.

As Montague recalled in a 1953 memoir teasingly titled *The Man Who Never Was,* the first order of business was to locate a body that under close examination would pass as a British officer who had died from exposure after an airplane crash at sea. The corpse of an otherwise healthy man in his early thirties who had just died of pneumonia—the liquid left in his lungs could suggest death by drowning—fit the bill perfectly. With the man's body hastily packed hermetically in dry ice, the intelligence teams went to work fashioning a bold plan that would craft, entirely with paperwork, a credible individual who just might bamboozle the Nazis with false information. The name selected for the victim was William Martin; his rank and branch of service would be major in the Royal Marines. Major Martin's fabricated mission, according to the script: to deliver face-to-face a highly sensitive letter written in the hand of Lieutenant General Sir Archibald Nye, the vice chief of the Imperial General Staff, to General Harold Alexander, an army commander in Tunisia serving under General Dwight D. Eisenhower.

Phrased in a manner that would explain why certain logistical requests supposedly being made by Alexander could not be fulfilled, the text, penned informally on official stationery, assumed the tone of a "friendly letter" that just might convey to the Germans "the indication that our next target was not Sicily, and yet could be found in the possession of an officer and not in a bag full of the usual official documents going from home to our army abroad." Once that key piece of correspondence had been prepared, there was then the supporting material—the legend, in professional parlance, or the "pocket litter" as it is also known—to construct around the courier, and these would spell the difference between success and failure. First off, a proper photograph for the identification card was needed. "I defy anyone to take a photograph of someone who *is* dead and to make it look as if he could conceivably be alive," Montagu wrote. Eventually a young naval officer was found who came close enough, and he agreed to the unusual request, no questions asked.

A chatty cover letter, written by Lord Louis Mountbatten, chief of combined operations, to Admiral of the Fleet Sir A. B. Cunningham, explained that Major Martin was carrying information too sensitive to go through normal channels. Another letter, from Lord Mountbatten to General Eisenhower, was placed in an envelope containing a newly printed public relations pamphlet describing the Battle of Britain, requesting that the supreme Allied commander in Europe write a blurb for an American edition, about to be published. A base pass that granted Martin restricted access to Combined Operations Headquarters was also slipped in.

Deciding that the major should be a man who was "fond of a good time," his creators supplied him with an invitation to a nightclub, "a probable result of a certain amount of extravagance," which just might explain why he would also be carrying "a letter from his bank about an overdraft." To these was added a paid bill from the Naval and Military Club, in London, and inserted nearby were two dated ticket stubs from a play then running at the Prince of Wales Theatre. Several well-thumbed letters from a fiancée, penned most affectionately by a young woman who worked in the XX office, were placed in the inside pocket of the ill-fated man's uniform, along with a photograph of the fetching young woman herself in a bathing suit. For good measure, there was a receipt from a New Bond Street jeweler for an engagement ring. An added touch was a letter from Martin's father inviting him to lunch at the Carlton Grill. "When we read all these documents together," Montagu recalled, "they conveyed the impression of a real person—of a real person who lived—of a man who really was."

The details of just how a corpse kept afloat by an inflated Mae West life jacket would be placed, under cover of darkness, in a sea current that would assure it coming ashore at a Spanish town known to be friendly to the German cause, the procedures taken to fake and report over radio channels the crash of a military aircraft in the Mediterranean, and how officials determined after the war that their deception had, in fact, tricked the Nazis—very likely saving many thousands of lives—provided the grist for a 1956 film, also titled *The Man Who Never Was,* with Clifton Webb cast in the role of Lieutenant Commander Ewen Montagu.

What the episode ultimately demonstrates, however, is how profoundly intelligence agencies have relied on paper to achieve their goals. Conversations I have had with a number of intelligence-gathering professionals past and present have emphasized how important this most basic of materials is to their operations, from creating bogus ration books and false identification cards to the fabrication of passports and special papers that can be dissolved quickly in water, or flash paper that can be burned in an instant without leaving any ash.

For twenty-five years, Antonio J. "Tony" Mendez worked at the CIA for what is vaguely called the Technical Services Division, known in-house simply as TSD; for fifteen of these he was their chief of disguise, an occupation he performed so masterfully that in 1997, he received one of fifty lifetime achievement awards given to "officers who by their actions, example or initiative helped shape the first half-century" of the agency's history, a commendation made especially significant by the fact that most of his triumphs are not likely to ever be known outside of the intelligence community. Mendez joined the agency at the age of twenty-five, in 1965, after working for Martin Marietta Materials, a manufacturer of aerospace equipment. Years later, Mendez would acknowledge that his two chief specialties had been "disguise and documentation," two skills that often worked in concert with each other.

A talented artist in civilian life, his start in the intelligence business came by way of the graphic arts. "I was an artist-illustrator working in Denver, and I saw a classified ad in the *Denver Post* that said, 'artist to work overseas with the U.S. Navy,'" Mendez told me during a wide-ranging conversation we had in his Maryland home. When he was interviewed for the position, the interviewer came right out and said, "Son, this is not the Navy," and showed credentials identifying himself as an employee of the Central Intelligence Agency. "The man—and he was a real Sam Spade type of guy, low-brimmed hat, raincoat, cigarette dangling from his lip—then asked me to read the recruitment guide for this artist position, and I was attracted to it instantly, because what I saw was what promised to be an intriguing application of art. It was different from anything I had expected. They wanted people who would be willing to subordinate their creative side to the service of their country. They were hiring forgers."

In time, Mendez would perfect skills that went well beyond the creation of document forgeries to include the modification of every manner of physical and personality attribute, be it the alteration of facial and body characteristics or eye, skin, or hair coloration, made all the more persuasive by clothing and personal accessories selected specifically for each operation. As chief of disguise, and later as head of the Graphics and Authentication Division (GAD), he supervised about a hundred specialists. "We called it identity transformation," he said of their collective work. "I came to regard myself as an espionage artist. If you're going to be involved in espionage, you've got to be able to cross international borders securely—and not just one time, but over and over again. That's quite a challenge. It's a lot harder than robbing banks." In the realm of document preparation, Mendez was careful to distinguish between forgery and counterfeiting, making clear in his interview with me that forgery is the making of very persuasive papers that can be taken for the "real thing," while counterfeiting is the replication of another country's currency, which is an act of war, according to the Geneva Conventions. There have nevertheless been instances, he acknowledged, in which the agency has made foreign currency, but that, he insisted, has happened generally when hostilities are already under way. He cited the amusing instance of CIA graphics experts having produced, during the Vietnam War, a representation of the kip, the currency of Laos, distributed by the Pathet Lao, a Communist insurgency group, with a portrait of Ho Chi Minh, the North Vietnamese leader, substituted for the image of an elephant that appeared on the authentic version. "We thought that by putting Ho Chi Minh's portrait there, it would show the Laotians that the North Vietnamese had designs on them, and cause a rift. So we printed all this Pathet Lao kip, and we dropped it from airplanes hoping to make everybody mad. It turned out that they just saw it as manna from heaven, and they started spending it. So that didn't work out at all."

Retired since 1990, Mendez and his second wife, Jonna, herself a former chief of disguise at the agency, live on a large tract of land in rural Maryland where both maintain separate studios, Tony as an artist, Jonna as a photographer. When I arrived for our interview, Tony Mendez had brought out a few items, each dealing, in one fashion or another, with the role paper had played in his intelligence work. The very first was an American $1 bill that was perfect in every way—the clarity of the type, the imagery, the coloration, the distinctive snap and feel of the rag paper—except that it had been reduced to about a third of its normal size. "It was a demonstration by our office to show that paper is mostly water. If you super-freeze currency, then put it in a press and quickly thaw it out, the water doesn't have an opportunity to find its way back into the fiber. So that's what a piece of currency looks like without the water."

He then showed me what he called his "flaps and seals tool kit," a pouch of paring devices and knives that he had used to penetrate envelopes without betraying that a surreptitious entry had been made. But the implements had many other applications as well. "You use these tools to manipulate paper," he explained. "Let's say you have to split a photograph onto a page. One way to do a photo substitution is to actually split the photo paper."

At this point, Jonna, who had been observing the demonstration carefully, chimed in that "you could also use that tool if you were splitting paper to put in a microdot," which prompted a vigorous nod in the affirmative from her husband. "This tool here is handmade by me. It started out as a stick with a blade in it, but I actually filed the blade and carved the handle. What it does is provide you with a means for splitting paper. If you want to bury something in it—like a microdot—you would use a tool something like this."

Jonna Mendez, whose duties at the agency also involved a range of technical applications, including clandestine photographic services, explained the operational function of microdots. "You start with a page of eight-and-a-half-by-eleven-inch paper with text, shrink it down four hundred times, and it comes out to be pretty much the size of a period at the end of a sentence that you might find in the international edition of *Time* magazine. That was a great place to hide microdots, by the way. Only you and the person you're sending it to know which page, which paragraph, which sentence, and it could go through any kind of censoring process, because if you didn't know exactly where it was, you could spend your entire career looking through that *Time* magazine to find it. So you take your microdot, and you just split it on top of the period. Sometimes we would put them in airmail envelopes: we'd split paper and just slip the dots in."

During his quarter-century with the CIA, Tony Mendez traveled to hot spots that included Vietnam, Laos, India, Russia, and various locations in the Middle East, applying the skills of his most uncommon profession directly in the field, more often than not as an "exfiltrator" assigned the task of getting someone out of a hostile environment. One of his most satisfying assignments—and, with the release of the 2012 Academy Award–winning film *Argo* based on its success, by far the best known—involved an audacious plan to secure the freedom of six American diplomats who had taken refuge with their Canadian counterparts following the 1979 seizure of the American embassy in Iran.

Mendez—the ace exfiltrator—was given free rein to come up with a scheme that could whisk the six out of Tehran before knowledge of their presence was leaked to the militants occupying the embassy. With the nearest border being that of the Soviet Union, liberating them by land was considered far too dangerous. "The only feasible way to slip them out was under everyone's noses—by commercial air," Mendez told me. For such a bold exit strategy to work, the immediate challenge was to justify the presence of six Westerners in Iran in a way that would make perfect sense to anyone examining their personal documents. "I had worked in the past with some Hollywood people," Mendez said, among them the late John Chambers, a special effects and makeup artist whose legendary triumphs had included the pointy Vulcan ears for Mr. Spock, on the *Star Trek* television series, and the eerily authentic appearances he created for the simian characters in the 1968 film *Planet of the Apes*. With few viable options available to him, and time running frightfully short, Mendez asked Chambers on a whim how many people would normally be involved in a film crew scouting locations for a movie to be shot abroad. About eight, Chambers said: a production manager, a cameraman, an art director, a transportation manager, a script consultant, a screenwriter, a business manager, and the director.

"That suited my purposes perfectly," Mendez said, and for the next few weeks he and his team worked nonstop to set up a deception that would enable the six diplomats to assume the identities of Canadian nationals working for a straw company Chambers helped them establish in Hollywood, called Studio Six Productions, with offices leased on the old Paramount lot, complete with telephones, desks, and file cabinets and staffed with a receptionist. For a further veil of authenticity, Chambers provided the script of an unproduced science fiction film, choosing as the title for their bogus production *Argo,* the setup line to an off-color knock-knock joke. To trumpet the project even further and give the sheen of authentic Tinseltown "buzz," they took out full-page advertisements in *Variety* and *The Hollywood Reporter,* describing their film-in-progress as a "cosmic conflagration" that would be shot on location abroad. "Obviously, we had to set all of this up before we went into Iran, and to close the deal, we had to create the paper," Mendez said.

Once completed, the new identity documents for the six stranded Americans—including authentic passports graciously provided by the Ottawa government—were brought into Iran by the Canadians, under cover of diplomatic immunity. Selecting the role of business manager for himself, Mendez and a CIA colleague arrived in Tehran on January 25, 1980, and began briefing everyone. Disguises were kept to a minimum—a few altered hairstyles, some dark glasses, appropriate clothing, but nothing shockingly over the top—with success or failure hinging entirely on the persuasiveness of the supporting documents. Three days later, the "production team" left for Mehrabad Airport to make a 5:30 a.m. Swissair flight for Zurich. After an excruciating delay to repair a faulty airspeed indicator, the passengers boarded the aircraft, and the flight departed. Once out of Iranian airspace, celebratory drinks were ordered for everyone. "It was the pocket litter, the business cards and whatnot—what we call window dressing—that sold it," Mendez told me. "When I went into Iran, I not only had all the documentation for the production, I had a printed film script that I could have used to actually pitch my movie, and I had a dossier in hand for every one of the six people we were taking out. We created motion picture credits for them, made Guild cards, and all the other stuff that they would have had on their person. I even had illustrations for the costume designs, and the sets that we would be making. It looked just like the portfolio that any production manager would need if he were trying to sell a movie to the Ministry of National Guidance. We had a whole gang of people working on it. You could do all the graphics in a few days if you had to, but we also had to go and set it all up first— and then create the paper to authenticate everything. That, in fact, is what we call authentication. And the artists who issue the paper with all the right inks and everything are called validators. So we call the whole process authentication and validation." In Ben Affleck's Oscar-winning film, Affleck himself played the leading role of Tony Mendez, who was a consultant during production.

Mendez stressed that all of the senses come into play when creating a false document—"the look, the feel, the smell, even the sound" of paper when snapped—which is why the fibers being used are so critical. He would not confirm outright whether or not the CIA operates its own papermaking unit, though he demonstrated extensive knowledge of the process, and he was not coy about discussing the lengths to which the Technical Services Division would go to make sure documents appear authentic in every way. "You try to get as close to the actual constituents that the paper is made out of in the first place. You actually reverse-analyze how this paper got to be what it is. What better way to get to the same place they are than to start from scratch? You end up doing foreign procurements of paper pulp, through people you use as cutouts. It becomes a clandestine operation just to get to the right substrates."

I asked if this meant that operatives would actually go into an unfriendly country for the purpose of acquiring native fiber. "We would have our ways," Mendez said vaguely. "Oh, someone would do it," his wife chimed in. "Let's say we would find out where that market is," Tony offered. "You know that there's got to be someplace somewhere in the world where this stuff is available, so you go to that place—somebody goes to that place—and purchases it. That would be a way to start." It was Jonna's turn to nod her head in agreement. "Nothing's impossible if you put your mind to it," she said brightly, which brought the conversation to the topic of secret ink, an invisible medium for writing on paper that becomes visible only when exposed to a substance chosen for the task at hand.

"It could be freshly squeezed lemon juice," Mendez said. "It could be goat's milk. It could be a very special brand of expensive vodka. If you make it really good—like we did, and like the Russians did—then the other guy can't find it unless he knows exactly what you're using. Each one is very specific—and very effective. There are certain things that happen to paper when it's being processed like that. So if you've got an arsenal of secret inks, and they come in different formulations— you can use paper as an invisible carbon, and write secret messages. It might be liquid, it might be something else. Now, on the other side of the pipeline—if you're receiving a secret message that you believe is from your asset—there are certain things you have to do to determine if the paper has been compromised."

Jonna Mendez picked up this thread of the conversation and explained how TSD technicians are able to determine whether critical letters have been intercepted by the wrong people and surreptitiously opened. "Whenever you get a message in an envelope—you know that's the envelope you're looking for, and that the message is in there—you have to be very careful before you open it to see if it has been read by somebody else. There's a chemical that you can literally paint on the envelope, and you have maybe a three-second window, because this thing will just flare up at you, and then it disappears. If that happens, it means that the envelope has been steamed open. And you can only do it once. I remember one of the first hits I ever got like that, somebody had been in an envelope. I was in Europe, and it was so important that our chief of operations came over from Washington to talk to me, and he said, 'Are you sure? Tell me again, what did you see?' And I told him again what I saw. In Paris, all these people got rearranged, people were sent out of the country, there were all kinds of things that happened, because somebody had been in that envelope that one time. It was pretty exciting work."

Mendez described for me the challenges posed by watermarks, citing the delicate representation of Mount Fuji on the Japanese passport as one example of a document that he would find a challenge to imitate. "What you have there is a three-dimensional watermark, which is not only positive but also negative, because there are actually two different kinds of watermarks embedded, one where you disperse the fibers and make it thinner, so that it is a lighter color, and another where you clump the fibers and make it more dense. So that's how you get that nice rendition of Mount Fuji: you're sculpting, actually, on a dandy roll."

These "new passports," as Jonna called the more recent productions, occasionally cause unexpected difficulties for those seeking to mimic their distinctive features. "I remember one of the problems we used to have is that our artists were perfectionists, as they should be, because they're forgers, after all. But sometimes perfection can be a problem. The last thing in the world you want to do is improve on what you're copying," a circumstance that occurred during the Civil War when forgeries of Confederate currency made by Northern provocateurs were superior in every respect to the official notes produced in the South, and thus easily identified as fakes. Taking a more recent example, her husband shared what he called "part of the urban lore of our business," a cautionary tale for all forgers, involving a Nazi reproduction of a Soviet passport during World War II—apocryphal, perhaps, but instructive all the same. "The Germans, being so precise, decided that they didn't want rusty staples like the ones in the document they were reproducing, they didn't want them to be shoddy, so they used stainless wire instead. Turns out that was the security feature—the rusty staples."

As chief of disguise during much of the Cold War, Mendez often found himself traveling to hot spots around the world to supervise sensitive operations and to be in position to improvise quickly as situations demanded. "A big part of what I did when I was in the Far East was to go up to that part of the world and design a leaflet program," he said, noting that in his experience, efforts aimed at "winning the hearts and minds" of the opposition by way of printed materials have, more often than not, been effective. "There was one surrender pass we did in cartoon form, because we knew that these people couldn't read any known language. We had a rather official-looking pass attached to the leaflet they could clip out and use as a safe-conduct pass to get to the other side." The design of a propaganda leaflet, he concluded, after a thoroughly stimulating morning in his company, "is a very precise thing—it has to be a certain proportion or it won't fly."

What Mendez was describing, for want of a better phrase, was a

*British gunners load twenty-five-pound artillery shells with propaganda leaflets in Holland, January 1945.*

kind of "flutter factor" to assure safe arrival of the paper on the ground when dropped from high altitudes. Sometimes called aerial propaganda bombardment, the practice of dropping leaflets from an aircraft is almost as old as human aviation itself, with roots traceable to the Franco-Prussian War of 1870–71, during the four-month Siege of Paris, when gas-filled balloons were deployed for a variety of purposes, including the dissemination of leaflets. The method reached full flower in World War I and has been a staple in what are known as psychological-warfare operations (PSYOPS) ever since.

Flush with the excitement of a decisive victory in World War I, Sir Campbell Stuart, the operational head of Britain's propaganda unit, wrote a lively memoir of the activities he had directed on "a new weapon of warfare" that was introduced during his tenure to counter "foolish falsehoods" that Germany had been spreading. Specialists were recruited to develop leaflets for each enemy nation, with some of the most capable minds in Britain brought in to assist, including the novelist H. G. Wells. On the American side, the renowned journalist Walter Lippmann became a propagandist for the Allies once the United States entered the war.

At its height, "a distributing capacity of almost a million leaflets a day was obtained," Stuart wrote, with success measured by the thousands of deserters who gave themselves up, announcing, "I have come because you invited me." One drawback was that airplanes were not used to deliver the leaflets, a concession to German threats that any captured airmen who were determined to have been dropping them would summarily be shot. Paper balloons made at the rate of two thousand a week were deployed instead, each equipped with a fuse that went off at about five thousand feet, releasing five hundred to a thousand leaflets. "The load of the balloons was chosen according to the direction of the wind. If it was blowing towards Belgium, copies of *Le Courrier de l'Air* were attached; if towards Germany, propaganda leaflets for enemy troops." One German writer described the flood of paper as "English poison raining down from God's clear sky," something more odious, to his thinking, than the deadly gases being used in the trenches.

But the most telling testimonial to their effectiveness came from Field Marshal Paul von Hindenburg, the defeated chief of the General Staff who would later achieve infamy as the man who appointed Adolf Hitler chancellor of Germany. "This was a new weapon, or rather a weapon which had never been employed on such a scale and so ruthlessly in the past," he complained in a 1920 memoir: a "shower of pamphlets" that convinced his men on the front lines that there was no point in continuing the struggle. "The soldier thought it could not be all enemy lies, allowed to poison his mind, and proceeded to poison the minds of others."

Significantly, the first offensive strike Britain made against Germany in World War II was not with bombs but with millions of leaflets dropped over occupied Europe during a period of fretful inactivity known today as the "Phony War," an eight-month lull that followed the German invasion of Poland in the fall of 1939. On September 3, RAF Bomber Command dropped six million copies of a "Note to the German People"—some thirteen tons of paper—over northern and western areas of the Third Reich.

The barrage continued throughout the war, though not everyone, by any means, regarded the missions as worthwhile, the most vocal opponent being Sir Arthur Harris, marshal of the Royal Air Force and a strident champion of strategic aerial attacks, including the massive bombardment of large populated areas. Known by friends and enemies alike as Bomber Harris, the air marshal had no interest in any approach other than the one he prosecuted with single-minded determination, often sending a thousand aircraft out on a single evening of nighttime raids to pummel German cities. Harris condemned the leaflet campaign, arguing that his airmen were risking their lives on missions that did nothing to bring the enemy to its knees. "My personal view is that the only thing achieved was largely to supply the continent's requirements of toilet paper for the five long years of the war," he wrote in a memoir of his experiences.

Six months after the Japanese attack on Pearl Harbor, the United States created the Office of War Information, and immediately began producing leaflets for deployment against all Axis forces. Up to two hundred million a month were delivered during the final weeks of the Italian campaign alone, sometimes reaching thirty million in a single day. In April 1944, General Mark W. Clark concluded that the effectiveness of the program "has now been established by actual field experience." According to one report, 84 percent of German prisoners captured in France admitted to having read the leaflets, and 67 percent said they "believed every word they had read." Although radio broadcasts were a favored medium in the Pacific Theater, paper operations were prosecuted with comparable aggressiveness there as well, with leaflet production reported in the hundreds of millions, along with the production of Japanese-language newspapers.

On the German side, specialists assigned to combat theaters produced materials with mobile printing units and devised numerous strategies for their delivery, including V-1 rockets to distribute leaflets over Great Britain, Belgium, and Holland. A catalog of German leaflets produced during the Italian campaign lists 780 items directed specifically to Allied troops. One of the most unusual collections of these materials was gathered on a single day, in the heat of battle, by an American liaison officer who took part in the action to take Monte Cassino, in southern Italy. On May 11, 1944, Captain Peter Batty was attached to the 8th Indian Infantry Division, one of several units mounting a unified assault on German soldiers holed up in the Monastery of St. Benedict. "The offensive against the Germans was international," Batty wrote in a small book of facsimiles aptly titled *Paper War*. "British, American, French, Indian, Moroccan, and Polish troops were all part of the effort," prompting the resourceful Nazis to reach out to the combatants in their own languages.

"At first the Germans thought we were a British Division and fired two pieces of propaganda at us in English. The Poles, who were on our right, were quickly identified, and the Germans then thought for a while that we were part of the Polish forces," prompting them to launch nine different leaflet salvos printed in that language. Once Batty's unit was recognized as Indian, a veil of paper in Urdu and Hindi began littering the ground. He scooped them up and stuffed them in his knapsack with the others. The message was pretty much the same in all of them, according to Randall L. Bytwerk, a Michigan scholar who has written extensively about psychological warfare and operates a clearinghouse known as the German Propaganda Archive. "Whether it was British soldiers whose girlfriends were being seduced by Americans back home, or Polish troops dying for England while being sold out to the Russians, or Indian troops bleeding for their colonial masters, the point was that soldiers were fighting for something other than their best interests."

# 9

## Hard Copy

Your Red Tapist is everywhere. He is always at hand, with a coil of Red Tape, prepared to make a small official parcel of the largest subject. In the Reception Room of a Government Office, he will wind Red Tape round and round the sternest deputation that the country can send to him. In either House of Parliament, he will pull more Red Tape out of his mouth, at a moment's notice, than a conjurer at a Fair. In letters, memoranda, and dispatches, he will spin himself into Red Tape, by the thousand yards. He will bind you up in vast colonies, in Red Tape, like cold roast chickens at a rout-supper; and when the most valuable of them break it (a mere question of time), he will be amazed to find that they were too expansive for his favorite commodity.
—Charles Dickens, "Red Tape," 1851

Alas I have failed. Red Tape has carried the day.
—Sir Francis Bertie, British diplomat,
to Sir Charles Hardinge, British diplomat, July 3, 1902

We can lick gravity, but sometimes the paperwork is overwhelming.
—Dr. Wernher von Braun, space pioneer, 1958

FOR ALL THE TALK of a world without paper, the impulse to "keep a hard copy" remains central to bureaucratic culture, and is sure to endure despite the arrival of electronic record keeping. My own involvement in this consuming melodrama is decidedly modest, but relevant nonetheless. As a young naval officer fresh out of graduate school during the Vietnam War, I worked on the executive staff of an aircraft carrier deployed to Yankee Station, in the Tonkin Gulf, ever mindful,

*An anti-littering sign in a Washington, D.C., metro station.*

throughout my two combat cruises, of advice hammered home to me repeatedly by seasoned shipmates: the letters CYAWP, an admonition to "cover your ass with paper."

Later, as an investigative journalist honing his reportorial skills during the Watergate era, I came to appreciate how the need to document is peculiar to every manner of organized entity, be it governmental, corporate, professional, ecclesiastical, or institutional, creating what amounts to graphic road maps in which seemingly trivial bits of information can often lead to others that are far more substantial, enabling probing reporters and prosecuting attorneys alike to follow what they call a paper trail. The aptness of the verb *document,* as another way of saying "authenticate," and its obvious provenance from a synonym for "paper," seems self-evident. To "paper over," by contrast, has come to mean concealment beneath a veneer of obfuscation and "gobbledygook"—yet another word spawned by exasperation with bureaucratic mindlessness.

Largely driven by an innate need for self-preservation, the ritual knows no cultural, national, geographic, or political boundaries, with the result that "proving" that something happened, more often than not, means locating the paperwork that backs it up. An article of faith shared by veteran investigators holds that once a file has been created, traces have a tenacious way of surviving; in instances where persistent efforts have been expended to make them disappear, the challenge is to find what remains, if only in teasing fragments.

This was the impulse, at least, that drove journalists determined to shed light on the military service of George W. Bush not long after the Texas governor declared his candidacy for the presidency, in 1999. The issue proved inconclusive when no solid evidence was unearthed, but it resurfaced in 2004, when Bush was seeking a second term in office—only this time around, with what veteran CBS news anchor Dan Rather would declare was black-and-white proof that the forty-third president had been suspended during his tour as a reserve lieutenant, more than three decades earlier, for "failing to perform to U.S. Air Force/Texas Air National Guard standards."

Aired on *60 Minutes Wednesday* two months before the election, the story was based on six "newly discovered documents," purportedly written by Bush's former squadron commander, that appeared to show that the young pilot had failed to fulfill his minimum obligations; it was further asserted that Bush had been grounded for refusing to take a medical examination. Not in dispute was the fact that Bush's hasty acceptance into the privileged stateside "champagne" unit in May 1968—a month in which 2,415 American servicemen died in Southeast Asia, the deadliest month of the entire war—ensured that he would not have to fight in Vietnam, and provided the backstory for reporters bent on ferreting out conclusive details clarifying his reserve service.

Within hours of the broadcast, conservative bloggers posting anonymously on the Internet were claiming that the memos had clearly been typed in a font and with proportional spacing that did not exist in the early 1970s, the time when they were dated. Whether the papers could have been copies of authentic originals became irrelevant to the prevailing belief that professional journalists who should have known better had been suckered into making an inexcusable blunder by what they believed were reliable sources. Five news executives were asked to resign or were let go outright within a matter of weeks by CBS, and Rather was forced out of his anchor slot on the *Nightly News* shortly after the 2004 election, though he has remained firm in his belief that the material itself is credible.

"What the documents stated has never been denied, by the president or anyone around him," he claimed when filing a $70 million lawsuit against CBS in 2007, for wrongful termination of his employment, and reiterated at length in *Rather Outspoken,* a memoir he published in 2012. But the grim fact remained that, true or not, the larger story had been cleverly discredited by what the great heavyweight fighter Muhammad Ali might have called a "rope-a-dope" tactic designed to lure clueless opponents in for swift annihilation. Such an irony was not lost on *60 Minutes* executive Josh Howard, who at the height of the controversy conceded to a *Washington Post* reporter that "I suppose you could say we let our guard down." The retired Texas Air National Guard official whom CBS identified as the person who furnished the memos to the network, Bill Burkett, became disquietingly vague when pressed to disclose on the record where, and from whom, he had acquired them, and the original source to this day remains unresolved. The ultimate authority in the matter, Lieutenant Colonel Jerry B. Killian—the man who supposedly had written them in the first place—could not confirm or deny their veracity: he had died in 1984.

Nothing is absolute, needless to say, and shrewd people with something to hide often protect themselves from serious unpleasantness by not writing anything incriminating down in the first place, an awareness not lost on unscrupulous bosses who pass unsavory orders on to underlings verbally, through trusted intermediaries. Giving someone "a layer of deniability" in this respect is another way of saying that there are no documents available to provide clear and convincing proof of that person's culpability. One confirmed instance of a government agency undertaking an operation of such extreme sensitivity that no damning paperwork was retained at all was disclosed in 1975, during hearings held by a special Senate investigative committee empowered to probe irregularities in the way American intelligence agencies gathered sensitive information. The panel called in a number of witnesses to testify, none more colorful than Dr. Sidney Gottlieb, a retired project director known early in his career at the CIA as the "Dirty Trickster."

Gottlieb was the man who had initiated experiments with LSD in the early 1950s, and he later headed up the unit known as Project MKULTRA (pronounced *M-K-ultra*), a code name for 149 furtive projects developed by the Office of Scientific Intelligence, involving drug testing, behavior modification, shock treatments, and the secret administration of mind-altering substances to hundreds of unwitting subjects at eighty American and Canadian universities, hospitals, research foundations, and prisons. He testified that no papers were ever kept of the agency's use of chemical agents such as anthrax and shellfish toxins, "because of the sensitivity of the area and the desire to keep any possible use of materials like this recordless."

Whatever records had been kept in those operations, it was further claimed, had been ordered destroyed in January 1973 by Richard M. Helms, who was about to retire as director of central intelligence and was the person who had given the initial go-ahead to the umbrella project. But a further search of the files, mandated by a Freedom of Information Act request, led to the discovery, in 1977, of sixteen thousand pages of reports itemizing payments to various institutions and companies that had provided material support to MKULTRA.

Testifying before a second Senate investigative committee, impaneled in 1979, Admiral Stansfield Turner, appointed director of central intelligence two years earlier by President Jimmy Carter, was asked how his predecessors could possibly have allowed such a massive oversight to take place. "It was the practice at that time not to keep detailed records in this category," Turner said, the hazy suggestion being that he was as surprised as anyone at the discovery of 130 boxes of overlooked documents gathering dust in a CIA storage facility he identified as the Retired Records Center. Senator Daniel Inouye of Hawaii asked Turner, a onetime Rhodes Scholar, whether that meant that knowledge of the hush-hush project had been "intentionally kept away from the Congress and the President of the United States." The admiral thoughtfully replied that there was "no evidence one way or the other" to make such a judgment. "There are no records to indicate," he repeated—which of course had been the original game plan outlined by Dr. Gottlieb during the agency's earlier go-round with the Senate.

Though certainly uncommon, MKULTRA was not without precedent as a state-sponsored operation of considerable magnitude that went recordless—not even the most egregious example in modern memory. For that distinction, we must go back to World War II and cite a project of prolonged complexity that resulted in the systematic extermination of six million people—the unspeakable horror we know today as the Holocaust—and consider where a program of such unparalleled mendacity got the bureaucratic support it undoubtedly needed to proceed so efficiently, on such a massive scale, and who gave the orders to do so. While many thousands of damning documents from that era have survived, trying to find the signature or initials of Adolf

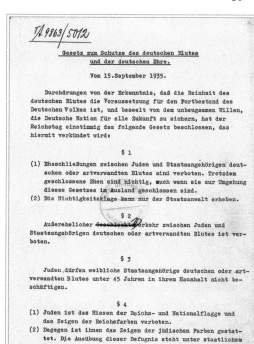

The Law for the Protection of German Blood and German Honor barred marriage between Jews and other Germans.

Hitler's signature on the Law for the Protection of German Blood and German Honor.

Hitler on any scrap of paper that might tie his name directly to the atrocities the world knows he sanctioned has been the Holy Grail of Nazi hunters since war's end.

But one document he signed, on September 15, 1935, that comes very close to doing exactly that did survive, and was turned over to the National Archives, in Washington, D.C., in 2010 by the Huntington Library, in San Marino, California, where it had been placed on temporary deposit in 1945 by George S. Patton Jr., its final disposition left in limbo for sixty-five years by the general's untimely death in an automobile accident a few months later. The second of two measures known today as the Nuremberg Laws, the four-page manifesto was drafted to assure "the protection of German blood and German honor" by stripping Jews of their citizenship and officially classifying them as inferior human beings, forbidden to marry or even have sexual relations with pure Aryans. The laws provided, in unambiguous language, a conceptual basis for the horrors that followed and, in that sense, can certainly be viewed as a generative document. Why Patton deposited them at the Huntington Library, near his boyhood home in Pasadena, California—he had appropriated two of the four original sets for himself—and not to the legal team then gathering evidence for the war-crimes trials soon to get under way, has never been fully addressed. One possible explanation may well be the most obvious: that Patton was an enthusiastic souvenir collector, a free-spirited one, who included among his personal trophies a large bronze eagle and gold swastika removed from the speaker's stand at Luitpold Arena, in Nuremberg, where the Nazis had staged their most elaborate rallies.

Once installed at the National Archives, the laws were added to Record Group 238, a substantial collection of documents that had been used at the Nuremberg Trials, held between 1945 and 1949, and were pivotal in securing convictions of Nazi Germany's most senior surviving leaders. The decision to rely overwhelmingly on paperwork in those cases was the brainchild of Robert H. Jackson, a sitting justice of the United States Supreme Court who was appointed by President Harry S. Truman as chief American counsel at Nuremberg. Called by one Pulitzer Prize–winning historian "the most important public figure of the twentieth century no one has ever heard of," Jackson negotiated the charter that established how the newly formed International Military Tribunal would conduct its proceedings, organized the evidence for the first trial, delivered the opening and closing statements for the prosecution, and assigned to himself primary responsibility for the cross-examination of Hermann Göring and Albert Speer.

"The case as presented by the United States will be concerned with the brains and authority back of all the crimes," Jackson declared in his opening remarks. "These defendants were men of a station and rank which does not soil its own hands with blood. They were men who knew how to use lesser folk as tools. We want to reach the planners and designers, the inciters and leaders without whose evil architecture the world would not have been for so long scourged with the violence and lawlessness, and wracked with the agonies and convulsions, of this terrible war." They would do this, he professed, with hard facts. "We will not ask you to convict these men on the testimony of their foes. There is no count in the Indictment that cannot be proved by books and records. The Germans were always meticulous record keepers, and these defendants had their share of the Teutonic passion for thoroughness in putting things on paper."

Not long after the first trial had ended, Jackson discussed his strategy in a talk at the National War College, in Washington, D.C. "In only two or three instances were any of the nearly four thousand documents" presented denied outright, he said. "These men were convicted, not on testimony by their enemies, they were convicted on their own signatures." In an introduction he wrote to a comprehensive selection of the documents used at the trials, Jackson offered further insight on the unorthodox approach: "The decision, supported by most of the staff, was to use and rest on documentary evidence to prove every point possible. The argument against this was that documents are dull, the press would not report them, the trial would become wearisome and would not get across to the people. There was much truth in this position, I admit. But it seemed to me that witnesses, many of them persecuted and hostile to the Nazis, would always be chargeable with bias, faulty recollection, and even perjury. The documents could not be accused of partiality, forgetfulness, or invention, and would make the sounder foundation, not only for the immediate guidance of the Tribunal, but for the ultimate verdict of history."

In the eleven trials that followed, other defendants included educators, civil servants, executives of companies that used slave labor, and various professionals, several of them physicians accused of conducting medical experiments on prisoners. Writing after the final proceeding had ended, Telford Taylor, Jackson's successor as chief prosecutor, predicted that the trial documents would prove invaluable to future scholars. "No well-rounded study of German or European affairs from 1920 to 1945 can be made without taking account of the revealing and profuse documentation offered in the trials of diplomats, industrialists and military leaders."

Robert G. Storey, another of Justice Jackson's principal aides, recalled how such a "surprising number of documents establishing the criminality of the Hitler regime" had been assembled, an astonishing circumstance, given their damning content. "When the war drew to a close no general order was issued for the destruction of documents, decisions in that regard being left up to individuals, offices, and departments," he wrote. "Attempts were made to hide, rather than to destroy, important documents. And sometimes we were able to recover entire caches of invaluable written evidence." The complete files of the "wordy Nazi philosopher" Alfred Rosenberg were found in an abandoned castle in eastern Bavaria, "hidden behind a false wall eighteen inches thick." In another vacant castle, records of the German Federal Foreign Office, weighing 485 tons, were recovered; the files of Heinrich Himmler describing the activities of execution units in the eastern territories were located as well.

FOR A FEW GIDDY YEARS after the fall of the Soviet Union, in 1991, barriers once considered impenetrable broke down, and granting access to records kept by the KGB and other intelligence agencies became something of a cottage industry, with well-placed insiders eagerly accommodating scholars, journalists, and publishers from the West who had deep enough pockets to pay the going price. Among publishing projects to benefit from this cornucopia of paperwork, certainly the most ambitious has proven to be the Annals of Communism series, begun by Yale University Press with seed money from George Soros, the Hungarian-born financial speculator, and championed, once it got started, by William F. Buckley Jr. in his syndicated newspaper column. Through 2011, twenty volumes had been released. Meanwhile, at the Woodrow Wilson International Center for Scholars, in Washington, the Cold War International History Project was established in 1991 to provide a Web-based clearinghouse for newly released documents from that period and to develop scholarly programs that facilitate their use.

Of all the papers from the former Eastern Bloc countries made public to date, none has caused more of a stir internationally than an order, released in 1992, that had been signed by Joseph Stalin in May 1940, authorizing the executions of 21,857 unarmed Polish reservists captured by the Red Army after it invaded eastern Poland in 1939—an atrocity known as the Katyn Forest massacre, for the remote region outside Smolensk, in western Russia, where the mass killings took place. For more than fifty years, the official Kremlin position had been that it was Germans, not Russians, who were responsible, an alibi never accepted by the outside world but, until the release of the Stalin document, never definitively disproved, either. The sudden mea culpa came hard on the heels of a highly publicized promise made by Mikhail Gorbachev during the heady days of glasnost, to fill in the "blank spots" of history kept hidden through seven decades of Communist rule; authenticated copies of the Katyn files were finally presented to the Poles at the direction of Boris Yeltsin, his successor. "We are witnessing the handing over of the most important documents concerning the cruel crime against the Polish nation," President Lech Walesa said on behalf of his people. "My legs are trembling."

Up to the time of its release, the death warrant existed in only one copy and was locked in the office of the Soviet premier, its whereabouts known to a select few and seen by them on a "for eyes only" basis—a textbook example of how governments routinely go about shielding extremely volatile information from prying eyes. In the United States, a rigid hierarchy of classification to control the circulation of sensitive documents uses the acronyms NODIS (no distribution), LIMDIS (limited distribution), and EXDIS (executive distribution). The number of copies is monitored, and in many cases reading can be done only under close supervision.

With so much material now being "born digital" and stored in computers instead of file cabinets, the likelihood of a security breach has increased exponentially. The posting on the Internet, in November 2010, of a quarter-million cables exchanged between the U.S. State Department and 274 of its embassies around the world over the previous decade—there for anyone with a laptop computer and a Wi-Fi connection to peruse at their leisure—was the realization of the government's worst fears. According to numerous published accounts, the massive trove had been downloaded onto a compact disc by a low-level Army analyst while seated at his office desk and pretending he was listening to music; the apparent motivation of Private First Class Bradley E. Manning, it was further reported, was unhappiness with the way he was being treated after disclosing his homosexuality in a "don't ask, don't tell" military environment.

The vast majority of the 251,287 dispatches Manning gave to the controversial website WikiLeaks were classified "confidential," the lowest level maintained in the American security system, so there was solace, at least, in the knowledge that the most sensitive cables had not been compromised. But since diplomats were seen to be discussing, frequently in very undiplomatic language, American operations in Afghanistan and Iraq, the sudden release of the exchanges caused untold anxiety all the same.

Paul Heinbecker, a career diplomat who once served as Canadian ambassador to the United Nations, wrote in the Toronto *Globe and Mail* that the most severe damage suffered was "to the practice of diplomacy, which depends on confidence and confidentiality." One probable after effect, he predicted, would be "greater secrecy, not less," along with a return to more "compartmentalization" of information and "much tighter discipline on its distribution, so that truly sensitive material is directed only to a small handful of people with a genuine and significant 'need to know.'" One senior intelligence analyst I spoke to expressed the ramifications even more succinctly than that. "Very simply stated," he said, "paper is safer."

While a quarter-million "confidential" cables is still a large number, it is minuscule when compared with the volume of classified material generated throughout the federal bureaucracy, day in and day out, as a *Washington Post* team of twenty staffers headed by two-time Pulitzer Prize–winning journalist Dana Priest pointed out in a series of investigative pieces published in 2010, titled "Top Secret America." Since September 11, 2001, Priest and colleague William M. Arkin reported, government operations created to combat further terrorist attacks have "become so large, so unwieldy and so secretive that no one knows how much money it costs, how many people it employs, how many programs exist within it or exactly how many agencies do the same work."

In and around Washington, D.C., alone, they found, thirty-three building complexes for top-secret intelligence work had been authorized since 9/11, together occupying "the equivalent of almost three Pentagons" and collectively producing many millions of documents. Analysts with top-secret clearances alone prepare fifty thousand published intelligence reports annually, "a volume so large that many are routinely ignored." One senior official who was authorized to access everything—and was thus known as a "superuser"—described the paperwork thus: "I'm not going to live long enough to be briefed on everything."

Still, as Paul Heinbecker emphasized in his *Globe and Mail* op-ed piece, "leaks are as old as democracy," a reality of public life that prompted some pundits in the media to compare the Bradley Manning–WikiLeaks incident to the Pentagon Papers disclosures of four decades earlier, though there was little in common between the two, beyond the obvious. In both instances, classified information had been compromised, but the material turned over to the *New York Times* and sixteen other newspapers by Daniel Ellsberg was far more sensitive, and the mechanics of its removal involved much more planning, deeper access, and far greater risk, demonstrating, in a convoluted sort of way, just how secure paper is—and why it remains the medium of choice for so much sensitive material.

Commissioned in 1967 by Secretary of Defense Robert S. McNamara, the narrative formally titled *Report of the Office of the Secretary of Defense Vietnam Task Force* involved the work of thirty-six researchers and analysts. The team relied entirely on documents generated by the Defense Department, the White House, the State Department, and the CIA to write a comprehensive overview of American involvement in Southeast Asia. No interviews were conducted, and no clarifications were sought from any federal agencies or any of the military services, thereby assuring total secrecy—everything they used for the study was derived from a paper document of one sort or other.

When completed, the text filled forty-seven volumes and seven thousand pages, every one stamped TOP SECRET across the top, with the word SENSITIVE added on for good measure. While there is general agreement today that it was probably overclassified, there were parts that were explosive enough, documenting in particular how four administrations, from Harry Truman to Lyndon Johnson, had continually misled the American public. They confirmed that the administration of John F. Kennedy had planned to overthrow South Vietnamese leader Ngo Dinh Diem before his death in a November 1963 coup, and that President Johnson had already decided to expand combat operations even while giving assurances during his 1964 presidential campaign that he would "seek no wider war." Only fifteen copies were made, two of which were placed with the RAND Corporation, a research center that did work for the Defense Department—and where Daniel Ellsberg, a senior military analyst who had contributed to the narrative while working previously at the Pentagon, was allowed unrestricted access.

In his memoir of the episode, Ellsberg told how he surreptitiously removed the material from a safe in small batches between October and December of 1969, photocopied the documents "one page at a time" at night in the offices of an advertising agency with the help of a friend, and returned the originals to RAND headquarters in Santa Monica, California, each morning. "As far as I knew, no one had ever leaked thousands of pages of top secret documents before," he wrote, and since only about a dozen people outside the Pentagon had seen the material, he understood that the prospect of his being discovered was high and that he was likely to spend many years in a federal prison.

That Ellsberg would spend no time at all behind bars came as a result of the zeal with which government operatives responded to the excerpts that began to appear in the *Times* on Sunday, June 13, 1971. The Nixon administration sought—and was granted—an immediate injunction ordering publication to cease. The *Times* appealed, and on June 30 the Supreme Court ruled 6–3 in its favor, allowing the presses to roll with the next installments; there would be nine in all. Twenty-five years later, a tape recording released by the National Archives allowed listeners to hear an incensed Richard Nixon ranting on the very day of the Supreme Court defeat, ordering his chief of staff, H. R. Haldeman, to arrange an entry into the Brookings Institution, where he mistakenly believed another copy of the Pentagon Papers was being kept.

"You're to break into the place," Nixon fumed. "Break in and take it out, rifle the files." In testimony given before the Senate Watergate Committee in 1973, Nixon aide Charles Colson had asserted that proposals to firebomb the liberal-leaning think tank were discussed by the White House staff. No forced action was ever taken, but a White House Special Investigations Unit of clandestine operatives informally calling themselves the "plumbers" was formed within a matter of days. Their twin duties, as they saw them, were to stem leaks damaging to the administration, on the one hand, and to create leaks devastating to its enemies, on the other. In both pursuits, documents would be central, and Daniel Ellsberg would be their principal focus.

What ensued from there has been fully chronicled and endlessly discussed ever since—the unsuccessful attempt by G. Gordon Liddy and E. Howard Hunt to plunder what they hoped would be blackmail-worthy files from the Beverly Hills office of Ellsberg's psychiatrist, the bungled burglary at the Watergate complex on June 17, 1972, the dismissal of all criminal charges against Ellsberg when details of the attempts to discredit him emerged, impeachment proceedings undertaken by the Congress in the summer of 1974, Richard Nixon's resignation, on August 9, 1974—and followed what was, it can be persuasively argued, a direct line of cause and effect. When reduced to these elements, of one key mishap inexorably precipitating another, the question can reasonably be asked whether it was the pursuit of paper that brought down a president of the United States. An oversimplification, perhaps, but like every other drama in which this medium has played a part, it is there, just off center stage, in a supporting role—but a forceful presence all the same.

TRADITIONS OF RECORD KEEPING have been in place for centuries, with roots that extend back to the first settlers of the region between the Tigris and Euphrates rivers, which we know today as Mesopotamia, where Sumerians, Hittites, and Akkadians introduced writing more than five thousand years ago, its primary purpose initially being to record the routine transactions of daily life, with storage problems in the heyday of clay and papyrus "similar to those confronting the archivist in the age of paper," the late Ernst Posner, a onetime director of the Prussian Privy State Archives, wrote in a history of ancient record keeping.

During pharaonic times, two divisions of a governmental body that we in the United States would call the Department of Agriculture were named the House of Measuring the Grain and the House of Counting the Cattle. Egyptian judicial practice required that written complaints and defense motions be filed in formal lawsuits, and all business matters, including purchases, leases, loans, and matrimonial agreements, written down in order to be valid. By sacred tradition, bureaucratic processes extended even to the afterlife, with the deceased required to present written statements of vindication on the day of final judgment. Surviving copies of the *Book of the Dead* typically picture the jackal-headed god Anubis weighing the heart of the departed on a scale against an ostrich feather, the symbol of truth and justice; always nearby is an image of Thoth, the patron saint of scribes and secretary to the deities, his stylus poised and ready to record the results on a writing board.

In classical Athens, government records were kept in a building known as the Metroon, at the base of the Acropolis, near the Agora. Recorded for the most part on papyrus scrolls, official documents were stacked in crowded but orderly spaces that were well maintained over lengthy periods of time, a custom praised indirectly in the third century A.D. by Diogenes Laertius, a biographer of Greek philosophers who told how the Roman historian and rhetorician Favorinus had been able to read the original allegation sworn against Socrates by his chief accuser, Meletus, some five hundred years after the trial had taken place, the case record "preserved even now," he wrote of the ancient proceedings, "in the Metroon."

Like the Greeks, the Romans made generous use of papyrus, too, but the wooden tablet also enjoyed widespread popularity among their official scribes. These hinged contraptions of layered panels were covered with white paint or gypsum, which could either be written or painted on or covered with layers of wax and incised with a stylus. A cluster of tablets was called a *caudex,* Latin for "tree trunk," from which derives the word *codex,* a synonym for the conventional book that is still in use today. The only examples of these early forms of writing surfaces to survive to our time were found preserved beneath the lava

*A bundle of nineteenth-century political petitions—tied in an original band of red tape—at the National Archives and Records Administration preservation laboratory in College Park, Maryland.*

at Herculaneum, though there is good anecdotal evidence to support their widespread popularity.

Though the exact derivation of the phrase "red tape" is uncertain—*The Oxford English Dictionary* cites a first printed usage in the *Laws of Maryland,* in 1696—one possibility is a legal practice traceable to the sixteenth century in which official papers were organized by subject and kept together in bundles secured by strips of crimson ribbon. English common law itself is firmly based on a tradition of written precedents that go back to the reign of Henry II, in the twelfth century, a practice that relied on ready reference to arguments and decisions that had been rendered years earlier and which were reapplied where appropriate.

Over time, the act of sifting through red tape became synonymous with poking through stacks of voluminous files, and the phrase itself has come to identify every manner of institutional paperwork, more often than not in a derisive context. During a visit I made to the National Archives preservation laboratory, in College Park, Maryland, for this book, bundles of nineteenth-century political petitions still tied together in the traditional fashion were being disassembled for conservation and refiling, with the old red ribbons set aside in a pile, their decades of use finally at an end; I was delighted to accept one as a small memento of my visit.

As immense as the National Archives and Records Administration may be—some eighty billion pieces of paper are maintained by the government agency at various locations throughout the country—its range is comparatively compact, embracing a mere two and a quarter centuries of one nation's official activity, beginning with the Declaration of Independence. Two other governmental repositories—the Ottoman Archives, in Istanbul, Turkey, and the General Archive of the Indies, in Seville, Spain—preserve records that in both instances document more than half a millennium of officially sanctioned activity, with consequences that extended well beyond each country's national borders.

In the instance of the Ottoman Archives, some 150 million documents pertaining to a dynasty that ruled on three continents for close to seven hundred years are preserved in Istanbul; it originally consisted of records kept by the Imperial Council and the Grand Vizier's office. Beginning in about 1300 from its base in Asia Minor, the empire eventually encompassed most of the Middle East, most of North Africa, and parts of Europe, including modern Albania, Bulgaria, Greece, Hungary, Romania, Croatia, and Bosnia and Herzegovina, reaching around the Black Sea and into the Caucasus, in Central Asia, including Armenia. In the Middle East, the Ottomans also ruled Syria, Palestine, Egypt, and parts of Arabia and Iraq; only Persia—modern-day Iran—and the eastern part of the Arabian Peninsula remained free of Ottoman rule.

The archival materials detail every manner of official activity, from international treaties and border disputes to wills, titles, privileges, trusts, gifts, court actions, property transfers, construction plans, demographics, taxes, crop reports, military records, and official correspondence, the vast majority recorded on paper that was supplied by mills that had been flourishing throughout the Islamic world since the eighth century. The language of the archives is an amalgam of Turkish, Arabic, and Persian known as Ottoman Turkish, which was legally abandoned by the Republic of Turkey in the 1930s in favor of a more Westernized tongue, rendering it unreadable today without benefit of a modern translation.

A shortage of translators fluent in the old language is frequently cited as just one of several impediments facing scholars; another is that, since printing was never sanctioned by the Ottoman government, almost all of the papers are in manuscript, and only about a quarter of them are classified and recorded electronically. Archives that remain to be categorized—as well as those deemed "too brittle for study"—are not made available for consultation at all. A good number of papers said to be in this category are documents believed to be pertinent to what is alleged to have been the first genocide of the twentieth century, the deaths of 1.5 million Armenians during World War I and immediately thereafter. The papers have been the object of intense international attention in recent years, particularly since the position of the Ankara government is that no systematic program of ethnic extermination ever took place, leading some scholars to speculate that any sensitive papers that might shed light on the episode have been expunged.

The General Archive of the Indies, in Seville, which I visited in 1997 while doing research for my book *Patience & Fortitude,* is a treasure trove of material produced during Spain's years of exploration and conquest—some eighty million papers that document the discovery, pacification, settlement, defense, and charting of lands that extended from what is now the southern United States to the lower tip of South America, with other materials relevant to Spanish activities in the Philippines and the Far East. Beyond documenting these adventures, the records demonstrate an administrative approach to absentee government that was perfected during the latter half of the sixteenth century by King Philip II and became more efficient in successive reigns.

"The replacement of the warrior king Charles V by the sedentary Philip II, who spent his working days surrounded by piles of documents, fittingly symbolized the transformation of the Spanish Empire as it passed out of the age of the conquistador to the civil servant," the historian J. H. Elliott wrote in a respected history of imperial Spain. With the advent of new bureaucratic protocols, he added, "government by the spoken word" was gradually replaced by "government by the written word," a long-distance approach to administration that amounted to what he called "government by paper." That this development accelerated at a time when Spain was a leading producer of paper in Europe may well be coincidental, but the ready availability of the product certainly facilitated the government's penchant for bureaucratic record keeping.

RED TAPE IS NOT the stuff of great fiction, though, like so many other aspects of paper, it has had its moments as a motif in popular literature. In more than one hundred farcical novels collectively known as *La Comédie Humaine* (*The Human Comedy*), the nineteenth-century novelist Honoré de Balzac reveled in pointing out the foibles of French society and was at the forefront of establishing social realism in European literature. Generally populated by large casts of well-defined characters, his books are at their best when poking fun at the establishment; not least among his targets was the ponderous bureaucracy, which in his cynical view was a "giant power set in motion by dwarfs."

In *Les Employés* (1841), a sweeping satire given the title *Bureaucracy* in its first English translation, Balzac offered the biting generalization that in France, governmental ministers are "better off than women or kings," since they have at their beck and call secretaries and clerks who cater to their every whim. "Perhaps, indeed," Balzac archly opined, "the private secretary is to be pitied as much as women and white paper: they must bear everything." Writing in the years following the fall of Napoleon, in 1815, through the middle of the nineteenth century, Balzac had an unobstructed perspective on the many ways that paper had come to "bear everything" in French society, a situation that had become institutionalized during the years of the French Revolution.

In 1851, a year after Balzac died, Charles Dickens expressed his own jaundiced opinion about the English way of doing things in an essay written for the weekly magazine *Household Words*. Unambiguously titled "Red Tape," the piece, cited in the opening epigraph to this chapter, singled out for special ridicule the various government employees "whose existence is to tie up public questions, great and small, in an abundance of this official article." An "invasion of Red Ants in innumerable millions," he continued, "would not be so prejudicial to Great Britain, as its intolerable Red Tape." Dickens continued his attack on bureaucratic paperwork in *Bleak House,* a dense novel that was published in twenty monthly installments between March 1852 and September 1853 and took as its central subject England's Court of Chancery, which had jurisdiction over all matters of equity, including trusts and land laws, and was notorious for taking years to resolve even the most trivial matters.

Inside Lincoln's Inn Hall, lawyers were seen "mistily engaged in one of the ten thousand stages of an endless cause," with piles of various documents stacked high before them: "bills, cross-bills, answers, rejoinders, injunctions, affidavits, issues, references to masters, masters' reports, mountains of costly nonsense." At the conclusion of a long and tedious case, there was an exhausting sense of futility. "Presently great bundles of papers began to be carried out—bundles in bags, bundles too large to be got into any bags, immense masses of papers of all shapes and no shapes, which the bearers staggered under, and threw down for the time being, anyhow, on the Hall pavement, while they went back to bring out more."

The one fiction writer above all others whom we would expect to take a go at mind-numbing paperwork, of course, is Franz Kafka, a haunted man whose very name has become a synonym for the nightmarish workings of the modern bureaucracy. *The Castle,* a novel left unfinished at his death, in 1928, is centered on a premise of paperwork run amok, a scenario that might have been suggested, in part, by the fourteen years Kafka spent working for the Austrian Workmen's Accident Insurance Institute in Prague, at the very time when government and private offices alike were "being suffocated by files and drowning in ink," according to the governor of Lower Austria, in a call for administrative reform put forth in 1906. Kafka himself complained in a letter to a friend that "the real hell is there in the office."

While certainly central to bureaucracy, paperwork has been treated in much the same way that paper itself has so often been regarded in the history of printing and publishing: as a marginal consideration at best. One scholar with the wonderfully appropriate though purely coincidental surname of Kafka has been at the forefront of a movement to elevate it to the level of an independent discipline. How I learned about Ben Kafka and his work is a story that is possible only in the electronic age: a Google search launched with the keywords "Kafka," "paperwork," and "bureaucracy" not immediately calling up Franz, as I had expected, but Ben, an assistant professor of media, culture, and communication at New York University and a member of the Institute for Advanced Study in Princeton, New Jersey. He is also, I quickly discovered, the author of several learned articles dealing with the "materiality of paperwork," the implications of which, he has eloquently argued, are "critical to understanding the powers and failures of the modern state." His book-length examination of how the French revolutionized the practice at the end of the eighteenth century, *The Demon of Writing: Powers and Failures of Paperwork,* was published in 2012.

A phone call to Kafka's office at NYU—begun with a good laugh about how I'd found my way to his doorstep—and we arranged to have lunch in New York. Though no relation to the Czech writer, Ben Kafka appreciates the irony of his name, especially since Franz has become such an iconic symbol of bureaucratic ennui. "Did you know that the Paperwork Reduction Act in Belgium is known as Project Kafka?" he asked when we met, a detail, it turned out, that I did not know but was eager to research.

Established in 2003, the Office for Administrative Reform, in Belgium, has abolished or streamlined more than two hundred laws and policies, according to the official government website, a good number of them the result of "ridiculous regulations and pointless pedantry" occasioned by excessive red tape. Embracing the credo that "simplicity is power," the agency claims to have accounted for an annual savings of 1.7 billion. Among the paperwork modifications imposed in the first four years were a few gems, including these: "quick visa for Chinese businessmen"; "elimination of the special authorization to take aerial photographs"; "electronic declaration for the compensation of breastfeeding pauses"; "elimination of the license for the use of a walking stick for the blind"; "elimination of inventory and annual count of pigeons by the military authorities"; "elimination of control booklet for butchers"; and my favorite—even though it has little, presumably, to do with paperwork—the "elimination of the prohibition to insult heads of state."

For Ben Kafka, as it happens, these kinds of regulations conform to his conception of what has historically constituted the concept of paperwork. "I use it to refer to any sort of document that's produced in response to a demand by the state, and it doesn't have to be a real demand," he said. "It can also be an imagined demand. People submit all kinds of things to the government all the time—petitions, applications, permissions, license forms. I use the term to cover any sort of document that's produced for that kind of reason or purpose." *The Demon of Writing*, he added, emerges from the "feeling of helplessness" that everyone gets when dealing with the bureaucracy. "Paperwork leads to a depersonalization of power that a lot of people find disconcerting, disheartening. Even the prospect of filling out a long form has a way of filling us with a feeling of helplessness. And with this comes a kind of depersonalization of power that is made possible by paperwork. Just the prospect of a long form itself has a way of alienating people and of rendering them helpless."

As a scholarly pursuit, Kafka said the study of paperwork has been around for only a decade or so and is a cousin of what has become known as the history of the book, or *l'histoire du livre,* in France, where it originated. Kafka cited the work of the anthropologist Miriam Ticktin, who has written of how illegal immigrants in France—known technically as people *sans papiers,* or without papers—manage to navigate the bureaucracy in search of documents that might allow them to remain in the country. "Whether it's a Senegalese woman trying to treat a medical condition," Kafka has written, "a Pakistani farmer trying to block commercial development on his land, or a Chicago trader trying to hedge a position, the essentials of life, health, and wealth continue to rest on paper."

Among his own contributions to the growing discipline is a riveting story of paperwork during the years of the French Revolution, and how one low-level functionary—"a simple employee of the Committee of Public Safety named Charles Hippolyte Labussière"—had managed to save twelve hundred people from the guillotine simply by making the necessary documents that had condemned them to decapitation go missing. The individuals themselves were never pardoned for their perceived crimes, nor were their cases forgotten by their unforgiving judges; it was simply a matter of not finding the documents necessary to carry out the orders as required by the new laws. The untenable situation was soon recognized by the very people who had sanctioned it, prompting Louis-Antoine de Saint-Just, a principal on the Committee of Public Safety, to call for the summary elimination of excessive paperwork and the imposition of dictatorial powers. "The prolixity of the government's correspondence and orders is a sign of its inertia; it is impossible to govern without brevity," he said on the floor of the National Convention in 1793. "The demon of writing is waging war against us, we are unable to govern."

THE ALMOST FRENZIED RUSH, early in 1941, to build a five-sided fortress of an office building in Arlington, Virginia, for what was then known as the War Department was exacerbated by the gloomy certainty that the United States would soon be drawn into another world conflict. With close to four million square feet of usable space, the Pentagon is the largest office building in the world, containing more than twice the area of the Empire State Building. Built on twenty-nine acres of land, its five inner rings are connected by a network of 17.5 miles of corridors, an odd design for a sprawling complex built to accommodate up to forty thousand workers, but ideal, President Franklin D. Roosevelt thought at the time plans were being finalized, for the ultimate use he envisioned "when this emergency is over." That long-term use, he asserted a few days before groundbreaking, was conversion to a "records building for the government," into which many millions of documents then being stored in a number of makeshift repositories around the nation's capital would be moved—records already too plentiful to be accommodated in the National Archives Building, opened just seven years earlier on Pennsylvania Avenue. But once installed in its spacious new headquarters, the military—renamed the Department of Defense in 1947—was not about to be displaced by an armada of paper pushers.

A person genuinely concerned about the underpinnings of history, however, and a determined bibliophile in his own right, Roosevelt is nonetheless the president who signed into law the National Archives Act in 1934, marking the first time that the federal government had delegated responsibility for maintaining the documents of all three branches of government to one central agency. His wish for a new records center would not be realized until 1994, when National Archives at College Park (Archives II), a 1.7-million-square-foot repository outside Washington near the campus of the University of Maryland, began relieving some of the burden.

Today, the National Archives and Records Administration, as it has been known since 1985, when it was separated from the General Services Administration and became an independent agency, has grown to thirty-seven facilities nationwide, a network that includes fourteen regional records centers and thirteen presidential libraries and has about three thousand employees. As 2012 came to a close, NARA estimated that it was custodian of ten billion separate files, comprising about eighty billion pieces of paper, a figure that does not include motion pictures, photographs, and audio recordings that are also part of the archives, or the rapidly growing inventory of electronic data.

As mind-boggling as that number may be—and it includes items as varied as income tax returns, military claim files, blueprints of government buildings, bankruptcy court filings, crop reports, federal prisoner files, immigration files, census reports, and maps of national parks, as well as the foundational documents of the nation—it represents only a fraction of the paperwork produced by the government. Quite apart from the National Archives is the Government Printing Office, a twenty-four-hours-a-day, seven-days-a-week operation that occupies a 1.5-million-square-foot complex on North Capitol Street, in Washington. As the official printing arm of the United States Government, the GPO churns out every manner of document and report, boasting among its better-known publications the *Congressional Record,* the Records of the Supreme Court of the United States, checks for the Social Security Administration, and passports for the Department of State, at an annual cost of about $1 billion. Of the immense volume of materials on paper that ultimately are submitted to the National Archives, only 2 to 3 percent is kept permanently.

In the years prior to the creation of the National Archives Establishment, in 1934, public documents were the responsibility of the agencies that generated them, with no uniform standards defining what papers had to be kept or even how they should be preserved. "For a nation whose government is based upon a written constitution and laws to neglect its public records for a century and a half is remarkable unto itself," noted H. G. Jones, a distinguished archivist who in 1967 conducted a detailed study of governmental record keeping. "For that same nation, once its conscience was awakened, to develop one of the world's foremost archival institutions in less than a generation is even more remarkable." Once a single set of standards was in place, the most pressing problem became one of having adequate space, not one of procedure. The nation's first archivist, Robert Connor, once described the inadequate system in grim terms, writing that governmental paperwork was "scattered throughout the country, stored wherever space can be found for them, in cellars and sub-cellars, under terraces and over boiler-rooms, in attics and corridors, piled in dumps on floors and packed into alcoves, abandoned car-barns, storage warehouses,

*One of many storage alcoves in Archives II, College Park, Maryland.*

deserted theaters, or ancient but more humble edifices that should long ago have served their last useful purpose."

At the time of his appointment by President Barack Obama, in November 2009, to be the tenth national archivist of the United States, David Ferriero was director of the New York Public Library, with operational control of the largest municipal library system in the United States and one of the most heavily used websites. I interviewed Ferriero a few weeks after he was sworn in, and was still adjusting himself to his new routine. We met in downtown Washington at Archives I, where he has his main office, and took the twenty-minute shuttle bus ride together out to Archives II, and continued the conversation there.

"How to handle the paper doesn't really bother me, because we know how to do that now, and the rules are the same for everyone," he made clear—and when he said "everyone," he was speaking specifically about the 256 federal offices and agencies that are required to turn their records over to his agency. "But most of the agencies have migrated to some form of electronic record, and each agency has been allowed to build their own operating system. Right now there are no standards that apply to everyone. My job is to make sure that we are capturing those electronic records. It's relatively easy in the paper environment, because of what we call the 'usefulness of the record.' We work with each agency to determine, basically, how long a useful life is supposed to be for a particular record, how many years must we keep certain kinds of paper, and what's going to be valuable over the long term. The more complicated arena now by far is in electronic communication."

Even though so much government business is transacted electronically today, Ferriero said, "there are a number of places where e-mail is printed to paper" as a matter of standard procedure, and that the hard copy becomes the archival copy. He said his ultimate responsibility is to ensure that the government records that eventually do become permanent are going to be available in perpetuity. "That means ensuring that the proper security both physical and virtual is in place which guarantees that documents don't leave our control, and are not altered in their use. I think when you strip everything away, my responsibilities are the same across my entire career, and that is to collect, protect, encourage the use of information, and to ensure that this content is available forever. Those are the principles, regardless of format, regardless of who the user is."

For all the many kinds of paperwork maintained by the National Archives, materials not stored in its vast warehouses include paper ballots from federal elections, which are the purview of the counties and states where the votes are cast, and are not kept much longer than twenty-two months after results have been certified. There are exceptions to this, most notably the 5.9 million ballots cast by Florida voters in the 2000 election, which for thirty-six days were at the center of a high-stakes dispute to determine who would be the next president of the United States. In 2003, ballots from sixty-six of the state's sixty-seven counties were turned over to the state archivist, in Tallahassee, at the urging of historians and lawyers who claimed they were important artifacts; ballots for Bay County had already been destroyed by the time the order was issued. One Florida official who argued for their preservation was Ion Sancho, elections supervisor of Leon County and a strident advocate of election reform. "They are the most important election records of the twentieth century," he told me in a telephone interview, dismissing arguments that 450 storage cabinets was a waste of valuable resources. One of his colleagues—former Palm Beach County elections supervisor Theresa LePore—had jokingly suggested a different approach: "How about a bonfire?"

In the absence of uniform standards, counties throughout Florida had been free to use individual configurations, some employing the notorious "butterfly" design, which had punch holes running down the center of the ballots, with the names of candidates confusingly listed to the left and right of the holes. During the surreal recount that followed the virtual deadlock—a difference of 1,784 votes in the first tally—a flabbergasted world was introduced to such terms as "hanging chads," "pregnant chads," and "dimpled chads" to describe the condition of improperly punched holes, all minutely examined to see whether the voter's intent could be discerned conclusively. "We are trying to determine what someone was thinking based on a piece of paper," one exasperated official explained of the dilemma.

When the U.S. Supreme Court summarily terminated the recount on December 12, 2000, in a sharply divided ruling, George W. Bush was declared the winner by a margin of 537 votes, giving him the majority he needed in the Electoral College to claim the presidency. Calls for reform were immediate throughout the country and led to widespread adoption of touch-screen machines that leave no paper trail whatsoever

and depend entirely on the word of the companies that provide them
to assure the integrity of the process. By 2006, about 30 percent of voters nationwide were using paperless electronic devices, but the systems
were soon determined to be vulnerable to tampering and most have
since given way to "optical scan ballots" that allow for computerized
tabulation while providing a verifiable record—on paper—of every
vote cast.

The extraordinary turnabout, paradoxically enough, was apparent
most dramatically in Florida, where touch-screen machines quickly
adopted after the 2000 travesty were replaced yet again in 2008, at the
urging of Governor Charles J. Crist. "You should, when you go vote, be
able to have a record of it," Crist had told a gathering in Delray Beach.
"It's not very complicated; it is in fact common sense. Most importantly, it is the right thing to do."

# 10

## Metamorphosis

The emperors of today have drawn conclusions from this simple truth: whatever does not exist on paper, does not exist at all.
—Czeslaw Milosz, Nobel laureate, *The Captive Mind*, 1953

THE SEIZURE OF the American embassy in Tehran by Iranian militants on November 4, 1979, sent shockwaves throughout the diplomatic world, causing profound embarrassment for the administration in Washington and contributing to the defeat of Jimmy Carter in his bid for a second term as president of the United States. For the fifty-two Americans held captive throughout the 444-day ordeal, freedom came within minutes of Ronald Reagan's inauguration on January 19, 1981, one final indignity for the outgoing commander in chief, who nine months earlier had green-lighted a failed rescue attempt that resulted in the deaths of eight American servicemen in a desert staging area. Beyond the great humiliation inflicted on a proud superpower, there was also a catastrophic loss of highly classified documents, which embassy staffers worked frantically to shred into incomprehensibility before being taken captive.

What nobody in the intelligence community had considered beforehand, however, was that a corps of Iranian carpet-makers skilled in the weaving of intricate Persian rugs would be called upon to reconstruct the thin slivers of paper left behind into readable texts, which were subsequently photocopied and issued by the Muslim Student Followers of the Imam's Line, the putative publishers, in seventy-seven volumes collectively titled *Documents from the U.S. Espionage Den.* "For a culture that's been tying four hundred knots per inch for centuries, it

wasn't that much of a challenge," Malcolm Byrne, executive director of
the National Security Archive at George Washington University, said
in mock admiration of the effort, which was made even easier by the
shredding method in place at the time —a simple strip cut, not the far
more effective crosscut method that minces individual sheets into bits
of confetti and is the approach now mandated by government agencies
everywhere for the destruction of sensitive papers.

As a piece of office equipment, the shredder is a fairly recent mechanical appliance, patented in 1909 by Abbot Augustus Low of Horseshoe,
New York, a prolific American inventor whose idea for a "waste paper
receptacle" remained just a concept until 1935, when Adolf Ehinger,
a German toolmaker and politically active purveyor of anti-Nazi literature, improvised a crank-operated gadget modeled on a Bavarian
noodle cutter to render the discarded offprints from his press unreadable to prying eyes. Convinced that he was onto something marketable,
after the war Ehinger established EBA Maschinenfabrik, a company
that found a ready outlet for his shredders among banks, law firms, and
government agencies, and that today, as a component of EBA Krug &
Priester GmbH & Co., produces high-capacity machines capable of
mincing up to a thousand pounds of paper an hour.

With growing concern over identity theft and protection of data
such as medical and financial records, a number of enterprising companies in the United States now produce full lines of machines that
not only eliminate paperwork but obliterate unwanted hard drives and
disks, the latter pursuit falling into a burgeoning category of "information destruction" known in the industry as "disintegration." The
disquieting knowledge, too, that trash and rubbish are fertile hunting
grounds for compromising information has spawned a booming service industry in secure document destruction, with many companies
deploying fleets of trucks specially equipped to shred tons of unwanted
paperwork on-site while providing strict "chain-of-custody" guarantees
that assure total confidentiality. An advertisement posted by Shred-
it International Inc., one of the leading firms in the field, offers this
caveat: "That memo you tossed? It could cost more than you think."

The public at large first became aware that such devices even
existed during the Watergate hearings of 1974, when it was disclosed
that G. Gordon Liddy, one of the White House "plumbers" involved
in the burglary of Democratic National Committee headquarters, had

gone to his office the day after the first arrests, two years earlier, and fed everything in sight into a Shredmaster 400, including a stack of $100 bills set aside to underwrite his group's illicit activities. A case of comparable notoriety came to light a decade later, when it was disclosed that key documents relating to a covert White House scheme intended to gain the release of seven American hostages being held in Lebanon by the terrorist group Hezbollah had been destroyed at the direction of Marine lieutenant colonel Oliver L. North, the Reagan administration aide in charge of what quickly became known as the Iran-Contra affair. Testifying in July 1987 before a joint congressional investigating committee, North said that he had neutralized a pile of key papers one morning on his Schleicher Intimus 007S crosscut shredder while agents from the Department of Justice were in an adjoining room reviewing other material. "They were working on their project," North said, "I was working on mine."

A bit of comic relief was provided by North's secretary, a willowy blonde named Fawn Hall, who admitted to having altered some documents and having smuggled others out of the Old Executive Office Building by stuffing them inside her chic leather boots and under her dress. Her biggest "mistake," she felt, lay in not having finished "eliminating traces of altered originals" from the files and replacing them with fabricated copies. "Sometimes," she explained airily of her illegal actions, "you have to go above the written law" in order to prevent "a lot of top-secret, sensitive, classified material" from circulating, particularly when operatives from the Soviet Union might be snooping about. "Well, it wasn't the KGB that was coming, Miss Hall," Senator Warren B. Rudman replied, we can assume with a straight face. "It was the FBI."

Shredding became a front-page story once again in 2002, when two accountants employed by the firm of Arthur Andersen LLP were convicted in federal court on charges of having destroyed audit reports that would have incriminated the Enron Corporation in a massive deception of consumers and stockholders. To expedite their own desperate efforts to obstruct justice, it was further disclosed that Enron executives had retained the services of Shredco Inc., a "document management" company whose motto was "Don't just throw it away. Destroy it." An immediate consequence was passage of the Sarbanes-Oxley Act, legislation sponsored by U.S. senator Paul Sarbanes and U.S. representative Michael G. Oxley that made it a criminal offense for anyone who "knowingly alters, destroys, mutilates, conceals, covers up, falsifies, or makes a false entry in any record, document, or tangible object with the intent to impede, obstruct, or influence the investigation or proper administration of any matter within the jurisdiction of any department or agency of the United States."

However flagrant those various paper capers may have been, they were minuscule when compared with the frantic measures undertaken by the East German secret police in October 1989 to prevent millions of salacious dossiers it had compiled over four decades of Communist rule from falling into the hands of a new government that was on the verge of assuming power. Beginning at about the time the Berlin Wall started to crumble, functionaries of the Ministry for State Security, the feared domestic surveillance agency known as the Stasi, launched a modern-day Labor of Hercules akin to the cleansing of the Augean Stables. But unlike the resourceful Greek demigod who pulled off his miraculous feat of mass sanitization in a single day, the German effort fell well short of completion when time ran out three months later.

Christened the "horror files" by the magazine *Der Spiegel,* the top-secret archive had been stored in 125 miles of compact metal shelving installed in the basement of Stasi headquarters, in East Berlin. Each mile contained about seventeen million sheets of paper, a mass of files that proved far too formidable for total destruction. When the rapacious shredding machines, known informally as "ripping wolves" by their handlers, broke down under the incessant workload, anxious operatives were forced to tear the pages apart manually. By the time the all-hands-on-deck operation ended, in January 1990, forty-five million sheets of paper had been torn into six hundred million fragments, but, with 98 percent of the archive still left untouched, a shocking picture of governmental venality began to emerge.

Acting under the direction of Security Chief Erich Mielke, the Stasi had systematically amassed damning information on the private lives of six million of its own citizens, about a third of the population of what was then the German Democratic Republic. Most of the material had come from a network of 175,000 civilian informants, in some instances husbands reporting on their wives, wives on their husbands, children on their parents, physicians on their patients, or priests on their parishioners, with every manner of personal detail considered fair

game. In 1992, the German parliament passed a bill that authorized
targets of the surveillance to access their dossiers, however painful it
might be for the aggrieved to learn what had been said about them
and, even more chillingly, by whom. As stories of outrage began to
appear in the German media, support grew for proposals to reconstruct the shredded documents, which had been stuffed into 16,250
trash bags, with the idea they would be hauled off for incineration, but
were impounded before they could be whisked away.

In an effort to piece together whatever they could, a team of thirty
civil servants was formed in 1995, their tools of choice adhesive tape,
tweezers, and magnifying glasses. Twelve years into the effort, 440
bags of material had been reassembled, a good start to be sure, but at
that pace the task was projected to take well over four hundred years to
complete—more Herculean a labor, by far, than the original destruction itself—which persuaded the Bonn government to invite proposals on ways to expedite the process. In 2007, the Fraunhofer Institute
for Production Systems and Design Technology, in Berlin, a nonprofit
research institute that works with private and governmental clients,
came forward with a pattern recognition machine called the ePuzzler
and put it to work on an $8.5 million pilot project to be completed by
2012. Its designers claimed the scanning device could compose digi-
tized images of whole sheets of paper from fragments by analyzing texture, shape, color, thickness, typeface, outline, and tear configuration.

One enormous stroke of good fortune had been the failure of Stasi
operatives to stuff the scraps randomly into different bags, a critical
oversight that enabled technicians to proceed with the assumption that
pieces found together had pretty much been shredded together. The
BBC reported in September 2012 that four hundred sacks of shredded files had been successfully reassembled during the testing phase
and that plans were afoot to continue with the project. It was further
reported by Agence France-Presse (AFP) that in the first twenty years
since limited public access was authorized by the Bonn government,
close to three million German citizens had submitted requests to see
their Stasi dossiers. If there is a lesson to be learned by bureaucrats in
all of this, it is that total security is assured only by burning, or, in the
instance of procedures in place at National Security Agency headquarters, in Fort Meade, Maryland—whose industrial-grade installation
I was allowed to view for this book—on-site pulping. In addition to

converting discarded paper into reusable fiber, this approach has the residual effect of being environmentally responsible, so much so that the NSA claims on its website that it saves the equivalent of twenty-two hundred southern pine trees each year through recycling.

I do not deny my own fascination for knowing, if only cursorily, how this shadowy agency, with an annual budget estimated to be any-where between $6 billion and $10 billion, goes about monitoring the millions of electronic transmissions that fly through the airwaves about the globe, and I very much enjoyed the opportunity I had to talk with the director of the National Cryptologic Museum, located just outside Fort Meade, Maryland, about its history. Pertinent, too, I thought, was the many ways paper has been involved in what the agency has accom-plished, not least among them use of the "one-time pad," which to this day remains arguably the most reliable method of communicating clas-sified information ever devised.

But above all, it was a desire on my part to see how a key federal agency goes about the task of handling sensitive documents no longer critical to its operations. "It's just like any other pulping plant you're likely to see," an NSA public affairs officer said in a withering attempt to cool my enthusiasm to have a look, and seven months after submit-ting my request, I was granted permission to visit. Reduced to its basics, the operation is designed to produce low-grade pulp out of office paper, yet the overall "mission," according to Craig Harman, chief of logistics services for the agency at the time of my visit, is the secure and system-atic disposal of highly sensitive documents, about one hundred mil-lion of them a year, by one estimate—down 30 percent from numbers reached in the 1980s and early '90s, but considerable enough, given the increasing use of electronic alternatives now being used throughout the government. Only about 10 percent of the paperwork generated by the agency's corps of cryptanalysts—said to be the largest pool of mathematicians employed anywhere in the world—is retained perma-nently. For the rest, disposal is accomplished by pulping, which is so reliable a solution that the NSA processes classified documents trucked in from dozens of other intelligence agencies and Defense Department offices located in the region—about six million additional pounds a year from those sources alone, accounting for a workload that can reach 27,500 pounds a day.

According to an official report issued by the Government Accounting Office, the volume of data generated by the National Security Agency judged sensitive enough to be classified is "probably greater than the combined total activity" of all other components and agencies of the federal bureaucracy. "With more secrets than are held by the CIA, the State Department, the Pentagon, and all other agencies of government combined, NSA likely holds the largest body of secrets on earth," James Bamford wrote in *The Puzzle Palace.* And while these secrets are increasingly being managed electronically, pencil and paper remain essential tools of the cryptologist's craft, David Kahn emphasized in *The Codebreakers* and reaffirmed to me in a telephone interview. "When they get down to work, they write on cross-ruled paper with colored pencils, shuffle pages, look for significant patterns, confer with colleagues, take coffee breaks," he observed of the daily routine. "Sometimes a yelp of joy will pierce the concentration as a cryptanalyst breaks through. They have one advantage at least over workers in more ordinary fields: they cannot take their work home with them at night."

For sheets that are no longer useful—and they constitute the overwhelming majority of the workload—standard procedure calls for their being disposed of in one of fifty-two "drop chutes" located throughout the NSA campus. "Our mission is declassification," Harman emphasized during the drive over to the pulping unit, located a short distance from the forbidding complex of four opaque glass buildings that make up the heart of the installation. The work performed in one of these Support Activity Buildings, identified simply by the designation SAB2 on the outside, resembles what takes place at any other paper-recycling plant, except that nothing quite like what is done here is replicated anywhere else in the world.

Instead of newspapers or corporate spreadsheets moving their way up a conveyor belt into a giant blue hopper, many thousands of highly classified documents are processed in a manner that allows for their rebirth in other forms. "If it's paper, it goes in a burn bag, and is sent on to us," Harman said, though incineration is used only in instances where materials not soluble in water must be destroyed by other means. When I entered the plant, the litter of a day's work was arriving by way of the Main Pneumatic Transport System, a network of underground tunnels more casually known among employees as the "suck pipes," for the turbine-driven vacuums that propel the material along at sixty miles an hour. During their brisk ride to the plant, the burn bags break up, allowing the contents to arrive as individual sheets. At one point during our walk around the facility, I was directed to stand back as a line of heavy-duty trucks arriving from other "customers" in the region, all of them plain and unmarked and looking for all the world like typical waste-disposal vehicles, queued up to unload their cargos into the yawning maw.

Inside the main control room, a technician seated before a schematic display known as the All Chutes Screen was monitoring the movement of every bag, indicating which of the "drop points" were being opened at any given time, and tracked the progress of each deposit along various branches of the network. Significantly, none of these documents, most of them on standard eight-and-a-half-by-eleven-inch office bond paper, are shredded. "We want to preserve the fiber," Harman explained, since a collateral goal is the production of a commercial-grade pulp that can be sold to an industrial contractor—Weyerhaeuser, I was told, had the contract during the time of my visit—which in turn uses it to make a variety of products that have included pizza boxes, egg cartons, and lesser grades of recycled-paper packaging.

So instead of shredding the sheets, a ten-thousand-gallon hydro-pulper converts them into a grayish slurry that consists, at first, of 90 percent water and 10 percent paper, the proportions being steadily reversed as the process proceeds and water continues to be extracted. At the end of the line, the fragments are baled into two-thousand-pound bundles of pulp and deposited onto a skid by a loading platform, all officially declassified and ready to be hauled away for more mundane uses in the civilian world. It was out there, on the dock, my visit concluded, that I was presented with two mementos of a most unusual morning: a small medal with the insignia of the NSA on one side and the motto "We Won't Back Down, We Never Have, We Never Will" on the reverse—and a plastic Ziploc bag filled with several ounces of the pulp, its prior life as bearer of highly sensitive government information entirely erased.

AS A CONTINUING NARRATIVE, the story of a woman who saw an opportunity to convert newsprint and scrap paper gathered from refuse dumps in the United States into cardboard packaging for products being manufactured by the millions in China—and, in the process, become one of the wealthiest entrepreneurs in the world—is irresistible. To accomplish this, the stars, it seemed, had to be aligned perfectly for Zhang Yin, the daughter of a Chinese army officer who in the mid-1980s was working as an accountant for a paper importer in Hong Kong when the company went belly-up, and she was in need of a new job.

Instead of going to work for another company, Zhang, in her thirties at the time, chose to pursue her destiny in California, where in 1990 she and her husband, a Taiwanese physician, used $3,800 in savings to establish America Chung Nam Inc. Using their apartment in Pomona as a base of operations, the couple drove about the United States in a secondhand Dodge Caravan setting up deals to purchase tons of scrap paper and ship it to China, where it was sold to mills in need of "recovered" fiber to nourish the explosive growth of the economy.

If there is an Achilles' heel in the Chinese success story, it is that wood pulp cannot be sufficiently supplied by domestic sources. It is one vital area, in fact, in which exports from North America far exceed imports, and this is traceable to the frenetic drive toward industrialization known as the Great Leap Forward, which took place between 1958 and 1962, a catastrophic undertaking that included among many ill-advised schemes the indiscriminate destruction of entire forests teeming with virgin wood. With no systematic environmental plan in place, and with the encouragement of the central government, trees by the millions were cut to fuel improvised smelters that had been installed throughout China, leaving much of the land that had been leveled open to erosion and contributing to a famine said to have caused the deaths of up to thirty million people. In the absence of a domestic supply of wood, China was forced to become the world's largest importer of pulp and timber products, sending enormous transport ships to such tree-exporting countries as Brazil and Indonesia, in many instances chipping logs as they were loaded aboard at the piers, to maximize available storage space for the voyage home.

Zhang's stunning success is rooted in having the perspicacity to recognize the critical need and for developing an ingenious strategy to exploit it. She made deals with the owners of junk and refuse dumps to buy mountains of newsprint and scrap paper and shipped it to China aboard ships that otherwise would have been returning with empty holds after offloading their cargoes. The American suppliers were thrilled to clear their lots, and the shipowners were more than happy to accommodate the "Cardboard Queen" (other journalists have called her the Paper Queen, the Trash Queen, and the Empress of Waste Paper) with preferential rates.

In 1995, Zhang established Nine Dragons Paper in China to broker the recovered fiber, and three years later she began producing her own cardboard. By 2010 the company was operating plants in four economic regions of the country, producing just under nine million tons of cardboard a year. Within fifteen meteoric years, her company had become the largest manufacturer of cardboard packaging in China and was listed among the five largest producers in the world. According to the Shanghai-based *Hurun Report,* which ranks Chinese entrepreneurs and industrialists in much the same way *Forbes* compiles its international list of the richest people, Zhang's personal fortune was estimated at $5.6 billion in 2010. When Nine Dragons went public on the Hong Kong stock exchange, in March 2007, its stock quadrupled in value in the first six months. "Chinese manufacturers were desperate for scrap paper," Zhang said at a news conference. "The business was just my husband and me, and I didn't speak a word of English. I had to learn from scratch. Other people saw scrap paper as garbage—but I saw it as a forest of trees. All I did was help fulfill a need."

AT A TIME when much of the world is thinking "green"—the word, in fact, has acquired a new patina of meaning in a very brief period, a metaphor no longer suggesting nausea or envy, but environmental consciousness—it is instructive to note that the first manufactured product to rely on recycled materials in a significant way may well have been paper. The Chinese, as we have seen, used frayed fishing nets in their earliest pulps, and for many centuries thereafter, cotton and linen rags—tons and tons of them—were the resource of choice in the Middle East, Europe, and North America. Today it is paper itself that goes back into the mix, which is why I arranged to visit Marcal Paper Mills, in New Jersey, an operation that was green, in the contemporary sense, decades before the word became fashionable.

Acquired in 2012 by Soundview Paper Co., an affilliate of Atlas Holdings LLC of Greenwhich, CT, Marcal was founded in 1932 by a Sicilian immigrant whose first job, as a machinist's apprentice in Paterson, paid $2 a week. Setting up shop in the adjoining community of East Paterson—known officially, since 1973, as Elmwood Park—the small company began by making consumer paper products conventionally, with fiber supplied by the wood and wood-pulp industry, but rationing imposed by World War II shortages led the founder, Nicholas Marcalus, to seek out alternative sources. "He looked at New York City as his concrete forest," his grandson and third-generation successor as president, also named Nicholas Marcalus, reminisced once with a reporter for the Bergen County *Record,* a reality that I found immediately apparent when I visited the mill in 2009, a few months after a new group of owners had introduced a line of toilet paper called Small Steps and adopted the phrase "A Small, Easy Step to a Greener Earth" as its motto, capitalizing, for the first time in the company's history, on qualities it had introduced for all of its products more than a half-century earlier.

Like every other mill I visited for this book, my tour of the Marcal plant began where hydro-pulpers of varying design and complexity commence the tried-and-true alchemy that transforms cellulose fiber into rolls of paper, but with a slight twist. At Marcal, the staging area is flanked not by wood chips, cotton, flax, or any of the other ingredients that normally produce pulp, but by twenty-foot mounds

*Scrap paper from Manhattan office buildings at Marcal Paper Mills, in Elmwood Park, New Jersey, where it will be recycled for use as toilet tissue and kitchen towels.*

of sales catalogs, supermarket flyers, magazines, "uncirculated mail"—papermaking code for junk mail that never got delivered—and piles upon piles of computer printouts, office reports, and whatever else of a paper nature workers in the concrete canyons of Manhattan and Northern New Jersey choose to deposit into the blue plastic bins that have become so commonplace in the office buildings of the twenty-first century.

"We don't use any virgin trees for our tissue at all, we use one hundred percent recycled fiber," Randall Suliga, director of research and development and a senior vice president for Marcal at the time of my visit, said as we got started. I had just asked Suliga to identify the abbreviations that marked the various bins that were supplying the "blend" for that morning's menu of products, which included kitchen towels, dinner napkins, bathroom tissue, and toilet paper. "COW," he explained, stands for "clean office waste," the abbreviation "MG" for magazines, "PW" for post-consumer waste, "ISG" for materials that include "insoluble glue" and thus require special attention, and "curbside," which was self-explanatory.

Not to be found anywhere on the Marcal lot were newspapers, which are sold to other companies that make newsprint and cardboard. "Newsprint is too coarse a wood fiber for our purposes," Suliga said, though books are perfectly acceptable, provided the hardcover bindings are stripped off beforehand. "We like telephone books, and we've had contracts with the Postal Service on Long Island to pulp discontinued stamps." Suliga said he did not know who got the contract to recycle *If I Did It,* the notorious memoir by O. J. Simpson that was canceled in the face of mounting public outrage shortly before its scheduled release in 2006, but he did say that if the four hundred thousand copies reportedly printed by HarperCollins were sent off to find a new life of sanitary service in the latrines of America, then they would have made "a whole lot of toilet paper." Assuming that each copy of the book weighed two pounds, there would have been about four hundred tons, "which is just about a day's worth of scrap paper at Marcal."

By using recycled paper exclusively for its products, Marcal saves about two million trees a year. The New Jersey plant makes between 400 and 425 tons of paper a day and uses two million to three million gallons of water every twenty-four hours, all of it drawn from the Passaic River. "You save seven thousand gallons of water for every ton of recycled paper you make, which means that we save close to a billion gallons of water a year by recycling. If all our lines are running full-out, this facility can do a million rolls of toilet paper a day." While other manufacturers boast of using recycled paper to varying degrees for their products, he pointed out that Marcal stands alone among the leading producers in that it uses no virgin fiber whatsoever in any of its processes, and has not done so since 1950. By no means a mega-producer in league with Kimberly-Clark, Procter & Gamble, and Georgia-Pacific, Marcal nonetheless manufactures in numbers significant enough to rank among the top ten tissue manufacturers in the United States, earning brand loyalty with a following of admirers who have bought into the company's all-out commitment to save trees, even if it may mean giving up some of the softness they have come to expect in toilet tissue.

When working with glossy magazines like *Vogue, GQ,* and *Vanity Fair,* there is the additional requirement of removing certain additives, particularly clay, that give them their distinctive feel and look. "Depending on the quality of the magazine, anywhere from twenty to thirty to forty percent of that weight is not good for making tissue products, because the slick coating and the heavy pages of the higher-end magazines usually yield a lower amount of fiber per ton of magazine received. Before you can pulp the fiber, you have to remove all those clays." At Marcal, the magazine wastes—"it's a sludge, really"—are repurposed to produce commercial absorbent used to clean up industrial spills and as biodegradable bedding for livestock; it is sold under the brand name Kaofin.

To whiten their paper and tissue products, Suliga said Marcal uses no chlorine bleach, but a proprietary process in which the main component is sodium hydrosulfite. "We go through a series of steps where we wash the fibers in very hot water, separate them, and clean them. Each company does something different—that's why I say that all paper machines are like fingerprints. No two machines make the same exact sheets. A true papermaker can look at a sheet and tell which mill it came from. An average person will never see the difference."

Suliga said, in fact, that he considers the best papermakers to be "artists" who deal with ingredients that are constantly changing. "Let's face it: the number-one raw material we are dealing with here, essentially, is crud. It's a different blend, a different recipe, all the time. One day we'll put so much of this in, so much of that, magazines versus office waste versus curbside collections from the towns, and the next day it might change. We have to tweak it constantly, yet still have a product that the everyday consumer is going to want, because nobody is going to buy our paper if it doesn't perform. You have to know how to work with the different fibers that are coming in twenty-four hours a day—hardwood papers, softwood papers, ash or maple, whatever— and when the combination changes, you have to be prepared to deal with it. We have bales of different kinds of wastepaper put aside for just this purpose that we call the 'spices.' If modifications are necessary, our technicians make adjustments on the spot, and that's where the spices—and where the art of making paper—comes in."

# 11

## Face Value

A verbal contract isn't worth the paper it's written on.
    —Attributed to the movie mogul Sam Goldwyn, 1879–1974

On a greenback, greenback dollar bill,
Just a little piece of paper, coated with chlorophyll.
    —Ray Charles, "Greenbacks," 1955

AS A KIND of show-and-tell exercise inspired by the old cliché that some things are not worth the paper they are printed on, I decided early in 2009 to buy through eBay—and as cheaply as I possibly could; otherwise what was the point?—some outlandishly inflated pieces of currency from recent decades that had fallen on stupendously hard times. Perhaps the best-known example of the last century—and, indeed, the one that jump-started my quest in the first place—is the German mark issued by the Weimar Republic in the years following World War I, a time when wheelbarrows filled with freshly issued bills were insufficient to buy so much as a daily newspaper. Before the outbreak of hostilities in Europe in 1914, German currency had shared equal value with the English shilling, the French franc, and the Italian lira; all had about the same exchange rate of four or five to the American dollar. By December 1923—the most severe month of the hyperinflation crisis—$1 had the buying power of 4.2 *trillion* marks.

One theory traces the collapse back to the Germans' having financed their participation in the Great War through borrowing alone, not by savings or taxation, and abandoning gold as the backing of their currency. Another attributes the breakdown more directly to the terms of

*A German citizen finds productive use for worthless Weimar reichsmarks during the height of the hyperinflation crisis, 1923.*

the Versailles Treaty, which required reparations in secured payments of such magnitude that Germany was unable to meet its obligations, leading France and Belgium to occupy the steel- and coal-producing regions of the Ruhr in January 1923. Either way, paper was no longer a surrogate for the real thing, and when nervous citizens attempted to withdraw their marks and convert them into goods and property, the central bank churned out more and more currency.

"So the printing presses ran, and once they began to run, they were hard to stop," the financial analyst George J. W. Goodman, writing under the pseudonym of Adam Smith, noted in *Paper Money* (1981), an examination of world currency. "The price increases began to be dizzying. Menus in cafés could not be revised quickly enough. A student at Freiburg University ordered a cup of coffee at a café. The price on the menu was 5,000 marks. He had two cups. When the bill came, it was for 14,000 marks. 'If you want to save money,' he was told, 'and you want to have two cups of coffee, you should order them both at the same time.'"

The Berlin publisher Leopold Ullstein wrote of an American couple who had tipped a domestic chef $1, a windfall that occasioned the establishment of a family trust fund. One of the most widely reproduced news photographs of the period pictures a man using reichsmarks to wallpaper a room in his house. In two other images, a kneeling woman fuels a furnace with bundles of notes pulled from a stack on the floor, and three boys build a sturdy pyramid with bricks shaped out of otherwise feeble bills. For an evocative Dada collage, the Bauhaus artist László Moholy-Nagy strung together a choice selection of vastly inflated notes, one of them indicating a denomination of a hundred thousand million marks. Similarly motivated, a clever vintner used thousand-mark notes as labels for his wine bottles—a vintage year to remember if ever there was one.

Given that many billions of reichsmarks were turned out nonstop by more than 130 printing firms hired by the government between 1921 and 1923—some five hundred quintillion in total currency was in circulation at the time of the collapse, or 5 times 10 to the 20th power—it seemed reasonable to assume that decent notes in presentable condition would be readily available at bargain prices today, if only as novelties. But as I quickly learned, some of the snazzier specimens being offered for sale by dealers can cost collectors a pretty penny to acquire. Like everything else we regard today as "printed ephemera"—one way of saying materials on paper not intended by their makers to last the long haul—the vast majority of Weimar Republic bills perished when their periods of utility were exhausted. And so now, in a bizarre kind of way, those that survive are worth more as curiosities than they ever were as currency, and thus outside the boundaries of my buying spree.

A similar fate befell paper currency issued by the upstart Continental Congress during the years of the American Revolution, which reached a level of depreciation so alarming that objects without value were often said to be "not worth a continental." In the early spring of 1779, an exasperated George Washington wrote John Jay, the recently elected president of the assembly, to report that his troops in the field were in dire need of food and supplies and that "a waggon load of money will scarcely purchase a waggon load of provision." Yet someone interested in acquiring an authentic "continental" note today will pay anywhere from $50 to $500 for a single bill—even more, depending on condition and scarcity. So those notes were outside the scope of my activity, too, as were Confederate States of America bills from the 1860s, ridiculed just as mercilessly in their day as continentals and reichsmarks were in theirs, but like them also coveted by collectors.

Settling, finally, on a strategy of the moment, I started at the end of the alphabet with Zimbabwe, where major news outlets had been reporting bleakly for several years on the collapse of the national economy, with Robert Mugabe's government frenetically printing new bills in an attempt to keep pace with inflation that was hopelessly out of control. "The price of toilet paper, like everything else here, soars almost daily, spawning jokes about an impending better use for Zimbabwe's $500 bill, now the smallest in circulation," Michael Wines wrote in the *New York Times* in 2006. Two years later, the London *Daily Telegraph* reported that the Zimbabwe dollar had been worth more than the American greenback at independence in 1980, "but Robert Mugabe's misrule has seen it plunge to a point where one pound is worth around Z$200 billion, and accelerating downwards." By then, the state-owned newspaper, the *Herald,* was selling for $25 billion a copy in local currency.

But other than the truly incredible denominations printed on the crisp bills I wound up buying for what might well be described as "chump change"—100 million, 200 million, 1 billion, 100 billion, 1 trillion, a mind-boggling 100 trillion Zimbabwe dollars—the notes themselves are quite attractive, with security threads and watermarks typical of other international banknotes. The manufacturer of the security paper was Giesecke & Devrient, of Munich, internationally respected

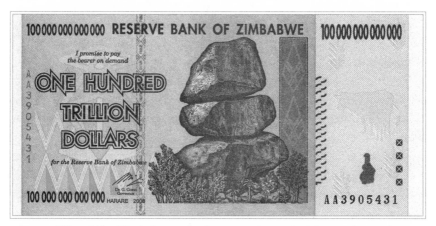

*A 100-trillion-dollar Zimbabwean banknote, 2006, acquired for pennies on eBay.*

for its high-end security note services and one of the firms that had supplied reichsmarks to the Weimar Republic during the 1920s.

The question of how many zeroes could possibly fit onto one little piece of paper became a nonissue when the government announced that it was suspending its own currency. Elton Mangoma, Zimbabwe's minister for economic planning, tacitly acknowledged the gravity of the dilemma by noting that there was "nothing to support and hold its value." The move came at the urging of the international community but was also influenced by the refusal of Giesecke & Devrient to furnish the hapless nation with any more paper. By 2010, barter had become a widespread medium of exchange for goods and services, though for most transactions the government was accepting the American dollar as legal tender.

Seeking out more dysfunctional examples, I then acquired a lovely note from Uganda bearing a regal portrait of the ousted strongman Idi Amin, valued at its time of issue at ten shillings. To that I added a handsome 100-dinar note from Iraq, featuring the benevolent smile of Saddam Hussein, and an Iranian bill from the 1970s lionizing the soon-to-be-deposed shah, Mohammad Reza Pahlavi. It was around this time that a band of pirates commandeered an American merchant ship off the coast of Africa and held the captain hostage for five days, before three of them were shot dead by U.S. Navy SEALs; since their ransom demands had been for American dollars—no big surprise there—I decided to get a note issued in Somalia, their refuge and haven, and a country without a stable currency of its own.

While occupying myself with these diversions, I was surprised to learn that no paper currency picturing either Adolf Hitler or Benito Mussolini had ever been issued by Nazi Germany or Fascist Italy. I thought that, surely, two megalomaniacs with such outsize egos would have been venerated in this way by their cowering acolytes. The two dictators were pictured on a multitude of postage stamps, but since this little riff of mine was all about the money, neither qualified for inclusion in my cabinet of curiosities, which was created in the first place to illumine, on an unambiguously literal level, the concept of "face value."

From the outset of my investigations, a guiding premise of this book has been to demonstrate that paper is a substance of utility, almost always defined by the task at hand. In instances where the function is of short duration—outdated magazines, advertising circulars, or junk mail, to cite a few of the more obvious examples—the material often finds a new life among recyclers for conversion to other productive uses. In one peculiar instance a few years back, weighty copies of a commemorative newspaper published by the *Beijing Evening News* were worth more in bulk for salvage than the price being charged for individual issues, encouraging vendors to bypass street sales entirely and deal directly with the scrap merchants.

But paper is still paper, and the far larger consideration is that the actual or implied worth of any document relies almost entirely on what has been written, drawn, or printed on its surface. While currency is the obvious example, attractive stock certificates representing shares in corporations that have ingloriously tanked, phony academic degrees sold by diploma mills to people anxious to pad their CVs, and commitments known as IOUs that are only as redeemable as the word of the people who sign them argue the case just as persuasively.

For more than three decades, an enterprise founded in 1979 by a Canadian advertising executive has been providing attractively embossed certificates "personalized" with "telescopic coordinates" as proof that a star in the sky has been named in the customer's honor and entered for posterity in a ledger the company prints for its clients, called *Your Place in the Cosmos*. Despite repeated assurances from the International Astronomical Union that none of these arbitrary designations will ever be recognized or used by any officially sanctioned body, the International Star Registry, as the company is legally known, claims to have sold "hundreds of thousands" of its certificates, for fees that vary depending on the degree of presentation desired. "You could call it a fraud," a Swarthmore College astronomer told *Time* magazine, but star-struck people continue to be charmed by the prospect of hitching their names to a heavenly body—and getting what they believe is the documentation to prove it.

One of my favorite movie scenes along these lines appears in the 1993 film *Searching for Bobby Fischer,* when Josh, the young chess prodigy at the center of the story, wonders ruefully when he might finally earn the "Grandmaster Certificate" his teacher gives out. The hardnosed mentor, played by Ben Kingsley, responds by tossing blank sheet after blank sheet of the form in front of the boy, telling him to just go ahead and write his name on the space provided, if that is the full measure of his ambition. Whether said outright or merely implied, the lesson of the "teaching moment" is unmistakable, and can be taken as axiomatic: "In the end, it's only a piece of paper."

Handmade paper can be quite beautiful and luxurious in and of itself, of course, and is the medium of choice among many respected artists, but as a vehicle of cultural transmission it conveys the considered expression of human thought, no more, no less. Whatever the thought being articulated might be, whatever configuration it may take—be it the tentative drawings of a master painter, the holographic drafts of a budding poet, the candid sentiments of a beloved public figure, the probing calculations of a molecular physicist, or simply the cogent reflection of a trenchant idea—I can think of no manufactured object that is valued more dearly for its intellectual content alone than this remarkably versatile material, which is the single element that separates billions of mundane specimens from the few that are truly extraordinary. A paradox in all this is that, while the enduring value of a document has little to do with its physical properties—and value can be measured in terms that are monetary, artistic, historical, theological, literary, or simply personal—it is the composition that more often than not determines authenticity, particularly in cases that may be in dispute. For people intent on making mischief in the marketplace of ideas—we know them as forgers and counterfeiters—success requires more than the replication of words and images; it also requires convincing examples of the paper itself.

Since finding unused paper made in prior centuries is not a simple task, one approach favored by the criminally minded has been to pillage blank endsheets from old books found on the shelves of most major research libraries. One of the most notorious episodes along these lines involved the creation, in 1985, of a bogus version of what was touted at the time to be a unique copy of the first text printed in British North America, a small broadside known, when it was issued in the seventeenth century, as "The Oath of a Freeman." The perpetrator of the hoax, an obscure memorabilia dealer from Utah named Mark W. Hofmann, had already tested his mettle as a cultural bandit by creating a series of potentially embarrassing documents relating to the early years of the Mormon movement and then selling them at very high prices to the Church of Jesus Christ of Latter-day Saints. Achieving heady success there, Hofmann set his sights on what is generally accepted to be the most celebrated printed document from colonial

times to have vanished entirely over the generations, and worth a modest fortune if one should ever turn up. Beyond the accomplished nature
of Hofmann's technical work—experts who were fooled by his forgery
included the late Charles Hamilton, a prominent New York autograph
dealer who later called the small broadside a "work of art"—what made
his pièce de résistance seductive was his skillful exploitation of the historical record.

Unlike the bizarre forgeries of William Henry Ireland, a minor
literary figure in eighteenth-century London whose creation, out of
whole cloth, of "lost Shakespeare plays" caused a sensation before being
demolished as nonsensical gibberish by the scholar Edmund Malone,
"The Oath of a Freeman" was not a figment of someone's imagination. Such a vow is known to have been drafted by members of the
Massachusetts Bay Colony to promote freedom of conscience, and has
long been regarded as pivotal in the evolution of American democracy.
About fifty copies of the original broadside, each the approximate size
of a modern postcard, are thought to have been printed in 1639, by
Stephen Day, at his Cambridge press. Because Day also printed the
Bay Psalm Book a year later—and since that hymnal survives in eleven
known copies—a credible font suggestive of his work could be fashioned by someone skilled in typography, and because the words of the
oath itself have also survived, an authoritative text was readily available as well. "He fooled me," Hamilton told the *New York Times*. "He
fooled everybody."

Hofmann maintained that he had stumbled across the document
while browsing through a bin of miscellaneous papers in the Argosy
Book Store, in New York, and he produced a cash receipt for $25 to
back up his story. He would later admit to having planted in the store a
nineteenth-century ballad that he had fabricated, with the words "Oath
of a Freeman" appearing at the top, and using the itemized invoice he
received to establish a chain of custody for the spurious broadside. The
asking price in 1985 was $1.5 million; among the interested suitors were
the Library of Congress and the American Antiquarian Society.

Hofmann's reckless antics—which included killing two people
with pipe bombs and seriously injuring another in a desperate attempt
to deflect attention from his rapidly unraveling enterprise—have been
thoroughly chronicled elsewhere and need not be explored in any
depth here, beyond stressing one salient point of relevance: none of

his forgeries would have been possible had he not been able to locate authentic sheets of paper from the periods he had targeted. In a sworn confession made as part of a plea bargain to avoid the death penalty, Hofmann admitted to having removed several blank sheets of paper from a seventeenth-century book he had found in the special collections library of Brigham Young University. He told investigators that the leaf he chose for his "Oath of a Freeman" had chain lines that were almost identical to those found in the paper used for the Bay Psalm Book, and were thus more likely to withstand a close examination by paper scientists.

Hofmann was by no means the first person who, in search of verisimilitude, had sliced blank sheets of handmade paper out of old books. The nineteenth-century artist James Abbott McNeill Whistler was constantly on the prowl for seasoned stock he could cannibalize for his work. Though best known for the oils of his mature years, Whistler had trained as a draftsman in the employ of the National Oceanic and Atmospheric Administration's Office of Coast Survey and had used the skills he developed there to master multiple techniques on paper. His proficiency in drawing, drypoint, lithography, etching, watercolors, and pastels were such that Joseph Pennell, his biographer, ranked him with Rembrandt and Albrecht Dürer as one of the outstanding printmakers of all time.

A perfectionist when it came to choosing the right surfaces for his prints, Whistler favored Italian sheets for etchings, and old Dutch leaves for lithographs, and often came up with innovative ways of finding them when money was tight. In 1879, Whistler accepted a commission to do a suite of etchings in Venice, where he struck up a friendship with the expatriate American etcher Otto H. Bacher. Bacher wrote years later about how Whistler often "wandered among the old, musty, secondhand book-shops, buying all the old books that had a few blank pages which he cut out for his printing," and how he exulted in his finds. "In London, you would have to pay a shilling a sheet for paper of this kind," he crowed of his acquisitions.

Bacher told how he had once come across a quantity of old paper bound in twine outside a junk shop and called his friend in to see the cache when he got back to his apartment. "He was quite impressed and immediately wanted all of it," and was so determined to make a deal that the famed artist offered a print he had recently produced in return, one that Bacher sold years later to the Metropolitan Museum of Art, in New York. "Whistler used the paper which he acquired at this time for pulling rare proofs. It had the rich mellow color of age with rare old watermarks delicately impressed upon its surface. Some sheets had been written upon in Italian script. Anything which had been left on by age, particularly if it were written, did not hinder him in its use, but added more to its charm."

For Whistler, the goal was to create original art of uncommon beauty; for Mark Hofmann, the motivation was to perpetrate fraud on a brazen scale. Had the Library of Congress paid the $1.5 million he was asking, it would have ranked as one of the most expensive sheets of paper ever sold, but it was hardly aberrational, and would not have stood very long as a record. Much higher prices have been paid since then, with the demand for exceptional items remaining steady, uninterrupted even by the worst economic downturn to maim the world economy since the Great Depression of the 1930s. And the enthusiasm has been apparent in a wide variety of genres.

In 2006, a man described as "a very advanced and sophisticated East Coast collector" of currency paid $2.3 million for a $1,000 American silver certificate printed in 1890, one of only two in the series believed to remain in existence. Among baseball card collectors, the Holy Grail is the T206 Honus Wagner rarity issued by the American Tobacco Company in 1910 as an advertising insert for packages of cigarettes, but quickly removed from circulation at the behest of the popular Pittsburgh Pirates slugger whose likeness it featured. Of the fifty or sixty to have survived, one example in particular—perfectly preserved for decades in its original transparent packaging, but a scrap of chromolithographed cardboard all the same—commands enormous prices whenever it shows up in the marketplace, making headlines in 1991 when hockey great Wayne Gretzky and an associate paid $451,000 to own the card, and again in 2007 when a California collector acquired it privately for $2.8 million. Another Wagner card in lesser condition—but still gorgeous in the eyes of collectors—sold for $2.1 million in an online auction in April 2013.

Collectors of postage stamps, known as philatelists, are not coy about the sums they are willing to ante up, either. Unlike currency, which circulates continuously until worn to tatters and then is quietly withdrawn, postage stamps exist for a single use and are "canceled" with a postmark whenever they are sent through the mails. Stamps are produced by the billions worldwide, their final disposition usually being the trash, but given the care and craftsmanship that often characterize their design, they have tremendous appeal as social artifacts. Prices for some of the most coveted prizes to change hands in recent years include $3.8 million paid in 1993 for a pair of rarities printed in 1847 on Mauritius, a British colony in the Indian Ocean; $2.3 million in 1996 for a unique Swedish stamp known as the Tre Skilling Banco, printed in 1855 on yellow-orange stock, not green, as intended; and $930,000 in 1988 for an 1868 one-penny American stamp depicting a portrait of Benjamin Franklin, with an embossed pattern of tiny squares called a Z-Grill, which survives in just two known specimens.

When introduced to the world by the British government in 1840, adhesive postage stamps were a novelty, and came as the result of an unprecedented effort to streamline an antiquated postal system that had relied, since the seventeenth century, on private vendors to deliver the mails. The procedure taken for granted today—paying modest flat rates in advance to send articles through the mails—was unheard of before Sir Rowland Hill, a former schoolteacher who became a greatly esteemed social reformer, came up with a solution made possible by the availability of inexpensive paper. In a famous report from 1837, *Post Office Reform, Its Importance and Practicability,* Hill described "small stamped detached labels—say about an inch square—which, if prepared with a glutinous wash on the back, may be attached without a wafer." Three years later, a stamp featuring a portrait of Queen Victoria was introduced, and the price—it is known to collectors today as the Penny Black—provided sufficient postage to mail a letter anywhere in the British Isles weighing up to half an ounce.

A far more recent development in the field of paper ephemera is the emergence of the comic book, a distinctively American form of mass-market entertainment that did not even exist before the 1930s. Because the target readership for these "low-brow" amusements has always been adolescent males, they have tended, like children's books, to be "read to death," and since they are printed on newsprint that is fragile and prone to decay, condition has always been a concern, which places a high premium on "mint" rarities whenever they appear on the market.

First to reach the seven-figure mark was a "near pristine" copy of *Action Comics* No. 1, the June 1938 debut appearance of Superman, to a

New York collector for $1 million on February 22, 2010. Just three days later, a fine copy of the May 1939 first appearance of Batman (*Detective Comics* No. 27) commanded $1,075,000; a month after that, another copy of *Action Comics* No. 1—one that had been stored inside the covers of a movie magazine for fifty years and shielded from heat and light—brought $1.5 million. In November 2011, yet another copy of what by then had indisputably become the "black tulip" of comic book collectibles—one formerly owned by the Hollywood actor Nicolas Cage—was sold for $2.16 million, or more than twenty-one million times its original newsstand price of ten cents and considerably more than the $150,000 Cage had paid for it in 1997. Reported stolen from the actor's house in 2000, the copy was found in an abandoned storage locker in California's San Fernando Valley in April 2011.

In the realm of manuscripts, the competition is just as fierce, and the prices people are willing to pay even greater, since the materials by definition are one of a kind, not mass-produced. On May 22, 2003, Bruce Kovner, founder of the hedge fund Caxton Associates, in New York, paid $3.48 million for the 465-page working draft of Ludwig van Beethoven's Ninth Symphony, adding it to 138 other musical high spots he donated, en bloc, to the Juilliard School of Music three years later. The extraordinary collection included holographic scores, sketches, and proofs of major works by Brahms, Schumann, Schubert, Chopin, Stravinsky, Bach, Liszt, Ravel, Copland, and Mozart and was acquired over an eleven-year period. "Clearly in some sense it was almost a primitive reverence for the thing that was created by a composer," Kovner, an amateur pianist and chairman of the Juilliard board of directors, said of his motivation to gather such unique materials. "It's kind of like an icon."

On February 9, 2009, another collector paid $3.44 million for the four-page draft of a speech Abraham Lincoln delivered in 1864 at the White House, following his reelection to a second term; in December of that year, a 1787 letter written by George Washington to his nephew, on the subject of the ratification of the Constitution, fetched $3.2 million. Early in 2010, an anonymous benefactor acquired, for the Bibliothèque Nationale, in Paris, the manuscript memoirs of Giacomo Girolamo Casanova de Seingalt, the eighteenth-century Venetian lothario known as Casanova.

Comprising thirty-seven hundred pages of yellowing sheets and written entirely in French, the papers had been owned since 1821 by the F. A. Brockhuas publishing company, in Germany, and were once thought to have been destroyed in World War II; they were later found safely stored in a bank vault. Though the purchase price was not disclosed at the time—a figure of 5 million was widely rumored—recent reports have placed the figure more precisely at 7.2 million. While certainly a considerable sum either way, it remains dwarfed nonetheless by the $47.9 million paid at Christie's in London on December 8, 2009, for a drawing made between 1508 and 1511 by Raffaello Sanzio, the Italian master of the Renaissance better known as Raphael. Called "Head of a Muse," the sketch was used as the basis for a figure in the *Parnassus,* one of four frescoes commissioned by Pope Julius II to decorate the Stanza della Segnatura, in the Vatican, and executed at the same time that Michelangelo was painting the ceiling of the Sistine Chapel.

Though not in the same league as the work of master artists, but occupying a respectable niche of their own, are original prints by major photographers. Unlike daguerreotypes, which are positive images fixed on silver-coated copper plates, and unique in each instance, photographic prints are made from negatives in multiple copies on specially formulated paper. Through 2012, the most money bid at auction for a photograph was $2.9 million, in 2006, for a copy of Edward Steichen's *The Pond—Moonlight,* a modernist image dating to 1904 and consigned to Sotheby's by the Metropolitan Museum of Art, which owns one of the two other known original copies. At the same auction, a West Coast dealer paid $2.83 million for two photographs Alfred Stieglitz made of the artist Georgia O'Keeffe. In February 2010, a bid of $1,082,500 was hammered down for a signed copy of Edward Weston's famed *Nautilus,* which had been purchased directly from the California photographer in 1925 for $10; a copy of *Nude,* another well-known Weston photograph, sold for $1,609,000 in 2008.

Since the very nature of ephemeral objects is that they are not meant to be forever, those that do escape disposal or incineration gradually acquire an aura of significance and are prized as relics from bygone eras. While putting the finishing touches on the first draft of this book, I learned about a graphic artist and professional designer from Tucson, Arizona, named John Grossman, who over thirty-five years had gathered 250,000 examples of the ephemera genre, rare items as diverse and varied as old calendars, cigar box labels, trading cards, valentines, greeting cards, calling cards, postcards, theater tickets, paper dolls, sheet music, hand fans—even grocery bags—and placed them all on long-term deposit at the Winterthur Museum, in Delaware. The library director at the museum, E. Richard McKinstry, told me that Grossman had acquired, on average, about twenty items a day over three decades of determined collecting. "Because it was ephemeral, so much has disappeared, and there are no examples left of so many things. So what has survived is remarkable—and only because so much of it was beautifully done that a few people did keep some of it."

For Grossman, the motivation was partly professional—he and his wife, Carolyn, were artists and graphic designers based in San Francisco for many years—but also visceral. The one inflexible rule Grossman applied over the years of his activity was that every item he acquired—and he bought from dealers, individuals, shows, and, when the technology arrived, online—represent the process of chromolithography as practiced between 1820 and 1920, the period when multicolor printing emerged as a creative way to promote goods and services. A good deal of the appeal for him was the "freshness and the unusual quality" of the artwork, which depicts a rich variety of customs, attitudes, and ideals of Victorian and Edwardian times in the United States and England.

One high spot in the collection is the first commercially produced Christmas card, commissioned in 1843 by the English artist and designer Sir Henry Cole. An album assembled in 1887 to celebrate the fiftieth year of Queen Victoria's reign contains several thousand chromolithographs picturing English life in the late nineteenth century; it weighs forty-one pounds. Prior to shipping their archive off to Delaware from Arizona in an eighteen-wheel tractor-trailer, the Grossmans had stored everything in twenty-nine legal-size fire safes and flat files, each weighing about 850 pounds when fully loaded. "When we moved out to Tucson from California, we were able to find a very large house," Grossman told me. "Everything out here is pretty much on concrete slabs," so there was no risk of having a building collapse on top of them from the sheer weight of their treasures. In February 2013, the Winterthur announced it had purchased the collection from the Grossmans for an undisclosed sum it acknowledged to be "the largest single gift purchase" in the museum's history.

———

WHAT HAS PROVEN over time to be the most sought-after sheet of printed paper of them all—and since it exists in more than one copy, uniqueness is not the driving impulse—is a first printing of the Declaration of Independence, issued on July 4, 1776, by order of the Second Continental Congress and hastily produced through that momentous night by the Philadelphia printer John Dunlap in a run estimated to have numbered no more than two hundred broadsides. Of twenty-six known to have survived into the twenty-first century—four previously unrecorded copies have come to light since the Bicentennial year of 1976—all but four are the property of government repositories, museums, historical societies, or research libraries.

The most money paid to date for a Dunlap Declaration came in August 2000, when the noted television producer Norman Lear and the Silicon Valley software mogul David Hayden together bid $8.14 million in an online auction conducted by Sotheby's for a copy said to have been found eleven years earlier, tucked in the back of an antique

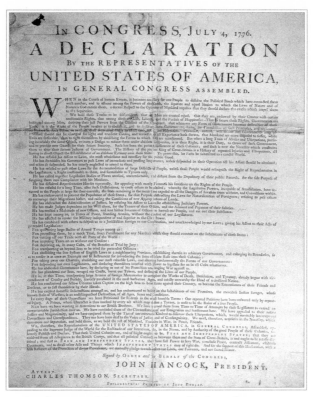

*A Dunlap copy of the Declaration of Independence.*

picture frame. The identity of the individual purported to have bought
the painting, for $4 at a country flea market outside Philadelphia, has
never been disclosed, leading some skeptical observers—myself admit-
tedly among them—to question the tidiness of such a vague story.
Details released by Sotheby's publicists at the time took pains to point
out that the lucky finder had admired the old frame, not the dreary
picture itself, which was why he disassembled it and found what was
hidden inside.

"The painting was trashed," the auction house further asserted, and
"so too was the frame when its owner decided it was crude and uninter-
esting; the document was kept only as a curiosity." The antiques dealer
was never identified, either, cutting off yet another link in what might
have established a traceable chain of custody. Because authenticity of
the document itself was never in doubt—it was said, in fact, to be a
superior copy—and with no recorded copies known to be missing, the
sale went forward as scheduled and the document found a new home.
Whether some small-town historical society may at some point have
had the copy tucked safely away in a cabinet of rarely used archives,
misfiled decades earlier and never properly cataloged in the first place—
and thus ripe for surreptitious removal—will never be known, though
such discoveries are not uncommon and frequently occur.

One recent instance, in fact, of a document resurfacing precisely
in this manner came on the eve of Independence Day in 2009, and,
amazingly enough, it involved yet another unrecorded copy of the
Dunlap broadside, spotted by an American bookseller doing research
in England at the National Archives. Reported to be in near-pristine
condition, the folded sheet was found nested among a passel of letters
written by American colonists during the Revolution and thought to
have been intercepted by British warships on patrol off the East Coast.
Once in England, the seized materials were promptly filed away and
not consulted again for decades. Their chance discovery brought to
three the number of first-issue Declarations held in England, the other
two having been dispatched to London in 1776 by General William
Howe.

Speculation quickly spread in the collecting world that this unexpected embarrassment of riches might tempt the British government
to sell what, to all intents and purposes, was a redundant item in its
holdings. "I'm sure if an American institution wanted to borrow it, we

would consider lending it," a spokesman told the *Daily Mail,* but otherwise the document would remain where it was. "This is an incredibly exciting find," another official told the *Guardian.* "The Declaration of Independence is effectively America's birth certificate, making it one of the seminal documents in world history." So once again, a single sheet of paper—one that exists in multiple copies, no less—was deemed to be priceless.

In 1975, the Library of Congress arranged to bring seventeen of the surviving Dunlap copies to Washington for close study by a team of experts headed by the eminent scholar and historian of book history Frederick Goff. An examination of the paper revealed slight variations in some of the copies, indicating that corrections were made pretty much on the fly, thus enabling the scholars to establish an order in which they probably came off the press. They also determined that twelve of the sheets bear Dutch watermarks, and were probably selected for the simple reason that they represented the best stock available. Closer study of the chain lines showed a slightly askew orientation of the printed text, suggesting "the urgency which prevailed that evening in Dunlap's printing office." Evidence of smearing indicated that the sheets were folded quickly and sent on their way before the ink was completely dry.

On July 8, the first public reading was made, in Philadelphia, by John Nixon, a lieutenant colonel in the local militia. The first public reading in Massachusetts was delivered in Worcester on July 14, by Isaiah Thomas, then it was proclaimed four days later in Boston from the balcony of the Old State House. At every stop along the way, the text was printed in local newspapers—some twenty-nine different publications in July alone—and reproduced in other broadside editions, most of which have long since disappeared. Over time, three-quarters of the Dunlap copies were lost. If an antiquarian sensibility was present, it was not applied in the majority of instances. Some, surely, were kept as mementos by those who had access to them—the copy read by John Nixon was presented by his heirs to Independence National Historical Park, in Philadelphia, in 1951; an upper fragment of what remained of General Washington's copy was given to the Library of Congress—while others either fell apart through improper handling or were simply lost or discarded through indifference or ignorance. The pair sent to London by General Howe, as well as the third English copy that surfaced in 2009 after spending 233 years in obscurity, have remained in single repositories.

Eight months before he died, in 1826, Thomas Jefferson called the Declaration of Independence "this holy bond of our union," its words so sacred that they are taught to every American schoolchild, a good number of us required to know them all "by heart" back when memorization was not frowned upon by educators. As a document of record, the Declaration marks the precise point in time at which the United States of America came into existence as a nation, and the handwritten copy on parchment in Washington, D.C., is among the top tourist attractions in the nation's capital. Encased in an apocalypse-proof cabinet, the "engrossed" copy, as it is known, is indeed unique, having been the only copy signed by the fifty-six delegates to the Second Continental Congress. But because those signatures were collected over a period of weeks after ratification, it is second in line of precedence, with the distinction of being first going to the copies printed in haste through a hot summer night by John Dunlap and sent off on their date with destiny by horseback.

IN THE COZY WORLD of antiquarian book and document collecting, it is fair to say that Kenneth W. Rendell enjoys a certain standing among those who have a particular passion for historical manuscripts. For close to fifty years, the Massachusetts native has built a reputation as the go-to guy for those in search of the choicest items, with a client list that has included Malcolm Forbes, Armand Hammer, and Queen Elizabeth II of England. Along the way, he established himself as an international authority in the field of document verification, making headlines when he exposed as hoaxes the fabricated diaries of Adolf Hitler and Jack the Ripper. A bookseller, too, Rendell was the person Microsoft founder Bill Gates turned to when he decided it was time to build a personal library that is rumored to include some of the highest of high spots to come on the market in recent years.

A side of Rendell not so well known is his activity as a collector of every manner of paper object relating to World War II. While very few dealers are private collectors on a grandly aggressive scale, Rendell is one of the notable exceptions, so driven to document the full sweep of the conflict that he built a ten-thousand-square-foot fortress of a building in a Boston suburb to house it all. Known as the Museum of World War II, the collection is viewable only by invitation or appointment. Rendell told me that he became a collector of these materials in the 1960s because he was unable to find buyers for objects that he knew were of historical significance. "It began with letters and documents I was buying to sell, but there wasn't any interest from anyone, so I began to keep them for myself. The big thing collectors very frequently don't understand—and people in museums and libraries don't always understand, either—is the value of opportunity. I saw what was in front of me, and I did not hesitate for a second." The range of materials he bought was extensive—ration books, propaganda, magnificently evocative posters, cables, dispatches, communiqués, newspapers, magazines, wartime leaflets, and prisoner-of-war diaries.

As he began to appreciate the distinctiveness of his holdings, Rendell started adding material objects, a quest that, to date, has added seven thousand artifacts that include weapons of every caliber and description, five Enigma code machines, numerous battle flags, uniforms of all the combatants, decorations, parachutes, even a Sherman tank. Two truly extraordinary items are the giant swastika and bronze eagle that once decorated Hitler's speaker's stand at the Luitpold Arena, which Rendell acquired from the estate of General George S. Patton.

I asked Rendell to give me a short list of the works on paper he keeps in his "collector's vault," and he ticked off a jaw-dropping inventory of documents he described as "iconic," but the one he wanted me to see and handle for myself was the draft copy of the Munich Agreement annotated by Adolf Hitler and Neville Chamberlain on September 23, 1938, before it was sent out to be typed in final form. This was the agreement in which Chamberlain agreed to the Nazi annexation of the Sudetenland, in a single stroke giving the word *appeasement* a new context in world history. Rendell bought the draft from the son of Neville Henderson, the British ambassador who attended the discussions and took it when he realized it was going to be discarded. To meet the purchase price, Rendell sold a minority interest he had in an antiquities business. "It was more money than I had in those days, but it was an opportunity I knew I would never see again. So when you ask me about the power of a piece of paper, I say the power of the document you are now holding in your hands is staggering. This is the document that starts World War II."

# 12

## On Paper

Without a minute Diary, your Travels, will be no better than the flight of Birds, throughout the Air. Whatever you write preserve. I have burned Bushells of my Silly notes, in fitts of Impatience and humiliation, which I would now give anything to recover. "These fair creatures are thyself." And would be more useful and influential in Self-Examination than all the Sermons of the Clergy.

　　　—John Adams to his grandsons
　　　　as they prepared to join their parents in England, 1815

CHARTERED IN 1791, during George Washington's first term as president of the United States, the Massachusetts Historical Society was the brainchild of the Reverend Jeremy Belknap, a Harvard graduate and Congregational minister whose single-minded purpose in life was to document the American experience. As an amateur scholar, Belknap achieved a modicum of renown with a painstakingly researched history of New Hampshire that drew heavily on obscure materials he had uncovered during the twenty years he spent as a village pastor in the Granite State, much of it dismissed by others as rubbish and not worth saving. "I am willing even to scrape a dunghill, if I may find a jewel at the bottom," he declared boldly of his research method. Issued in three volumes between 1784 and 1792, his history earned the esteem of Alexis de Tocqueville, who wrote that "readers will find in Belknap more general ideas and more forceful thinking than in any other American historian to date," while a duly impressed Noah Webster anointed him the "American Plutarch."

Belknap's zeal to preserve every manner of written artifact was decades ahead of its time, and he was clear about the way he wanted the nation's first historical society to go about the task. "We intend to be an *active,* not a *passive,* literary body," he wrote in a letter to a colleague who had pledged assistance, "not to lie waiting, like a bed of oysters, for the tide to flow in upon us, but to *seek* and *find,* to *preserve* and *communicate,* literary intelligence, especially in the historical way." One foresighted strategy was to encourage prominent people of the day to donate their family papers, a precedent that led to the acquisition of numerous domestic archives, most spectacularly four generations of documents maintained by the Adams family of Brighton and Quincy, as well as those of such founding New England dynasties as the Winthrops, Mathers, Cabots, and Lodges. He was similarly keen on acquiring the papers of clergymen, entrepreneurs, and everyday people like Peter Brown, a soldier at the Battle of Bunker Hill whose letter to his mother on June 25, 1775, has been described as "the fullest account that survives of the feelings and observations of a participant in the ranks."

Though its name suggests that it is the repository of a single state, the Massachusetts Historical Society set a mandate for itself that embraced the entire country, and as pretty much the only game in town during this formative period of the early republic, Belknap's labor of love established the foundation of an institution that today numbers among its holdings some twelve million pieces of manuscript, most of them coming as gifts, the vast majority in the form of letters, diaries, notebooks, journals, sketches, or drawings. I have over the past several decades been shown through the vaults by two of the institution's chief librarians, the first time in 1988, when I was starting research for what seven years later would become *A Gentle Madness.*

My guide at that time was Stephen T. Riley, then the director emeritus of the MHS and esteemed by colleagues as one of the outstanding librarians of his generation. Among the treasures Riley showed me that day were George Washington's Newburgh Address of 1783; Cotton Mather's seventeenth-century "Biblia Americana," an unpublished ecclesiastical history comprising 4,500 manuscript pages; the holographic copy of Richard Henry Dana's *Two Years Before the Mast;* a number of Revolutionary-era documents in the hand of Paul Revere; and the detailed journal the nineteenth-century historian Francis Parkman kept while researching what became his magnum opus, *The Oregon Trail.* Riley selected as his favorite item of them all a pair of letters

exchanged between Abraham Lincoln and Edward Everett immediately following their respective addresses at Gettysburg on November
19, 1863. "I should be glad, if I could flatter myself, that I came as near
to the central idea of the occasion in two hours, as you did in two
minutes," Everett wrote the president within hours of their remarks.
Lincoln's reply, posted the next day from the Executive Mansion, was
magnanimous. "In our respective parts yesterday, you could not have
been excused to make a short address, nor I a long one. I am pleased
to know that, in your judgment, the little I did say was not entirely a
failure."

My host twenty years later was Peter Drummey, a young librarian on the staff when I first visited, by this time the Stephen T. Riley
librarian, appointed to that position in 2004. Like Riley before him,
Drummey lives with paper; the older it is, the better. His passion for
the task is palpable, his knowledge of the materials encyclopedic. In
the acknowledgments to his Pulitzer Prize–winning biography of John
Adams, the historian David McCullough paid tribute to the "incom-
parably knowledgeable Librarian of the Massachusetts Historical
Society, Peter Drummey," for helping him navigate his way through
the collections. When I interviewed McCullough in 2004, for *Every
Book Its Reader*—we met on that occasion, in fact, at the Massachusetts Historical Society—he told me that what impressed him so much
about Drummey was the dedication he has for placing in context every
document he retrieves from the stacks, and the way pivotal events and
great minds intersect across a quarter-millennium of American history through their interpretation. "It all comes alive in Peter's hands,"
McCullough said.

Drummey led my wife and me to the most secure area of the library,
an inner sanctum aptly named the "treasure vault." He directed our
attention first to a single sheet of paper that he declared straightaway
to be his personal favorite. A good-size document measuring twelve
inches by just under eight inches, the sheet bore creases where it had
been folded many decades earlier. "This is a letter by William Bradford, the first governor of Plymouth Colony, to John Winthrop, the
first governor of the Massachusetts Bay Colony," Drummey explained
and noted the date written to the left of the signature at the bottom:
April 11, 1638. "Plymouth is only forty miles south of here, but at the
time of the writing, they were independent colonies."

The main body of the letter discusses in a firm but cordial way a disputed border, a matter that remained unresolved, even though the two colonies had united the year before in a war against the Pequot Indians. At issue still was whether Scituate, considered by the Pilgrims to be the northernmost town in Plymouth Colony, actually lay within the bounds of Massachusetts Bay, and whether Hingham, settled by Massachusetts Bay, actually fell within territory assigned by the Crown to Plymouth. Bradford used the occasion to express mounting concern over whether the religious dissident Anne Hutchinson, who would be expelled from Massachusetts Bay shortly after the Antinomian Controversy of 1636–38, might move with her followers into Plymouth, and he asked Winthrop for more information about Mary Dyer, a supporter of Hutchinson who would die as a martyr to religious freedom in 1660.

All in all, it is a letter of some substance, penned in a tight, careful hand on a large sheet of rag paper, handmade in Europe, of course—as the establishment of the first paper mill in British North America was still fifty-two years away—and in remarkably good condition. The considered response Winthrop drafted for Bradford was summarized on the reverse side of the same letter, on which the recipient's address had been written but which otherwise was left blank. "Paper was very scarce in the colonies, not something to be wasted, so precious that

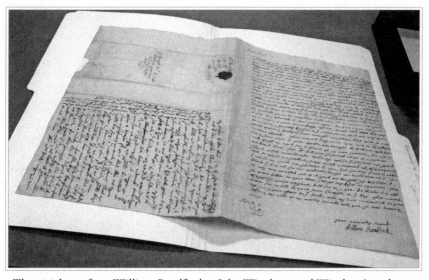

*The 1638 letter from William Bradford to John Winthrop and Winthrop's reply, on the same sheet of paper, in the collections of the Massachusetts Historical Society.*

an important exchange between two governors—two heads of state, really—would be written on a single sheet," Drummey said.

"This profound respect for paper is by no means restricted to the seventeenth century, either," Drummey continued, and he cited the example of Horace Mann, who was a distinguished reformer, abolitionist, and politician in the 1800s. "Horace Mann was born in the small town of Franklin, Massachusetts, in 1796, and he was brought up in the frugality of the countryside. So when he writes out lectures or speeches, he'll do it on the back of a letter he has received, or something else that might be lying around, because no piece of paper goes unused. What you have so often with him are two different documents on one sheet of paper, more often than not unrelated to each other. It can be very problematic if you're an archivist: you go looking at one thing and wind up trying to decipher another. My point is that you may say William Bradford—that's the 1630s. I'm saying Horace Mann—1830s. It's still doing the same thing."

The respect early Americans had for paper was evident yet again in the next item Drummey had laid out, a small volume, bound in leather, that he identified as an early diary of John Adams. "It dates from 1755, when Adams graduated from Harvard and moved out to Worcester to be a schoolteacher." He invited me to pick up the fragile octavo and examine the pages. "Look how tight the writing is," he prodded, noting how Adams had written with extraordinary concision and economy. "Once again, paper is dear, so you write small. We have thousands of diaries in this building, probably hundreds from the time of the Revolution alone, and what is striking is that they are all little books just like this—and not an inch of space is wasted in any of them."

We then turned to another John Winthrop item, one far more famous than the response to William Bradford we had examined a few minutes earlier, this one showing the physical effects of continued consultation over the previous three centuries. "This has magnetized people for hundreds of years; everybody has handled and touched it," Drummey said, and he allowed me to go ahead and add my fingerprints to the vellum binding. It was one of the two surviving volumes of the journal Winthrop kept from the time he set sail from Yarmouth on the ship *Arbella,* in 1630, and maintained through 1649, the year of his death, by common consent the most important firsthand account relating to the earliest years of European settlement in North America.

"This is the third volume, at the end of Winthrop's life, and what I suggest you observe is how thoroughly the book has been read. Once you get into the meat of his descriptions, you can sense the number of people who have actually turned the pages of this volume; what you are looking at is the human effect on documents."

In 1984, Richard S. Dunn, a University of Pennsylvania historian and at that time the most recent editor of the Winthrop journal, described the problems a scholar encounters when beginning a project of this complexity. "This set of texts is surely the most baffling of all major early American documents to decipher or to edit," he wrote. "The handwriting in the two surviving volumes is notoriously hard to read, the ink is faded, the paper is often stained, worn, or torn, and the text is studded with marginalia, insertions, cancellations, and underscorings." Other scholars who worked directly with these texts over the decades have included William Hubbard and Cotton Mather, in the seventeenth century; Thomas Prince, Ezra Stiles, Jonathan Trumbull, and Jeremy Belknap in the eighteenth; and John Savage, in the nineteenth. Three separate editions preceded the 1984 effort—in 1790, 1825–26, and 1908. The second volume of the journal, containing 366 manuscript pages and the largest of the three, was destroyed in a fire at Savage's home in 1825, a grievous loss, although a modernized transcription he had made of the text survives to preserve some sense of the content. Twentieth-century historians who consulted the journal include Bernard Bailyn and Walter Muir Whitehill.

Once again, Winthrop's profound appreciation for paper is immediately apparent: when he formally began the chronicle of his great adventure to the New World on March 29, 1630, he started at the back of a journal he had already been using for other purposes. He simply flipped the volume upside down and wrote in reverse direction from the back, filling up all the pages before resuming his narrative with the now lost volume 2. Only volume 3—the copy I handled—began on paper that had not been written on previously.

As we moved away from this cubicle, Drummey paused to indicate an alcove that contained a teeming archive of correspondence, letter books, diaries, literary manuscripts, speeches, and assorted legal and business documents—some half a million pages of materials generated primarily by four generations of the Adams family—and took a moment to appreciate the enormousness of what is preserved in this

*A volume of John Quincy Adams's diary. "I cannot indulge myself the luxury of giving two hours a day to these two writers; but to live without having a Cicero and a Tacitus at hand seems to me as if it was a privation of one of my limbs."*

compact space. It begins with John Adams, the second president of the United States, and continues with his son, John Quincy Adams, the sixth president. Next come John Quincy's descendants, including his son Charles Francis Adams, the ambassador to Great Britain during the Civil War, in the third generation, followed, in the fourth, by Charles's sons, who included the author Henry Adams and the historian Brooks Adams.

The archive came to the MHS in 1956, and editing it for publication has occupied a team of textual scholars for more than half a century now, with fifty-two volumes published by Harvard University Press through 2010. A microfilm edition of the papers, issued in 608 reels before the move to digital preservation began in the 1990s, runs to more than five miles in length. But far more impressive than sheer size is the realization that this is arguably the most significant gathering of documentary material relating to one family to be found anywhere in the United States. "Of its kind, the collection known as the Adams Papers is beyond price and without peer," L. H. Butterfield, who served as editor-in-chief of the project during its earliest years, wrote. "No such assemblage of historical records touching so many aspects of American life over so long a period—just short of three centuries (1640–1920)—has ever been created and kept together by any other family in this country."

For Drummey, the personal impact of the archive is beyond words. "This is where history lives," he said simply. Certainly the best-known component is the 1,160 letters exchanged between John Adams and his wife, Abigail, from 1762 to 1801—they were the centerpiece resources for David McCullough's 2001 biography and for a greatly admired seven-part miniseries that aired on HBO in 2008—but there are other high spots equally as compelling, not least among them the two-way correspondence between John Adams and the man who succeeded him as president, Thomas Jefferson.

"The reason the Jefferson–Adams correspondence is so wonderful—and the reason we know it so well—is because John and Abigail kept every letter Jefferson wrote to them, and made copies of all the letters they sent to him. So we have both sides of the correspondence—and we have it here, in one collection of papers." And every bit as vital as the John–Abigail letters and the Jefferson–Adams letters is the diary kept by John Quincy Adams, begun in 1779, at the age of twelve, and maintained faithfully for close to seventy years. The final entry was made just a few weeks before Quincy Adams collapsed on the floor of the House of Representatives, in Washington, in 1848, dying two days later. L. H. Butterfield regarded the diary as "probably the most extensive and faithful record of its kind ever compiled." During one period of half a century, there are no breaks at all in the daily journal—365 entries a year, 366 during leap years—prompting Quincy Adams to complain, in one instance, that the marathon effort was "like the race of a man with a wooden leg after a horse," creating, in his irritated view, "a multiplication of books to no end and without end."

Comprising some fourteen thousand pages, the fifty-one volumes were first prepared for publication in a heavily truncated edition by John Quincy's son Charles Francis Adams (himself a committed diarist), and more recently in its entirety, as part of the ongoing collaboration with Harvard University Press. "This is another interesting thing about paper records, be it faithful letter writing or the keeping of a diary across many decades," Drummey said. "It is not simply a record, but a form of discipline. Someone who keeps a journal like this with an unbroken series of entries is doing a lot more than maintaining a diary. It represents so much of who he was. John Quincy Adams's diary was so famous that people would refer to it in his own lifetime. A question would come up about some obscure matter before Congress, and someone would say, 'Well, John Quincy Adams must have that in his diary.' And it was considered to be probative."

Before leaving the Adams Papers, we spent some time with two of the most frequently quoted letters from the archive: one from John to Abigail, announcing the formation of the new nation in Philadelphia, the other from Abigail to John, urging him in clear language to "remember the ladies" in whatever plans might be formulated for the new republic. Drummey also pointed out a number of letters that lacked the usual salutations—"my Dearest Friend"—not through any oversight but because they were written over several days for purposes of paper conservation—sometimes twice on the same day—until the entire surface was used up.

Drummey encouraged me to read aloud the letter from John, dated July 3, 1776, in which he discussed the momentous events of the previous day. "Adams thinks that July 2, the day they voted for independence, will be the one celebrated for generations to come, not when it was publicly declared," he said. "When this letter was written on July 3, the Declaration had already been drafted and approved—but it had not yet been set in type or printed. So here you have a person who is on the committee to write the Declaration of Independence, he's a direct participant, and what is most remarkable about this letter is that he predicts precisely the way the day will be remembered—only he's got the exact day wrong."

At this point I picked up the letter, ever so gently, and read into my digital voice recorder the following excerpt: "I am apt to believe that it will be celebrated, by succeeding Generations, as the great anniversary Festival. It ought to be commemorated, as the Day of Deliverance by solemn Acts of Devotion to God Almighty. It ought to be solemnized with Pomp and Parade, with Shews, Games, Sports, Guns, Bells, Bonfires and Illuminations from one End of this Continent to the other from this Time forward forever more." I took several photographs of the document and waited for Drummey to summarize what I had just held in my hands. "John Adams describes Independence Day exactly as we celebrate it," he said. "Only he doesn't know just yet that it is going to be the Fourth of July."

Though written privately to his beloved Abigail, it seemed clear to me that Adams was aiming for a much wider readership. "He's documenting everything for posterity," I said. "Exactly," Drummey replied, "and perfectly, too. Once again, this is a letter without an introduction, because he's writing to his wife more than once a day on the same sheet of paper. Notice that the handwriting is more compact, neater, and more controlled." The paper was smaller, too, than most of the others, undoubtedly a consequence of the shortages brought on by the war.

From the Adams Papers we turned to an archive of materials central to the life and career of Thomas Jefferson, including approximately 8,800 pieces of correspondence, of which 3,280 are letters written by Jefferson. Other materials include a number of journals Jefferson kept for more than fifty years, various legal papers, a catalog he compiled in 1782 of his personal library, and five hundred architectural drawings. It is, in fact, a larger collection of Jeffersoniana than the one held at the University of Virginia, in Charlottesville, an institution that the third president founded and where another considerable collection of his papers is preserved. The materials Drummey was about to show us had been given to the Massachusetts Historical Society in 1898 by Thomas Jefferson Coolidge of Boston, a great-grandson.

We began with a journal Jefferson kept on beautifully made rag paper that bears no formal title but is cataloged by the society as Thomas Jefferson's Farm Book, a generic way of identifying what is essentially a record of the minutiae that went into the operation and management of a considerable Southern estate—some 10,600 acres, according to the journal—from 1774 to 1824. How many hogs may have been slaughtered in a certain month, whatever repairs had to be made on the outbuildings, provisions that were purchased and the amounts paid, all the plowing, sowing, planting, and cutting activities that were performed, the crop forecasts, and the harvests realized—all are part of the seasonal chronicle.

"If you want to understand how a plantation operates at this point in American history, this is where you go," Drummey said. "Scholars today want to know how everyday life was lived; I won't say this is unique, but it's extraordinarily detailed." My wife was taken by an entry that itemizes the precise number of turns a water-powered grinding wheel made over a certain period of time. "He's an engineer, remember," Drummey said, "so he's fascinated by that stuff." I marveled at the excellence of Jefferson's handwriting. "And it sustains throughout his life," Drummey said. "The last letter he writes is as clear and as legible as the letters he writes as a young man." Also in the society's collection is a companion volume to the Farm Book called the Garden Book, in which Jefferson recorded the varieties of vegetables, fruits, flowers, and trees planted at Monticello and at Shadwell, a fourteen-hundred-acre tract along the Rivanna River that he inherited from his father, as well as data on sowing locations, harvesting dates, and weather conditions; it spans the years 1766 to 1824.

Of consuming interest to people who examine the Farm Book are the names and personal details of the many hundreds of tenant farmers and "servants" who tended Jefferson's fields and maintained his household. "The central dilemma of American history is on almost every page of this journal," Drummey said. "These are slaves that belong to Jefferson, and you can't disguise it. There are hundreds of people listed here." The journal—Jefferson refers to it as a "diary"—includes lists of the names and locations of his slaves, including Sally Hemings, who was determined through DNA testing in 1998 to have been the mother of a son by Jefferson, and of her other children, who are listed on numerous pages. There are also itemizations of the cloth, bedding, and food—generally fish, bread, and beef—that was distributed to the slaves. "It's all here, in his hand, and the record, again, is meticulous. It also includes data for Poplar Forest, the retreat he owned about eighty miles south of Monticello, and a number of other places that he owned as well."

Among other items Drummey showed us was paper money printed during the Revolution, a good deal of it designed by Paul Revere, and a sheet of stamps of various denominations issued by the British government in accordance with the Stamp Act of 1765, materials that would be regarded as ephemeral for the periods in which they were produced, and thus very rare today. "These revenue stamps are vanishingly small in number and almost impossible to find," he said. "Just about all of them were destroyed, most of them in anger by the colonists." How these examples managed to be preserved goes back to principles put in place when the historical society was established, in 1791. "The only person I can think of who made any effort to preserve them was our founder, Jeremy Belknap. He kind of got what it was all about—right from the beginning," Drummey said in summation, his presentation finally finished, a three-hour tour de force in every way. "You know," he said as we headed back downstairs to his office, "I sometimes wonder if you can love these documents too much; I say that because I haven't found one among the twelve million yet that bores me."

A VISIT TO the subterranean vaults of the Folger Shakespeare Library, in Washington, D.C., begins with the understanding that you are about to see an array of materials relating to England's national poet that is truly one of a kind, its core collection—the earliest editions of William Shakespeare—without peer in the world. Unlike other research libraries that are built around original manuscripts covering a multitude of diverse subjects—the Massachusetts Historical Society, in Boston, and the Harry Ransom Humanities Research Center, in Austin, being just two of many examples—or broad categories of exceedingly rare books such as those to be found at the Houghton Library of Harvard, the Beinecke Rare Book and Manuscript Library, at Yale, or the Special Collections Research Center, at the University of Chicago, the Folger came into existence in 1932 by virtue of a single transformative literary figure and his era.

In the years that followed, the library branched out, and its holdings today boast an archive of sixty thousand manuscripts and fifty thousand artworks on paper that are notably strong in the Elizabethan and Jacobean eras, plus 256,000 research-level volumes that are quite respectable in and of themselves. But the heart and soul remains William Shakespeare, and because nothing of substance survives in the playwright's hand—six signatures on a few legal documents preserved in England is all, and possibly a 148-line fragment of an unfinished play at the British Library—it is through printed books that his genius endures.

Today, the ownership of a copy of the 1623 London edition of *Mr. William Shakespeares Comedies, Histories, & Tragedies,* published in an edition believed to have numbered 750 copies and known as the First Folio, is the literary equivalent of having a personal copy of a Dunlap broadside of the Declaration of Independence. Like the Dun-

*Entryway to the subterranean treasure vault of the Folger Shakespeare Library, in Washington, D.C.*

lap broadside, the First Folio is not overly scarce—232 copies survive worldwide—but only a handful are in private hands, making competition for those that remain keen on the infrequent occasion that one is offered for sale. The book contains thirty-six plays, half of which had not previously appeared in print, among them *The Tempest, Macbeth, Twelfth Night, Measure for Measure, Love's Labour's Lost,* and *Antony and Cleopatra.* The heroic endeavor to collect all of these works in one volume was undertaken shortly after Shakespeare's death, in 1616, by John Heminge and Henry Condell, two of the dramatist's colleagues from the King's Men group of players. The texts, they asserted unequivocally in the extended title of the book, were rendered "according to the true original copies," qualifying them for what can be argued was an authorized edition of the works.

An anonymous buyer bidding by telephone in 2001, later disclosed to be Paul G. Allen, of Seattle, paid $6.16 million for a copy being sold in New York by Christie's, surpassing by close to $1 million what would be paid for a First Folio at Sotheby's in London five years later. The spirited interest in this copy was due partly to the fact that it is essentially "complete," meaning it has no missing pages; partly for the seventeenth-century blind-tooled brown calf binding over pasteboard; and partly for an extraordinary provenance that includes prior owner-ship, through several generations, by the poet John Dryden's family.

Yet as breathtaking in every respect as that one copy may be—and I handled it several times when it was the property of the late Abel E. Berland, a Chicago bookman I wrote about in *Patience & Fortitude*—it is still just one copy of this great book. Multiply the impact it has on the beholder by eighty-two and what you have is the Folger Shakespeare Library collection of First Folios, all of them shelved behind a barred steel door of the type you would expect to see at Fort Knox, lying flat on their sides and appearing for all the world, as I mused the first time I saw them, in the early 1990s, like so many bars of gold bullion.

The founding spirit of the library was Henry Clay Folger, a one-time president and chairman of the Standard Oil Company of New York, and his wife, Emily Jordan Folger. In a brief sketch he wrote of himself in 1909 for Amherst College, his alma mater, Folger noted that, since he had no offspring of his own "to brag about"—the couple was childless—he took enormous pride instead in the collection of Shakespeariana he and his wife had assembled that was "probably the largest and finest in America and perhaps in the world." He credited an inspirational lecture given at Amherst thirty years earlier by Ralph Waldo Emerson with sparking what would become his lifelong obses-sion. Equally engaged by the hunt, his wife was sufficiently motivated during this time of frenetic pursuit to write a master's thesis for Vassar, her alma mater, titled "The True Text of Shakespeare." Together they had spared no expense or energy in their quest to acquire as many First Folios as possible, buying up what today comprises more than a third of all the copies that remain in the world; the British Library, in London, by contrast, has five; the Bodleian Library, at Oxford, just one.

"This is our reading copy," Stephen Enniss, the Folger librarian, joked as he guided me into the vault for my second visit there in fif-teen years, indicating a volume not nearly as luminous as some of the others—most spectacularly a copy bearing the prior-ownership signa-ture of Isaac Jaggard, the London printer of the book, and regarded, unofficially, as "number 1" in the world among First Folios—but a First Folio all the same. While these books are the undisputed centerpiece of the library, there is also an outstanding collection of Shakespeare

plays that were printed in smaller quarto editions, many of them unauthorized piracies published well before the appearance of the collected
works and thus, in those instances, the earliest surviving texts.

In a famous passage in the First Folio directed to the "great variety
of readers," Heminge and Condell dismissed the unauthorized quartos as "stolen, and surreptitious copies, maimed, and deformed by the
frauds and stealthes of injurious impostors." Sold unbound and often
read to tatters, they are among the most ephemeral books of the age
and exist today in very low numbers. In the absence of any surviving manuscripts, the quartos offer the earliest known evidence of what
Shakespeare might actually have written and, just as pertinent, what
probably appeared in performance on the early modern English stage.

Scholars also find the quartos useful when seeking evidence of variations in the texts. Easily the scarcest of these—indeed, it is the rarest
Shakespeare quarto in the world, surviving in a single copy—is the
1594 *Titus Andronicus* Henry Clay Folger bought in 1905 for £2,000
from a Swedish postal worker who had found it among some items
he had inherited from his father, wrapped in two eighteenth-century
Dutch lottery tickets. How this quarto made its way from England
to Sweden, why it was wrapped in antique gaming certificates from
Holland, and how it came into the hands of an obscure civil servant
remains a tantalizing mystery.

Before he was appointed librarian of the Folger, in January 2009,
Stephen Enniss (see endnote) was head of the Manuscript, Archives,
and Rare Book Library at Emory University, in Atlanta, where he
was responsible for a comprehensive collection of materials that has
been growing by leaps and bounds, becoming very quickly—with
the help of millions of dollars bequeathed by Robert W. Woodruff, a
longtime president of the Coca-Cola Company—one of several outstanding research centers specializing in twentieth-century literature.
While certainly rich in printed books—the acquisition, in 2004, of a
75,000-volume library of twentieth-century poetry, said to be the finest
collection of its kind in the world, is but one example—the strength
of the Emory collections lies in the manuscripts and archives of such
figures as William Butler Yeats, James Dickey, Flannery O'Connor,
Seamus Heaney, Ted Hughes, and Anthony Hecht.

"It has been quite a remarkable transition for me in many ways,"
Enniss said when I asked him to compare Emory with the Folger. "I've

moved from a university special collection to being the librarian for an independent research library. I've moved from a collection that was largely focused on manuscripts to a collection whose greatest strength is in rare books. I've moved from collections that were oriented on the twentieth and twenty-first century to collections focused around the sixteenth and seventeenth centuries. I've moved from a collection that measured authors' archives in linear feet to a collection where the most central author left behind no manuscripts whatsoever."

What both libraries do have in common is that each is committed to the preservation of cultural achievement as it has been recorded on paper, though my purpose on this visit to the Folger was to consider not the content of these materials, but the medium upon which they have been transmitted, and to spend some time in a quiet area on the third floor of the library that is responsible for ensuring their physical well-being. There I met with J. Franklin Mowery, an internationally respected innovator in the use of various paper restoration strategies, who served as head of the Werner Gundersheimer Conservation Laboratory from 1977 until 2011, when he established a private practice that includes as clients art galleries, museums, libraries, dealers, and private collectors. Mowery graciously offered to demonstrate some of the conservation techniques he had helped pioneer, but before he did that, there was the incidental matter of four books he had lying side by side on a worktable in the laboratory—each of them a First Folio brought up from the vault in the basement.

"This is what we play with every day," Mowery quipped, and he allowed me to handle and photograph each one. These particular copies were being examined as part of a world census then being conducted of all First Folios. "I'm up to fifty-six," he said, adding that he expected to be finished with all eighty-two Folger copies in another month. "What is required is a complete physical description of every folio, a collation of each volume. What I'm doing right now is making a very detailed description of each of the bindings, their structures, and their tooling." Because the vast majority of books in the Folger collections were printed in the years before wood pulp was introduced, the quality of the stock is generally good. The First Folios were all printed on imported paper of decent quality, most likely from Normandy. "The beauty of working at this place, as opposed to next door at the Library of Congress, is that most of the paper in this library is generally superb to start with," Mowery said. "We deal here with sixteenth-century, seventeenth-century, eighteenth-century materials, and the paper is wonderful—all of it is rag paper."

In instances where the goal is to repair a tear invisibly, Mowery said his material of choice is an ultrathin tissue that he developed in the 1980s based on Japanese principles of hand papermaking. For pulp, he favors a mixture of 70 percent mitsumata and 30 percent kozo, the former for its long fibers, the latter for strength. "I called it gossamer tissue, because, literally, it floats," he said, and thereupon mended a tear in a seventeenth-century book to show me how it works. "The beauty of Japanese paper is that it's remarkably strong for its thinness; you can't find anything even remotely like that in anything else." Mowery said he had been inspired to develop the tissue by the woeful state of a 654-page illuminated manuscript that had been given to the Folger in 1945 and was in dire need of aggressive conservation.

Known as the *Trevelyon Miscellany* of 1608, the volume was the handiwork of Thomas Trevelyon, an obscure Englishman about whom very little is known except that he produced, entirely by hand, two books of the early seventeenth century consisting of material he had copied and adapted from a wide variety of graphic sources, and which together offer an uncommon view of everyday life in Elizabethan and Jacobean England. The other Trevelyon miscellany, which dates to 1616, was acquired by the late J. Paul Getty Jr. for the remarkable library he formed at Wormsely House in Buckinghamshire northwest of London.

Badly in need of attention when it came to the Folger, the 1608 miscellany remained untouched for fifty years, waiting, as Mowery put it, for technology to advance sufficiently to address its specific needs. The gossamer tissue he developed proved most useful in this case, though some of the sheets required additional intervention. One approach involved a process Mowery learned in Germany, in which sheets of decaying paper are split into two longitudinal sections, then reinforced with another sheet of paper that is inserted between the halves and reassembled.

To demonstrate another technique in his arsenal known as "leaf casting," Mowery walked me over to a corner of the laboratory where he had been working on a collection of domestic documents known as the Papers of the Ferrers Family of Tamworth Castle. Acquired by

*Harvard College Library charging book for 1786, being restored at Weissman Preservation Center, in Cambridge, Massachusetts.*

the Folger in 1977, the archive dates from 1500 to the mid-seventeenth century "and was in horrific condition when it got here, moldy, falling apart, and could not even be handled by the catalogers. Nobody really knows what's in here, even now." The equipment Mowery was about to use included a custom-made electronic system built to his specifications in the 1980s, using as principal components a vintage digital camera and an old Atari computer that runs on five-inch floppy disks. "A friend of mine who was an oceanographer and a computer whiz and is now a professor at MIT helped me pull this together. It's better than any other system out there, guaranteed." The electronics work in tandem with a modified water basin, which he identified as his leaf caster but to my eyes looked like a basic sink.

"It's a simple papermaking machine is what it is. We have this very fancy deionized, recalcified water system, and it will get filled up with filtered water. The document gets placed on a screen, and you lay out as many pages as you can at a time to be efficient." One severely damaged leaf had already been placed on the screen, along with a couple of other fragments. Mowery then made a digital image that indicated, by way of black pixels, the areas to be filled. After measuring the thickness of the paper, he determined how much slurry he needed. "It fills in all the holes—I can leaf-cast this in five minutes—and I can lay out as many pages as I am able to fill into this screen." Given the lengths to which the Folger and other research libraries go to preserve single sheets of paper—I observed similar procedures at National Archives II, in College Park; the Getty Research Institute, in Los Angeles; and the Weissman Preservation Center, at Harvard University—I asked Mowery if he agreed that it is the content, not the medium itself, that makes what he was doing so special. He was amused by the question—how do we measure value, after all, when it comes to paper?—but gave it some thought all the same.

"So you're asking if these are sheets of paper that are valuable in and of themselves? I guess the answer is no—probably not. But that is a very interesting point you raise, because what we do often find here when we examine very old printed books—and we have, what, a quarter of a million volumes or so of them in the library altogether?—are old sheets that had been discarded as valueless, and were used as waste to reinforce the bindings of other books. Instead of throwing them away, they would reuse them in the structure of the books for support. The material itself was valuable and not to be wasted; the writing, the printing, was irrelevant at that point. We run across these things all the time—and this happens everywhere."

Mowery cited an exhibition he helped organize in 2009 called *The Curatorial Eye: Discoveries from the Folger Vault* that included some obscure religious and political tracts from the seventeenth century printed on single sheets of inexpensive paper in France and the Low Countries he found while disassembling some of the library's old books for conservation. Known in-house as "bound ephemera," the Folger collection of these items—described by some scholars as the "blogs" of their day—numbers about ten thousand pamphlets altogether, most of them uncataloged and largely unexamined. "But they're all right here," Mowery said, "where they belong—in this library."

# Part III

# 13

Things Unknown

The poet's eye, in a fine frenzy rolling,
Doth glance from heaven to earth, from earth to heaven;
And as imagination bodies forth
The forms of things unknown, the poet's pen
Turns them to shapes, and gives to airy nothing
A local habitation and a name.
—William Shakespeare,
*A Midsummer Night's Dream,* V.i.12–17

INCREDIBLE AS IT MAY SEEM, the realization that notebooks kept by artists, writers, composers, scientists, architects, inventors, engineers, choreographers—inspired thinkers of every conceivable discipline— might provide a window into the wonders of the creative process is a relatively recent avenue of scholarly inquiry, beginning in the latter years of the nineteenth century and coming into full bloom in the twentieth. "Of all forms of expression, the sketch is the most closely linked to the artist's inner vision," the art historian Claude Marks wrote in a 1971 survey of the sketchbooks of master painters and sculptors, words that could be applied to every manner of probing mind. "It is a kind of handwriting," he continued, one that reveals the "thoughts, intentions, and interpretations of the world" of creative people, and one not likely to be found anywhere else. Marks's study took in the full sweep of sketching, tracing its modern applications to the drawing of preparatory images on parchment in medieval times and citing a small volume of pen-and-ink adaptations of scenes from the New Testament

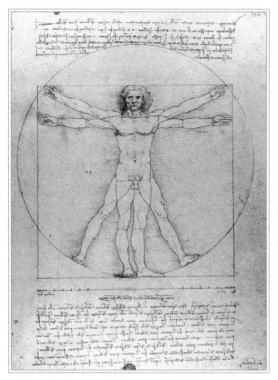

*Leonardo da Vinci's drawing on paper known as*
*"Vitruvian Man," c. 1487, depicts a male figure in*
*two superimposed positions with his arms and legs*
*apart and simultaneously inscribed in a circle and*
*a square, based on the correlations of ideal human*
*proportions with geometry described by the ancient*
*Roman architect Vitruvius.*

by the French artist Adémar de Chambannes, circa 1025, as being the
oldest known artist's sketchbook.

The consummate practitioner among them all, however, was Leonardo da Vinci, the universal genius whose graphic excursions included
wide-ranging ruminations in science, mathematics, architecture, sculpture, anatomy, engineering, hydrodynamics, music, optics, botany,
music, and all aspects of the visual arts. It is no stretch to suggest that
this, the archetypical Renaissance man, is perhaps the most diversely
gifted person to have ever lived—and virtually all of his creative energy
achieved expression on a writing surface that had arrived in Italy two
hundred years before his birth, in 1452, which coincided precisely with

the time that Johannes Gutenberg was developing the idea for movable metal type in Germany. An exhibition mounted at the Victoria and Albert Museum, in London, in 2006 took special note of this unusual circumstance; of consuming interest to me, of course, was that the stated goal of *Leonardo da Vinci: Experience, Experiment, Design* was to demonstrate, in the words of Martin Kemp of Oxford University, the curator, how Leonardo "thought on paper."

By the blockbuster standards of today, this show of sixty pieces, arranged in one small room, was modest, showcasing, for the most part, "a few fragile, sometimes faded, often soiled and stained bits of very old, brownish paper, all displayed in dim light," according to a reviewer for *The Guardian*. "Yet how alive Leonardo's drawings are. The whole world seems to be there, writhing and spilling and turning on page after page, each filled with notes, observations, speculations, analysis and fantasy."

In the detailed monograph he wrote for the exhibition, Kemp acknowledged that ingenious people had been sketching well before Leonardo, "but no one used paper as a laboratory for thinking" on his scale. "No one covered the surface of pages with such an impetuous cascade of observations, visualized thoughts, brainstormed alternatives, theories, polemics and debates, covering virtually every branch of knowledge about the visible world known in his time." And regardless of how limited the paper supply might have been—it was not readily available everywhere in fifteenth-century Europe—Leonardo did not skimp when it came time to record his thoughts. Indeed, the level of his activity was so enormous it would have been judged exceptional "in later years of paper plentitude," according to Kemp.

Paper was not merely a tool, in other words, like a chisel or a hammer in the hands of a stonemason or a carpenter, but a vital instrument that Leonardo relied on to give his fertile thoughts "a local habitation and a name." Suitably energized by this premise, I telephoned Kemp one morning at his home in Woodstock, Oxfordshire, to discuss his own encounters with Leonardo's notebooks and drawings over the previous four decades.

I was, needless to say, keenly interested in finding out how a person allowed frequent access to these astonishing documents—a privilege rarely granted by the various repositories that have custody of them, to even the most worthy of supplicants—approaches the task of "reading" Leonardo in the flesh, so to speak, but my first question for Kemp was far more straightforward, and directly to the point of this book. Would any of this unparalleled productivity have been possible, I wondered, without paper? "You cannot envisage Leonardo doing what he was doing without it" was his unequivocal reply. "Parchment is a much scarcer commodity, and could not be used as prodigally, so that wouldn't have worked. Drawing on a more ephemeral medium like tile—which would have required Leonardo to rub off his jottings as he proceeded—would never have allowed for the accumulation of material that was so essential to his way of working, either. So he could never have done what he did, or in the way he did it, without paper."

This predilection of Leonardo's is particularly relevant, since what we know directly of this supremely talented man's genius has survived primarily by way of his private notebooks. As accomplished as the oils of his mature years may be—the *Mona Lisa* remains by far the number-one tourist attraction at the Louvre, in Paris—no more than twenty paintings believed to be by him are known today. Leonardo's most celebrated mural, *The Last Supper,* moreover, endures in Milan in a condition that is barely reflective of the original, while none of his sculptures survive in a finished state of any kind. The only illustrations he drew that were published in his lifetime were a series of ink drawings on vellum from 1498 that were issued as woodcuts in Luca Pacioli's *De Divina Proportione,* in 1509, and very few of his inventions ever went beyond the drawing board.

In the absence of a comprehensive body of completed work—or a critical mass, in today's terminology—the "key" to grasping Leonardo's genius, the noted Renaissance scholar Carmen C. Bambach has asserted, "is without doubt to be found in his extant drawings and accompanying manuscript notes." That such an "enormous body of drawings by Leonardo survives" at all, she added—"more than four thousand if one counts every scrap of paper with sketches and diagrams, and all the pages bound in his notebooks"—is "nearly miraculous." The kind of paper Leonardo used for his many projects varied. The stock for the life-size preparatory drawings he made of his larger artistic works, known as cartoons—from the Italian *cartone* and the Dutch *karton,* meaning strong, heavy paper, or pasteboard—came from Bologna. He generally favored large sheets that he acquired in bulk, probably from local merchants in the various cities where he lived, then folded and bound himself. There is some evidence to suggest that Leonardo may have hoped to publish this material in some coherent order, but nothing ever came of that, and at his death in 1519, everything was left in the care of Francesco Melzi, a devoted assistant.

Because of their beauty and virtuosity, the drawings were prized by collectors, a boon in one respect, in that they were recognized for their value not long after his death, and thus more likely to survive over time, but disastrous, too, in that Melzi's heirs, who inherited them in 1570, allowed so many of the notebooks to be cut up and dispersed individually. A further complication involved Leonardo's quirky disposition to write in what is known as cursive mirror script—words that appear backward to the naked eye, and were set down left-handed on top of that—a circumstance that made sheets without illustrations less desirable. As an unfortunate consequence, 80 percent of what is surmised to have existed has been lost.

A handful of appreciative collectors—the Italian sculptor Pompeo Leoni; the librarian Cassiano dal Pozzo, of Rome; the seventeenth-century British collector Thomas Howard, 2nd Earl of Arundel; and the critic and biographer John Forster, a determined bibliophile who passed his precious acquisitions on to the Victoria and Albert Museum—are credited with preserving the notebooks that do remain. Other collections are to be found today in the Royal Library at Windsor Castle; the British Library; the Bibliothèque de l'Institut de France, in Paris; the Biblioteca Nacional de España, in Madrid; and the Biblioteca Ambrosiana, in Milan, which holds the twelve-volume Codex Atlanticus, gathered by Pompeo Leoni—1,119 pages dating from 1478 to 1519 and covering a breathtaking range of subjects, from flight to weaponry, from musical instruments to mathematics, from anatomy to botany. The Codex Leicester—acquired by Microsoft founder Bill Gates at Christie's in 1994 from the estate of Armand Hammer for $30.8 million—is the only major scientific work by Leonardo in private hands. The purchase price remains the most money ever spent for a single book, which in this instance is eighteen sheets of paper, each folded in half and written on both sides, forming a seventy-two-page journal.

How Leonardo managed to be so prolific with paper at such an early age can only be surmised, but a good place to start, in terms of logistics, at least, would be through the connections of his father, Ser Piero di Antonio da Vinci, who for thirty-five years was a notary in Florence, and undoubtedly on good working terms with suppliers of the materials necessary for his line of work. It was Ser Piero, too, who brought his young, illegitimate son to apprentice at the workshop of the renowned Florentine sculptor Andrea del Verrocchio, probably in 1469, when he would have been seventeen. As bona fides of Leonardo's competence, he presented a sheaf of sketches, since the youngster "never ceased drawing and working in relief, pursuits which suited his fancy more than any other," according to the sixteenth-century art historian and critic Giorgio Vasari. During these years of apprenticeship, Leonardo "practiced not one branch of art only, but all those in which drawing played a part, and having an intellect so divine and marvelous that he was also an excellent geometrician," Vasari further noted.

Trained as a sculptor—he spent a decade in Verrocchio's studio—Leonardo worked to create works of art that were truly three-dimensional in every medium he undertook. "No one was ever more inventive at devising the graphic means to accomplish visual thinking than Leonardo, and no one was more skilled at inventing presentational methods to let the spectator see what he was thinking," Kemp pointed out, and while the drawing of diagrams involved illustrating on an even surface, his flat geometrical images were revolutionary. As "one of the greatest visualizers of forms and space in three dimensions," Kemp asserted in yet another monograph, "he stands alongside Michelangelo and Bernini as sculptors, and with Kepler and Einstein as scientists. Like them, he could manipulate forms and space within his mind as a form of mental sculpture of the most fluid and plastic kind." Leonardo used the word *disegno* to describe what he was setting down on paper, a word that translates either as "drawing" or "design" but was used by him to mean mastery of the principles and practices of what we would call draftsmanship.

"I have had the supreme privilege of being face-to-face with most of the notebooks, and there is no single answer as to how you read Leonardo," Kemp told me. "Different notebooks—even those that have survived in reasonably original form—must be tackled in different ways. Sometimes he'll start with characteristic mirror writing at what we would think is the front, but he will quickly turn it upside down if he decides that he's got a different topic, then start at the back. Things appear, reappear, some are crossed out, ideas are introduced from other notebooks, and he will interpolate things at later dates. They are extraordinarily erratic and impulsive in how they go about laying down their material, which is both terrifically exciting but also frustrating, because getting a coherent train of thought out of all that is hard work. It's absolutely different from reading most people's notebooks."

Because very few researchers are allowed access to Leonardo's notebooks, scholars have had to rely on surrogate copies. To assist these efforts, Kemp has been at the forefront of an international collaboration known as Universal Leonardo, which aims to make all of the materials now in institutions available online, an important first step for world scholarship, though there is still no substitute, he told me, for studying the actual artifacts. "There are the intangible things such as the sheer feel of the original that you get," he said. "If you're also asking hard questions about the composition of a sheet, of how that sheet developed in the way that it did in the mind of Leonardo, you can often deduce some of that from the density of the lines, the chalk, the different inks that he used; you can get a feel for how the sheets have been worked up in very complicated ways. A facsimile is flat; there is no texture at all to it. People tend to think of paper as a surface on which you simply draw. But it's actually more complicated than that."

And beyond the feel and composition of the object is an appreciation of scale and immediacy. "When you pick up one of his pocket books, these very fat but very small-in-page-dimension pocket books, you can get a real sense of the urgency and intensity, and the shared mental vigor with which he filled these pages with tiny sketches and tiny bits of writing. You get an amazing sense of his thought cascading onward. Then, when you take one of the big double-folded sheets—these were done when he was sitting down in the studio, not outside looking at people and observing his surroundings—you can see a slower and more varied pace. There is this extraordinary sense of size, and one can grasp the physical nature of it all. But your first impression is the speed at which something has been done."

For Leonardo, everything was validated by vision—"seeing is believing," in one iteration or another, could easily have been his motto—and drawing was his principal tool of close examination. As a designer whose form of visual thinking depended largely on the creation of three-dimensional models, Leonardo would frequently employ "swirls of crashing lines," sometimes augmented by midtone wash and white heightening to "virtually sculpt" forms on the surface of the paper. "The mixture of visual and verbal thoughts pouring out onto paper was an incredibly complex compound of what was going on in Leonardo's brain," Kemp stressed in his interview with me. When Leonardo was designing what Kemp calls his "theory machines"—devices that existed solely in his mind and were visualized entirely on paper— his brain was working overtime. "In other instances, we can observe when the 'theory machine' did not work, even on paper." Leonardo once drew a container fed by a vertical pipe that has a spout passing above the top of the neck. Realizing on further observation that this could not work, he crossed out the spout. On other occasions, he might sketch variants of the same device, or he would concoct a dialogue with both text and illustration to disprove one of his working theses.

Kemp's work with Leonardo began in the 1960s and has been ongoing ever since, along with other work that has taken in many related themes. He is emeritus research professor in the history of art at Oxford University and has written and broadcast extensively on imagery in art and science from the Renaissance to the present day. Kemp also has taken what can be described as a hands-on approach to Leonardo's corpus of work. In 2000, he served as consultant to the British skydiver Adrian Nicholas in the construction of a parachute made by following details outlined in a drawing scribbled in the Codex Atlanticus in 1485 and fabricated from materials that would have been available in the late fifteenth century. Tethered on June 26, 2000, to a hot-air balloon over South Africa, Nicholas detached at ten thousand feet and, with a black box recorder measuring his descent, glided for five minutes before cutting himself free at three thousand feet and descending the rest of the way with a conventional parachute. The 187-pound apparatus—built with wooden poles, ropes, and canvas—made such a smooth and slow descent that the two jumpers who accompanied Nicholas under canopy had to brake twice to stay level with him; the device itself landed without incident.

William Shakespeare, according to his dear friend and First Folio eulogist Ben Jonson, was said to have "never blotted out" a single line while writing his dramatic works, to which his old comrade from the London theater crustily opined, "Would he had blotted a thousand." But if this is true—and in the absence of any verifiable literary manuscripts in the Bard's hand, we have to take Jonson at his word—this supreme skill suggests a creative genius whose blank verse went straight to paper without any need of substantive revision. Such was not always the case with Leonardo, however. The writing instruments he typically used were pen and ink and various colored chalks, and while wooden pencils and rubber erasers had not yet been invented, Kemp said that Leonardo occasionally tried to remove certain things from his pages.

"There are signs in some of the drawings that he erased things, not as extensively as if he had had pencil and rubber, which is more convenient, but there is no question that he clearly had changed his mind. And he did an enormous amount of work in blank stylus—that is to say, a sharp instrument which leaves a groove in the paper that is visible to a degree. On many of the pages, both geometry and freer-hand ones, he used a blank stylus so that he could see the evolving design without it being a definitive mark."

While there is some suggestion that Leonardo might have intended his notebooks to be read by others, there is no evidence, Kemp said, that he considered publication of them in any traditional sense. "In one way they're very private notebooks, but he does say, occasionally, 'Reader, do not blame me if this is a collection without order,' so I do think he's certainly thinking about getting things into the public domain in some shape or form. This is really one of the more puzzling things about them. He is deeply ambiguous in terms of his intended audience."

A word Kemp uses over and over to describe what Leonardo was doing on paper is *brainstorming,* which I asked him to define for me. "Brainstorming, as I use it, is basically that turbulence from which ideas emerge, in more or less coherent form, which we all do to some extent, and it's kind of preverbal, previsual in a way. In Leonardo's case, it also relies upon the serendipity of the image that appears, which may suggest other things. There are famous passages where he talks about seeing images in stains on walls, so he realizes that by crashing things down on paper, the kind of graphic collisions that result can themselves suggest inventions. Leonardo, for all that brilliance and fertility, is a very concrete thinker. If he couldn't see it, ideally, or touch it or taste it or smell it or hear it, then it was of no interest to him."

For all the creative expression paper has helped facilitate, Kemp is quick to emphasize that there are limits to just how far a person can go with the form. "There are very few people who visualize effectively in three dimensions and also have the graphic skill to get that down on a flat surface. I think here of Kepler in a different way, I suppose, or somebody like Einstein, for whom it's less a graphic visualization and almost more a somatic one. These are the great 3-D modelers, who in a sense can do it in their minds. I can even do it a bit. But their ability is just awesome. Einstein resolves the problem by thinking about it in quasi-physical terms, particularly in bodily terms, as he stressed himself. But then he has to go to mathematical formulas. He has to communicate his ideas through formulas, such as $E = mc^2$, although that precise form of what has become a visual icon was not actually formulated by Einstein himself."

Kemp said that as dimensions are added to formulations, the process becomes a matter of having to invent conventions for representing things on paper. "It's pretty good that we can get three dimensions on a two-dimensional surface, but when you get to four dimensions and above, you're beginning to operate in realms where you have to either suppress one of the dimensions or have some kind of a convention you can use to express it. In a way, Einstein faced the difficulty that you can't represent relativity visually—you can't even represent the notions of space-time involved adequately—on a flat piece of paper. So there are limits to what you can do with drawing on paper. But that sort of problem never seems to have hindered Leonardo."

One area of visual thinking that I did not discuss with Kemp but that very definitely involves dealing with four dimensions in a two-dimensional format is choreography, a creative exercise that involves not only a third dimension, space, but a fourth: movement. The word *choreography* itself derives from the Greek words for dancing and writing, one of several fairly modern coinages that use the metaphor of writing for an innovation or expression of some sort that extends the senses: *phonograph* for sound and *photograph* for direct imagery being the two best known. Others, similarly conceived and equally colorful, are *lithograph, telegraph, ideograph, seismograph,* and *hydrograph.* In each instance, the operative root is *graph,* "to write," and the object is to do so with some exotic medium other than paper.

Classical ballet is interesting in this respect, in that the dancers express themselves entirely by way of movement—they never speak—making what they do artistically onstage a purely visual presentation, and far more reliant on instruction. In place of graphic transmission, dance has been handed down from generation to generation by means of imitation and oral tradition. The Canadian historian Iro Valaskakis Tembeck has written that, while the art form "is a universal phenomenon" that has existed throughout history, "it often seems to have done so in isolation." The underlying problem, she explained, was the absence for so long of "a written text of some kind" that could have enabled later generations to appreciate the niceties "without having to actually witness a performance." Although written records of dances have existed since the fifteenth century, it is only since the late 1820s that several well-defined attempts have been made to record their movements.

The difficulties were put in further perspective by Ann Hutchinson Guest, a founder, in 1940, of the Dance Notation Bureau, in New York, and author of several works on the subject that are regarded as definitive. Various devices have been used to diagram dance steps on paper, but few had much success until the introduction, in the twentieth century, of the Laban system, named for Rudolf von Laban, a Hungarian dance theorist whose work in "movement analysis" laid the foundation for a standardized method of notation, which Guest fully articulated in her 1970 book *Labanotation: The System of Analyzing and Recording Movement* and developed further in four subsequent works. "Dance has been called moving architecture, a truth which the complexities of contemporary choreography may mask," she wrote in an essay for the Yale School of Architecture. "While the recording of movement on paper—dance notation—does not look like movement (disregarding primitive stick figure drawings), there is an 'architecture' in the sequence of graphic symbols used to record dance patterns."

IN THE SPRING OF 2008, the University of California, Los Angeles, mounted an eclectic exhibition of high spots selected from its vast assortment of "special collections," a storehouse of treasures that includes 333,000 rare books, thirty million pages of manuscript, and five million photographs, all maintained apart from the institution's total holdings of 8.3 million volumes. The exhibition was called *From Aldus to Aldous*—cute references to the fifteenth-century Italian publisher Aldus Manutius and the twentieth-century English writer Aldous Huxley, both of whom were represented in the display cases.

The curator of the exhibition was Victoria Steele, at that time director of special collections for the library and, since May 2009, director
of acquisitions strategy for the New York Public Library. She told me
during a walking tour of the show that her personal favorite was the
five-line note from Michelangelo Buonarroti written to a friend on September 22, 1533, telling of a visit he had just had with Pope Clement.
"Because it is so precisely dated, we know that it was at that meeting
with the pope that Michelangelo discussed the commission for the *Last
Judgment* in the Sistine Chapel," Steele said. The letter was given to the
university in the 1980s by one of the great booksellers of the twentieth
century, Jake Zeitlin, whose papers are also at UCLA.

But it was another gift to the university—a single leaf of music with
notes scrawled out along sixteen staves—that reinforced my conviction that every cultural artifact has an inner narrative waiting to be
revealed, and that there is a peripatetic nature to paper objects in particular that sometimes defies credulity. The unadorned sheet had no
name signed or written on it anywhere, and there were no companion
documents to give it context or explanation, either, which probably
explains why it had remained stored and forgotten in a box of miscellaneous musical autographs given to UCLA in 1947 by Walter Slezak,
an Austrian-born actor whose movie credits were substantial enough to
earn him more than forty-five thousand dedicated Google hits when I
checked him out afterward.

In 2006, a member of Steele's staff had brought the document to
her attention. "First of all, it wasn't lost—there was a label on it, written back in the 1940s, that said BEETHOVEN MANUSCRIPT, so there was
a finding aid, even though it was somewhat embedded in the collection," she said. "I couldn't authenticate it myself personally, but being
UCLA, we have people who know about everything, and Robert Winter, one of the three-person team who compiled the mammoth census
of Beethoven sketches back in the 1970s and '80s for the University of
California Press, is right here on the faculty. He's seen thousands of
pages of Beethoven manuscripts. When we were on the phone, he said,
'Well, tell me, does it have ink?' I said yes. 'Is there pencil on it?' I said
yes. Then he said, 'Is there red pencil on it?' And I said yes. Then he
asked a few questions about the sheet itself, and said, 'I'll be right over.'
When he got here and took a look at it, he said, 'This is indisputably a
Beethoven manuscript.'"

With that as a teaser—along with the fact that I already knew of Winter's work two decades earlier on *The Beethoven Sketchbooks*—I immediately got in touch with the professor when I returned to Massachusetts. Winter holds the presidential chair in music and interactive arts at UCLA and is himself an accomplished pianist who has hosted and performed in classical radio broadcasts for American Public Media. Before joining the UCLA faculty, he spent three years in Europe researching his doctoral dissertation on Beethoven's sketches for the late quartets. In 1974, he and two colleagues—Douglas Johnson and Alan Tyson—began what would turn out to be a fifteen-year project to examine every known musical sketch of Beethoven, many of them held in repositories throughout Europe, a good number of them still in their original notebooks and others long since removed from whatever semblance of order they might once have had. Their goal was to compile a census and to determine the place of each sketch in the oeuvre. Constantly alert for the slightest nuance that would help them get a grasp on the maestro's technique, the three scholars became the equivalent of paper scientists, documenting every watermark they encountered in what turned out to be thousands of leaves, studying the types of ink that Beethoven used, the thickness of pencil marks, even the placement of stitch holes.

Winter told me he had been able to make a quick confirmation of the UCLA sheet on the strength of several factors. "When you see a Beethoven leaf, there is absolutely not the slightest confusion about whether it is or it isn't," he said. "This is stuff that not even the most skillful forger could ever replicate. It would be absolutely impossible." The reason for that, he explained, is that the way Beethoven composed music "is so free and impulsive, the note heads are not in the right place, and there are ideas scattered around seemingly randomly. This particular leaf is very complex; there's not much continuity, so you have to pick out the areas that are musically coherent." On the strength of what he saw—and on what he heard when he played the notes out on a piano for himself—Winter expressed his considered belief that the leaf "contains early ideas for the slow movement of the monumental 'Hammerklavier' Piano Sonata, Opus 106."

Winter was able to date its composition to 1817 or 1818, based on several factors. Beethoven's custom during those years was to take large sheets of paper and fold and cut them along two horizontal seams.

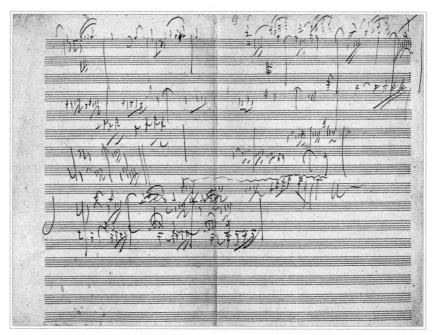

*Piano Sonata in A Major, Opus 101 (Allegro), manuscript sketch in Beethoven's handwriting, 1816.*

"This was a period when Beethoven didn't buy big notebooks," Winter said. "He seems to have either used up the scraps that were lying around, or he just bought small allotments of paper. This particular leaf doesn't have a clear watermark, which is typical for him during those two years. In 1819, he started to buy larger books again, and the paper quality improves. You judge the quality at this time based on the relative whiteness of the paper. The papermakers would bleach the rags, but they wouldn't knock themselves out to get every bit of color out. So with Beethoven, we've got green paper, we've got brown paper, and sometimes we've got the real high-quality stuff, which is whiter, because they spent more time bleaching it. The timing turns out to be good, too, for the 'Hammerklavier'—that's exactly the period when he would have been working on it."

Most people who are not familiar with the full biography of Beethoven's life nevertheless know that he was deaf during a good period of his adulthood and that he composed some of his most important works, including the "Hammerklavier," when he was unable to hear his own compositions performed, raising the question of whether he could "hear" in his mind what he was setting down on paper. "On the surface, musicians hear like anybody else," Winter said. "But Beethoven heard far more acutely than everybody else, and what's so astonishing about the works composed from 1818 on, when he is clinically deaf, is their originality. That is, he was creating sounds that did not previously exist. You could imagine easily being able to re-create sounds you already knew, but he creates, in his string quartets and elsewhere, sounds that we didn't have before, that he himself had never heard audibly but could surely hear in his inner ear, which was extraordinarily imaginative and skilled and highly trained."

During the years of Beethoven's clinical deafness (1818–27), he relied on a parallel form of notation to communicate with his friends and colleagues. Unable to hear others speak, Beethoven asked people to write down what they had to say to him in small notebooks he kept on hand for precisely that purpose. Unfortunately, they do not contain what Beethoven's responses may have been—only the questions were written down—but they offer keen insight into the topics of discussion, and 137 of these "conversation books," containing 5,523 leaves, are known to have survived.

Winter was not coy as to whether he feels paper was necessary to the way Beethoven worked. "It was the essential tool," he said. "What Beethoven did was write down thousands of pages of musical ideas about which you and I would say, 'I don't need to write that down, that's so obvious, that's so simple.' The very act of writing in Beethoven's case was central and therapeutic to his creative process; it was totally essential. He was compulsive about setting everything down. If you were to write out Beethoven's complete works, they would consume some eight thousand pages. Yet the sketches run to even greater length—not to mention that we've lost at least a third of them. And during his entire life, Beethoven never uttered a single preserved remark about this fascinating but eccentric habit."

This practice of his apparently began in adolescence, when, surviving documents from his youth show, he would refine tunes not by tapping out various versions on the keyboard but by moving notes back and forth on sheets of paper like so many pieces on a game board. Later, when he was producing his most famous compositions, it was not uncommon for him to put a melodic fragment through as many as sixty or seventy stages before he was satisfied he had a finished theme.

Beethoven was forever buying huge quantities of manuscript paper, and when he could not afford notebooks, he stitched sheets together to make his own. "He was never to be seen in the street without a small notebook in which he jotted down whatever occurred to him at the moment," his friend Ignaz von Seyfried recalled, "and whenever conversation turned to this he would facetiously quote the words of Joan of Arc: 'Without my banner I dare not come.'"

Over the final thirty-five years of his life, Beethoven changed residences frequently, the only constant when he moved from one place to the next being his ever-growing cache of sketches, which he required to have hauled along with him. At his death, in 1827, more than fifty volumes of material, along with several hundred unbound leaves—the earliest dating to 1792—were found in his flat. One of Beethoven's visitors recalled walking into an apartment that was "as disordered as was his hair," a lead pencil "with which he sketched out his work" lying on the keys of an upright piano, "and beside it on a scribbled sheet of music-paper I found a number of the most divergent ideas, jotted down without connection, the most heterogeneous individual details elbowing each other, just as they may have come to his mind. This was the material for his new cantata."

Once the compositions were written down, another distinctive step in his routine followed, one that also required the use of paper. Beethoven was making music he had every expectation would be heard by audiences, but before any of his creations could be performed by musicians, they had to make the transition from holographic draft to printed score. Winter said that Beethoven "did his best" to work compatibly with the professional copyists retained to do that highly specialized work for him, but, given his compulsive inclination toward constant revision, he frequently created chaos. Legendary for being a taskmaster, Beethoven carried on what Winter described as an "ongoing war" throughout his lifetime with his copyists. "He couldn't keep copyists; he abused them. He once said, 'The only decent copyist I've had in my life was Schlemmer, and he's dead.' This was Wenzel Schlemmer, one of the most gifted copyists of the nineteenth century—he worked with Beethoven for several decades and possessed an uncanny ability for ferreting out what the composer actually meant. And Beethoven never once thanked him."

And once again, Winter emphasized, essential to this process at every turn was for Beethoven to get it all down on paper. "I've worked a lot on the Ninth Symphony, for example, and you may remember the phrase 'continuity draft' from our book? You start at the beginning and try to get through in some shape, whether it's one line or a piano score or short score or full score, or what have you. Beethoven may have a half a dozen continuity drafts for just one movement. So you might say, 'Why don't you skip a couple?' Well, he couldn't get to the next one unless he wrote every stage down in its entirety."

Despite the profusion of sketches, Winter does not believe Beethoven was documenting his work for posterity. "It was strictly for his own utility, of that I am certain. So why, you might ask, didn't he just toss the false starts like everyone else? Because he would go back from time to time and mine them for ideas. It's so obvious. In the famous Pastoral Symphony Sketchbook, in the British Museum, let's say, you might find all these sketches for the 'Pastoral' Symphony, but in between movements, and occasionally within a movement, you'll find all these other ideas that were orphans who were occasionally adopted." Further evidence that Beethoven was not concerned whether future scholars would pore over his sketches is the fact that none of them are dated. "He didn't make it easy for us," Winter said, "but he made it more fun, because then you have to argue from musical merits."

I asked Winter if he thought that the reason Beethoven was so insistent on writing ideas down as they came to him was that he feared they might otherwise be lost. "Yes, I think he did have a concern that it might not be there again. What you see with Franz Schubert, by comparison, are ideas that are already finished and brilliant, and you are depressed that you could never come up with an idea like that in your whole life; so Schubert hardly writes anything down, because he just goes straight to the finished work. The central nugget of Beethoven's genius—and I think that the reason he is such a universally loved and admired composer—is because he starts out with ideas that you or I could have come up with, and then slowly, degree by degree, raises them from banality to sublimity. That's his great, celestial gift. And we witness that exhilarating journey in his sketches."

AS TOURIST ATTRACTIONS GO, the Thomas Edison National Historical Park, in West Orange, New Jersey, does not command top billing with the Grand Canyon, Yosemite, Big Sur, or Niagara Falls. Unlike those breathtaking wonders, the chief selling point of this drab complex of brick buildings, a few miles off the Garden State Parkway, is not unparalleled displays of natural beauty, but insight into the creative process of a probing thinker, a mechanically gifted genius whose endless tinkerings with things unknown were recorded on paper in meticulous detail.

An autodidact once deemed by his grade-school instructors to be too "slow" to learn, Edison gained fame early in his career for the electric light, developed at his first laboratory, in nearby Menlo Park. When that workshop proved much too small to contain the great inventor's inexhaustible imagination, a three-story brick building ten times larger was erected, to Edison's exacting specifications, in West Orange and began operations in 1887. Edison was granted 1,093 patents in his career—an astonishing rate of two per week, according to the *New York Times*—many of them for ideas that were worked out in these buildings.

Opened to the public in 2010, after a six-year, $13 million renovation, the complex began allowing visitors for the first time to see the upper floors and other working spaces and laboratories where teams of innovators once worked to develop such modern marvels as the phonograph, a fluoroscope for viewing X-ray images, machines to extract iron from rock, cylinder recorders for office dictation, and nickel-iron-alkaline storage batteries. The ground floor of the main building is filled with lathes, pulleys, belts, and machines on one end and a substantial library of ten thousand books where Edison maintained his formal office at the other. Between two bookcases in an alcove off to one side is a small bed, placed there by Edison's wife so the great thinker could take an occasional catnap. On the second floor are chemical laboratories, a photographic studio and darkroom, and a quiet area where ideas that had been sketched out in haste were set down in greater detail by professional draftsmen. A motion picture projector synchronized with a phonograph, which Edison called the kinetophone, led to the opening of the world's first movie studio, complete with a Steinway piano once used to audition people who had dreams of making it big on the silver screen.

Kept in one of several annexes not open to the general public, but available for use by researchers, are the copious files that document the

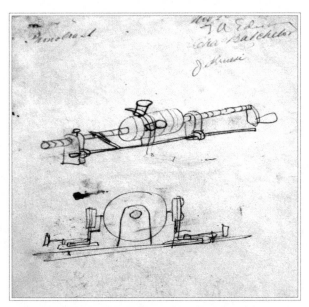

*Thomas Edison's first drawing of a phonograph
apparatus, 1880, in one of his laboratory notebooks.*

activities of what has been described as the first professional research-and-development operation of the modern world. Elevating it to an even higher level are the contributions of Thomas Edison that are to be found in so much of the paperwork—most revealingly, thirty-five hundred notebooks in which his thoughts and ideas had their first incarnations, many of them hastily sketched out crudely as they formed quickly in his mind. I had the opportunity to examine a few of these, and I must admit I had a bit of disappointment at first, expecting, perhaps, to see instances in which flashes of insight are dramatically evident. But the expression of genius is very often a process, and divining that from technical materials such as these is the mandate of scholarship.

To get a sense of that, I drove to the main campus of Rutgers University, twenty miles away in New Brunswick, where a team of textual scholars has been working since 1979 to compile, edit, and publish a definitive edition of *The Papers of Thomas A. Edison,* which through 2010 had issued seven volumes and expects to be done about a half-century after the work was started. A five-part microfilm edition of 288 reels—about three hundred thousand pages—and an online edition that combines material from the first three reels and documents

*Two of Edison's laboratory notebooks, at the Thomas Edison National Historical Park, in West Orange, New Jersey.*

from other repositories have also been produced; together, these include about two hundred thousand images. The marathon effort is directed by Paul Israel, a research professor at the university who has been involved with the project since 1980 in several capacities and has served as general editor since 2002. In that time, he has also written several books related to the ongoing work, most notably *Edison: A Life of Invention* and, with colleagues Robert Friedel and Bernard S. Finn, *Edison's Electric Light: The Art of Invention*—monographs that would have been impossible, he told me, without all the archival material that was readily available to him.

"Everything is very definitely based on paper; everything is initially a document," Israel said. "And while that may sound formidable, it is intimidating only if it's just an undifferentiated mass—which all this most definitely is not." When the Edison Papers project began, it had proceeded under the assumption that there was something on the order of 1.2 million pages of material in the archive, not the five million or so that are believed to actually be there today. "There was no good inventory ever done beforehand, and perhaps that was fortunate, because if we realized at the time the magnitude of what we were looking at, we may never have undertaken the project. But once it began, what we did realize was that we didn't have a really good handle on it. It turned out there were papers all over the place—every building at the site had historic papers." Israel said the job of his team is assisted measurably by the fact that about two-thirds of the paperwork was produced by Thomas A. Edison Inc., which lies outside the purview of their project. "As you generate a large bureaucracy, you generate a lot of paper, so there's a lot that's more marginal there in terms of the papers of Thomas Edison. This project we are doing at Rutgers is all about Thomas Edison, the individual thinker." Edison was a true stickler for detail, and "a very mindful documentarian," Israel continued, though some materials did get waylaid among the various laboratories. "We've discovered things related to each other that became separated. But over time, he became more careful about his own records. He finally went to a standardized notebook for everybody, and he required this of everyone in the laboratory." Edison can be seen constantly recording things, with very little in his mind regarded as trivial. "You see this pattern with the storage battery, later on. There are a lot of notes for all the ideas and designs." And the convention of note-keeping was impressed upon the secretaries, who were required to follow a certain pattern that Edison imposed on them. "It's been quite a challenge to organize the material in ways to make a selection for publication. The one constant for us in making a choice has been to assure ourselves that Edison's involvement is crucial—his involvement in the process—and what came out of it."

Beyond its usefulness as a writing surface, paper was also a resource Edison turned to in his inventing, as a material of function—in particular, in the ticker tape machine, which relied on a narrow spool of paper tape to receive stock data from Wall Street, giving brokers the ability to follow trends on the floors of the major exchanges as they occurred. In 1876, Edison patented an "autographic printing" machine that made low-cost copies of documents by forcing ink through a stencil onto sheets of paper. With refinements, the first commercially successful duplicating machine became known as the Mimeograph, under license from Edison to Albert Blake Dick, whose A. B. Dick Company of Chicago sold millions of them over the years. They were so popular that the word *mimeograph* itself became generic. Edison's first trials with the phonograph used as a recording surface a strip of paper coated with paraffin—a sheet of waxed paper, basically—that produced a pliable surface upon which grooves could be embedded.

For his electric lightbulb, he tried numerous filaments, the early successful experiments including carbonized cardboard that he cut in a horseshoe thread. He worked with other fibers before settling finally on bamboo, which proved longer-lasting.

"Edison was always thinking about technology in very creative ways, and he was very skilled at marshaling large groups of people to work on problems for him," Israel said. "He tried out a great variety of materials and chemicals, but always within certain parameters. He was never wedded to a single approach, and whenever something failed, he quickly moved on." Because so much of what Edison did involved mechanical technology, his diagrams and sketches can often be impenetrable to the uninitiated. "A lot of the electrical technology was involved with moving something—a generator, a telegraph key, whatever. Some of it was about the way a signal goes through a circuit, and that's all drawn out. He's very good about sketching out a variety of different possibilities with any technology he's working on."

Israel said that whenever Edison wrote out instructions to his machinists, there typically was an "interesting mix of written information and embodied knowledge" present. "We might not know exactly what they're doing, because the mechanic already had that knowledge in his head." The American patent system, he noted, was the first in the world to place publication at the center of the formal process, elevating the importance of the draftsman. "At some point, someone in the building has to get it all down on paper. In the American system, you published the patent and disseminated it. This country was willing to provide a limited monopoly in exchange for the technology."

If there is a common thread discernible in the mass of paperwork, Israel said, it is ultimately the "voice," in a sense, of Edison himself. "If you look at almost all of the things that emerge out of the laboratories, they begin with Edison's kind of conceptual framework, and throughout the process, he's always there at the center, moving the research in directions that he thinks are most useful. There is almost a visual thread you can see, and a kind of style he has that is distinctively his, and his alone. So much of the initial idea of how the technology ought to be designed comes right out of his mind—through his pen—and onto a piece of paper."

# 14

## The Drawing Board

I cannot so well set it forth in words as I see it in my mind's eye. But the picture will show it.
>—Guido da Vigevano, Italian physician and inventor,
>in *Texaurus Regis Francie*, 1335

Nor did he rest until he had drawn every sort of building—round, square, and octagonal temples, basilicas, aqueducts, baths, arches, colossea, amphitheaters, and every temple built of bricks . . . and so zealous was his study that his intellect became very well able to see Rome, in imagination, as she was when she was not in ruins.
>—Giorgio Vasari, writing about Filippo Brunelleschi
>in *Lives of the Artists,* 1550

Now regard this pure white sheet of paper! It is ready for recording the logic of the plan.
>—Frank Lloyd Wright, *An Autobiography,* 1932

The Creator created paper for the purpose of drawing architecture on it. Everything else is, at least for my part, to misuse paper.
>—Alvar Aalto, *Sketches,* 1978

TRADITION HOLDS that the brilliant scientist, mathematician, and engineer from antiquity Archimedes of Syracuse was killed when he refused to move on the orders of a Roman soldier in 212 B.C. "Do not disturb my circles," the great thinker is reported, by numerous ancient sources, to have growled when interrupted at his calculations, an act of impertinence deemed so haughty that it was silenced with the thrust of a sword. The geometric shapes the old man was drawing on the ground were probably being sketched out on a firm dirt floor—a writing surface of expediency, to be sure, but all that was within reach of the originator of the lever, the compound pulley, a hand-powered screw to raise water, and numerous mathematical formulas, including one for the ratio of the circumference of a circle to its diameter, known as pi.

Legendary in his lifetime for becoming totally absorbed in the task at hand, Archimedes was single-minded when it came to his work, the most celebrated instance, by far, being the time he ran naked through the streets of Syracuse shouting "Eureka!" at the discovery of displacement mechanics, the flash of perception having come while taking a bath in a full tub of water. Plutarch marveled that, if suitably inspired, Archimedes would rake ashes out of a fireplace, or poke figures with a fingernail on his freshly oiled skin after washing, to make an impromptu drawing board. In the best of times, he had waxed wooden tablets, the erasable blackboards of their day, or papyrus to use for his computations, but nothing so practical as paper.

Plutarch is the source for a somewhat similar scenario believed to have attended the planning of a great city at the mouth of the Nile River, named Alexandria, for its founding spirit, Alexander the Great.

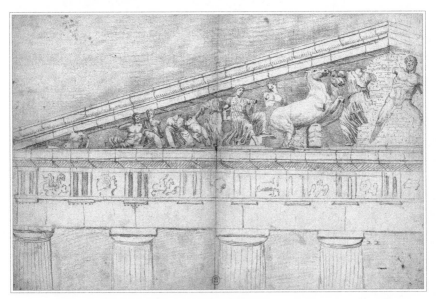

*Jacques Carrey's drawing of the west pediment of the Parthenon, showing Athena and Poseidon competing for Athens, prepared on-site in 1674.*

Coming ashore in 334 B.C. to survey the site, Alexander is said to have made up his mind quickly about what he wanted done and, with no chalk nearby with which to draw lines on the ground, ordered some grain brought forth from his detachment's food supplies and spread out on the shore. Using a stick to make lines, he sketched out "a pretty large compass of ground in a semi-circle," then drew "into the inside of the circumference equal straight lines from each, thus giving it something of the form of a cloak or cape."

Alexander carefully indicated where he wanted avenues, piers, fountains, and temples erected and was altogether pleased with his handiwork until a flock of birds rose like a "black cloud" from a nearby lagoon and devoured "every morsel" of the grain. Assured by his augurs that the sign was good—their prudent reading of the unfortunate feeding frenzy was that Alexandria would be the "nurse and provider" of many nations—Alexander directed his architect Dinocrates to proceed with plans prepared in a manner more consistent with the times—but, once again, without the assistance of paper sheets to draw on.

No plans survive for the Parthenon, either, though it can be fairly well assumed that construction of that quintessential Greek temple was conducted under the constant supervision of the project designer, the sculptor Phidias, with day-to-day direction provided by the master architects Iktinos and Kallikrates. How they drew, with what instruments, and on what kinds of material is pure speculation, since only the ruins remain, and even then in a skeletal state. It is thus only by way of paper that we have any idea of what the Parthenon looked like before a munitions explosion reduced much of the edifice to rubble in 1687. Thirteen years before that great calamity took place, a young draftsman from Troyes named Jacques Carrey spent two weeks at the Acropolis preparing sketches of the building for the French ambassador to the Ottoman Empire. Carrey's drawings picture the exquisite friezes that were victims of the Venetian attack—about 20 percent of the sculptures were destroyed—as well as those removed during the early 1800s by agents for Thomas Bruce, the 7th Earl of Elgin, and installed in the British Museum.

Unlike the Parthenon, where at least the exterior frame of the structure still strikes a majestic figure above Athens, the destruction of Old St. Paul's Cathedral, in London, is an example in which an architectural masterwork from the distant past has been preserved entirely by

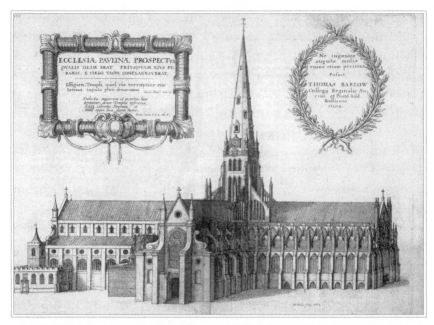

*One of Wenceslaus Hollar's illustrations in William Dugdale's* The History of
St. Pauls Cathedral in London *(1658).*

paper, if only in a virtual state. The miracle worker in this case was Sir
William Dugdale, an English antiquarian and herald whose *History of
St. Pauls Cathedral* was published eight years before the medieval landmark was leveled in the Great Fire of London in 1666. In preparing his
monumental study, Dugdale wrote of having consulted "no lesse than
ten porters' burthens' of unsorted, mouldering charters, rolls and other
documents" he found lying in neglected disarray in various "baggs and
hampers" at Scriveners' Hall, which also was destroyed in the conflagration. Dugdale's meticulous study included detailed descriptions of
every monument and inscription in the cathedral, which had been built
between 1087 and 1314 by the Normans and their successors; he even
identified books and manuscripts that were shelved in the library. As
a bonus, Wenceslaus Hollar, the preeminent illustrator of seventeenth-
century London, provided forty-five sketches of the cathedral's original
details and of alterations made in the 1630s by the architect Inigo Jones.

   In his introduction to the history, Dugdale recalled how he had
been "often and earnestly incited" by Christopher Lord Hatton, comp-
troller of the household to King Charles I, to undertake a "speedy view"

of monuments and churches that had been victimized by the religious upheavals of the Reformation and the English Civil War. It was only through the availability of "inke and paper," he wrote, that the "shadows" of historic buildings then decaying throughout the realm "might be preserved for posteritie."

While indisputably catastrophic, the St. Paul's disaster nevertheless made possible the defining triumph of Sir Christopher Wren that followed, a milestone in the history of architectural design that was attended by careful planning and set down with painstaking precision on sheets of drafting paper that survive to this day. Wren's thirty-five-year effort to build a newer and greater cathedral was the focal point of *Compass and Rule,* a 2009–2010 exhibition mounted in London and New Haven, Connecticut, that paid rich tribute to the development of architecture after its emergence as a branch of practical mathematics that employed designs drawn proportionally to scale. None of these revolutionary principles would have been possible, asserted Anthony Gerbino and Stephen Johnston, the authors of the exhibition catalog,

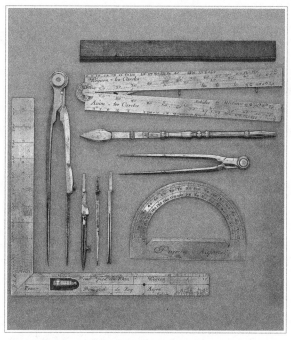

*A set of eighteenth-century French architectural drawing instruments from the Andrew Alpern Collection at Columbia University.*

without a "paper revolution" that had swept its way through Europe between 1500 and 1750, allowing for unprecedented advancements in architectural technique everywhere it went. Though separate processes today, design and construction were inextricably interconnected in medieval architecture, and any plans that may have been set down on parchment were schematic at best, and done for the purpose of communicating "the idea" of a building to patrons and workmen. Exact dimensions were determined directly at the building site, with poles and rope, and any planning issues that arose were "resolved not by erasing lines on paper, but by moving stakes" back and forth on the ground.

At almost the same time that Arabs were beginning to learn paper-making techniques from the Chinese, ambitious plans were being made by the Abbasid ruler Caliph Abu Ja'far al-Mansur to build a new capital city on the west bank of the Tigris River in Baghdad. In A.D. 762, according to a ninth-century Arab historian, the entire infrastructure was sketched out full-scale, directly on the ground it would occupy, by teams of laborers indicating exactly where the various buildings, roadways, walls, and gates would be situated. When all of the lines were traced out, the cuts were packed with a mixture of ashes and cotton-seeds that had been soaked in naphtha, then ignited simultaneously at night so that the caliph—standing at the center of what became known as the Round City (it was a full four miles in circumference)—could fully appreciate the majestic design.

As architecture matured into an independent discipline and as geometry came to define its character, various instruments were devised to assist the process: the compass and the rule, most famously, but also protractors, dividers, triangles, ruling pens, and straightedges. While the *Compass and Rule* exhibition featured several examples of these devices, a presentation at the Avery Architectural & Fine Arts Library, at Columbia University, in New York, that same year dealt entirely with drawing tools that had been developed for use exclusively on paper. Assembled over thirty years by the New York architectural historian Andrew Alpern, the collection includes 170 drawing instruments made in Europe and America over three centuries, many of them attractively crafted in silver, ivory, steel, and brass, each one a precision tool designed to transfer precise details from the eye of the architect to the page.

"Before a thing is made, it exists as an idea," the noted historian of technology Eugene S. Ferguson stressed in a detailed explication of the manner by which material objects are coaxed into being, a key phase being one that is devoid entirely of language, issuing forth initially as more of an image in the "mind's eye" of its creator than as a fully articulated entity. For close to six hundred years—during a period that roughly parallels the emergence of paper in Europe—the principal means by which these concepts were conveyed was through drawings; even today, in the age of highly sophisticated computer-aided design (CAD), final plans are still printed out and distributed among work crews, not downloaded as files to be referenced at construction sites on laptop computers.

"The idea of drawing out a building entirely before you begin it was born during the transition from the Middle Ages to the Renaissance, and that is precisely when the transition away from vellum occurred," James F. O'Gorman, a professor emeritus of Wellesley College and former president of the Society of Architectural Historians, told me in an interview for this book. "Beginning in the late fifteenth century in Italy, all architectural drawings, until the computer, have more or less been made the same way: on paper. Paper thus becomes the standard medium through which architects communicate their ideas to the builders and the clients. So it becomes sort of the currency of architecture. Before the Renaissance, buildings were begun without a clear overall picture of how they would end. They took many decades to build a cathedral, often more than a hundred years, and they improvised and modified what they were doing constantly over time."

Now, by contrast, "everything is drawn with hundreds of documents, the lawyers are involved, they become legal instruments," O'Gorman continued. "All this is a modern concept. In the Middle Ages, there was nothing at all like that. You mention Archimedes—he was writing on sand, right? Or dirt? Whatever it was, there was nothing permanent at all about it, was there? Well, paper changed all of that. Parchment does not offer flexibility—you can't really sketch on it, and many drawings were not even done on parchment; some were drawn on stone. So a temple in Athens is nothing like a skyscraper in Dubai. What the Greeks were doing was producing an overall envelope. The cost of buildings today is all in the infrastructure: heating, ventilating, plumbing, the tremendous services needed for computers. All of this has to be meticulously drawn and planned out in advance. In order for an architect to get a concept approved, it has to be put on something solid and portable. In the modern era, that something has been paper."

Drawing precisely to scale is a concept that came along with these changes, and it is responsible for the development of the dividers, compasses, and rulers displayed so attractively at the Avery Library, in New York. "Some architects, like Frank Lloyd Wright and Ralph Adams Cram, said they knew in their mind what they were going to do before they got to the paper," O'Gorman said. "That may be a bit of wishful thinking. But the idea was first recorded in a preliminary drawing architects often call a napkin sketch, sometimes a back-of-the-envelope drawing or a matchbook drawing, but basically something that is inspired and drawn in a rush on whatever scrap of paper is within arm's reach." O'Gorman mentioned in this context the architectural musings of Leonardo da Vinci. "They're like snowflakes almost, aren't they? There's just one after the other, every variation on the theme that you could possibly want, all on one piece of paper—and it's probably done in, what, twenty-five minutes?"

O'Gorman has written more than a dozen books, including biographical examinations of Henry Hobson Richardson, the noted nineteenth-century American architect who created what is known as the Richardsonian Romanesque style and is best known for his 1872 design of Trinity Church in Boston's Copley Square, which was conceived in this high-octane manner of improvisation. "Richardson never went beyond napkin drawing, really; he had a handful of draftsmen working for him, and they would whip his little sketches up to scale, then he'd scribble all over them and tell them to go back and iron it out and get back to him. But the thing that carries those ideas from one person to the other is the paper. Ultimately, these are the visual arts. You can't really tell anybody verbally what you want—it has to be accessible visually."

Perhaps the best-known example of this freewheeling approach, O'Gorman said, is the design the English architect and landscape gardener Sir Joseph Paxton came up with in 1850 to house the Great Exhibition of the Works of Industry of all Nations, scheduled to open the following year in Hyde Park, London. As the story has been related by a number of contemporary sources, Paxton was attending a board meeting in London of the Midland Railway company, on which he served, and mentioned to the chairman, John Ellis, a member of Parliament and head of the royal commission appointed to organize the exhibition, that he had an idea that might work. He had just completed designing an innovative greenhouse that utilized recent advancements in the manufacture of glass and cast iron, a concept he felt might be modified for the exposition. Ellis told him to submit his idea on paper, with the understanding that he needed to see something within nine days.

Paxton had other business obligations to attend to first, but at a conference in Derby, he spent most of his time doodling with pen and ink on a blotting sheet that was lying on the table. At the end of the meeting, he held up the first sketch of what an editor for *Punch* magazine would later dub the Crystal Palace—a building 1,848 feet long and 408 feet wide, set on nineteen acres, and rising to three levels on a skeleton of cast-iron columns, with a glass transept that peaked at 103 feet. The structure's modular design and prefabricated elements allowed for an on-time opening the following year. Having been moved to another location after the exhibition, it was leveled by fire in 1936; Paxton's nineteenth-century precursor to the cocktail napkin sketch, meanwhile—the original piece of blotting paper—is housed today in the Victoria and Albert Museum.

Some historians of technology credit the Italian Renaissance architect and engineer Filippo Brunelleschi with pioneering the linear perspective techniques that are standard in modern architectural designs. He was also the first to prepare plans of such specificity that workers were able to perform their tasks entirely as instructed. This technical advancement liberated the designer from having to supervise every phase of assembly on-site and allowed for the delegation of assignments among separate assembly teams.

Commissioned to accomplish what was considered at the time an almost impossible task—completion of the great masonry dome of the cathedral of Santa Maria del Fiore, in Florence, without the benefit of scaffolding—Brunelleschi solved a key logistical problem by designing an ingenious hoisting machine for the vertical delivery of construction materials. He maintained security by sending drawings of vital components off to different job shops outside the city and had the sections joined as they were returned to the construction site. Only the architect himself and his immediate subordinates were privy to the overall scheme, a close-to-the-vest mentality that prefigured the way things would be built in the future, and anticipated the utilization of what we know today as subcontractors.

While certainly close cousins, architecture and engineering are separate disciplines nonetheless. Derived from the Greek word *architekton,* for "chief builder" or "master carpenter," architecture is concerned primarily with the design of buildings but takes in a multitude of other structures such as bridges, highways, and aqueducts. The earliest engineers were people who were involved in the making of military machines such as catapults and battering rams, a diversion pursued by Leonardo in his notebooks, or in developing clever defensive instruments for sieges, a specialty of Archimedes. As recently as the 1600s, the term *engineer* identified a person responsible for managing fortifications and military logistics, particularly firearms and gunpowder.

Technological developments changed the connotation of the word considerably, and it reached full flower during the Industrial Revolution, when the making of machines or "engines" of commercial utility became the order of the day and the engineer emerged as a kind of applied scientist who focused on the nuts and bolts of the trend toward mechanization. Aptly, the word itself, from the Latin verb *ingeniare* (to devise), identifies "an ingenious contrivance," a perfect description for what these professional enablers came to regard as their reason for being.

In Eugene Ferguson's view, the engineering process typically starts with a series of freehand sketches, none of which are drawn to scale; the initial goal is to try out new ideas, compare alternatives, and, most important, "capture fleeting ideas on paper." The sketch can then take on several aspects. The first of these Ferguson called the "thinking sketch"—with Leonardo being the prime exemplar—used mainly to "focus and guide nonverbal thinking." Sometimes drawn to scale, the "prescriptive sketch" directs a drafter in the making of a finished drawing. And a third, what he called the "talking sketch," is generally something drawn spontaneously and used to help explain ideas and goals to colleagues.

Another form of graphic representation is the three-dimensional model, which has been in architecture and design since the Renaissance. Ferguson pointed out that such renderings "show designers how their ideas appear on paper" and, when complete, give workers "all the information needed to produce the object." What professionals call "plans" are imaginary horizontal slices taken through buildings, while "sections" are slices usually taken vertically. "What both plans and sections do is draw to our attention spatial relationships that, in fact, can be seen only in the mind's eye."

A British historian whose specialty is industrial art and graphics makes the point that engineering drawing as we know it today is a product of the Industrial Revolution, its origins reliant on the development of new forms of manufacture and consolidation. "Although it is possible to trace roots back to naval and architectural draughtsmanship and to scientific and technical illustrations at the time of the Renaissance, it was a distinctive form of production—the division of labor—that made engineering drawing essential," Ken Baynes writes in *The Art of the Engineer.* Though this assertion is largely ignored by cultural historians, Baynes argues that the essential link between conception and reality "made possible a new relationship between management and manufacture and separated the process of design from the process of production."

*The Art of the Engineer* grew out of two exhibitions, mounted in Cardiff and London, in the late 1970s. Curated by Baynes, both were concerned with the key role played by this type of industrial art in the technological developments that came to define much of the modern world. Most of the engineering drawings selected for the exhibitions were made for the transportation industry during the nineteenth and twentieth centuries, with the central focus being on locomotives, ships, automobiles, and aircraft. Formerly head of the Design Education Unit at the Royal College of Art, Baynes is himself an artist and designer who has written extensively about the subject. Like so many other people I interviewed for this project, Baynes said he had always regarded the availability of paper as a given in this context; he intuitively understood and accepted its role, but he had never fully examined it in terms of its indispensability.

"I think, on reflection, that very definitely you could make a strong argument that the Industrial Revolution depended on the ability to make images on paper. If you hadn't been able to do that in profusion, you wouldn't have had a practical way of storing the relevant technical expertise and passing it on to other people. And because the engineers very quickly developed a particular language—their own language, in which they could communicate with each other and (very interestingly) with the people who would actually build the machines and the railways and the canals—they needed an appropriate vehicle. So there had to be a way in which they could convey to them what should be built. I think that architectural craftsmanship, and in particular the way that they rediscovered perspective in the Renaissance, had a powerful creative effect on engineering drawing as well."

Without a form of visual communication incorporating signs and symbols that among professionals are as "readable" as words on a page, the ability to construct highly complex machines would not, in his view, have been possible, either. "Locomotives *definitely* couldn't be built without them," Baynes said. "A ship of the eighteenth century probably couldn't have been built without them, either, but that's closer to the origins of ships built with things like templates. When I went to Turkey to look at traditional shipbuilding, where they build a kind of Mediterranean sailing vessel without any plans at all, what they do have are templates that outline the basic shape of the ship. They keep these just lying on the ground where they are building them. If the ship you are building today is the same as the ship you were building yesterday, you don't need a drawing—what you need is knowledge of how to do it. As soon as you have technological change, you need a drawing. By the eighteenth century, the pressure for innovation, particularly in warships, was such that you had to have the drawings."

Because any large-scale project—a railroad stretching across hundreds of miles of changing landscape, for instance, or a multi-engine airplane built for commercial use—can involve the making of many thousands of drawings, no other medium could have been used besides paper. The work became so accomplished that some of the drawings were done in color, and many finished pieces were lithographed, which is why Baynes describes so much of the work he gathered for the exhibitions, and reproduced in his book, as "engineering art." "I think that these people felt so strongly that they were in the forefront of progress, and that what they were doing was dignified and important, so there was no question but that the drawings would be beautiful," Baynes told me. "It just wasn't discussed. It was how they would be in order to capture the essence of the machine which was going to result from the drawing."

What made possible the building of the projects that did result was the requirement that all relevant drawings be made precisely to scale, a convention that evolved over time to assure that every component would mesh as intended in the final assembly. With enormous undertakings being produced by separate work groups, there had to be certainty that everyone was proceeding "on the same page," to assure that all the pieces would fit together. In the earliest days of the industrial boom, engineering firms maintained large staffs of draftsmen who made accurate copies of drawings for distribution to the work crews.

The vital role played by the drawing was underscored early in the Industrial Revolution by Charles Babbage, the British mathematician and inventor who came up with a design for what is argued by some historians to be the genesis of the modern computer, a machine that existed entirely on paper before a prototype was successfully built, in the early years of the twenty-first century, from his plans. "The drawings are intricate and detailed," Doron Swade, the engineer and historian of technology who headed up the project for the Science Museum, in London, recalled of his first viewing. "They show a machine eleven feet long, seven feet high, and eighteen inches deep, with eight columns, each with thirty-one figure wheels." The successful venture Swade spearheaded—which took five years for his team to achieve—came in the aftermath of an epiphany: "The attempt to build the Engine was not the physical realization of an abstract ideal embodied in the drawings. It was instead the resumption of a practical engineering project that had been arrested in 1849 and remained in limbo for 140 years."

Writing in 1832, Babbage had discussed at length the essential role of drawing in making revolutionary machines of unprecedented complexity. "When each process has been reduced to the use of some simple tool, the union of all these tools, actuated by one moving power, constitutes a machine. In contriving tools and simplifying processes, the operative workmen are, perhaps, most successful; but it requires for other habits to combine into one machine these scattered arts. A previous education as a workman in a peculiar trade, is undoubtedly a valuable preliminary; but in order to make such combinations with any reasonable expectation of success, an extensive knowledge of machinery, and the power of making mechanical drawings, are essentially requisite. These accomplishments are now much more common than they were formerly; and their absence was, perhaps, one of the causes of the multitude of failures in the early history of many of our manufactures."

In his interview with me, Ken Baynes picked up on that observation, noting how large engineering firms in the early nineteenth century "developed a kind of institutional approach to design, which they had to do because they were designing quite a lot of things at the same time, and they needed to be disseminated to many different people. So you had armies of copyists, and they were skilled not only in drawing—they were technically skilled, too, since they had to understand what the drawings meant."

Baynes said one aspect of the phenomenon that "really fascinates" him is how the instructions on paper drawings were then transferred to a block of metal, known as the workpiece. "We're talking here now around about the 1900s or so, and what would happen, generally, is that the foreman would come along and he would mark on the sheet metal precisely where the cuts were going to be made. He translated that from the drawing he had—which was not full size—into a full-size representation, which he made in chalk, directly on the workpiece. When you think about it, that's an extraordinarily skilled thing for him to do, and yet all that respect for this kind of skill, of translating from drawing to workpiece—we really have not documented that, and we really don't celebrate it at all. There's something interesting to be said about the relationship between the paper and the metal, if it's a ship or a locomotive, or between the paper and bricks, if it's a building—whatever the material. There's a kind of existential relationship between them, which I think deserves more thought and more interpretation."

What makes the relationship existential, Baynes continued, is a progression that extends "from the visual to the actual, and probably what we've all forgotten is that there is a person who had to do that in his mind so that the thing could be built. I'm astounded by the ability we have to look at a tiny drawing, a scrap of paper, and somehow it is possible for the human mind to say, 'Well, okay, this is a locomotive,' 'this is a city,' whatever it is, and that must, I think, account to some extent for our success as a species in shaping, for better or for worse, the environment to our own plan rather than to evolution's plan. That definitely hasn't been all good news—but we have been able to do it."

Like scribes in the years before the invention of print, draftsmen were subject to occasional error, which was especially unforgiving in a trade where such a high premium was placed on precision and exactitude. What changed the dynamic dramatically was the introduction, in the late 1800s, of the blueprint, a process of graphic duplication discovered at the dawn of photography that allowed for the copying of documents identical to the originals. The breakthrough for its practical use was made by Sir John Frederick William Herschel, a younger colleague of William Fox Talbot, who developed what he called the cyanotype process (from the Greek word *kuanos,* for dark blue, the color of the prints that were made). Its commercial applications were developed in Paris in the early 1870s and introduced at the Philadelphia Centennial Exhibition in 1876.

"The blueprint, if you think about it, was a kind of precursor to the computer," Baynes said. "It was not computer-aided drafting in any way—not even close—but blueprints did make it possible to multiply these drawings cheaply and precisely. That was quite a step forward." They became such a fixture in the world of engineering design that the word was soon an idiom in and of itself, so pervasive that, like all expressions that begin their existences as lively word images, it lost its metaphorical impact through repeated and oftentimes illogical use. To argue that some politician's vapid plan for economic recovery is a "blueprint for disaster," for example, or that a DNA sequence provides a "genetic blueprint" for the building of an organism's genome, makes for good sound bites, but both lose sight of the original purpose the documents served, which was to build durable objects with a minimum of error.

EMERGING FROM a strong German tradition that has always placed a high premium on documentation, Dr. Wernher von Braun, the father of modern space travel, was no stranger to paperwork. In fact, it was the careful preservation of the most important blueprints and memoranda prepared by his rocket team during World War II at Peenemünde, the secret German missile production center on the Baltic island of Usedom, that made him a particularly attractive prize for whichever Allied power might secure his services at war's end.

A member of von Braun's elite corps of scientists described the limited options they had to consider as peace finally drew near: "We despise the French; we are mortally afraid of the Soviets; we do not believe the British can afford us; so that leaves the Americans." And so the Americans it would be, at least for the most gifted of the team; one memorable line from *The Right Stuff*, the film based on Tom Wolfe's 1978 book of the same title, has the von Braun character declare confidently of America's greatly hyped space race with the Soviet Union that "our Germans are better than their Germans." How such a coup came to pass is also traceable, in considerable measure, to the anxious delivery of fourteen tons of plans, designs, and production reports to the Americans by von Braun and his team as a way of gaining favor with their new employers.

With Russian forces closing in from the east and American troops driving up from the southwest, the outcome of the war became more a matter of when Germany would fall, not if, prompting von Braun and his associates to plan appropriately. On April 1, 1945, with the surrender in Europe barely five weeks away, he instructed one of his key aides, Dr. Dieter K. Huzel, to find a suitable hiding place for the mass of reports and drawings that had been central to the building of the V-1 and V-2 rockets over the previous thirteen years. Loading everything of importance that they had into three panel trucks and two trailers, a select crew of ten men hauled the treasure trove to an abandoned quarry outside Goslar, a village forty-five miles north of Bleicherode, using as their cover a set of top-secret orders conveniently issued by von Braun that required any suspicious SS officers they might have encountered along the way to assist the convoy by every means possible. Finding a suitable location—a dry storeroom at the end of a thousand-foot tunnel, serviced by an electric rail cart—they drove the trucks inside in the dead of night and worked through noon the next day unloading the hoard.

After sealing off the chamber with dynamite, Huzel joined up with von Braun at a Bavarian city on the Austrian border, where together they made their way to the American lines. The papers were promptly recovered and became the underpinning of a program that soon got under way at Cape Canaveral, Florida, and eventually landed astronauts on the moon, in 1969. "These documents were of inestimable value," Huzel would later attest in a memoir. "Whoever inherited them would be able to start rocketry at that point at which we had left off, with the benefit not only of our accomplishments, but of our mistakes as well—the real ingredient of experience. They represented years of intensive effort in a brand new technology, one which, all of us were convinced, would play a profound role in the future course of human events."

WHERE I GREW UP, in Lowell, Massachusetts, in the early 1950s, it was accepted as an article of faith in the public schools I attended that the "Spindle City," as it was known, had been established in the 1820s as the world's first planned industrial community, all of it made possible by the surreptitious introduction of technology into the United States at a time when England fiercely protected its manufacturing secrets. Beginning in the early 1780s, it was a criminal offense to export any piece of industrial equipment from Britain or Ireland, or to remove any technical information that might assist in mimicking or improving it. No plans of any sort could be copied, no notes of any kind sketched out.

While traveling abroad with his family between 1810 and 1812, the Boston entrepreneur Francis Cabot Lowell, a brilliant son of privilege with impeccable letters of introduction, was allowed to tour a number of textile mills in England and Scotland. Although his hosts were gracious in showing him around, it was understood that he could take no notes on the power looms then being used to weave cotton yarn into finished cloth. But, being gifted with what we would today call a photographic memory, and a standout student of mathematics while at Harvard, Lowell sketched out the essence of what he saw during the sea voyage home. On his return, he engaged the services of Paul Moody, a "thorough, practical machinist," according to one early account, with a knack for creative thinking. A biographical sketch published in 1847 would describe Moody as being "fully acquainted with all that was then generally known of cotton-spinning and weaving." Even more to the point was this attribute: "It is a remarkable fact, and illustrative of the strength and peculiarity of his mind, that most of his calculations were made in his head, with but little use of pen and paper."

No record survives of how Lowell and Moody pooled their respective skills, but in very short order they had fashioned a system of water-driven power looms that attracted the financial backing of some wealthy Massachusetts businessmen brought together by the merchant Nathan Appleton. In a matter of months, they converted a former

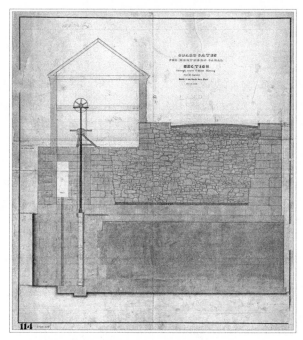

*A Locks and Canals engineering drawing, dated
December 10, 1846, showing a section for "Guard Gates
for Northern Canal" in Lowell, Massachusetts.*

paper mill on the Charles River in Waltham into the nation's first vertically integrated textile-manufacturing plant. By the end of 1814, the
enterprise, called the Boston Manufacturing Company, was converting
bales of ginned raw cotton into bolts of finished cloth, in one contained
process.

Limited by insufficient waterpower in Waltham, the merchants
soon turned their attention to East Chelmsford, a rural farming village twenty-five miles north of Boston on the Merrimack River. They
would name their new community for Lowell, who had died in 1817,
at the age of forty-two, but whose "entirely new arrangement," according to Nathan Appleton, had made possible "all the processes for the
conversion of cotton into cloth, within the walls of the same building."
That same principle would be brought to bear a few decades later in the
production of paper from wood pulp.

While little documentation survives of Lowell's early collaboration
with Moody, the planning that went into the design and construction of the bold industrial experiment that came to bear his name

was minutely detailed by the engineers and draftsmen enlisted to the task, much of it preserved in ten thousand plans and drawings that to this day remain in the city where they were executed. Viewed as a form of visual narrative, they offer a unique window into the physical development of an unprecedented social experiment that included the recruitment of young women to work in the mills, a kind of Yankee paternalism that would earn the approbation of Charles Dickens when he visited the city in 1842.

Three hundred of the earliest drawings are held by the Center for Lowell History, the special-collections library of the University of Massachusetts Lowell, located in what was once a boardinghouse for "mill girls." The far larger concentration is maintained by the National Park Service in the Cultural Resource Center of the Lowell National Historical Park, established in 1978 by an act of Congress. The very survival of these materials is fortuitous unto itself, a circumstance made possible by the longevity of the Proprietors of Locks and Canals on Merrimack River, a business enterprise (commonly called Locks and Canals) that was incorporated in 1792 for the express purpose of building a canal around a stretch of the Merrimack River known as the Pawtucket Falls. Once the Boston merchants decided that the falls had the potential to provide all the power they needed—the Merrimack drops thirty feet in less than a mile before it merges with the Concord River—they began to buy up large blocks of land in the area, and in 1821 they acquired the Locks and Canals company itself.

By 1850, nearly six miles of freshly dug waterways snaked their way through what was by then the state's second-largest city, turning turbines designed and fabricated by Locks and Canals machinists and driving the wheels, pulleys, and belts of forty multistory brick mills built by Locks and Canals construction workers, which together housed 225,000 spindles and ten thousand looms made by Locks and Canals mechanics. It is a fascinating episode in the industrial heritage of the United States, and a good deal of it has been richly examined, but what few of the histories explore in any depth are the engineering plans prepared during the most dynamic years of the company's activity. It was only in 1960, when a dramatically downsized Locks and Canals was relocating its headquarters, that the first batch of drawings was given to what was then the Lowell Technological Institute, now part of the University of Massachusetts system. Included were materials attributed to James B. Francis, the visionary engineer who devised numerous methods to deliver, measure, and, most important, bill for water. A talented draftsman and surveyor, Francis began working in Lowell in 1834 as assistant to George Washington Whistler, the chief engineer and also the father of the artist James Abbott McNeill Whistler. Francis took over the top position in 1837, when Whistler accepted an offer to supervise construction of the Moscow–St. Petersburg Railway, in Russia, and remained a major figure in Lowell until his death, in 1892.

The far more substantial portion of drawings was turned over to the Lowell National Historical Park in the 1980s. Included in that collection were working and presentation drawings, pencil and ink drawings on linen and paper, blueprints, machine models, photographs, and manuscript records. During my visit to the research center, the curator of the archive, Jack Herlihy, showed me the original incorporation papers of the company, signed boldly on June 27, 1792, by Massachusetts governor John Hancock. But the highlight of the day was without doubt a sampling of the early drawings rendered on large sheets of high-quality rag paper made in England by the famed firm of J. Whatman, whose founder, James Whatman, had developed the process for making wove paper in the 1750s. With a rigidly smooth surface devoid of chain lines, Whatman paper has been a favorite of watercolor artists, printmakers, and lithographers for more than two and a half centuries. It counts among its most famous devotees John James Audubon, who used it for the double-folio etchings he made for his monumental *Birds of America,* and William Blake, who utilized it in four of his illuminated books. During the American Revolution, Benjamin Franklin acquired through an intermediary in London two reams of Whatman paper for an elegant run of impressive loan certificates he printed on his press at Passy, outside of Paris, while serving as minister plenipotentiary to France. Other appreciative customers have included the artists Thomas Gainsborough and J. M. W. Turner, the emperor Napoleon, and Queen Victoria.

In 1994, twenty-two of the most attractive Lowell drawings were mounted and displayed in a joint exhibition called *Art of the Draftsman: 19th Century Plans and Drawings,* some of them signed, initialed, or attributed to James B. Francis, most of them unsigned, but all beautifully rendered, and many hand-colored. Plans for basins, gates, feeder engines, flumes, turbines, guard locks, waterwheels, bridges, and cofferdams are carefully drawn out. One overhead view, prepared in 1824, shows the projected location of ten mill buildings and about ninety boardinghouses for the female workers. I discussed the subtlety of these drawings with Christine M. Wirth, a conservation specialist with the National Park Service, who has also worked with the Frederick Law Olmsted National Historic Site collection of 150,000 landscape drawings and manuscript papers, in Brookline, Massachusetts. "What you see in so many of these nineteenth-century drawings is how meticulous they were about documenting their work," she said. "They recorded precisely what they had designed, they used it for their work, and then they passed it on. It survived because it's on good paper, and in many cases it's beautiful. But the point is that nobody threw it out."

# 15

## Sleight of Hand

In the days before the cabaret New York boasted a considerable number of popular dining clubs which brought together a host of people who could "do entertaining things." At one of these dinners I observed an Americanized Japanese folding a leaf of the menu card in a peculiar manner. Gradually all those within "seeing distance" became interested, and before he finished he was quite surrounded by spectators who applauded him roundly when, from that scrap of pasteboard, he at last produced a little paper bird that flapped its wings quite naturally.
—Harry Houdini,
*Houdini's Paper Magic,* 1922

One of my dreams is to go up into the mountains and learn to make paper from trees the way people did in the old days. I want to go with the young people and start my own origami village, and there we will make and dye paper so it will last a long, long time.
—Akira Yoshizawa,
quoted in *Folding the Universe,* 1989

Anything is possible in origami.
—Robert J. Lang, e-mail to author, 2011

RARELY DO WE THINK of paper as anything other than a material of pure utility, a marvel of happenstance that functions best when attracting no attention whatsoever to itself. While certainly this is true for the most part, there are some notable exceptions in which paper stands out on its own and becomes more than just a medium and very much a part of the message. Such an anomaly is apparent in the book arts, where exquisitely crafted volumes become beautiful objects in and of themselves and where every physical detail is essential to the making of the artifact—not least among them the quality and malleability of the paper.

Several names stand out in this field, none more distinguished than Claire Van Vliet, of Newark, Vermont, a one-woman dynamo of creative energy whose Janus Press has produced a significant body of watercolors, drawings, etchings, lithographs, woodcuts, and broadsides since 1955 that have all explored the infinite possibilities of paper, some of them using pigmented pulps applied directly on handmade substrates to create images that are distinctive and unique in each instance. In Madison, Wisconsin, the experimental use of handmade papers has been explored in surprisingly inventive ways by Walter Hamady, a printer, teacher, and papermaker celebrated for his readiness to "juxtamorph" art with literature, typography, letterpress printing, papermaking, and assemblage. "I think all life is a collage," he has said, a conviction that animates his highly individualized work.

On a far broader scale, various paper trinkets provide their measure of amusement, too, be it kites sent straining against the wind, decorative lamps hung from porch rafters, elegant fans emblazoned with bucolic scenes, ingenious pop-up books designed by clever "paper engineers" such as Robert Sabuda and David Carter, or decks of cards—foretelling the future for some, creating wagering opportunities for others. In parts of the Far East, Buddhist and Shinto cultures make paper offerings to assorted spirits and deceased ancestors, and molding paper by hand with a variety of vegetative fibers prepared to individual specifications, as we shall explore in the next chapter, is a richly gratifying skill enjoyed by many enthusiasts worldwide.

For a clear instance in which it can be argued that form and function become one and the same, however, the traditional handicraft known as origami stands alone as the archetypal example, not only in terms of massive global appeal but for its reach across all age and social barriers. Dismissed by some, perhaps, as mere child's play, the making of complex sculptures from single sheets of paper is one of those rare activities that have the power to engage preschoolers and scientists alike with comparable appeal, its range of possibilities limited only by one's imagination and manual dexterity. In each application, the object is to construct a multisided figure of some complexity out of a flat piece of paper, and to do it without the use of scissors, tape, or glue. Therein lies the challenge, and therein lies the satisfaction.

A refrain expressed often in these pages is that paper is plentiful, inexpensive, and portable; if made well, it resists tearing and can be creased into compact shapes that are useful for currency, correspondence, and cleverly conceived three-dimensional objects. Such alchemy is made possible by yet another characteristic that is often overlooked when discussing the manifold properties of paper: what we might call foldability. This peculiarity is the industry standard used to measure strength, and it was at the core of *Double Fold,* the writer Nicholson Baker's searing examination of recent library policies regarding the disposal of old newspapers deemed redundant and irrelevant to institutional collections.

Baker's title referred to a test used by conservators to determine the brittleness of various grades of paper by folding down the corner of a book or newspaper page, then folding it back in the opposite direction, constituting one *double fold*. The action is continued until the sheet breaks or is about to break, and the number of repetitions it can endure establishes a relative measure of strength. As the twentieth century drew to a close, numerous libraries used this procedure as a way to justify discarding many artifacts judged too frail to keep on their shelves—and, in the instance of archival newspapers, replacing them entirely with microfilmed copies that scholars everywhere agree make for inferior surrogates.

Baker's response to the practice was heated and confrontational, and he is credited with having forced many institutions to reconsider the wisdom of dumping primary materials once substitute copies were made. "A leaf of a book is a semi-pliant mechanism," he argued. "It was made for non-acute curves, not for origami." That glib observation is relevant because the essence of origami is indeed the folding of paper, though the far larger objective is to do so in ways that are aesthetically satisfying, and in some instances to solve complicated mathematical problems. *Origami* is a Japanese coinage that combines *ori,* the word for fold, with *kami,* for paper. In the vast majority of instances—origami done by children as part of structured educational programs, for instance, or the casual making of paper airplanes, which is a related form of the pastime—the quality of the paper is not of overriding concern. But in cases where the goal is to produce a work of art, quality is very definitely a factor, not only for a particular sheet's suitability to accept multiple creases but for strength and permanence.

Though no one knows for certain, the likelihood is that the first paper sculptures were crafted in Japan in the sixth century, as ritual containers for Shinto offerings, but hard evidence of origami is not readily discernible until around the seventeenth century. While origami historians concede there is no precise chronology, the practice eventually appeared in other parts of the world, arriving either through undocumented migration or as activities that emerged independently along with the introduction of paper.

The German educator Friedrich Fröbel introduced the folding of colored papers into ornamental designs as an integral feature of his program of constructive play and self-activity in early childhood. Fröbel never used the word *origami*—it is possible he never even heard of it—favoring instead the German expression for paper folding, *Papierfalten,* in his development of the kindergarten (meaning, literally, a garden for children) during the early years of the nineteenth century. Similarly, the Italian educator Maria Montessori applied the principle in the innovative program she developed for early learners, making various folding routines integral to the practical life exercises that remain vital to her theory of education.

In the early decades of the twentieth century, the Bauhaus, an influential school of commercial design established in Germany by Walter Gropius, stressed the folding of paper as a method to be used in training students. The artist and educator Josef Albers stressed the necessity of learning everything possible about the materials at hand and preached the gospel of experimentation in courses he taught in the United States and Europe. His custom was to arrive on the first day of class with an armful of newspapers, which he passed around the room. "Try to make something out of them that is more than you have now," one of his students, Hannes Beckmann, recalled him saying. "I want you to respect the material and use it in a way that makes sense—preserve its inherent characteristics. If you can do without tools like knives and scissors, and without glue, the better."

Among other devotees was the Reverend Charles Lutwidge Dodgson, an Oxford University mathematics instructor best known by the pen name Lewis Carroll. In one memorable scene in *Alice's Adventures in Wonderland,* Carroll outfitted his young heroine in a paper dress.

Another paper folder was the Spanish writer and philosopher Miguel de Unamuno, who was so proficiently devoted that a number of animal constructions he invented are still studied today. A satiric novel he wrote in 1902, *Amor y Pedagogía* (*Love and Pedagogy*), includes as an appendix a humorous paean to origami. The legendary magician Harry Houdini's 1922 guide to at-home conjuring, *Houdini's Paper Magic,* had for its subtitle "The Whole Art of Performing with Paper, Including Paper Tearing, Paper Folding, and Paper Puzzles."

As noteworthy as these milestones have been, none has done more to recruit new devotees than the heartbreaking story of Sadako Sasaki, a survivor of the atomic bombing of Hiroshima who contracted leukemia in 1955, at the age of twelve, and was persuaded to take up paper folding by a Japanese proverb passed on to her by a playmate shortly after learning the grim news of her diagnosis: "If a sick person folds one thousand cranes, the gods will grant her wish and make her healthy again." During Sadako's final days—her supply of paper having been exhausted—she used the wrappings from medicine bottles and get-well gifts. When time ran out, on October 25, 1955, Sadako had folded 644 cranes, but her will to press on inspired others to complete the task. Before long, children worldwide were making paper cranes, and statues honoring Sadako's memory were erected in both Hiroshima and Seattle. Today, the girl's tale—like that of Anne Frank—is synonymous with the unspeakable suffering of children during wartime, and also like Frank, whose memory was preserved through the miraculous survival of a handwritten diary, Sadako had her moving message of hope passed on by way of paper.

LIKE MANY THOUSANDS of origami enthusiasts, Michael G. LaFosse came to paper folding as a youngster, captured by the magic of what can be accomplished with a minimum of materials and a wealth of imagination. Acclaimed internationally today as one of the most creative origami artists of his generation, LaFosse regards the choice of paper as critical, so much so that he makes his own by hand, having learned the basics in the 1970s, through trial and error, and later mastering the craft in workshops offered by Elaine Koretsky in Brookline, Massachusetts.

As he became more skillful, he learned to select various fibers that were suited to specific projects, perfecting the craft to the point that the sheets he makes commercially today are in demand among other master paper folders. When we spoke for the first time, by telephone to set up an interview, he suggested I visit his studio and gallery, in a converted mill in Haverhill, Massachusetts, on a Saturday morning, when he would be making a batch of his special paper with a student. I would be welcome to try my hand at a bit of origami, an invitation that I eagerly accepted. I was early for the meeting, and while waiting for LaFosse to arrive, Richard L. Alexander, his business partner, offered to guide me through the making of a paper puppy.

"Let's go ahead," he said cheerfully. "I'll pretend you're a seven-year-old." Following Alexander's patient directions, I did just fine, and to this day I keep the little canine I assembled under his guidance on a bookshelf by my desk. But the larger point to be made is that in this instance, the process was geared to the abilities of a second-grade class, which would probably have done a far more accomplished job at the task than I did. Indeed, the success of Origamido Studio, the company LaFosse and Alexander established in 1996, has been based on teaching origami to students of every age.

"When I was five years old, I saw a man on a television program showing how to fold a balloon out of a piece of paper, and I was totally mesmerized," LaFosse told me, recalling when he was introduced to origami. "Bookmobiles would come to my school, and I took out every book they had on paper folding. I was passionate about it, and by the time I was seven years old I had solved all those folding problems." LaFosse said the paper birds, water bombs, airplanes, jumping frogs, and flowers he was making as a boy came from his willingness to follow written instructions. What changed everything in his approach was the chance discovery of a lavishly illustrated article in the August 1970 issue of *Reader's Digest* by the Pulitzer Prize–winning writer Leland Stowe about a Japanese innovator of the form, Akira Yoshizawa, regarded by master folders everywhere as the godfather of modern origami.

The article told how the onetime ironsmith had taught himself the essentials of the craft, and how so much of his technique involved close study of animals and plants in nature. "Master Yoshizawa approached what he did from a scientific point of view," LaFosse said. "He studied the anatomy, even some of the chemistry involved, and from there he invented new forms, even if it took him years to accomplish—the cicada, one of his best-known figures, took him twenty years to perfect. And the photographs—in the opening spread, there was a picture of his face, and then next to it a self-portrait in folded paper—I had never seen anything like this before. It was brilliant." The article also noted that Yoshizawa moistened his paper while making figures, a revelation for LaFosse, who had always assumed that origami was folded strictly with dry sheets.

"I had thought origami was like crossword puzzles: you get the book, you learn the fundamentals, you do it, you're done. But when I looked at those photographs, here was this man *inventing* his own designs. I had always wanted to be an artist, and I had always wanted to be a scientist. People had been telling me, 'You can't be both. You either go to art school or you study to be a scientist.' But here I could see both art and science coming together. Master Yoshizawa was acting as a scientist, to study these creatures and plants, and as an engineer, to invent the origami. His beautiful results, with the handmade papers of Japan folded so sensitively, were truly works of art. So as a kid, at age ten or eleven, I said, 'I want to be like him. That's what I want to be.' That day—that very day—I started inventing. And the first thing I invented was this penguin."

That penguin, which to this day occupies a prominent place in the Origamido studio, was developed conceptually over a two-year period that LaFosse traces to that flash of insight in 1970, the breakthrough moment coming one Sunday while he was attending church services in his hometown of Fitchburg, Massachusetts. "There was a flier there—there's always a flier of one sort or another in church—and I started folding it. It was pastel mint green, and it occurred to me while I was folding that I could somehow use colors to my advantage. Before the service was over, I had basically come up with the idea that became that penguin. I saw the possibilities." What is immediately impressive about the giant bird LaFosse ultimately created is how the natural coloration of the animal was achieved with a single piece of paper—it has a white neck, ears, chest, and feet, and a black beak, head, and body.

"A piece of paper has two sides to it," LaFosse explained. "So if one side is white, and the other side is black, then you can get two colors when you start folding it up. So that's the engineering side, isn't it? It's all very methodically planned." He was able, finally, to achieve his goal through the mail-order purchase of some origami paper that was black on one side and white on the other. "When I folded up my penguin for the first time, it turned out to be a white bird with a black belly. So I unfolded it, reversed all the folds, and got it right—and realized right there that I had created this two-color entity that correlated to the penguin's real pattern."

LaFosse compared the making of an original origami figure to a chess game in which each move is considered many steps in advance. "There's a lot of trial and error, and the fingers need a laboratory to puzzle all these designs. An abundance of paper is an absolute must in origami when you are just getting started." Fitchburg, a working-class community on the Nashua River in north-central Massachusetts, was at one time a hub of commercial papermaking in the United States, and home to numerous companies.

"My grandmother worked in one of the plants and was always bringing beautiful paper home. Not having to worry about having paper around was a great advantage for me; I must have burned through thousands of pieces when I was a kid," LaFosse recalled. After high school, he entered the University of Tampa, in Florida, with the idea of becoming a marine biologist, an area of study that would prove useful years later in developing designs for his figures. "But origami was tugging at me. At the end of my third year, I moved out to the Berkshires to put my priorities straight, and started developing my art there." LaFosse worked in a bookstore in Williamstown, then got a job as a cook, all the while honing his folding skills. In 1991, he met Yoshizawa at a master class in Ossining, New York, and they began a friendship that continued until the master's death, in 2005. "Master Yoshizawa was a religious man who didn't take credit for the designing and folding of his creations. He felt like he was a paintbrush, and God was working through his hands. He would pray before he folded and designed things."

In 1996, Richard Alexander, an environmental consultant and a great admirer of LaFosse's work, came up with a plan for a business enterprise they decided to call Origamido, which adds the Japanese word *do,* for "way," to *origami,* to suggest "the way of folded paper." LaFosse, meanwhile, stayed in touch with Yoshizawa, visiting him at his home in Japan on several occasions and collaborating with him on four exhibitions. The master's most important advice, he stressed, was the admonition to always use the best available materials. "Having the right paper makes all the difference in the world. The only way you can control strength, thickness, color, texture, longevity, and colorfastness is by making your own sheets." LaFosse's fiber of choice is a blend of cotton and abaca, a plant in the family *Musaceae* that's indigenous to the Philippines. Known also as Manila hemp (but not of the hemp family), abaca is esteemed for its strength and resistance to moisture and is ideal for the kind of origami LaFosse practices, which uses wet-folding techniques. It is for this reason, too, that abaca is used for tea bags, which need to resist dissolving in boiling water, and was an important source of cordage used on oceangoing sailing vessels in the nineteenth century.

LaFosse varies the proportions and the thickness of the sheets he molds to suit the figures he has in mind. "If it isn't the right paper, then it isn't going to happen in my fingers. It's a very logical and very satisfying process. I love the feel of folding paper under my thumbnail, I love to hear it crinkling, and there's that tactility with the textures. I've been making my own paper for more than thirty years, so I really am alert to the touch. I feel that I am creating a living thing."

LaFosse is always on the lookout for images that he can transform into sculptures, and he recalled a trip to a county fair in nearby Topsfield that gave him the idea to make one of his favorite pieces. "I saw all these lively piglets running around, and I thought, 'I've got to capture that.' I made a particular quality of textured paper that was just the right color of a piglet's skin. The interesting thing is that I made a whole batch, and I went through every piece until I put my fingers on the one piece that I felt was really going to work. I cut it into a twelve-inch square. I was being very engineer-like and analytical—'I need four legs, I need a tail, I need a nose, I need two ears, and I need them to be proportionate.' "

Beyond the engineering aspects, however, were concerns not so easily resolved. "I needed something lyrical and lively, so I wound up putting it aside for a week. When I felt I could do it, I picked it up, and it took about five or six hours before everything finally came together—and the secret was in having the right sheet of paper. Because the paper I made was fairly stiff and fuzzy and soft, I was able to shape the figure into a very fuzzy, soft little piglet. Now, over here, I have a bat; for that, I needed a different texture. The bat's wings are thin, crisp, and glossy—it needed paper that was thin, crisp, and glossy. What you see in both animals is permanence. They're not ephemeral objects. They're here to stay."

While LaFosse has made many versions of the same subjects over the years, he readily acknowledged that no two can ever be the same and that true replication is impossible. "I can certainly retrace what I did, but never to the degree of subtlety that each piece really exhibits. For instance, I know how I folded that pig as far as its basic structure goes, but then what I do to it after that, it's like a drawing or a painting: there's no way to reproduce it exactly. So yes, I have a folding sequence that will bring me up to a point where I then have to bring it to life."

For the California origami master Robert J. Lang, on the other hand, scientific analysis is very much a part of creating a three-dimensional sculpture, so much so that he has developed sophisticated software, known as TreeMaker, that assists him in the search for complex solutions to folding problems that would have been regarded as inconceivable twenty years ago. In addition to Lang's celebrity as an artist—he has been the subject of lengthy profiles in *The New Yorker* and *Smithsonian* and, along with Michael LaFosse, was a central figure in the television documentary *Between the Folds,* which won a Peabody Award in 2010—he is acclaimed as a pioneer in computational origami, which has been coming into its own as a greatly esteemed scientific discipline since the 1990s.

With a Ph.D. in applied physics from the California Institute of Technology, Lang has authored or co-authored more than eighty professional papers, holds fifty patents in lasers and optoelectronics, and has written a dozen books on his distinctive form of paper folding, including *Origami Design Secrets: Mathematical Methods for an Ancient Art,* regarded as a modern classic. His oeuvre includes the creation of six hundred original origami designs, and his finished works have been exhibited at the Museum of Modern Art, in New York, the Carrousel du Louvre, in Paris, the Nippon Origami Museum, in Kaga, Japan, and many others.

Of Lang's many breakthrough designs, one of his better known, even outside of origami circles, is a full-scale replica of a Black Forest cuckoo clock folded from a single one-by-ten-foot sheet of paper that features a deer head with antlers, a bird perched on a platform, a face with hour and minute hands, dangling weights, and a pendulum. He spent three months working out the design details and devoted six inten-

*Origami master Robert Lang in his Alamo, California, studio.*

sive hours to the folding. Other notable creations—all, again, made by deft movements of his hands, and with single sheets of paper—include a snake with one thousand scales and a pteranodon with a sixteen-foot wingspan, installed at the Redpath Museum of McGill University, in Montreal. The algorithms Lang has developed for folding are so advanced that they have proven useful in the designs of a compact lens for a proposed space telescope and airbags for automobiles.

But what makes Lang most appealing, from my standpoint, at least, is that tinkering with paper is his day job, not an absorbing diversion he enjoys as an after-work hobby, and while scientific inquiry remains in his repertoire, it is something he now does on the side. This unlikely reversal of priorities took place in 2001, when Lang was working in San Jose for JDS Uniphase (now known simply as JDSU), a company that designs and manufactures products for optical communications networks, including lasers and fiber optics. Before that, he worked for NASA's Jet Propulsion Laboratory and Spectra Diode Laboratories, and from 2007 to 2010 he was editor in chief of the *IEEE Journal of Quantum Electronics,* a scholarly journal published by the Institute of Electrical and Electronics Engineers. In 2009, he was awarded Caltech's highest honor, the Distinguished Alumni Award, for his work in computational origami.

We met in the freestanding studio Lang maintains behind his home in Alamo, California, an East Bay suburb of San Francisco. My first question, as usual, was directed at the medium: Why paper and not something else? "Paper is the means for realizing the structure, plain and simple," he said without hesitation. "The driving challenge is the intellectual challenge: coming up with the designs. In some sense, you might even think that paper wouldn't even be necessary, that you could create a computer rendering of a folded shape. But in practice, the texture in the paper and the way it is manipulated, the curves, the non-ideal aspects of paper are what lend character to the real folded model. So there's two aspects of folding: the real physical, tactile properties that contribute to the model and also this abstract concept—the geometry that's involved, of how it goes together, what the patterns and the symmetries and the folds are, and how the parts on the square sheet of paper take on new relationships once it's all folded."

Lang recalled for me the invitation he received from the Lawrence Livermore National Laboratory, in Livermore, California, in 2000 to work on the Eyeglass space telescope project, the challenge in this instance being to figure out how to fold a three-hundred-foot-wide flat plastic lens into a compact package that could be launched into space and unfolded once in geostationary orbit, twenty-two thousand miles above the earth. The prototype using Lang's pattern folded from an initial size of sixteen feet down to about five feet, following a precise series of controlled creases designed to ensure the integrity of the optical elements.

"I had written a paper for a computer science conference in 1996, and the Livermore engineers who were developing this telescope had already come to the conclusion themselves that this big flat sheet of telescope needed to be folded into a small shape, and since folding was involved, maybe origami could make a contribution. So they did what all good engineers do: they did a literature search, they looked for people who had written technical papers that had to do with origami, and they found my article, which was how they got in touch with me. What I did for them was develop folding patterns that would be appropriate for their telescope. They ended up using one of them for their first prototype."

Attractive to them, too, was the expertise Lang had developed in both origami and laser physics. "I'm predominantly a theoretician, meaning I analyze how lasers work, the optical properties, how the electrons and the photons interact and so forth. What I've done for many years is to figure out a mathematical description of a laser, or of some aspect of a laser, and then, by using the rules of mathematics, to manipulate that description, and thereby figure out how to build a better laser. So it seemed a pretty natural extension to try that with origami, to develop a mathematical description of origami. What does it mean to make a fold? What are the constraints, what deformations are possible, and still be a fold? And then, once I've developed that mathematical description, how can I work with that description to design new, interesting origami figures?" Lang's solution for the lens package resembled a collapsible umbrella in the furled state, and the fifteen-foot-diameter prototype using his fold pattern passed all preliminary tests. The mission to launch such a monster project—the telescope itself would be a mile long—remains very much on the drawing board.

Proficient in mathematics at an early age, Lang began folding as a boy growing up in Georgia, encouraged by an elementary school teacher while he was in the first grade. Hooked from the beginning, he began creating his own designs in his teens and kept at it through college and graduate school. "I've always been interested in making things, figuring out how things work. As far as my family was concerned, this was just another hobby. As hobbies go, this one was fairly cheap and innocuous. By the time my wife met me, I was reasonably well known and had already designed a lot of very nice pieces, so she thought it was pretty impressive."

Working in areas that cover a broad range of subjects, it figures that Lang would have favorites, but even then, there are no hard-and-fast rules. "When I'm creating an art object, my favorite subjects are birds, insects, and wildlife, and when I'm working on one of those, I am doing something that serves no practical purpose. But when a client says, 'I need a design that folds into a packet for transportation, opens out completely flat, and then can be refolded into a bundle as a container for something,' then I'm folding an object of function that may have nothing to do with art. It may be rather pretty-looking, just because of the neat geometric planes and angles, but the goal for that project is utilitarian. Whether practical or artistic, when someone asks for something, whatever it is, I usually start by trying to visualize how the paper's going to fold together, what parts of the paper are going to turn into what parts of the subject, and how will they move relative to one another."

Although Lang does not make his own paper, he has dabbled a bit with it under the guidance of Michael LaFosse. "I spent a couple sessions with him, where, essentially using his recipes, I actually made some sheets. It's fun, but it's really hard, and you come to appreciate so much of the craftsmanship of papermaking. I'm pulling sheets out, and they're breaking up as they form, and I'm going, 'Why is this happening?' Michael sticks his hand in the water and says, 'It needs some formation aid. It needs some additive.' He could tell that just from the feel of the pulp, because he's been making paper for so many years."

Lang then walked me over to a cabinet in his studio that was well stocked with a variety of sheets, a good many of them from Japan, and an entire drawer filled with stock from LaFosse's Origamido Studio. "You find tremendous diversity in paper choice among origami makers, because we're looking for different things, and that often requires a different feel. Folding can be very demanding on the paper's strength, so you need very long fibers, and often very uniform fibers, especially if you're doing something that requires thin paper. The nonwoody plant papers—abaca, hemp, flax—all make good origami papers." He showed me some lovely handmade stock of 100 percent rag that he bought from Papeterie Saint-Armand, an artisan paper mill in Montreal. "It's heavier paper than most, and it makes the best elephants. I did two elephant commissions with this—it's just fantastic." He also used a custom-made sheet of Saint-Armand paper to make the flying reptile with the huge wingspan that hangs at McGill University.

"Here's a wood-based commercial paper called Wyndstone Marble, very heavily calendared, that I use a lot. I like it because it has almost a plastic holding quality when it's dampened, and it shapes really well. Wood-pulp paper can be long-lived, as long as they take care to buffer and pH-balance it. It may still eventually fade, but at least it won't become brittle. For my most complex works I will use plant fiber papers; for example, hanji paper, from Korea, which, like Japanese washi, is made from kozo fiber. Japanese paper has an interesting texture: they use a very thin slurry and do multiple dippings. Every time I go to Japan, I buy tons of paper. I'm something of a pack rat when it comes to papers."

We turned then to some of the sculptures he has made. "I spent a lot of years focusing on insects, because it's quite a challenge to get all the legs just right, but I've been moving more to birds, because birds are more challenging artistically. Every bird is basically a head, tail, maybe wings, maybe feet, so there's no challenge in just getting the parts right; the challenge is in capturing the character of the individual birds." To illustrate the point, he indicated the shape of a crane standing on one of the shelves. "The crane here is in the middle of its courtship dance. The trick is to catch that sense of motion. You want to get details that stand out, like the feathers, or the wings, and the feet, but in a way that retains the delicacy of the form. You don't want huge tyrannosaurus feet. The delicate parts have to be delicate, and the feathers splayed."

With so much planning, there is still, he said, always room for improvisation. "Again, it depends on what I'm doing. In a lot of cases, I will do things on the fly. If it's a really complex piece that has a lot of parts, I will plan it out completely in advance, or do a mixture of the two. Generally, the more complicated the pieces, the more thoroughly it's planned out. In some cases I'll improvise portions separately and work them out using individual sheets of paper. Once I figure out how the various parts of it will fold, then I will plan out all the crease patterns on one sheet of paper. Before I fold the whole thing, it is completely planned out. There are designs where software helps me on some parts. But then I will improvise on the individual parts."

Looked up to internationally as one of the most articulate proponents of origami, Lang said there is a good deal of friendly competition that goes on among master folders. "We have a challenge we've been doing for a number of years now, in conjunction with the OrigamiUSA convention, in New York. Every year we pick a topic. We say, 'Next year we're each going to try and fold this subject,' and we'll get back together the next year and see how we did. One year we did a beetle, another year a hermit crab, another year a plant. So it's competitive, but there's no prize, there's no award. All you're competing for is the respect of the people you respect."

THREE YEARS AFTER Lang showed me around his California studio, he was in Cambridge, Massachusetts, spending ten days at the Massachusetts Institute of Technology to collaborate on a project with Erik

Demaine, a professor of electrical engineering and computer science and himself a folder of considerable skill. While in the city, Lang gave two public programs, one a workshop for advanced origami folders, arranged by OrigaMIT, the university's folding club, and another for a general audience. I attended both, not only to catch up with Lang but to spend a little time with Demaine, who has achieved widespread celebrity in his own right. The faculty and students who participate in OrigaMIT workshops call what they do "extreme origami," and I sat in on several of their sessions over the next few months, including one in which a film crew from Japanese public television followed every move, every step, and every fold Demaine made with his nimble fingers. The sessions are open to the public, and on the day of Lang's presentation, there were as many adolescents present as undergraduates, many of them busily multitasking on sheets of origami paper.

Demaine had been appointed an assistant professor at MIT in 2001, at the age of twenty, the youngest person ever selected for that post in the 150-year history of the institution. Named a MacArthur Fellow two years later, he is also a member of the Computer Science and Artificial Intelligence Laboratory. Through 2011 he had written, either by himself or collaboratively, twelve books and more than two hundred journal articles, in fields that range from computational geometry to combinational game theory. One of his MIT classes, "Geometric Folding Algorithms: Linkages, Origami, Polyhedra," concerns the reconfiguring of physical objects. At the heart of the course are joint projects intended "to solve open problems in folding," which in the past "have led to important new results and published papers."

Like Lang, Demaine also develops geometric folding algorithms, but the shapes he makes that draw the most attention to what he does are such objects as polyhedra and curved-crease sculptures. The title of the book in which he explains this process, *Computational Origami*—written with his father, Martin Demaine—"refers to our underlying the algorithmic goal of determining the mathematical curved surface that results from different kinds of pleated folding," which, they write, is a form of "self-folding origami" that "may have applications to deployable structures that can compress very small by folding tightly and later relax into its natural curved form." Three paper figures he posted on his website to illustrate this concept are part of the Museum of Modern

Art's permanent collections and were featured in the New York exhibit *Design and the Elastic Mind* in 2008. Demaine told me that he was drawn to the infinite possibilities of origami while in graduate school. "I was fifteen when I started my Ph.D.," he pointed out when I asked if that was a bit late to get started in paper folding. "I was looking for interesting problems to solve. I heard about Robert Lang's work with computational origami and started forging my own path." The "big thing" he and Lang were working on during this visit to MIT was "formalizing the tree method of origami design. This has been developed over many years by many people, but Robert has been the one to get it so formal that it's in a computer program, and together we're making it so formal that you can prove that it works."

Demaine said he likes that "origami speaks to many different kinds of people," and indicated with a nod the youngsters who had gathered in the MIT classroom to hear Lang speak. "For me, it was attractive because I am a mathematician. The kids here are attracted to the art forms, and I am, too. Everyone enters this world at some level, and that is part of its attraction. You don't have to care one bit about the engineering or the geometry to find it compelling." For all the scholarly papers he has written, and the joy he clearly takes in grappling with concepts and problems of pure intellect, there is a youthful genuineness to Demaine. He may well be blazing new frontiers in artificial intelligence, but he makes it a point to never get bored with what he is doing.

With his father, Martin, artist in residence in the Department of Electrical Engineering and Computer Science at MIT and an instructor in the Glass Lab, he enjoys solving sophisticated puzzles and making glass sculptures. The two also have tried their hand at doing stand-up routines at an improvisational comedy club in Cambridge. Having a sense of humor is important, Martin Demaine told me when we had a chance to chat, something he always tried to instill in his son when he was homeschooling him as a single parent in the 1980s and early 1990s, while they were living in Canada. It was in this spirit, Erik told me, that they agreed, in 2004, to make some furniture at the invitation of the MIT library, and that their material of choice for building blocks was discarded books that had failed to sell in several secondhand sales.

"It started as a joke," he said, noting that both he and his father have expertise as structural engineers and as artists, which they applied to the task. "We built a whole bedroom—bookshelves, lampshades, beds, quilts—all made out of discarded books. One of the motivations for this—we discovered that a lot of the books in the world had become trash. They were being thrown away, many of them not even being pulped because the bindings and the glue make them expensive to recycle, so they're just tossed out. This was one way to save a few of them. We love books, both of us, but I've got to tell you, there's no feeling like taking a book to a band saw and cutting through it. It feels so wrong: this precious thing, and there you are, slicing it to pieces."

Demaine conceded that he is not passionate about paper in and of itself, but uses it simply because it is the ideal medium for what he is trying to accomplish, and because there is such a body of established technique to build on. Put another way, there are constraints by which he must abide. "There's a fine line—you want things to be interesting, but not impossible. You don't want to find a cheating solution, either, since that's not interesting at all. And if it's a one-line answer, then you can't write a paper about that, can you? So you try to make it as interesting as possible, as challenging as you can, without becoming ridiculous to solve."

An additional incentive, he said, is that rewards come on multiple levels. "What's special about origami is that you get the aesthetic satisfaction and the physical satisfaction from actually building something out of paper. So it's really nice to be able to do both, the artistic things and the science things, with the same material. And you have the limitations of paper culture to help you along there, too. You can't stretch paper, which is very important, because that would destroy the underlying geometry. There are other materials that behave like paper, but they don't have the same folding aspects. We've experimented with metal and some plastics on problems dealing with scale and structure, and we've had some success—but they're a lot harder to fold."

Demaine said he adheres to the convention of using a single sheet of paper for his constructions, because "it is more fun," and having fun, he made clear, is what makes it such an intoxicating exercise. "To me, mathematically, it's more interesting when you can't cut, all you can do is fold. The starting shape, the piece of paper, it's just more challenging if you do it from one square. So you start with the idea that you can fold a square into anything. I like that constraint. I don't feel wedded to it, but from a mathematical perspective, it's the most impressive. Mathematically, you try to come up with the simplest statement of what you can do—and what can be more simple than a single piece of paper?"

# 16

In the Mold

The machine age has unfolded before my eyes, a prosaic period that has not appealed to me. I have long been an advocate of hand craftsmanship and have struggled against mass-production methods, but my efforts have been no more effectual than the exertions of a lone termite in a petrified forest. The discovery of oil in the ground, which made the gasoline engine possible, was the turning-point. Before the advent of automobiles—and the natural sequence of airplanes, tanks, bombers, and guided missiles— the world was more at ease. There is no gain in quarreling with machines, science, and technology, but the question persists: have they brought more peace and contentment to the world?

—Dard Hunter, *My Life with Paper,* 1958

TO READ the autobiography of the paper historian and fine-press printer William Joseph "Dard" Hunter is to get the unmistakable sense of a man who had a difficult time coming to terms with the twentieth century. Like the subdued reflections of Henry Adams, half a century before him, Hunter made no bones about his preference for earlier times, declaring outright that, if given the opportunity, he would have been born toward the end of the eighteenth century and lived out his years entirely before 1830, a compact interval that would have allowed him to skip altogether the burgeoning innovations of the Industrial Revolution.

"Had the choice of place in which to live this span of years been mine, I would probably have selected rural Scotland, the seat of my forebears," he added wistfully. But after much casting about the United States and Europe as an inquisitive young man in search of a muse, he finally chose to use Chillicothe, Ohio, where he had spent much of his youth, as home base for a number of enterprises that even the most sanguine of observers would have regarded as quixotic at best. Setting up shop on a hill overlooking the city, in a grand mansion he called Mountain House, Hunter produced eight limited-edition books between 1922 and 1950, on the subject of hand papermaking, that are greatly coveted by collectors today, all the while securing his position as the world's leading authority on the subject. His efforts had the additional result of reviving a tradition that had been abandoned as an obsolete anachronism in the United States, and of giving life to what is known today as the book arts movement.

By the time Hunter embarked on what became his lifelong obsession, America had fully adapted to the new ways. With mechanization, the mass production of paper had become commonplace, and when coupled with the seemingly limitless availability of wood pulp, the reliance on cotton rags was eliminated almost entirely. The transformation was so decisive that by the early 1900s, not a single hand-papermaking mill was operating in the United States. The downside to this new abundance was a general decline in quality. Beyond his contributions as bookmaker, author, and collector of important artifacts is the extraordinary influence Hunter wielded on successive generations of like-minded spirits, beginning with his son Dard Hunter II, who committed his life to perpetuating his father's legacy, and extending to a remarkably diverse sphere of men and women who followed his example in a variety of productive ways.

Born into a prominent Ohio newspaper family in 1883, Hunter spent considerable time as a boy in the composing room of the Steubenville *Gazette,* becoming adept, by the age of ten, in the "art and mystery of typesetting," as he put it. When the Hunters moved 170 miles west to Chillicothe in 1900, to take over the *News-Advertiser,* Dard—a nickname from his youth that stuck—became his father's staff artist, but before long, a streak of wanderlust had him touring the United States with his older brother, Philip, a professional magician who had gained a modicum of celebrity as "the Buckeye Wizard." During a gig in Riverside, California, and a stay at the chicly appointed Glenwood Hotel (what is today the Mission Inn), he began to appreciate the Arts and Crafts movement, introduced several decades earlier in England by William Morris, the legendary proprietor of the Kelmscott Press.

In 1904, Hunter traveled to East Aurora, New York, outside Buffalo, hoping to spend a summer at the Roycroft Shops, founded by Elbert Hubbard, a pioneer of Arts and Crafts in the United States, and worked there intermittently over the next few years. After studying lithography, book decoration, and letter design in Vienna, he found work as a commercial designer in London, and would cite a trip to the Science Museum as forever changing his life. "I saw for the first time a pair of moulds for forming handmade paper; and also was able for the first time to examine the punches, matrices, and hand moulds that in previous centuries had been used in making type," he wrote in his memoir. "It was my desire to have my own private press, but I wanted my work to be individual and personal, without reliance upon outside help from the typefounder or papermaker. I would return to America and attempt to make books by hand completely by my own labor—paper, type, printing."

If anything of the personal history of Dard Hunter makes him stand out in the early decades of the twenty-first century as a decided throwback to earlier times, it is this audacious commitment of his—eccentric when he first considered it, a century ago, and even more odd today: to produce a printed book in every significant detail of production entirely by himself. Nobody, so far as anyone could say, had done such a thing before him, and given the realities of where the publishing industry is headed today, the prospect of anyone else making such an effort now is similarly unlikely.

In 1912, Hunter bought an eighteenth-century house sixty miles north of New York City, in the village of Marlborough, and converted an old gristmill on a small waterway called Jew's Creek (see endnote) into a traditional workshop, appointing it with antiquated tools and equipment he had acquired in England and restored to working condition. To give it an authentic Devonshire look, he even installed a thatched roof made from rye that he harvested himself. It was here, at the place he called Mill House, that Hunter mastered hand papermaking, experimented with watermarks and produced his own font of type.

The publication, in 1916, of *The Etching of Figures,* commissioned by the Chicago Society of Etchers as a keepsake for its members, combined all of these special skills in a single undertaking, an achievement so unprecedented that it and a similar production Hunter completed later that year are thought to be unique in the annals of publishing. "In making these two books," he wrote to a colleague in 1921, "I used no tools, appliances, or materials that were not in use during the first two centuries of printing." In a bibliographical survey of the private press movement published in 1929, the graphic designer Will Ransom marveled that Hunter's accomplishment "stands as a symbol of the ideal he has maintained for many years, the revival of pure, unaided, individual art and craftsmanship."

Hunter's insistence on using a traditional waterwheel at Mill House had an unfortunate downside in that it provided insufficient power during the winter months, forcing him finally to sell the New York property in 1919 and establish the Mountain House Press in Chillicothe, which became his permanent base of operations. At various intervals over the next forty-six years, he would travel extensively to the most isolated regions in the world, all the while interviewing native papermakers and gathering tools, equipment, raw materials, and samples for a massive collection of artifacts.

In 1927, Hunter decided to take one more stab at commercial papermaking, and chose an abandoned iron foundry in Old Lyme, Connecticut, for his mill, which on this go-round would be staffed by a family of skilled artisans he persuaded to come over from England to run it. With the stock market crash of 1929, the enterprise could not have been more poorly timed. The hopeful effort went bankrupt in 1932, but not before a considerable supply of handmade paper had been produced, which Hunter was able to acquire at the foreclosure sale in sufficient quantity to make 180 copies of *Papermaking by Hand in America* eighteen years later.

"I would not go through all this again," he confided in a letter to a friend. "I can see why there will be very few handmade paper mills in America." While it lasted, the Old Lyme undertaking—called a "noble experiment" by Cathleen Baker in her exhaustive biography of Hunter—was the only hand-papermaking mill in the United States then operating as a commercial enterprise.

On a more immediate level, Hunter's continuing legacy is to be found most profoundly in his books, which endure as classics of papermaking literature, and for the enormous archive of papermaking implements he acquired during his travels about the world, which from 1938 to 1954 were housed at MIT on long-term loan. The artifacts are now the principal resource of the Robert C. Williams Paper Museum, at the Institute of Paper Science and Technology, in Atlanta, an interdisciplinary research center within the Georgia Institute of Technology that is devoted entirely to the study of paper in every manner of preparation and is custodian of one hundred thousand objects, said to be the largest collection of its kind in the world. But the motivation to collect at this level went well beyond the impulse to stock a museum, since having these exotic molds, deckles, vats, pestles, beaters, dandy rolls, and every other imaginable device within arm's reach contributed to the writing of a richly informed body of work.

Today, books bearing the Mountain House imprint sell for thousands of dollars when they appear on the antiquarian market and are available to the wider public only in the reading rooms of special collections libraries. Given their rarity and general inaccessibility, the books Hunter wrote that have proven lastingly influential are the ones he produced for the general trade, most notably *Papermaking: The History and Technique of an Ancient Craft,* first published by Alfred A. Knopf in 1943, featuring numerous illustrations from his artifact collection, and still in print. By word and by deed, Hunter set an example for those who believed themselves to be his kindred spirits, and while his enduring achievement as a fine-press printer speaks eloquently enough for itself, it is this book as much as anything else that helped revive hand papermaking in North America.

The first such effort came in Pennsylvania in the years following World War II, when a commercial job printer in search of a hobby began making rag paper by hand for the simple reason that it presented a challenge. "I learned because I was fascinated by it," Henry Morris told me when we got together at his home in Newtown, Pennsylvania, about forty miles north of Philadelphia. What happened after that—establishment in 1958 of the internationally renowned Bird & Bull Press—came about because, once he had learned how to make beautiful paper by hand, he needed a practical way to make use of it.

A child of the Great Depression, Morris was raised in a working-class Philadelphia neighborhood by a single mother, and he appreciated early the importance of getting a steady job. Applying for admission to the Murrell Dobbins Vocational Technical School in 1939, at the age of fourteen, he chose printing only because he thought it "less sloppy" than being a plumber, the other trade he had considered pursuing. Once he had mastered the fundamentals of setting type, Morris dropped out of school entirely in the tenth grade and got a job printing envelopes for $18 a week. Not long after World War II started, he was hired by the William Cramp & Sons Shipbuilding Company to work on submarines and oceangoing tugs. "With overtime, I was making forty dollars a week, and I was still living with my mother. When my brother Ralph went into the Navy, I decided to do the same. I got a birth certificate, doctored it, and joined up."

Not long after his return to civilian life, in 1946, Morris and a boyhood friend opened a printing business together. "My mother had a small corset shop in Philadelphia, and we bought a little Chandler & Price press for $150 that she let us set up in her basement." They printed business forms, cards, stationery, advertising flyers, and the like, and before long they were able to buy out a competitor, City Wide Press. "Pearl and I were married in 1949, and we were in the printing business, just scraping by and barely making a living. She was working as a payroll clerk in a brewery, so we were able to buy a little roadhouse in Philadelphia where we lived for thirty years."

In 1956, Morris bought a piece of old furniture from an antiques dealer, who sent along on speculation a page from a law book that had been printed in 1491 by a grandson of Nicolas Jenson. "It was flexible, it had a wonderful texture, and was expertly printed on paper that was in absolutely marvelous condition. I thought nothing that old could be that beautiful. So I brought it over to the Philadelphia Public Library, where the rare books curator was a woman named Ellen Shaffer. I said, 'I think this is a fake.' She looked at it and said, 'It's not a fake. Let me show you a few things.'"

A recognized authority on incunabula—books printed before 1501—Ellen Shaffer got her start at Dawson's Book Shop, in Los Angeles, in the 1930s and was well known in antiquarian circles. After leaving Philadelphia, in 1970, she spent the final twenty-four years of her life in St. Helena, California, as curator and librarian of the Silverado Museum. "I was hooked on the spot," Morris told me of what she showed him. "I said right there, 'I'm a printer. I need a hobby. I want to make some paper that looks like this.' Miss Shaffer said, 'There's a man named Dard Hunter—you should get his book.' I did—and that was the beginning of the whole thing."

Morris made his first batches of pulp in the most basic of ways, using a hammer and anvil to pound linen half-stuff he bought in bulk from a paper salesman. Amazed at just how intensive that kind of manual labor could be, he tried using a kitchen blender and, failing there, experimented unsuccessfully with an electric mixer and a food grinder. "There was a lot of guesswork, and my first attempts were really dreadful," he acknowledged, at which point he looked more closely at Hunter's book. "I was a shipfitter in the Navy, so I could do these things," he said, and by studying the various photographs in *History and Technique,* he began, in 1957, to build his own Hollander beater. "I sold my antique gun collection, which broke my heart, but I was really into this idea of making my own paper. The electric motor for the beater alone cost me thirty-five bucks." He bought rolls of copper sheeting and industrial-grade steel bars and began forging metal blades in his cellar; in one instance, a neighbor, frightened by the sight of sparks shooting outside from an exhaust system he had jury-rigged, called the fire department.

Later, to make a vat, he modified a forty-six-gallon galvanized bathtub, and to squeeze water from couched sheets, he modified a second-hand screw press he had bought from a bookbinder. It took several attempts before he finally had a wooden mold that he felt could withstand the stress of repeated immersions in water. "It was strong enough to support an elephant," he said. "It was pretty much guesswork on a lot of this—just me and Dard Hunter's book. I actually wrote to Hunter at one point and started asking him some questions. He wrote back, and we had a very nice little correspondence. But basically, it was all trial and error."

Morris still worked as a commercial printer, but the evenings he set aside for papermaking. "I would get everything ready on the weekend. I was able to make two pounds of pulp at a time on my little beater. I had a stopwatch. I'd get down there at seven a.m., it took two and a half hours for each load, and my goal was to make eight pounds of pulp that I could use during the week when I came home at night. After I'd finished that, I'd go out and cut rags. I was thirty-eight or thirty-nine years old at the time, and I did this because it gave me something interesting to do. I had a bunch of these eleven-by-seventeen sheets, and someone said to me, 'What are you going to do with all this paper you made?' I mean, nobody makes paper down in their cellar, right? So I said, 'I'm a printer. I'm going to print something on them.'"

His first effort—issued under the imprint of City Wide Press, the name of his job-printing business—was *Receipts in Cookery,* a reprint of an eighteenth-century cookbook Morris had found in the public library, and which he set into type by hand. "The paper was the only good thing about it. Nobody downtown would buy them, so I got a list of people who sell cookbooks, and I wrote them all a letter on my handmade paper. People started asking me about this beautiful paper—where did I get it? So it is fair to say that I backed into fine-press printing by way of the paper I was making in my basement. That's how Bird & Bull Press actually got started."

In 1980, Morris and his wife moved to Newtown, and Bird & Bull went along with them. The name he had chosen for his imprint has no significance other than his interest in following the example of early English papermakers who used various animals as models for their watermarks. Over the years, he has produced a variety of broadsides, books, and other printed materials that are now recognized as an important part of the contemporary American private-press scene. Of the seventy-eight titles printed by Bird & Bull through 2011, most of them deal with various aspects of paper, papermaking, and bookmaking.

As handsomely crafted as his paper was, it was never something that Morris made for anyone but himself—and even then, only for eleven of the books published under his imprint. For the others, he has for the most part used what is called "moldmade paper," a product imported from Europe that is produced by machines that simulate the handmade process by using a cylinder to rotate the pulp. The result is a matrix of fibers that are more randomly intertwined. (Paper made on Fourdrinier machines aligns only on a north–south basis.) He named Arches paper, from France, Zerkall, from Germany, and Wiggins, from England, as particular favorites of his.

Morris is more than mindful of the fact that his books are represented in special collections libraries throughout the world and eagerly coveted by collectors. His archives are installed at the University of Delaware and include original typescripts, text samples, metal engravings, woodcuts, tear sheets, and, of course, many paper samples. "I don't mean to sound immodest here, but it is fair to say, I think, that I started something," he said when I asked him to assess his place in the book arts movement. "There was a little fine-press printing going on when I was getting started, but I was the only one making any paper, certainly the only one here in the United States." And as nicely done as

Bird & Bull publications may be, Morris said he has no illusions about the fact that it was the paper he was making "that really got everyone's attention. I have no doubt whatsoever about that."

TWELVE YEARS AFTER Kathryn and Howard Clark went into the business of making paper by hand for a full range of artistic and fine-press clients, a small exhibition of their evolving accomplishments was mounted near their home and base of operations in the prairie community of Brookston, Indiana. Called *Making It in Paper,* the 1983 show featured lithographs, engravings, hand-printed letterpress books, broadsides, original works of pulp art, photographs, carbon prints, and calligraphy—thirty-six striking objects, all told, a good number of them executed by visiting artists working collaboratively with the Clarks at Twinrocker Handmade Paper, the ambitious enterprise they had established in 1971 with those very goals in mind.

The central premise of the exhibition was underscored by John P. Begley, the curator. "Artists have ceased to think of paper as an uncontrollable, minimal, or even neutral element," he wrote in his foreword to the catalog. "Formerly regarded as a necessary and monotonous evil, it has come to be seen as an independent, elegant medium that can, without further embellishment, fully express an artist's statement." And Twinrocker, he continued, "has been in the vanguard of the artists' dialogue that has produced this new consensus about paper." As Twinrocker celebrated its fortieth anniversary, in 2011, with another exhibition at the Robert C. Williams Paper Museum, in Atlanta, the idea of a new attitude toward the creative function of the medium remained relevant to the conversation.

Before Twinrocker opened for business, the last mill to make paper commercially by hand in North America had closed in 1929, so when the Clarks began, forty-two years later, they essentially were starting from scratch. There were no mentors for them to enlist for advice, no one to buy commercial-grade equipment from, and no instruction manuals to consult. Dard Hunter had died in 1966, so even the driving spirit of the twentieth-century renaissance was out of the picture as a possible source of guidance. Henry Morris had been operating the Bird & Bull Press in Pennsylvania since 1958, and he did make paper with devices of his own design, but on a very small scale and for his own use only. What Morris did provide, however, was an example, and that was encouragement enough for the young couple as they started out.

"Henry was a giant in our view, because he proved it could be done," Kathryn Haugh Clark made clear to me when I paid a visit to Brookston to talk about their experiences as the "Ma and Pa" of the modern movement. "His paper was exquisite, and we looked up to him tremendously. Our feeling was that if he can make paper of this quality in his basement, then there was hope for us. But Henry was only making one kind of paper—book paper—and just in one standard size. Once we decided to get into this, our intention was to make paper for other people commercially, and because I am by training and experience an artist and a printmaker, our concentration began in that area."

The Clarks had met in the 1960s, when both were graduate students at Wayne State University, in Detroit, Kathryn pursuing a master's degree in fine arts, Howard a master's in industrial design, to go along with a bachelor's degree in mechanical engineering he had earned from Purdue—skills that would prove useful to him when it came time to build papermaking machines. "I was looking toward a career as an artist, and planned to print my own work," Kathryn said. Nothing in her game plan had pointed to a career in papermaking, but a course she took at Wayne State with Aris Koutroulis, a master printer who had studied at Tamarind Lithography Workshop, in Los Angeles, introduced her to the principles. "Part of his instruction method was to have us collect old rags and cut them into little pieces and make a pulp. It didn't matter what the color was; the idea, basically, was to make some paper, then create a print that complemented it." The paper they made for Koutroulis "became something of a found object" in its own right, she said. The concept was "totally backward from the whole notion of what lithography is supposed to be, of course, but that's how we went about it. Nobody was actually teaching us how to make paper in any systematic way, since nobody really knew how to make it. What we were learning was how to become printers. But this was my first exposure to papermaking—and Howard's, too, since it was his first look at the equipment involved."

Kathryn's opportunity to ply her printing skills professionally came in 1969, when Howard accepted an offer to work on the West Coast with a start-up company involved in computer program development.

As Howard began his new job, Kathryn was hired by the Collector's Press lithography workshop, in San Francisco, under the direction of Ernest F. de Soto, another Tamarind alum. Their arrival in San Francisco came at a time when the Bay Area was emerging as a nexus of creative activity, with poetry, livres d'artistes, fine-press printing, and music all part of a vibrant cultural scene. It was also a time when a number of movements in the visual arts were gaining momentum on both coasts, in each instance creating a demand for high-quality paper.

The first initiative along these lines was undertaken on Long Island, New York, by Tatyana Grosman, a Russian émigré whose family had been prominent publishers in Russia. In 1957, she and her husband established Universal Limited Art Editions with the express goal of introducing European-style printmaking traditions to the United States. She began collaborating with such artists as Larry Rivers, Grace Hartigan, Jasper Johns, Robert Rauschenberg, Jim Dine, Sam Francis, Cy Twombly, James Rosenquist, Edwin Schlossberg, Helen Frankenthaler, and Barnett Newman to create prints of original works executed exclusively for lithography. In time, Grosman also produced limited editions of artists' books using the intaglio process and relief printing from woodblocks, both of which also required all-rag artist's paper, at that time available only from European suppliers, in limited formats.

While Grosman was building her reputation in New York, June Wayne was developing the Tamarind Lithography Workshop Inc., in Los Angeles, which she set up in 1960 with the full financial support of the Ford Foundation, her explicit goal being to "rescue" what she called the "dying art" of lithography. A visual artist who had worked in Paris with the master printer Marcel Durassier, Wayne felt that the only way to achieve an enduring renaissance of the form in the United States was to train skilled artisan-printers in a rigorous program of practical instruction that incorporated a system of apprenticeships, a strategy that would later be adopted by the Clarks in Indiana. After operating for ten years in Los Angeles—on Tamarind Avenue, hence its name—Wayne accepted an invitation from the University of New Mexico to move her workshop to Albuquerque, where the Tamarind Institute was established in 1970 and thrives to this day.

"The idea of a limited-edition print is a French concept, and what it is, basically, is an artwork that is made to be a print," Kathryn Clark explained. "It's not a reproduction of a painting; in fact, there is no painting at all. It can be an etching, a woodcut, or a lithograph, with the lithograph probably being the purest form, since it's very painterly and in layers, and every layer has a different color, or stone. But what happens is that the print becomes an original artwork produced in direct collaboration with the artist. Tatyana Grosman and June Wayne knew that, for the print to be collectible, you had to be able to put it on the wall, and that the colors would not fade. The modern history of handmade paper in America is tied into this."

The immediate impact on Kathryn was that Tatyana Grosman and June Wayne had created a "huge market for original prints," and business was booming. "When Ernest de Soto saw that I could do the work just fine—there is an awful lot of heavy lifting involved in stone lithography—he took me on." With a lithographic press at hand, it was only a matter of time before she pulled an original print on one of the sheets she had made at Wayne State. "I brought the biggest sheet of paper I made with me to San Francisco, twenty-four inches square, and I made a large print. It was all thready, and basically the image was already in the paper, since it was made from dyed rags. Ernest took one look at it and said, 'If you can make paper like this, I will be your first customer.'"

Further encouragement came at a San Francisco arts fair, where Kathryn's print was entered as an exhibit. "Everyone said, 'The print is fine, but wow—where did you get that paper?'" Then another inducement came with the sudden availability of Howard to join the project. "My friend's business collapsed in the aerospace recession, and there was a whole sea of engineers out there without work," he said. "I was standing in unemployment lines with vice presidents, and Kathy had her job printing lithographs. So I was all for it."

To get himself started, Howard read everything he could find on commercial papermaking at the San Francisco Public Library, but in the end the most important reference was Dard Hunter's *History and Technique,* which includes many photographs to go along with the expert commentary. Over the years, Howard would make about forty Hollander beaters for other papermakers, and sixty or so hydraulic presses. "I have blood on every one of them," he said when I asked him to describe the degree of difficulty involved in charting what in the beginning was terra incognita for them.

The date the Clarks give for the formal beginning of Twinrocker is

April Fools' Day 1971, when they received a license from the city of San Francisco to operate a business at 3156 Turk Street. "It was a preposterous idea, of course, but we were young, we were living in San Francisco, and people we respected encouraged us to take a stab at it," Kathryn said. "Our whole purpose was to make high-quality paper not just for prints, but for books, too, because there were lots of other things that would push it aesthetically. Actually, the fine-press book printers in San Francisco really encouraged us to think about making paper."

There was an additional incentive, too, in that they just might be fulfilling a pressing need in the arts community. "All handmade paper was imported from Europe back then, and was available in two colors—white and cream—and in just one size, twenty-two by thirty. When we started Twinrocker, we did it with the intention of doing what you can do in a small studio that a big machine mill can't do, and that was to be like a microbrewery, in a sense: making small batches of higher quality, with more interesting colors and more variety. We wanted to make papers that had a natural deckle edge so people could enjoy and appreciate it. Handmade paper is so much more alive than machine-made paper."

Howard took on the task of making papermaking equipment, meanwhile, "by the seat of my pants, basically," in the basement of the apartment they were renting. "I had a workbench. I bought a cheapo table saw, and I had a real press where you clamp the drill in. So I got a piece of metal out of the junkyard and built a beater." A first-place prize that September, for a process booth they set up at the twenty-fifth annual San Francisco International Arts Festival, and the enthusiastic response they received from area printmakers and fine-press publishers at yet another fair, in nearby Walnut Creek, where they exhibited, gave them hope for the future—which they soon decided to play out on a twenty-acre corn farm in Indiana where they could make ends meet on a modest income and where they had room to grow and nurture the aspirations of others. "All that is accurate enough," Kathryn agreed, "but we came here primarily because Howard's father had just died, and this had been the family farm through five generations. We were kind of at the end of our rope financially in San Francisco, too, so coming here seemed like a pretty solid option for us."

Once they were up and running again in 1972, their fortunes would hinge on the pairing of two dramatically contrasting sets of skills, each

*Papermaker Travis Becker, at Twinrocker Handmade Paper, Brookston, Indiana.*

impeccably suited to the task at hand, and each critical to the overall scheme. "I am the papermaker, and Howard is the engineer," Kathryn made clear, as if there had been any doubt on my part about the roles each had assumed in the partnership. She made the sheets, one dip at a time, and her husband made the machines, one bolt at a time. "I can tell you that, whatever we were doing when we began Twinrocker, we were doing wrong," Kathryn said. "Our teachers were all pieces of paper."

As they became more proficient, Howard would help develop technical strategies for special paper projects. His work with Claire Van Vliet, to perfect the use of dyed pulp in the formation of original artworks produced under her Janus Press imprint, was one notable example. The Twinrocker watermark incorporates back-to-back rocking chairs, producing a symmetrical design that appears correctly from either side of the sheet. The use of the word *twin* in the name is a tribute to Kathryn's identical twin sister, Margaret Prentice, who was involved in the business for a brief time, along with her husband, Kit Kuehnle. "We weren't business people," Kathryn said, "but we were committed to reviving hand papermaking in America." Part of that commitment included the recruitment of apprentices who have since contributed to the long-term prospects of hand papermaking.

In the late 1980s, the Chicago filmmaker David McGowan shot a short documentary about Twinrocker, "The Mark of the Maker," which was nominated for an Academy Award in 1991. The Clarks' on-site work with the calligrapher Janet Lorence, the watercolorist Jim Cantrell, and the scholar-printer Michael Gullick made up central segments of the film, and in each instance the quality and texture of the paper was considered critical. By that time Twinrocker had moved into an old International Harvester tractor showroom that provided more space. And in 2005, terms were worked out with Travis Becker, a Brookston native and master papermaker trained by Kathryn, to take over the business and keep it going well into the twenty-first century.

"Papermaking by hand is one of the true pure crafts," Kathryn said of her determination to see the work continue. "Practically every other craft has more design to it. Papermaking has design, too, but it's subtle and minimal, since it's there to enhance the image on the surface. It's kind of like an instrument in an orchestra: you don't see the violin in the music, but the violin is creating the sound. Papermaking is like a musical instrument—only it's visual."

# 17

## At the Crossroads

The paperless society is about as plausible as the paperless bathroom.
—Jesse Shera, *Library Journal,* 1982

Paper is still the best medium of preservation, and libraries still need to fill their shelves with words printed on paper.
—Robert Darnton, *The Case for Books,* 2009

AS THE TWENTY-FIRST CENTURY SHIFTED into high gear, paper manufacturers began to appreciate more than ever the need to have an open mind about the markets they were trying to serve, and how they might go about reaching them. Times had changed, and the paper industry was forced to cope along with them. The increasing popularity of e-books, the declining circulation of newspapers, soaring energy costs, increased recycling of recovered fibers, aging equipment, foreign competition, uncertain world markets, heightened environmental concerns, and the unending transition to electronic record-keeping were just a few of the factors contributing to steady reductions in demand. It became increasingly clear that the key to success in the modern economy was to be alert to opportunities as they arose; to rely exclusively on old models was to risk falling by the wayside.

Those were some of the issues, at least, that confronted George H. Glatfelter II in 1998, when he was named president and chief executive officer of P. H. Glatfelter Inc., a company established by his great-great-grandfather in Spring Grove, Pennsylvania, a quiet borough of two thousand residents ten miles southwest of York and twenty-four miles due east of Gettysburg. During the dozen years that followed, 120 paper mills in North America closed, and one-third of the workforce was idled—some 240,000 jobs lost in the United States and Canada. "All pretty sobering realities," Glatfelter told me when we met to discuss his eventful life in the pulp and paper industry, and realities, it turned out, that he had foreseen with a degree of perception described to me by several outside observers as "visionary."

During George Glatfelter's stewardship—or on his "watch," as he preferred to put it—P. H. Glatfelter almost tripled its sales, acquiring along the way several smaller companies in seven countries that were complementary to the new direction he had pursued. In short order, the company became the leading producer of more than a thousand different specialty papers for a varied cluster of "niche" markets. Products made with Glatfelter paper now include postage stamps and Priority Mail paper envelopes for the United States Postal Service; Hallmark greeting cards; Salada, Tetley, and Twinings tea bags; Crayola crayon wrap; Band-Aid adhesive bandage components; Reese's Peanut Butter Cups wrappers; Heineken and Carlsberg beer labels; Post-it notepads; Kotex release liners—the list goes on and on. And while that reinvention of purpose was taking place, P. H. Glatfelter's bread-and-butter business—high-quality paper for the publishing industry—remained on its front list of products, giving the company a remarkably balanced position in the industry. Traded on the New York Stock Exchange under the symbol GLT, the company had combined earnings in 2011 totaling $1.6 billion; eleven years earlier, they had been $579 million, and growth remained steady through the financial crisis of 2008–9.

I met with George Glatfelter in the company's corporate headquarters, in York, three months before he was to retire, in 2010, at the age of fifty-eight. Though he was certainly young enough to continue on the job, he was content with the state of the company as he prepared to step aside, and it was a perfect time to let his successor, Dante C. Parrini, take over. "It's been quite the journey," he said when I asked him to explain his rationale for going "beyond paper," as the company's new motto proclaimed it would do when he became CEO, and what he saw that persuaded him to range so boldly outside such a historically reliable comfort zone.

"When I looked at the U.S. market in the late 1990s, what I saw was a large number of pure commodity paper producers out there, with eighty-five percent of what is called uncoated free-sheet paper—those are the types of printing papers that we make—being manufactured by fifteen large companies. From what I saw, it was pretty clear that there was going to be consolidation in the commodities base, and today that number of commodity paper producers is, in fact, down to five. As that happened, the big companies—International Paper, Domtar, Boise Cascade, Georgia-Pacific—got larger, but their focus remained on commodities. So their ability to serve the smaller niche business dissipated—and we envisioned that was going to happen, too."

As understood in the industry, "commodity paper" includes any grade made in high volume with minimal technical specifications, typically on very large machines, and sold in mammoth rolls or large skids of sheeted paper to multiple users across the market. The end users convert the base material into a countless variety of consumer products, chief among them paper for copiers, desktop printers, commercial offset printing, writing tablets, and the unending flow of unsolicited stationery many of us know contemptuously as "junk mail."

During the period of frenetic consolidation George Glatfelter had so acutely projected, the largest commodities producer of them all, International Paper Company, absorbed three of its competitors—Champion, Federal, and Union Camp—and sold four aging mills in Maine, Michigan, and Minnesota, which it had operated to produce glossy stock for magazines, high-end catalogs, and food packaging, to a spin-off company created in 2006 from its coated-paper division, Verso Paper. Through all this, International Paper's sales in 2011 reached $26.2 billion, an increase of $2 billion over the two previous years.

For close to a century and a half, P. H. Glatfelter had made high-quality paper for just a few targeted markets, most successfully printing stock for hardcover trade and academic books. As the first major manufacturer to convert entirely to an acid-free alkaline kraft process, in the 1970s, the company became a leading supplier of archival-quality paper to the American publishing industry. Today, every major imprint in the United States, including the publisher of this book, prints on Glatfelter paper, many of them exclusively, and most—probably all—use an even heavier Glatfelter grade for their endleaf sheets.

By the time he was named president and CEO, George Glatfelter had already spent twenty-two years working at the company's flagship mill, in Spring Grove, paying close attention all the while to what was going on in the industry. "I was about to be the fifth generation of my family to lead the business, and to be perfectly frank, I had become very uncomfortable with the state of the industry and our positioning in it. Historically, the American paper industry had been characterized by periods when demand would increase, and then capacity would come online that would mute demand until the next cycle. When demand would increase, the more capacity, and the cycle would be muted again. It was like clockwork through the 1970s and '80s."

The challenge to all papermakers, as a consequence, was to know when to enter the cycle and when to back off. "If you could define a solid market position for yourself and ride that cycle, understand it, you could do pretty well, and the reason you could do pretty well was because what drove the cycle was continuing improvement in paper consumption—and that's what you placed your bet on. So you'd invest a hundred million dollars in a paper machine to be ready for that inflection point in terms of the consumption. But through the decade of the 1990s, when I was really more on the operational side of the business, I watched as the industry went through tremendous change and the cycle became fractured, and we all went through the entire decade of the nineties continuing to invest capital in the belief that the next cycle was just around the turn. Like a lot of other companies, we became way overinvested with the idea of preparing for a demand upswing that really never happened."

When he was interviewed for the CEO position, Glatfelter recalled, he told the board of directors that "if all we do at this point is focus on markets that we already serve, to operate the business the same way we always have, then we will fail." He then proposed that P. H. Glatfelter expand into a company that would be global in reach, and target niche markets where it could dominate, not just dabble. Commodity papers would not be abandoned, but there would be a new emphasis on sophisticated engineering, with products produced pretty much to order, and in lower volumes. "I believed that the company had to reposition itself into specialized niches very deeply. That meant not just test the waters, but make the commitment to become a pure paper specialist. I told the interview committee that was the only way I would agree to do the job. And what we have done since then started there."

A full decade before George Glatfelter had an opportunity to shake things up, *Forbes* magazine published an appreciative profile of the company that took particular note of the knack the Pennsylvania paper-

*A poster announcing the forthcoming sale of Glatfelter's Spring Grove paper mill, in 1863.*

maker had for staying a step or two ahead of the competition, to "not just survive" over the generations, "but thrive." Christopher Power, the author of the piece, suggested it had been a combination of "good luck, good management, frugality, honest dealing," and, most important, "a remarkable family whose members have retained an owner-operator mentality and have never allowed their attention to drift too far from Spring Grove and the business at hand." Philip Henry Glatfelter III, the company president when that article was published, in 1986, told Power that being smaller than his major competitors gave the company a tactical advantage, one that would prove prophetic a decade later when his nephew, George Glatfelter II, was at the helm. "We like to see the big boys get bigger, because the bigger they get, the softer they get. If you're too soft, you take too long to move."

George Glatfelter is a passionate outdoorsman, and when Connie and I visited, the walls of his York office were adorned with a number of photographs taken in the fields and streams of North America, but he took special pleasure in pointing out an antique poster that had been distributed during the Civil War to publicize the forthcoming sale of a certain "valuable paper mill" in what was then Spring Forge, Pennsylvania. The property, according to the announcement, would come complete with a "Frame Machine House," a "first class Fourdrinier" machine, two "improved Burnham water wheels," a rotary boiler "carrying 2000 pounds," four engines, a stock house, four tenant dormitories, and more than a hundred acres of land. It was to be sold at a probate proceeding called an "orphans' court sale" on December 23, 1863—a month after Abraham Lincoln would pass through the area on his way to dedicate the Soldiers' National Cemetery, at Gettysburg. If there is a foundational document in the P. H. Glatfelter Inc. company history, it is this framed broadside circular.

The Spring Forge Paper Mill, as it was known under the ownership of the late Jacob Hauer, had operated since 1851. Before that, it had been home to an iron manufactory, whose founders had been drawn to the area in 1754 by the plentiful water supply and an abundance of ore in the nearby hills. During the American Revolution, the forge had supplied musket balls to the Continental Army, and by the middle of the nineteenth century it was producing two hundred short tons of iron bar each year. That background, along with the village's location, on Codorus Creek, accounted for the name Spring Forge; it would formally become the borough of Spring Grove in 1882, nineteen years after Philip H. Glatfelter, a twenty-six-year-old descendant of Swiss immigrants to Pennsylvania, paid $14,000 for the old mill at the orphans' court sale.

No neophyte to papermaking, Glatfelter had already spent seven years learning the business at a mill on the Gunpowder River, in Maryland, that was owned by his in-laws, and he seized the opportunity to branch out on his own. He was described in an 1886 history of York County as being a man of "abundant native energy, natural adaptability to the business, and judicious care in management," qualities that enabled him to have "continually increased his trade until he gained a reputation equal to any manufacturer in the same business."

The founder concentrated at first on newsprint, which he made initially from a pulp of rye straw mixed with lesser amounts of rags. By 1868, his production had increased from fifteen hundred pounds of newsprint a day to four thousand pounds. In 1874—two years before rail service arrived in Spring Grove—he relocated the mill farther north along the creek and invested $200,000 in a new building outfitted with an eighty-two-inch paper machine. By 1880, his capacity had expanded to ten thousand pounds a day, and another Fourdrinier—said at the time to be the largest in the world—was installed, allowing production levels to reach 110,000 pounds a day. Modernized and refitted several times over the decades, that same machine, known respectfully as Old Number 5, is still employed in the manufacture of specialty papers; on the day I visited, it was turning out a heavy grade of greeting-card stock.

Philip H. Glatfelter I (there would be two more Philip H. Glatfelters to lead the company over the ensuing years) made a sagacious decision early on that proved pivotal—as game-changing, perhaps, as the unorthodox moves undertaken a century later by George H. Glatfelter II. Continually frustrated by the scarcity of rags, he was among the first papermakers in the United States to convert over to the new soda processes then being introduced for cooking chips, and by 1881 he was making his own pulp from jack pine and poplar. It was the beginning at Spring Grove of what is known today as a vertically integrated plant, a configuration in which trees arrive at one end of the mill and finished paper goes out the other, giving the company an advantage over smaller competitors that rely on outside suppliers for their pulp.

To supplement the freshly harvested wood bought on the open market from private tree farms, the company began to acquire its own tim-

*A nineteenth-century engraving depicting industrial papermaking at P. H. Glatfelter, on Codorus Creek in Pennsylvania.*

berlands in Pennsylvania, Maryland, Delaware, and Virginia, leading to the formation, in 1918, of a separate entity, the Glatfelter Pulp Wood Company. In 2006, the company began selling off its woodlands, some 81,000 managed acres by then, using the proceeds to underwrite its various expansions. Another modification that would be key was Philip Glatfelter's decision, in 1892, to discontinue the making of newsprint altogether and concentrate on producing higher-quality paper for books, lithography, and business forms.

In a similar spirit of decisive action, one of George Glatfelter's earliest moves came with the $158 million purchase, in 1998, of the Schoeller & Hoesch Group, the world's leading producer of papers for the tea bag industry, based in Gernsbach, Germany. The new unit also held a major share of the European markets for cigarette paper, metalized label paper, and overlay paper. Attractive, too, was the pulp mill it owned in the Philippines to process abaca pulp from Manila hemp. Six years later, the company discontinued making cigarette paper, yet another move that framed the way business was about to be conducted under new leadership. "It was purely a case of our not getting acceptable returns," George Glatfelter told me. "Cigarette paper is very highly commoditized, and the big boys had all the business. So we moved out of the cigarette paper market and converted that capacity over to tea bags."

In 2006, P. H. Glatfelter acquired a division of the NewPage Corporation, located in Fremont, Ohio, that produces chemically coated duplicates known as carbonless business forms. Included in the $80 million deal was Chillicothe Paper Inc., a wholly owned subsidiary in Chillicothe, Ohio. Grades of paper manufactured at a Glatfelter plant in Neenah, Wisconsin, were then transferred to Chillicothe, a more modern mill with pulping on-site, and the Neenah mill was closed. The company also closed the Ecusta mill, in North Carolina, which it had purchased in 1987.

"You learn a few things after 144 years of being in business, and certain things are indelible," Glatfelter said when I asked about the Neenah and Ecusta closings. "You might change the products you make, and you might change the market you serve; you might even change the people—that's an evolutionary process. But you don't change the value system. That's what you preserve, and so when we went about the transformation of the company beginning in 1998, we had two commitments. First of all, change everything and anything about the company that no longer creates value, and adhere to those things that do, which are the core values of this company." Core value number one, he continued, is integrity. "It's the way I was brought up, and it's the way that my father and his father and his father approached the business. Number two core value is respect—we call it mutual respect across all layers of the organization. And there's an element of financial discipline in there that has to happen as well. You have to be able to make the tough financial calls. But if you can make them in a manner that's consistent with being respectful and honest, at least they can be understood."

To help him execute his plan, Glatfelter persuaded the global technology manager for the Avery Dennison Corporation, Scott L. Mingus Sr., to head up his research-and-development division, and it was Mingus who was our principal guide for the Spring Grove phase of our visit. Recognized as a pioneer in the making of what are called variable-information printing papers, Mingus holds patents in self-adhesive stamp and bar-code label products, and was heavily involved in Avery Dennison's manufacture of postage stamps for the federal government. At Glatfelter, his first assignment was to assemble what he told me was an "all-star team" of American papermaking. "George challenged me directly to come up with new ideas. Being a customer myself for twenty-three years before coming here, I had contacts with seventy-five or eighty paper mills around the world, so I knew where the really good scientists were. We went out and hired people with experience in the specialty sectors and brought them all here."

Because the company has never dealt directly with end-use consumers, it has minimal name recognition in the world at large. "Nobody knows who we are, because we are one hundred percent business-to-business," Mingus said. "Glatfelter has always sold directly to printers or directly to converters. Working exclusively with businesses allows us to give them our full attention." Regardless of name recognition, Glatfelter products are handled every day by millions of people and in multiple ways. "We have become number one in postage stamps. Our composite-fibers business unit in Germany, France, and England produces seventy-five percent of the paper used for tea bags in the world. Ten years ago, we started with playing cards; now we're number one. Since most brands buy from Glatfelter—Hoyle and Bicycle are the big names—every casino playing card in North America is probably on our paper. Greeting cards is another market we targeted. In just five to seven years, we became the supplier of choice to Hallmark. So 'when you care enough to send the very best,' more often than not you send Glatfelter."

What is known in papermaking as the "conversion process" is best explained, Mingus said, by the example of postage stamps and other label stocks. "We will sell roughly eighty-inch-wide rolls of paper that are forty, fifty, sixty thousand feet in length to the big pressure-sensitive companies like Raflatac and Avery Dennison. They in turn will then unroll them, put the sticky stuff on the back, marry it all to the release liner—we also make half of the stamp liner in the United States, by the way—and sell that to the print shops. In Avery's case, they also print, finish, perforate, and distribute final U.S. postage stamps to the government."

I asked Mingus what the secret was to achieving such extraordinary coverage in such a brief period of time, and he said simply that there is none. "We didn't find a lot of new applications for paper; we found applications that other guys already did, we just did them better. Here's another great example for you. In 2007, we decided we wanted to be number one in FDA-compliant cup stock—Solo cups and Dixie cups. So we figured out how to make them better, cheaper, stronger, and with better properties, and now we're number one in that market. We send the paper to Solo and Dixie, they coat it with paraffin or other materials and make it into a cup."

And there is also the paper for what he called "soufflé cups," the little containers used for condiments like ketchup and mustard in fast food restaurants everywhere. "We're also doing those little white trays you get when you buy a hot dog from Nathan's or from a street vendor. A couple of years ago, we didn't make any of that stuff. In the cleaning industry, Swiffer is probably the biggest known brand name of dusting pads that we manufacture for that market."

As another example of creative opportunism, he cited the company's acquisition of the NewPage unit in Fremont, where chemically coated duplicate forms are manufactured. "You might say that's a dying product, and maybe you would be right," he said, the inference being that what are known in the trade as "carbonless papers" are being marginalized by the more efficient use of computerized accounting procedures.

"But there's still a pretty fair demand out there for three-part and multipart business forms. You see them a lot in the automotive industry and in the medical field. We now sell more carbonless business forms in North America than anyone else. As long as it's profitable, we'll continue to make them." And when demand finally does recede, there will always be other opportunities to pursue. "George made it very clear to us that fifty percent of our sales have to come from NPD— new product development—from now on, in perpetuity. We spend a lot of time studying markets, and if we can't be a leader, we won't do it. We don't have the manufacturing base to run with the big guys, so we don't experiment. If we're going to get in, George's commitment was that we better dominate those markets. And so far we've been pretty successful."

The same dedication, he said, carries over to the manufacture of the company's "old reliable" grade of high-end printing stock for the publishing industry. "We don't make pulp fiction, we don't make comic books, we haven't made newsprint in over a hundred years. If you're looking for a paper that meets all Library of Congress archival standards for permanence—and not just books for the general trade, but legal books, medical books, reference books, college textbooks, elementary school books—this is where you go. We have the dominant position in hardback permanent book paper, and we've been number one since the 1920s. We make one of the smoothest print surfaces you will find anywhere. We give you quality in the old-world, Pennsylvania German tradition of craftsmanship. It's just a gorgeous sheet of paper."

In keeping with the image of a company with old-fashioned values holding its own in the twenty-first century, the equipment in P. H. Glatfelter's Spring Grove mill was built to produce paper for the demands of a bygone era but has been modified to master the needs of today. "We're pulling this stuff off on small commodity paper machines that were never built to do the grades that we make now," Mingus said. Because requirements vary dramatically, juggling a day's operation schedule can be tricky, with formulations constantly changing as different papers are set up and sent rolling through the machines. "The lightest sheets we make are below ten grams per square meter, with heavier products that can be more than three hundred grams."

Spring Grove operates five uncoated paper machines, Chillicothe four—all traditional Fourdriniers—and both mills produce their own

*Rolls of postage stamp paper being produced at the Glatfelter mill, Spring Grove, Pennsylvania.*

pulp. One thousand tons of paper are made at Spring Grove every day, another 1,250 tons at Chillicothe. To generate steam, Spring Grove makes 100 percent of its own electricity, with 75 percent of it generated from biomass fuel derived from papermaking waste products. No coal, gas, or ethanol is used, and excess power is sold to the local grid in a cogeneration arrangement. About thirteen million gallons of water a day are drawn from company reservoirs fed by the Codorus Creek, with several impounds and dams in place to maintain volume and regulate the flow.

Mingus began our tour of the mill in the woodyard, where logs brought in by long truck were being unloaded, debarked, chipped, and screened for impurities. As that was happening, two gargantuan mounds of wood chips—one softwood, the other hardwood—were being fed onto a rising conveyor belt, destined for the towering spire that dominates an otherwise rural landscape; this is the mill's batch digester, where they begin the transformation into pulp. Once inside the mill, the long fibers of the softwood pine and spruce are blended with the shorter fibers of the hardwood oak, maple, and mineral filler products, to produce many different grades of paper.

As we walked toward two of the Fourdriniers, Mingus told me that the Great Depression–era machine chugging away on our left was making paper for postage stamps, and the one laboring noisily to our right was working on a kind of saturated sheet for food handling. "Each of these rolls weighs about one and a half tons," he said, every one of which had a product label to identify its likely function and destination. One cluster of rolls, marked "end-leaf," would go off to a book publisher; another, "archival folder," to a distributor of office products. Grades of "lace paper" would find service as place mats in restaurants. Nearby, a consignment of "natural book" spools awaited shipment to a printing company in New York. A colorful touch, I thought, were the stacks of pastel-tinted rolls—envelope stock, Mingus said, for greeting cards.

"To me, this is one of the wonderful stories of the paper industry, and, to be very frank, the only reason I left an extremely lucrative, secure career at Avery Dennison was because I bought into George's vision," he said when we were back in his office. "I think everyone in the business knew that if George and his team could pull this off, this was going to be *the* place to work in the paper industry. In a world where everyone else was shrinking to their core business, we went the opposite way. We diversified."

AT A DAYLONG ACADEMIC CONFERENCE organized by Yale University Press in the fall of 2008 to discuss the future of scholarly publishing, one of the panelists began his prepared remarks by noting that at least 60 percent of the technical monographs in his personal library were "obsolete" and not likely to be of any use whatsoever to him in the foreseeable future. The statement was not framed as a call to action of any sort, so the matter was left for others to ponder in silence. But there, dangling heavily in the air all the same, was the unspoken inference, put forth by a prominent member of the Yale faculty, that up-to-the-minute options available at the flick of a fingertip have made a certain class of books a waste of valuable shelf space.

When questions were invited from the audience a few minutes later, a glib young man who identified himself as a Yale undergraduate offered the depressing comment that most of the time he spent in the labyrinthine stacks of Sterling Library was devoted to flirting with female students and playing vacuous games with like-minded classmates, his point being that most serious research these days is done

*Robert Darnton, university librarian of the Harvard University
Library System.*

electronically, not between the hard covers of printed books. "Students
of my generation regard the library in much the same way that tourists
regard the great cathedrals of Europe," he added, with a further twist
of the knife: "greatly admired—but seldom used."

There were other observations put forth that day, a good deal of
them reflections on what kinds of steps academic publishers might take
at a time when digital alternatives are pushing so many of them closer
to oblivion, but those two comments in particular seemed to summarize a view that has become more and more evident with respect to the
shape books are likely to take in the years ahead. Disconcerting from
my standpoint was that they were expressed openly on the campus of
an Ivy League university that holds close to thirteen million volumes in
its various repositories, making it one of the largest research collections
in the world.

My role at the conference—called "Why Books Still Matter"—was
simply that of interested observer. I had just completed a commission
to write a centennial history of Yale University Press, widely acknowledged to be one of the outstanding scholarly publishers in the world
and one that—unlike fully 90 percent of its brethren among American
academic imprints at the time—is able to operate, more often than
not, in the black. Indeed, Yale had emerged during those key tran-

sitional years as one of the notable examples of savvy survival in the face of widespread cutbacks. The moderator for several of the panels that day was Robert Darnton, a scholar, teacher, best-selling author, and pioneer in a field known as history of the book, who, from 2007 to 2011, was the Carl H. Pforzheimer university professor and director of the Harvard University Library before being named university librarian in 2011. As caretaker of the world's largest gathering of printed materials held by any academic library, Darnton occupies an influential position in the field of books and information technology. There are seventy-three separate collections in Harvard's system, with total holdings, in 2012, hovering around seventeen million volumes. What Harvard does with these books sets an example that other institutions are often inclined to follow. Policies of ongoing concern among all of them include such matters as collection development, the discarding of books and journals deemed redundant, off-site storage of seldom used materials, the preservation of materials regarded as being at risk, and the integration of traditional collections with new technologies.

"It really is a very heavy responsibility, and I feel responsible not just to the faculty and to the students of Harvard, but to the scholarly world in general," Darnton said when I interviewed him in Cambridge a year after the Yale conference. We met to talk specifically about his involvement with paper as an agent of cultural transmission, but also to discuss his role as chief custodian of such a priceless collection. I was curious to know, too, what had gone through his mind twelve months earlier in New Haven when he heard those two dour comments expressed, and it was there that we began our conversation.

"I totally reject that premise," he said unhesitatingly when I asked about the Yale professor's suggestion of obsolescence. "I can't understand how a book can be obsolete, unless you have a very utilitarian view of what a book is. If it's the user's manual about how to start, let's say, a lawn mower of a model that is no longer available, you could say the user's manual is obsolete—it's useless, it has no function anymore, okay. But that kind of book represents a tiny fraction of a fraction of the books that exist. In what sense is a novel ever obsolete? Any book, it seems to me, even if the quality of the writing isn't great, is nonetheless a testimony to somebody's version of events, view of the world, understanding of his or her condition. So I think that a book, virtually every book, is a cultural product, and cultural products give us information about the surrounding culture."

With respect to the Yale undergraduate's statement of indifference to the relevance of libraries, Darnton was equally dismissive. "There is this tradition, certainly, of libraries being great cultural symbols on the order of medieval cathedrals, which I don't denigrate at all," he said, citing the New York Public Library, where he is a trustee, as one of many examples he could give of a building that represents, as a structure of stone and mortar, much more than its intellectual content. "But if the student is saying something else as well—which I think probably he was—namely, that he doesn't go in there anymore, or that he doesn't use what it has to offer, because it is irrelevant, then he has my sympathy. I can say, however, that here at Harvard we can measure the use of the libraries with some precision, and we do that all the time. What we have found is that all of our libraries are active, and that they are relevant. In fact, we have adjusted to the demand by keeping one of them, Lamont Library, open twenty-four hours a day, five days a week. Students are there at three in the morning, and they are using every manner of research tool we have provided for their use—including, very definitely, printed books."

Other changes have been made, too, in response to the way students gather to study. "The library is not simply a warehouse for books," he said. "I think that was never true, but it's especially not true now. We are redesigning libraries to a certain extent so that they operate more as nerve centers for the exchange of ideas. Students work more often than not now in groups than they used to. When I was a student here, I never worked with groups. 'Group study' to me was a contradiction in terms. I had to bang my head against the books by myself. But we've discovered that often group study is actually quite effective, and to the students it's normal. So we have set aside certain areas in the library where groups can get together, where there are places for them to plug in their computers, but where they also bring their books and discuss things."

Darnton's honors and accomplishments, by any yardstick, are extraordinary—Harvard Class of 1960 magna cum laude after three years of study, Rhodes Scholar, MacArthur Fellow, president, in 1999, of the American Historical Society, chevalier of France's Légion d'Honneur, the author of numerous critically acclaimed books—but nowhere in his curriculum vitae is there an entry for "librarian," a circumstance, oddly enough, that reflects the commanding stature books have enjoyed at Harvard since it was founded, in 1636, with a gift of books from the estate of the Reverend John Harvard. "I never dreamt I'd be the director of a huge library like this, and never set out to do this," he said. "So yes, to answer your question, I sometimes do ask myself how I got here."

But when considered as part of a continuum, his appointment is consistent with the role books have played in Harvard's history, particularly its willingness to occasionally go outside the community of professional librarians for a director. It is a "peculiar position" at Harvard, Darnton agreed, one that is typically given to someone "who is not a librarian, but a senior scholar at Harvard. In my case, they brought me in from Princeton, but the principle, I think, was the same: that is, someone who has scholarly interests that are very compatible with libraries. And I've also spent many, many years trying to develop this field that we now call the history of the book. Perhaps that made me seem, in the eyes of the provost and the president of Harvard, eligible for the job, though it is hard to imagine anyone being worthy of such a position."

A similar philosophy of going outside the box, so to speak, has been followed by the Library of Congress, whose top librarians in recent decades have included the poet Archibald MacLeish and the historians Daniel Boorstin and James Billington, and the New York Public Library, with direction entrusted successively to the scholars Vartan Gregorian and Paul LeClerc, and the Amherst political scientist Anthony W. Marx.

The person credited with masterminding Harvard's most aggressive program of library expansion during the early years of the twentieth century, Archibald Cary Coolidge, was quoted often as saying "there is no such thing as a dead book at Harvard." A colleague of Coolidge's, the eminent literature professor George Lyman Kittredge, summed up the prevailing attitude best when he told friends that if, by some catastrophe, every building in Harvard Yard except the Harry Elkins Widener Memorial Library were to be destroyed, "we would still have a university."

When Darnton was invited, in 2007, to succeed Sidney Verba as university scholar and library director, he was completing his thirty-ninth year on the faculty of Princeton University. At the time of his appointment, he was a professor of European history and director of Princeton's Center for the Study of Books and Media. Printed books, he felt then—and emphasized again when we met in 2009—are measurably more than bearers of information, and fulfill a multitude of functions. "Books belong to economics because they are commodities—they are bought and sold," he had told a writer for the *Princeton Weekly Bulletin* in 2005. "They belong to art history because they are works of aesthetic value. They belong to philosophy and intellectual history because they are carriers of ideas. They belong to English as a form of literature, and they belong to history because they mobilize public opinion and often prove decisive during political conflicts."

Mindful, too, of what is going on in the world with electronic media, Darnton has been at the forefront of formalizing strategies for the use of emerging technologies. As president of the American Historical Association in 1999, he developed protocols for the electronic publication of doctoral theses, and his work on the Gutenberg-e project with Columbia University Press produced a number of open-access scholarly books, one of which, Bin Yang's *Between Winds and Clouds,* is cited in the endnotes to Chapter 1 of this book.

Darnton told me that the overriding goal of his tenure as director of the library at Harvard was to ensure that "we maintain this library at an appropriate level, which isn't easy in a world where you have to be purchasing digital everything, while at the same time keeping up with the printed book, and journals of all sort, electronic and in print, not to mention objects and recordings of music and film and so on—it's just enormous. I have spent a lot of time working on various electronic projects, so it's not as if I'm just someone who loves old books. But I do believe that the new media offer possibilities for expanding the books, for creating new kinds of books, for doing things that weren't possible with the old sorts of books." In 2011, Darnton was named university librarian, a redefined position that allows him to concentrate more fully on the formulation of general policies and less on administrative functions—a change, he told me in an e-mail, that has enabled him to work more actively on the Digital Public Library of America (DPLA), established in 2010 by the Berkman Center for Internet and Society at Harvard. The goal of the national collaborative, according to a mission statement, is to create "an open, distributed network of comprehensive online resources that would draw on the nation's living heritage from libraries, universities, archives, and museums in order to educate, inform, and empower everyone in the current and future generations." In April 2013, Darnton himself announced the formal launching of the DPLA in a lengthy essay published in the *New York Review of Books.*

As a scholar, Darnton has done pioneering work in the movement developed in France during the 1960s known as *histoire du livre*—history of the book—which led to the publication of numerous monographs, most notably *The Business of Enlightenment: A Publishing History of the Encyclopédie, 1775–1800,* in 1979, and *The Forbidden Best-Sellers of Pre-Revolutionary France,* a study of the underground book trade and winner of the 1996 National Book Critics Circle Award. Darnton began his research in 1965, amid a "sea of paper" he virtually stumbled across in the village of Neuchâtel, Switzerland, when he was beginning research for a book about a key figure in the French Revolution—a book he never finished.

"I had run across a footnote to the manuscripts in Neuchâtel suggesting that they had material concerning a man named Jacques Pierre Brissot," he said. "Brissot was the last of the extreme Republicans before the Reign of Terror, and before the French Revolution he was a hack writer and would-be philosopher who was fascinated with America. I had recently arrived at Oxford, where I did my Ph.D. I was twenty-six, I had done a brief stint as a reporter for the *New York Times,* and was just given a position as a junior fellow here in Harvard. I had three years in which to do postdoctoral research, and I thought this would be a nice subject."

Neuchâtel had been home in the eighteenth century to one of many firms that took advantage of strict censorship laws that restricted the content of books allowed to be published within France. In the absence of copyright laws, printers were free to print whatever titles they wished and ship them surreptitiously across the border into France, where they were sold to an eager readership. "We're not talking here about manuals or law or medicine or theological works, but all of current literature, and most of that was produced outside of France at this time, and marketed in France," Darnton said. A good many of these projects were outright piracies, and there was little recourse for the aggrieved to seek any sort of satisfaction.

"It was a fairly major industry, these publishing houses, and in virtually every instance their archives have disappeared. But the exception happens to be in the city of Neuchâtel. There were three families involved, three main directors of the company, called the Société Typographique de Neuchâtel. One of them had a large house with a great big attic, and when the company finally broke up, he just put the papers in the attic, and they sat there for many years." Darnton traveled to the city with no expectations other than the task at hand—to illuminate the early life of a man who was a major figure in the French Revolution.

"I went there, and sure enough, there were the 115 Brissot letters I had been told I would find, with the replies, which were all very revealing. But they were surrounded by fifty thousand *other* letters that had to do with everything concerning books. Papermaking was front and center, but also the workers who composed the type, and pulled the bars of the press, the book wagoners who transported the finished books, not to mention authors and booksellers everywhere in Europe, including Moscow and St. Petersburg and Budapest. It had everything you could imagine, and it was all so fresh and untouched."

Darnton wrote five hundred pages on Brissot before he stopped and put the manuscript aside. "This is a case of something I never published. What I have stands on its own, but it only takes the story up to 1789, when Brissot begins to be important. That's when the Revolution starts, and he plays a role in it. For that, I had a lot more research to do using other sources. But I was too much interested in this material I had just found in Neuchâtel. I said to myself, 'You know, more important than Brissot's biography is the *book*—the *book* is the subject.' And so, instead of taking another five years to get up the rest of Brissot's life, I dropped it, and I began concentrating on books. And I've been doing it ever since."

Darnton would spend summer after summer in Neuchâtel, finishing his work there finally in 1990. "I read all fifty thousand documents," he said, and among the many rewards was an enriched appreciation for paper. "I found to my amazement that people are talking about paper all the time. By 'people' I mean the publishers, the booksellers, even the readers. I found letters from readers who complained about the quality of a particular kind of paper used in a particular book. Now, to a modern reader, that's amazing. It's so unexpected. I became convinced that not just book professionals—that is, printers and booksellers—but readers paid attention to paper. And there's lots of evidence for this. If you look at advertisements for books, they often say, for example, 'made from the very best paper.' So I think there was a paper consciousness that existed two to three hundred years ago that you don't see today."

Darnton said the Neuchâtel archives contain, moreover, "dozens and dozens and dozens of letters" from all sorts of other people connected with the paper trade—the millers, the merchants, "even the paper scouts who go around to mills and report on the quality of the water and the rags. Not everyone used rags from Burgundy, which were terrific, but sometimes they had lesser rags, and there's talk about rag pickers and the quality of rags. So it's a whole world, the world of paper, that is enormously rich and complicated. And people talk about the water, because water, as you know, is very important. The Jura Mountains, for instance, are very good for papermaking, because they have wonderful water there." In reading these letters, Darnton said, he became intrigued with the whole subject of paper as the physical material of literature, and its central importance in the book trade of the early modern period. "So I decided I would include a little chapter about paper in this book I was writing about the publishing history of the *Encyclopédie,* called *The Business of Enlightenment,* but the chapter ran away with me and it became about a one-hundred-page monograph—which to date is still sitting in my desk drawer along with the Brissot biography."

Though that manuscript also remains unpublished, Darnton said the experience was instructive for him on a number of levels. "When I was a student here at Harvard, I read books and never paid any attention to the paper. I took paper for granted until I got to know it. When I first wandered into those archives, in 1965, I had no interest in paper, and the history of books as a field of study had hardly existed. The expression wasn't even used yet. And I didn't think I was writing the history of books, either. I was just going to do another monograph. But the more I got into it, the more I realized that, first of all, if I like anthropological veins, which I very much do, then I should try to understand how printers and publishers actually thought. Well, turns out, they thought a lot about paper. And to me, that was surprising. And whenever I come upon something that is essentially counterintuitive, then I feel I'm onto something, and I try to pursue it."

# 18

## Elegy in Fragments

Au fond, le papier, le papier, le papier.
—Jacques Derrida, *Les Cahiers de Médiologie,* 1997

IN A DAY fraught with searing images, none was more horrifying on September 11, 2001, than the sight of two colossal buildings crumbling thunderously to the ground, each releasing massive plumes of office paper beneath shrouds of sickly gray dust. Reported later to be hip deep in places, most of the fragments landed on the streets closest to what quickly became known as Ground Zero, but thousands of others fell in neighborhoods throughout the five boroughs of New York City and across the Hudson River in New Jersey. Described by some witnesses as a surreal kind of "paper rain," the visual effect in Lower Manhattan drew grim comparisons to the ticker-tape parades staged over the previous century in the Canyon of Heroes, nearby. Though scorched around the edges in many instances, the tattered sheets were still the only artifacts of consequence to emerge from the Twin Towers in any recognizable form.

One of the more moving responses to the phenomenon came in the form of a video prepared by Blue Man Group, an avant-garde ensemble of musicians and pantomime artists based in New York. Presented online within months of the terrorist attacks, the segment, called "Exhibit 13," was later adapted for live presentation onstage and included as the final track in the group's 2003 album *The Complex.* Other than one introductory sentence—"The following pieces of paper blew into the Carroll Gardens neighborhood in Brooklyn, New York"—there is no coherent text, just the muted recitation, underneath the music, of words that appear on fifteen of the recovered scraps, which intermittently become legible. No date is mentioned, no further information is offered, no additional commentary is provided. Context, in this sublime mélange, is entirely by way of circumstance; each sheet had floated across the East River and come to rest in the same neighborhood.

The progression begins with a single piece of paper fluttering gently downward on a black background, joined before long, in measured succession, by others, with the steady, ominous beat of percussion and synthesizer strings driving what finally becomes a crescendo of falling fragments. "Exhibit 13" refers to the two words that appear on one of the recovered sheets, probably a cover page for a professional presentation of some sort that will forever remain a mystery. Others include a square of memorandum paper embossed with the words "while you were out," a shard of computer copier paper with sprocket holes, a leaf from a daily calendar, a shorn-off section of a spiral notebook, a page of Japanese characters printed in vertical columns, and a list of instructions for bank employees to follow in the event of a robbery. As the first anniversary of the attacks drew near, a film critic for the *New York Times* singled out the three-and-a-half-minute video for the "poetic, imagistic, and simple" way it "draws viewers in, inviting us to reflect rather than telling us what to think."

In the weeks and months that followed the attacks, journalists and photographers who covered the story offered a multitude of impressions, and some made mention of the paper that was everywhere to be seen. David Horrigan, a contributing editor of the *National Law Journal,* wrote about how he had been sent downtown to "cover the story." Within minutes of arriving at the intersection of Park Place and Church Street, he noticed that "the ground itself bore witness to the reality that this place also was home to the legal community—lawyers, paralegals, legal secretaries, and other professionals working in New York City's two towering icons. The tools of their trades—pleadings, interrogatories, legal memoranda, and legal research printouts—snowed to the streets."

As a colleague of his shot photographs, Horrigan took notes. "Some documents, once urgent, were not so urgent anymore. A law firm's fax was marked, 'RUSH.' A deposit slip for a payroll account was ready for the bank." As he was looking through these documents, a "consent to change attorney form," prepared for the Supreme Court in Queens, "blew through the air," and then he noticed a cluster of pleadings that were lying by his feet. "One insisted that an opposing party's testimony was 'nothing more than the rankest of speculation.' Another was damaged so badly all that could be deciphered was that the author believed the opposing party's conduct violated Connecticut's unfair trade laws."

One of the more haunting photographs to be made that day was of a bronze statue of a Wall Street businessman seated at a park bench in Liberty Plaza, a fixture in the neighborhood since 1982 and the only recognizable object in what was otherwise a sea of paper. The picture was taken by Susan Meiselas, a New York photographer affiliated with Magnum Photos, a professional cooperative established in 1947 by Robert Capa and Henri Cartier-Bresson. Meiselas is well known for her diverse body of work, which has brought her numerous awards and international recognition. She told me in an interview for this book that she arrived at Ground Zero by bicycle just after the first tower collapsed and remained on the scene until after dusk. "Of all the pictures I took that day, this is the one that stays with me the longest, because

*Liberty Plaza, near Ground Zero, after the paper from the Twin Towers had settled. The sculpture of the businessman on the park bench, called* Double Check, *is by John Seward Johnson II, and was installed in 1982.*

it captured the total chaos, and at the same time a bizarre calmness, to something very traumatic that had just happened," she said.

"All the dust and all the paper was definitely the landscape through which everyone flowed that day. Paper was flying everywhere, and when I framed that picture, it was starting to settle, and we were all beginning to assimilate the enormity of what we had just witnessed. I have a number of pictures of firemen and policemen in the midst of all this, and paper is strewn everywhere in each of them. But this one really summarizes for me the disorientation of the moment. It was an interval of quiet to absorb the profundity of what had just taken place."

Once cleanup efforts got under way, the rubble was hauled off to the massive Fresh Kills Landfill, on Staten Island. Other than a small number of material objects—a fire extinguisher, an assortment of elevator door signs, a pile of office keys, and the crushed remains of a personal computer among them—very few items were readily identifiable, though efforts to document what did remain began almost immediately. Mark Schaming, director of exhibitions and programs for the New York State Museum, in Albany, told me that within days of the devastation, he and his co-workers were developing a plan of acquisition.

*A recovery worker examines a piece of printed paper from the Twin Towers rubble at the Fresh Kills Landfill.*

"This was an attack on the United States that happened in New York, and the two big questions for us, of course, were what do you collect, and do you wait until the dust begins to settle? We agreed that we had to get right on it. We knew, for instance, that the missing-person posters that began to appear almost immediately would be important. People were putting these faces all over the city, and after a few weeks, when it was clear that the search for the living was futile, a good many of them became memorials. We at first photographed the memorials from a distance. When the city finally said these things had to come down, we collected an entire block of fence at Broadway and Liberty Street, and everything on it. We also have missing-person posters from Pier 94, probably the biggest single collection of individual personal memorials."

Posters were just one phase of a much larger accumulation, with the most intensive selection to be done at Fresh Kills, which began receiving wreckage on September 12. The municipal landfill there had been closed permanently since March 2001, but it was reopened and designated a crime scene, making it off-limits to anyone without proper credentials, including the press. Over the next ten months, 1.8 million tons of debris were ferried in by barge, each vessel carrying up to 650 tons per load, with as many as seventeen shiploads arriving on a single day. One hundred and seventy-five acres were used to sort and sift through everything, the three priorities among investigators being to locate human remains, recover personal effects, and gather evidence for the ongoing Federal Bureau of Investigation probe.

Found among the mounds of material was $76,318.47 in cash, most of it paper currency. Of the fifty-four thousand personal objects recovered by investigators, about four thousand were photographs, most of them presumed to have been on people's desks; they were sent to Kodak labs for decontamination and turned over, when possible, to relatives. Some three thousand identification cards turned up, too, in many cases the only trace of a victim that was left behind.

"I spent forty days out there—two days a week for ten months," Schaming said. "The only thing I recognized that first day was a FedEx envelope. We returned the next week and worked with the police and FBI. They were looking for remains and evidence. What really struck me was that everything had paper embedded in it—steel, vehicles, everything. We ended up choosing two thousand objects for our col-

lections, some of it paper—ledger books from a fire company, stationery, newspapers, things blown into cars. We collected a number of
vehicles, and we have about fifty pieces of the planes. We did a lot of
photographing out there as well." A third paper element his museum
acquired was "an enormous sympathy collection of things sent to New
York from people all over the world."

One artifact that Schaming said he found profoundly moving
among those acquired by the Abany museum was the "Family Trailer,"
a construction-site vehicle brought to the World Trade Center by the
Port Authority of New York and New Jersey for the exclusive use of relatives of those who had died. "They could go in there and look out the
window, and they would leave tributes of people lost, memorial photographs, posters. The families plastered every inch of the walls. You
will find cards in there—'Happy Birthday, Dad,' that sort of thing. We
have the whole trailer. When you stand in there, you're just immersed
in the magnitude of it all. It's thousands of faces looking back. It's a
very sacred place that families are now sharing with the public."

With some fifteen million objects pertinent to the history and
culture of the state included among its holdings, the New York State
Museum collects much more than 9/11 artifacts, of course. At Ground
Zero itself, on the other hand, the mandate of the National September
11 Memorial & Museum, incorporated in 2003, is devoted to documenting the historic event and its aftermath, and the museum has been
gathering material and developing a detailed exhibit plan since 2006,
when Jan Seidler Ramirez was appointed chief curator and director of
collections. Her previous experience included positions at the Museum
of the City of New York, where she was deputy director and chief curator, and the New-York Historical Society, where she served as vice president and director.

As a developing concept, the 9/11 museum may be unique among
major institutions in that its mission is to document and interpret the
events and consequences of a single day, and to do much of it by creating a narrative out of artifacts. I first met with Ramirez and Amy
Weinstein, the associate curator, one February morning in 2009, in
their temporary offices at 1 Liberty Plaza. Outside the windows twenty
floors below, the gaping enclosure at Ground Zero was abuzz with trac-
tors and cranes, their new home still several years away from being a
reality.

"It was so incomprehensible," Ramirez said. "What a good number of people are telling us is that for about ten or twenty seconds they couldn't process what they just saw. They looked up into the blue sky of that gorgeous morning and the paper was catching the sun. A lot of employees just arriving for work off the subways recall asking themselves, 'A ticker-tape parade?' 'A flock of birds?' Some described it as an iridescent rainbow. These buildings were meant to be the epitome of modern work habits, and lo and behold, what is it that we see coming out of them in their great moment of extremis? All this paper—a geyser of confetti."

In developing their scheme for the museum, Ramirez said, the curators designed an opening sequence where visitors will experience some of the prevailing sense of helpless disbelief that was so endemic that day, and that "paper is ubiquitous" in the overall plan. "We have some paper retrieved from rooftops, balconies, some very interesting things from all over the city. We will have in the opening sequence exhibition some of the paper that flew out of the towers. We have some other things that came from the airplanes, and we're working on getting items from the Pentagon, in Washington, and from Shanksville, Pennsylvania, where Flight 93 went down." Two artifacts recovered from the wreckage in Pennsylvania were the personal logbook of senior flight attendant Lorraine G. Bay and an in-flight manual annotated with personal notes to clarify actions to be taken in the event of emergencies such as hijackings.

An invoice mailed from Essex, Massachusetts, to a company in California, postmarked September 10, was picked up by a law student who had been evacuated from a building. "He took some papers he found on the ground home with him—a lot of people did that—and he had this unopened envelope that was in a mailbag on one of the planes that had left that morning from Boston. He turned it over to us, we contacted the addressee, and they were gracious enough to say we could keep it." Ramirez said that a good deal of the collection depends on materials that people have given them, and so much of what has been considered worthwhile is paper. "Paper badges, for instance: here's one from the lapel of a man who was a computer technology guy there on a job. He had just gone down the elevator to get a cup of coffee, and because of that, he survived. He gave his badge to us."

One of the precious few stories of miraculous survival belongs to

Mickey Kross, a New York City Fire Department lieutenant who had rushed, with his Engine 16 crew, to the burning towers. He was helping a woman down the stairs of the north tower when the building collapsed, trapping them and a dozen others in a small void beneath the crumpled fourth floor for five hours. How they survived, and how so many hundreds of others perished, remains a mystery—but escape came by following a shaft of light to the outside. Among the materials Kross gave to the National September 11 Memorial & Museum is a playing card—the two of clubs—that was the first object he saw when he led the group to safety. He also donated the "call slip" that had been tucked into his pocket, with the names of the four men who rode with him that day—all survived—and a note he left for his girlfriend, telling her he was all right and not to worry.

Like Schaming at the New York State Museum, Ramirez and Weinstein have made missing-person posters a priority. "This is believed to have been the first missing-person poster," Weinstein said, showing me one that was put up on the afternoon of September 11. "By that evening, there were hundreds. It is part of the paper story of the day," Ramirez said. "You see people, over time, rethinking what they want to put on the poster. What was she wearing that day? Where were her scars or tattoos? There is this incredible sense of urgency, where people are beginning to pick up any piece of paper, just trying to make a statement. They write notes, they post notes. Given the complete crippling of the telephone and electrical systems, what also fascinates me, sociologically, is that paper becomes the only urgent and most efficient mode of communication. Thank God for paper, because we turn to it again and again."

An artifact that the museum does not have but has been tracking with interest, in the event the FBI no longer needs it, is the scorched passport of one of the terrorists that was picked up on Liberty Street before the towers collapsed. "There are some incredible stories of the effort that people made to get paper back to other human beings," Ramirez said. "It might be a transaction with the signature on it of a name that appeared on the victims list. Sometimes this kind of gesture has led to friendships."

Ramirez then showed me a photocopy of a business card bearing the name Pablo Ortiz, identifying the man as a construction inspector for the Port Authority of New York and New Jersey, owner of the buildings. It appeared heavily soiled and singed lightly around the edges and had been found, according to the transmittal letter of the person who donated it to the museum, "perched upon the ledge outside" a window of his Park Slope apartment, in Brooklyn, in the early evening of 9/11. "It was difficult to conceive how a business card could have traveled such a distance and to have landed safely on my window ledge," the man wrote. He had kept it for six years, "knowing I wanted to find a more permanent home for it."

Ramirez said that shortly after the museum received the card, they did a Google search on Pablo Ortiz "to see what had happened to this man" and were astonished by what they found. "It turns out this man was one of the great unsung civilian heroes of that day. He was on the eightieth floor, and he was training new people. As all hell starts to break loose, Pablo Ortiz and another man from the Port Authority, Frank De Martini, grab some simple tools and order everybody else to go down. But they go up, and they burst through doors, saving a lot of people. Just an incredible story. And how his business card gets to Brooklyn is just astonishing."

A search I subsequently conducted on the LexisNexis database of full-text newspaper articles turned up a wealth of stories on the heroism of Ortiz and De Martini, acts that were confirmed by people whose lives they had saved and on transcripts of emergency 911 calls released by the Port Authority in 2003. "With their tools, the two men—

*The business card of Pablo Ortiz, a Port Authority inspector credited with helping more than fifty trapped people escape. It was recovered in Brooklyn.*

Frank De Martini and Pablo Ortiz, an architect and a construction inspector—attacked the lethal web of obstacles that trapped people who had survived the impact of the airplane but could not get to an exit," Jim Dwyer wrote in the *New York Times* on August 29, 2003. "At least 50 people stuck on the 88th and 89th floors of the north tower were able to walk out of the building because Mr. De Martini, Mr. Ortiz and others tore away rubble, broke down doors and answered calls for help. Everyone above the 91st floor died," as did De Martini and Ortiz.

Ramirez then showed me a photograph taken by a prominent Magnum photojournalist, Larry Towell, picturing a man in a business suit standing in the middle of a street, intently reading a piece of paper he had just picked up. Ramirez said there are other photographs of people picking up paper before the north tower fell, "trying to make sense of what was happening," then she slid another photocopy across her desk for me to look at. It pictured a single sheet of common bond copy paper, largely intact and bearing a dark red smear at one extremity on the left. The original document had been given to the museum a few months before my visit, its chain of custody since the moment of discovery beyond reproach. There were seven words written on it, scrawled out hastily in pen: "84th floor west office 12 people trapped." Ramirez said that she and Weinstein had heard accounts of people throwing notes out of windows, but this was one that had actually been recovered.

"We assume this is a bloodstain, and that the person who wrote the note broke a window to get air," Ramirez said. "It was picked up by a woman who was evacuating the area down on Liberty Street. She handed it to a security guard outside of the Federal Reserve Bank, and as he looked up, the south tower began to collapse. So by the time anyone had an opportunity to process what they were looking at, there was no eighty-fourth floor in either building. It was a matter of a person on the street picking up a plea for help and handing it over to a man in uniform. It was kept in a safe-deposit box in the bank until just recently, when the decision was made that we were the appropriate people to take custody of it."

Considerable work had been done to try to identify who the twelve victims were, she said, with speculation centering on a cluster of Euro Brokers employees who worked on the eighty-fourth floor of the south tower, but nothing at the time of my visit was conclusive. "We are

*The photojournalist Larry Towell recalled of this image that many people "just stood and stared" incredulously at the devastation, while some "sorted through the debris."*

hopeful that perhaps, at some point, the medical examiner can extract DNA from the stain, and if that can be done, then there is a chance that an identity can be established. We've talked about that with the medical examiner's office, and they are open to this possibility in the near future, as part of their ongoing effort to make new identifications. We're also looking at the handwriting."

When Ramirez first showed me this document, in February 2009, the thought that an identification might in fact be possible was remote but hopeful, and if the name of the individual remained forever anonymous, so be it—the prevailing feeling was that it represented, in a poignantly powerful way, all the innocent victims of the terrorist attacks. "It speaks for all the people who died, and who can't speak for themselves," Ramirez said. "I think sometimes the *not* knowing is just as important as the knowing."

When I contacted Ramirez in the fall of 2011 to get an update on the museum, I learned about some exciting new collections that had recently been acquired; there were two in particular that documented the public response to 9/11, but in fundamentally different ways that

are remarkably complementary. One of them, called the Michael Ragsdale 9/11 Aftermath Paper Ephemera Collection, was gathered over a
fourteen-month period by Michael Ragsdale, a videographer at Columbia University, starting the day after the attacks. "It's basically flyers
and posters and pamphlets that were freely available that he picked up
in the course of his work," Ramirez said.

"He collected every piece of paper he could find in the tri-state area
that had anything to do with 9/11 except missing-person flyers and
photographs of the destruction. He wouldn't take anything that wasn't
intended to be public or given away." There are about 2,800 items,
and they include such materials as Red Cross leaflets, religious and
United Nations reactions to the attacks, calls for peace and tolerance,
and offers of help for people in distress and need of counsel. "Like all
ephemeral materials, these things tend to disappear pretty quickly, so
it's something we're really pleased to have."

On a more global scale, Ramirez said the museum was delighted
also to have acquired what has been called the Dear Hero Collection of
correspondence maintained over an eight-year period by Tanya Hoggard, of Cincinnati, Ohio, a Delta Air Lines flight attendant who in
the early months of the recovery effort shuffled her work schedules so
she could spend time with the Salvation Army in Lower Manhattan
serving refreshments and offering support to the rescue crews. After
a while, she began to pin on the side of the respite tent, where she
volunteered, cards and letters received from children, and she struck
up friendships with a number of firefighters who told her that piles of
similar material had been flowing into their firehouses from all over
the world. Before long, she became determined to gather as many as
possible and preserve them until a permanent home could be found.

With the help of other airline employees willing to tote an extra
suitcase or two on her behalf—and with the grateful acquiescence of
the first responders to whom the warm and moving greetings were
being sent—Hoggard began to take custody of what turned out to be
about three tons of correspondence, and transported it all to Cincinnati, where several businesses provided free storage space. She cataloged
each piece individually and kept it packed in eighty archival storage
bins. When the gift was announced, a New York firefighter who had
helped Hoggard gather the material told a reporter how much the letters had meant to everyone who received them. "It was a very dark time

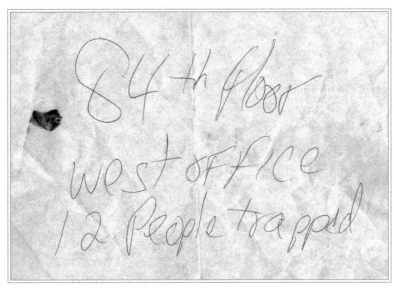

*The eighty-fourth-floor note safeguarded for ten years by the Federal Reserve Bank of New York, now on long-term loan to the National September 11 Memorial & Museum.*

for us," said Joe Tisbe, whose fire station—Engine 40, Truck 35—had lost twelve people on 9/11. "Emotionally, mentally. It was physically draining. And to see that kind of support, to see the letters kids had written, was a bright spot. It's like saving your kid's first painting. It means a lot more than the paper and ink that's there."

I then asked Ramirez whether she had ever been able to get a forensic analysis of the handwritten plea for help she had shown me two and a half years earlier. "We did have the medical examiner analyze it—and it did match somebody who worked for a financial services company on the eighty-forth floor of the south tower," she said after a lengthy pause. "The medical examiner reached out to the next of kin, the man's wife, and out of sensitivity to her, she will decide when, and how, the identity is to be disclosed. So this will all come out at an appropriate time, and in an appropriate manner." Ramirez did agree with me, however, that there was now an entirely new context attached to this simple sheet of paper, one that held its ultimate secret for ten years, and which she put into fuller perspective.

"We have a woman, a terrified evacuee on Maiden Lane, where the Federal Reserve Bank is located, and there is a security officer outside helping people. She runs up to him and hands him a piece of paper. 'I just found this—please help these people.' He opens the note, he assumes the south tower, he turns to go into the bank, and as he turns to go inside, the tower collapses. At that moment, the man on the eighty-fourth floor who writes the note and throws it out the window dies while desperately trying to help the people he is with. It *is* an entirely different narrative, now that we know his name. And it speaks eloquently for all the other victims who perished that day."

# Epilogue

AS UNITED AIRLINES FLIGHT 175 approached the World Trade Center from the southwest on September 11, 2001, it passed over the Hudson River at an altitude of one thousand feet, then banked sharply to the left before striking the south tower with cataclysmic force at 9:03 a.m. The plunging airliner's rate of descent had momentarily reached a frightful ten thousand feet a minute, and its speed at impact was 587 miles an hour. A horrified air traffic controller who followed the flight path of the fully fueled Boeing 767 on his radar screen later described what he witnessed as a "power dive" into the 110-floor building.

Investigators would determine that, because the hijacked aircraft ripped into the tower at an angle—not head-on, as had been the case seventeen minutes earlier with American Airlines Flight 11 at the north tower—one smoke-filled passageway to the northeast, Stairway A, remained marginally passable. That circumstance allowed for the escape of four survivors from the upper floors and another fourteen from just below the immediate point of entry, and it might have been a lifeline for others who remained trapped, if only that detail had been known to them during the rapidly deteriorating crisis.

In its official report of the day's events, the 9/11 Commission estimated that at least a hundred people in the south tower had been killed on impact. The commission further found that, of the 599 people known to have died in the building, all but twenty had the fateful misfortune of being in or above the strike zone, which extended from the seventy-seventh floor to the eighty-fifth. A number of companies suffered grievous losses, five of them alone accounting for nearly half of those killed. Of these, Euro Brokers Inc., an international trading firm with offices at the epicenter of the strike, on the eighty-fourth floor, suffered sixty-one fatalities.

The last person to escape the south tower before it collapsed, at 9:59 a.m., was Ron DiFrancesco, a Euro Brokers money market trader whose decision, minutes before the second jet hit, to evacuate the building without waiting for further instructions was the difference between life and death. He was in the eighty-fourth-floor lobby, where he was shielded by heavy machinery housed in a central elevator shaft, when the right wing of the aircraft sheared just overhead. Able to grope his way into Stairway A, he teamed up with Brian Clark, a Euro Brokers vice president who had already been attempting to organize an evacuation. How these two men became separated yet still found a path to safety was thoroughly reported in the aftermath of the attacks, but both credited being away from their desks at the time of impact as crucial to their survival. This was not the case with one of their colleagues, forty-eight-year-old Randolph Scott, of Stamford, Connecticut, who was believed to have died instantly when UAL 175 tore into the company's offices.

Shortly after the north tower had been struck, Randy Scott called Springdale Elementary School, in Stamford, where his wife, Denise, taught first grade, and left a message to assure her that he was all right. Like so many others in the south tower that morning, Scott is presumed to have remained at his desk during that critical interval, as directed over loudspeakers by Port Authority officials, who declared their building safe. Confirmation of his death would come in the months that followed, by way of fragments recovered periodically, thirty of them through the autumn of 2011.

"I took some comfort in believing that Randy had died instantly, that at least he wasn't in pain," Denise Scott told me when we met in August 2012 to discuss an extraordinary turn of events we had both learned about at roughly the same time—that forensic analysis of a bloodstain had identified her late husband as the person whose hastily drafted appeal for help was picked up on Liberty Street by a fleeing passerby moments before the building fell. "You spend ten years not knowing what happened—I mean *exactly* what happened—and you pray that your loved one doesn't suffer," she explained. "I was told that the impact site was his floor, so my thought was that the plane hit—

done. My hope—honestly—was that he had gone in an instant. I had three kids who just lost their father, and I was in shock; I had to focus all my strength on putting our lives back together. So yes, I was at ease with my own little fantasy, with my own little belief—that at least he hadn't gone through any of that unspeakable horror."

Denise recalled for me the phone call she had received from Dr. Barbara Butcher, the chief of staff and director of forensic investigations in the Office of the Chief Medical Examiner in New York City, informing her of the discovery. "I thought at first it was another fragment they had found, but she said, 'No, it's something written.' Something *written*? After ten years? I was absolutely stunned." A couple of days later, she drove into New York with Steve Ernst, her late husband's best friend, to see the note for herself and to be briefed on the DNA results. "I brought a sample of Randy's handwriting with me, ready to dispute it, but just looking at the document, right away I knew. There was no doubt: it was his handwriting. So of course, when you see something like that, there are ten thousand things running through your head."

The words on her husband's note, moreover—"84th floor west office 12 people trapped"—told her not only that Randy had survived but that others had survived with him, and that he was doing everything he could to get them all out alive. "When I showed this to our daughters, one of them said, 'He must have been so scared.' I said, 'No, your father wasn't scared. He was trying to rescue people.' If there is one consolation now for me, it's the knowledge that Randy died trying to save the people he was with, and I think it speaks for everyone who was trapped in those buildings that day. He never lost hope, he fought to the end—and I wouldn't have expected anything less of him."

Denise said her reluctance at first to disclose the identification publicly had been driven only by the timing of the verification, which had come a few weeks before the tenth anniversary of the attacks. "I couldn't bring myself to tell my daughters about it at that time; it was traumatic enough already. And you don't want to sit them down at Thanksgiving or Christmas and show them something like this then, either. So I told them in January, and it was after that I said, 'Okay, the girls know, so it's not a secret anymore.'" A month after we spoke, she gave an interview to the *Stamford Advocate,* her hometown newspaper, which ran an article on the identification to coincide with the eleventh anniversary of the attacks, and it quickly became a national story.

When I met with Denise in her home in Stamford, she was putting the finishing touches on a sequence of slides to be included in a National September 11 Memorial & Museum tribute honoring all 2,982 confirmed victims of the attacks, a number that includes those who were killed that day at the Pentagon and in Shanksville, Pennsylvania. One of the images is of Randy Scott as a youngster growing up in Brooklyn, New York; another shows him and Denise at the time of their marriage, in 1979, and still another is of the couple with their daughters, Rebecca, Jessica, and Alexandra. The most recent had been taken on Sunday, September 9, 2001—two days before the terrorist attacks—and pictures Randy astride a Honda Shadow motorcycle, a twentieth-anniversary gift to him from his wife.

Denise said that on those occasions when she visits the private room set aside for 9/11 families, she pays her respects to all the victims whose photographs cover every inch of wall space. "And every time I go in there, I find the guest book, I sit down, and I write Randy a little note. I tell him, 'The girls are good, we all miss you.' It's the only place I do anything like that. I don't know why. But I always let him know how the girls are doing." And she emphasized that, while she has agreed to place the eighty-fourth-floor document on deposit with the museum, her family retains ownership. "It's on loan to them for as long as they want it there—but it doesn't belong to me. It belongs to my daughters. It's their legacy from their father."

# *Acknowledgments*

This book has been quite a few years in the making, beginning from scratch in what for me was uncharted territory, and drawing on the good counsel and expertise of many people who not only suggested productive avenues of inquiry, but helped pave the way with their sound advice.

First and foremost, MacArthur Fellow Timothy Barrett, my host during a speaking visit to the University of Iowa Center for the Book in 2002, whose enthusiasm and extraordinary grasp of hand papermaking techniques gave me the initial idea for what became this project. Tim's willingness to put me in touch with his colleagues proved invaluable, and the course he teaches at Rare Book School at the University of Virginia with John Bidwell of the Morgan Library that I later took was a magical experience. Both men generously read segments of the book in manuscript, and offered useful suggestions for their improvement. Many thanks, also, to Michael Suarez, the brilliant director of Rare Book School and a great champion of books as material objects.

I am especially grateful to Martin H. Hubbe, professor and distinguished scientist in the Department of Biomaterials at North Carolina State University and founding co-editor of the online peer-reviewed journal *BioResources*, for his careful reading on matters related to the chemistry and process of industrial papermaking.

My deepest thanks to the National Endowment for the Humanities for a generous fellowship in 2008 that helped me focus my full attention on this project, and to the Vancouver philanthropist Dr. Yosef Wosk, a champion of the literary arts and a keen advocate of independent scholarship, for hosting a lecture tour I made to British Columbia, and for a thoughtful grant in support of this book.

The "Common Bond" chapter turns, in large measure, on the three-week trip I made to China in 2007 in the company of Elaine Koretsky, her husband, Dr. Sidney Koretsky, and their daughter, Donna Koretsky, the owner of Carriage House Paper in Brooklyn, New York; my appreciation to them for inviting me to come along. My gratitude as well to Guan Kaiyun of the Kunming Botanical Garden, our principal guide; to Christine Harrison, a paper historian from Lincolnshire, United Kingdom; and to Anna-Grethe Rischel of Copenhagen, president of the International Association of Paper Historians, for their cheerful camaraderie on our lengthy drives along the Burma Road in Yunnan Province and through the Bamboo Sea of Sichuan Province.

A flawless trip to Japan was arranged by Paul Denhoed, lecturer in paper-making techniques at the Asia University in Tokyo. I recognize, too, the assistance during that journey of Paul's wife Maki Yamashita, the expatriate American artist and papermaker Richard Flavin, the Echizen paper artist Rina Aoki, and the master paper conservator Nobuaki Mishima.

My son-in-law Michael P. Richter, an intelligence officer for nearly a decade and now an attorney in private practice in New York, coordinated my visits to the Central Intelligence Agency and National Security Agency, and read relevant portions of the book in manuscript. Mike's thesis advisor at the National Intelligence University, retired senior intelligence officer Jon A. Wiant, suggested the centrality of paper to intelligence operations; Peter Earnest, for thirty-five years a case officer with the CIA and in 2002 the founding director of the International Spy Museum in Washington, D.C., put me in touch with Antonio "Tony" Mendez years before the general public had an inkling of what the clandestine operation known as "Argo" was all about.

The California laser physicist and master origami artist Robert Lang offered suggestions that proved essential in the "Sleight of Hand" chapter. Others who graciously reviewed segments of the book at various stages include: Terry Belanger, Jonathan Bloom, Scott Brown, Paul Israel, Ben Kafka, Martin Kemp, Franklin Mowery, James O'Gorman, Pradeep Sebastian, and Robert Winter. Douglas Johnson, professor of geography at Clark University and a leading authority on the soils of the Middle East and North Africa, shared some splendid insights on the clay of Mesopotamia.

Four distinctively different industrial papermaking operations are profiled in these pages. For their knowledgeable assistance in making that possible,

I recognize Peter Hopkins at Crane and Company in Massachusetts; Dan Lachmann and Bill Welsh at Kimberly-Clark in Connecticut; Scott Mingus and Heath Frye at P. H. Glatfelter Inc., in Pennsylvania; and Randall Suliga at Marcal Paper Mills, in New Jersey. Kathryn and Howard Clark, founders of Twinrocker Handmade Paper, were most hospitable during my stay at their home in Brookston, Indiana; Dard Hunter III provided an informative private tour of The Mountain House, his grandfather's legendary residence and studio, in Chillicothe, Ohio.

My trips to various research libraries, archival repositories, and conservation laboratories were facilitated by the able assistance of the following: Ellen S. Dunlap and Georgia Barnhill at the American Antiquarian Society, Worcester, Massachusetts; Victoria Steele, Virginia L. Bartow, and Michael Inman, at the New York Public Library; Cindy Bowden, the former director of the Robert C. Williams Paper Museum at the Institute of Paper Science and Technology, in Atlanta; Susan Brynteson, director of libraries at the University of Delaware; Leonard DeGraaf, the Thomas Edison National Historical Park, West Orange, New Jersey; Peter Drummey, Massachusetts Historical Society; Stephen Enniss, the Folger Shakespeare Library; James N. Green, the Library Company of Philadelphia; Jack Herlihy, Lowell National Historical Park, Lowell, Massachusetts; Miriam Kleiman, the National Archives and Records Administration; Martha Mayo, the University of Massachusetts Center for Lowell History; Jan Seidler Ramirez and Amy Weinstein, the National September 11 Memorial Museum, New York; and Marcia Reed, the Getty Research Institute, in Los Angeles.

I would like to extend thanks also to the following individuals for sharing their time and insights: Cathleen A. Baker, paper historian, biographer of Dard Hunter, and publisher of The Legacy Press in Ann Arbor, Michigan; the photographer, printer, and retired director of the Yale School of Art, Richard Benson; Ann Blair and Leah Price of the Radcliffe Institute for Advanced Study at Harvard, who hosted a superb conference on early papermaking techniques and transmissions, and arranged an informative visit to the Weissman Preservation Center in Cambridge; John Chalmers of Chicago, for his help in locating some obscure bibliographical references; the hand papermaker Evelyn David, of Edmonton, Alberta; Merrill Distad, associate university librarian in charge of research and special collections services at the University of Alberta; Donald Farnsworth, founder and director of Magnolia Editions in Oakland, California, and his colleague, the master papermaker David C. Kimball; Jodee Fenton, director of special collections at the Seattle Public Library, who spent several days introducing me to the paper industry of the Pacific Northwest; Kit N. Funderburk, formerly head of paper manufacture for Eastman Kodak in Rochester, New York, and historian of the medium; William A. Gosling, retired university librarian, University of Michigan; Webb Howell, publisher of *Fine Books & Collections* magazine; Paul Messier, conservator and collector of vintage photographic paper in Boston; Brian Queen, Alberta College of Art and Design, for an excellent tutorial on watermarks; Claire Jeanine Satin, book artist and sculptor, of Dania Beach, Florida; Matthew Shlian, paper engineer, of Ann Arbor, Michigan; the Washington, D.C., artist and papermaker Lynn Sures, for arranging a research trip to Fabriano and Amalfi, Italy, in 2003; and Peter Thomas of Santa Cruz, California, known to one and all as "Peter Papermaker."

Yet again, James P. Feeney, Jr. at the Boston Athenæum, James Hogan and Patty Porcaro at the Dinand Library of the College of the Holy Cross, and Mary Hartman at the Robert H. Goddard Library of Clark University, made sure I always found the elusive materials I needed.

My literary agents Glen Hartley and Lynn Chu of Writers Representatives, Inc., have looked out for my best interests now for twenty-five years. I am especially pleased that they found a home for this book at Alfred A. Knopf, and placed me in the expert care of Victoria Wilson, my editor, whose reputation for bringing out the very best in her authors is richly deserved. Thanks go out, too, to copy editor Will Palmer for his rigorous reading of the manuscript, to Vicky's able assistants Daniel Schwartz, Charlotte Crowe, and Audrey Silverman, jacket artist Jason Booher, Cassandra Pappas in design, and promotion specialists Gabrielle Brooks and Erica Hinsley.

The many textual translations of Barbara Basbanes Richter, my daughter, were beautifully nuanced and splendidly on point, and the bibliographical talents and online savvy of her younger sister, Nicole Basbanes Claire, the family librarian, a godsend. I am so proud of them both. Thanks, too, to Billy Claire, Nikki Richardson, and George Basbanes, for their continuing encouragement.

I salute also the unwavering friendship over the past five decades of my *Oriskany* shipmates, with particular gratitude to Eugene O. Hester of Torrance, California; Joseph M. Mason, Jr. of Brooksville, Florida; and Thomas N. Willess of Oakton, Virginia—we few, we happy few.

My mother, Georgia K. Basbanes, missed publication of this book by two years, but she was a ferocious champion of my work from the very beginning, and had regular updates on its progress. She was the last of our parents to leave us, and we miss them all dearly.

Every voyage needs a steady hand on the tiller, especially one that takes on the range and scope of a Homeric odyssey. For that task, as always, there has been the dedicatee of this book, my wife, Connie, whose calm wisdom and strength of character are present on every page. May the journey continue with fair winds and following seas.

# Notes

### PREFACE

xiii **Paper Museum:** See Décultot, catalog of *Musées de Papier,* an exhibition at the Louvre, in Paris, Sept. 25, 2010–Jan. 3, 2011.

xiv **J. D. Drew:** Quoted in Dan Shaughnessy, "Sox Are for Real . . . But Nothing in Sports Is Certain," *Boston Globe,* April 1, 2011.

xv **"were bitter enemies":** William Wan, "U.S., Vietnam Build Trust Through Exchange of Tender Relics," *Washington Post,* June 4, 2012.

### I. COMMON BOND

3 **"The Emperor's Mint":** Marco Polo, *The Travels of Marco Polo,* book II, chap. XXIV (The Khan's Paper Currency).

3 **"Paper is a tenacious":** Francis Bacon, *Novum Organum Scientiarum,* book II, aphorism 31.

4 **gunpowder, printing, and the magnetic compass:** Karl Marx also singled out those discoveries for being "the three great inventions which ushered in bourgeois society. Gunpowder blew up the knightly class, the compass discovered the world market and founded the colonies, and the printing press was the instrument of Protestantism and the regeneration of science in general; the most powerful lever for creating the intellectual prerequisites." *Economic Manuscripts of 1861–63, Division of Labour and Mechanical Workshop, Tool and Machinery* (XIX-1169).

4 *khipu:* Some six hundred of these cords are known to survive in private and institutional collections. For a thorough examination of their history and function, see Gary Urton, *Signs of the Inka Khipu* (Austin: University of Texas Press, 2003).

4 **clay:** From the German verb *kleben,* meaning to stick, cling, or bind. For more on its many uses in Mesopotamia, see Handcock.

5 **these small tablets:** When Baghdad was looted in the aftermath of the American invasion in 2003, many hundreds of cuneiform tablets were plundered from the National Museum of Iraq. One grouping alone comprised an entire collection dating from the sixth century B.C., called the Sippar Library (recovered from a site southwest of Baghdad), is believed to have been the oldest surviving library in the world. See Basbanes, *Splendor of Letters,* epilogue.

5 **"sources of our knowledge":** Mozi (also known as Mo Tzu), quoted in Tsien, *Bamboo and Silk,* vi.

6  **"human civilization depends"**: Pliny, *Natural History,* vol. 3, chap. 21, "Papyrus," 13. *Cyperus papyrus* is a member of the Cyperaceae, or sedge, family of plants. Modern researchers have demonstrated its buoyant qualities, most notably the Norwegian adventurer Thor Heyerdahl, who crossed the Atlantic in 1970 in a craft made entirely of papyrus, according to ancient models. See Heyerdahl, *The Ra Expeditions* (Garden City, NY: Doubleday, 1971); Parkinson and Quirke; and John J. Gaudet, "When Papyrus Ruled: The Versatile Plant That Strengthened Pharaohs of Egypt," *Washington Post,* April 8, 1999.

6  **"chew the papyrus"**: Theophrastus, book 4, chap. 8, verse 4, quoted by Donald P. Ryan in "Papyrus," *The Biblical Archaeologist* 51, no. 3 (Sept. 1988): 132–40.

6  **Pliny**: For a full account of the circumstances surrounding Pliny's death and the recovery and modern examination of the Herculaneum scrolls, see Sider. The Villa dei Papiri (also spelled Papyri) inspired the design of the J. Paul Getty Museum, in Malibu, California, which today houses its collections of Greek and Roman sculpture and earthenworks.

7  **"making paper from the bark of trees"**: Fan Ye, quoted in Tsien, *Bamboo and Silk,* 136.

7  **the Silk Road**: The name (*Seidenstrasse*) was coined by the nineteenth-century Austrian geologist and explorer Ferdinand von Richthofen (1833–1905).

7  **fifty thousand scrolls**: See Wood and Bernard; Whitfield et al.

8  **"a mat of refuse fibers"**: Tsien, 35.

9  **Cassiodorus praised papyrus**: Cassiodorus, *Variae* (XI.383–86). The quotation on papyrus continues: "a writing surface which takes black ink for its ornament; on it, with letters exalted, the flourishing corn-field of words yields the sweetest of harvests to the mind, as often as it meets the reader's wish. It keeps a faithful witness of human deeds; it speaks of the past, and is the enemy of oblivion. For, even if our memory retains the content, it alters the words; but there discourse is stored in safety, to be heard for ever with consistency."

9  **papyrus sheets**: See Pliny, *Natural History,* vol. 4, book XIII. Dard Hunter reproduces the entire segment in *History and Technique,* 19–23; see also Pedersen, 57.

9  **"from Pergamum"**: See Basbanes, *A Gentle Madness,* 64–65, 68, and Basbanes, *Patience & Fortitude,* 23–30.

11  **Hydrogen bonding**: Dard Hunter discusses the process at length in *History and Technique.* For an excellent overview, see also Martin A. Hubbe and Cindy Bowden, "Handmade Paper: A Review of Its History, Craft, and Science," *BioResources* 4, no. 4 (2009): 1736–92, http://ojs.cnr.ncsu.edu/index.php/BioRes/article/viewFile/BioREs_04_4_1736_Hubbe_Bowden_Handmade_Paper_Review/482; and F. Shafizadeh, "Cellulose Chemistry: Perspective and Retrospect," *Pure Applied Chemistry* 35, no. 2 (1973): 195–208, http://dx.doi.org/10.1351/pac197335020195.

11  **a book from bamboo**: Tsien, *Bamboo and Silk,* 30.

11  **animal-hair brush**: The major resources were the white goat, black rabbit, and yellow weasel, though hair from wolves, horses, and mice were used as well. Goat-hair brushes were found to be soft, flexible, and absorbent; rabbit-hair brushes produce bold, vigorous lines, and are best suited to calligraphy.

11  **"books that belong to the scholars"**: Tsien, *Bamboo and Silk,* 11; see also his footnote.

11  **hauled before him for executive action**: Carter, 2.

12  **Buddhist canon carved on stone**: See Tsien, *Paper and Printing,* 13, 28, 48, 42, 112, 115.

12  **quickly gained in popularity**: One of the most powerful ministerial departments established during the Ming Dynasty (1368–1644) was the Office of Transmission (Tongzheng si), an autonomous bureau charged with coordinating the massive exchange of official information throughout the government. "All documents constituting the paper flow, both in and out, were expected to pass through this single office," F. W. Mott wrote in *Imperial China: 900–1800* (Cambridge, MA: Harvard

University Press, 1999, 642–646). "Because paper was power, this office controlled the flow of paper."

13  **Burma Road:** See Patrick Fitzgerald, "The Yunnan-Burma Road," *The Geographical Journal* 95, no. 3 (March 1940): 161–71.

13  **"urban revolution":** Thomas J. Campanella, *The Concrete Dragon: China's Urban Revolution and What It Means for the World* (New York: Princeton Architectural Press, 2008), 14.

13  **network of road construction:** See Thomas Fuller, "In Isolated Hills of Asia, New Roads to Speed the Trade of an Empire," *New York Times*, March 31, 2008.

14  **most diverse province:** Kunming is home to the Yunnan Museum of Minority Nationalities (Yunnan Sheng Minzu Bowuguan).

14  **cultivated in Yunnan:** See Bin Yang, *Between Winds and Clouds: The Making of Yunnan, Second Century BCE to Twentieth Century CE* (New York: Columbia University Press, 2008), http://www.gutenberg-e.org/yang/index.html.

23  **"Directly behind me":** Elaine Koretsky, "Along the Paper Road," *Hand Papermaking Newsletter*, no. 84 (Oct. 2008). See also her "Along the Paper Road" article in no. 83 (July 2008). For my response, see "The Paper Trail: Hand Papermaking in China," *Fine Books & Collections*, March/April 2008. Just six months after our trip to Sichuan, much of the area we had visited was in the heart of a devastating earthquake that killed ninety thousand people. The center of the tremor, which measured 7.9 on the Richter scale, was northwest of Chengdu.

### 2. GODDESS BY THE STREAM

27  **"cultural property":** Workshop figures from *Current Handmade Papers of Japan*, essays by Yoshinari Kobayashi, Yasuo Kume, and Kenicki Miyazaki, 3 vols. (Kochi-shi, Japan: All Japan Handmade Washi Association, 1992). Source also for Count Friedrich Albrecht zu Eulenburg quotation in the epigraph.

28  **the concept of a threshold:** See Dorothy Field, *Paper and Threshold: The Paradox of Spiritual Connection in Asian Countries* (Ann Arbor, MI: Legacy Press, 2007).

28  **"a product of nature":** Hughes, 35–36.

30  **Kawakami Gozen:** The story of the papermaking goddess as recounted by Dard Hunter in *Papermaking: The History and Technique of an Ancient Craft*, 55–56, differs in several respects from the one cited here. Hunter suggests that the deity was actually a god disguised as a woman and describes it as "a fanciful local legend that purports to be ancient" (even though the Okamoto shrine itself has been in place in various forms for more than a thousand years). My source for the quote in the epigraph and the legend is Makoto Kobayashi, *Echizen Washi: The Ancient Japanese Art of Papermaking* ([Imadate-cho], Japan: Imadate Cultural Association, 1981), a beautiful boxed volume with a number of samples tipped in, which I acquired during my visit to Echizen in 2008 (the last copy available for sale, I was told).

30  *Kami no Matsuri:* See Paul Denhoed, "The Echizen Washi Deity and Paper Festival," *Hand Papermaking* 26, no. 2 (Winter 2011) 10–13.

31  **"He who repeats it":** Quoted (as is "Whoever wishes . . .") in Carter, 36–38.

32  **2008 Bloomsbury auction:** Bloomsbury Auctions, New York, April 5, 2008, Lot 24B.

32  **clear plate glass:** See Macfarlane and Martin, 74, 112.

33  **transoceanic balloons:** See Mikesh. See also "Balloon Bombs Hit West Coast in War," *New York Times*, May 29, 1947; and Stan Grossfeld, "An Air of Reconciliation Over 51 Years, Japanese Balloon Bombing in Oregon Changed Lives," *Boston Globe*, Dec. 8, 1996.

36  **Timothy D. Barrett:** See Mark Levine, "Can a Papermaker Help to Save Civilization?" *New York Times Magazine*, Feb. 17, 2012. Barrett's website is paper.lib .uiowa.edu.

44    **"a mind that is more Japanese-like"**: Kyoko Ishihara, Toyko art gallery owner, quoted in Miya Tanaka, "American Artisans Try to Help Japan Appreciate Its 'Washi,'" *Japan Times*, Jan. 6, 2007.

### 3. ROAD TRIP

48    **Battle of Talas:** The waterway is known today as the Tharaz River.

49    **workshops opened up:** See Mariam Rosser-Owen, *Islamic Arts from Spain* (London: V&A Publishing, 2010), 14.

49    **notation:** See Ann Blair, "Note Taking as an Art of Transmission," *Critical Inquiry* 31, no. 1 (Autumn 2004): 85–107. For more on migration of paper during this period, see Bloom, chap. 2.

49    **Abu Ja'far al-Mansur:** Freely, 72–73.

49    **"paper bazaars"**: From *waraq,* a common Arabic word for "paper," derived from the word for "leaf"; Karabacek, 41; Bloom, 47; Pedersen 52.

49    **copied in 970:** Bloom, 87.

50    **Their first compilation:** Pedersen, 54.

51    **Samarkand:** See Roya Marefat, "The Heavenly City of Samarkind," *The Wilson Quarterly* (Summer 1992), 16, No. 3, 33–38; Michael T. Dumper and Bruce E. Stanley, *Cities of the Middle East and North Africa: A Historical Encyclopedia* (Santa Barbara, CA: ABC-CLIO, 2007), 318–323; Trudy Ring, Robert M. Salkin, and Sharon La Boda, *International Dictionary of Historic Places,* vol. 5, Asia and Oceania, (Chicago: Fitzroy Dearborn Publishers, 1996), 718–22.

51    **"paper is among the specialties"**: *A Book of Curious and Entertaining Information,* quoted in Bloom.

52    **Ibn Khaldun:** Quoted in Bloom, 49.

52    **watermarks:** Introduced in Italy in the thirteenth century, watermarks provide a way of identifying papermakers and verifying the authenticity of documents such as passports and banknotes. The traditional method is to sew wire of a certain design onto the surface of a wire-mesh-covered mold. The design then leaves thin areas in the pulp during papermaking that can be seen when dried sheets are held up to the light. Alternatively, a "light and shade" watermark is produced by pressing a low-relief sculpture into the wire mesh before it is attached to the mold surface, leaving both raised and sunken areas that produce a range of thick and thin areas in the paper, and thus a "light and shade" watermark image. In mechanical papermaking, a watermark is made with a cylinder of wire gauze (a dandy roll) that is pressed on moist pulp before it starts its way through the rollers of the machine. The term *watermark* itself is fairly modern, its first use in English traceable to the early eighteenth century. It is called *wasserzeichen* in German, *filigrane* in French, *papiermerken* in Dutch, and *filigrana* in Italian. Indeed, an outstanding collection of watermarks can be viewed at the Museo della Carta e della Filigrana in Fabriano, Italy (http://www.museodellacarta .com), where the formal research for this book can be said to have started, during a 2003 visit. Well worth seeing, too, while in Italy is the Museo della Carta in Amalfi (http://www.museodellacarta.it); located nearby on the same stream is the Amatruda Paper Mill (La Carta di Amalfi, http://www.amatruda.it), owned and operated by successive generations of the Amatruda family since the fifteenth century. For more on the specifics of watermarks, see Hunter, *History and Technique,* 258–308.

52    **a code of laws established in Spain:** The *Siete Partidas* of King Alphonso X of Castile.

52    **"cloth parchment"**: *Encyclopaedia Britannica* (1888), 218.

53    **100,000 or so papyrus documents:** For more on the collection known as the Cairo Ginezeh, see Hoffman and Cole, and Basbanes, *Splendor of Letters,* 51–53.

53    **"a period of 600 years"**: *Das Arabische Papier* (1887); translated into English by Don Baker and Suzy Dittmar as *Arab Paper* (London: Archetype Publications, 2001).

53   **"definitely an Arab invention"**: Karabacek, 41–42.

54   **made of rags**: A. F. Hoernle, "Who Was the Inventor of Rag Paper?," *Journal of the Royal Asiatic Society of Great Britain and Ireland* (Oct. 1903): 663–84.

55   **the Taj Mahal**: See Wayne E. Begley, "The Myth of the Taj Mahal and a New Theory of Its Symbolic Meaning," *The Art Bulletin* 61, no. 1 (March 1979): 7–37. He identifies Ustad Ahmad as the man who "seems to have been" the lead architect. "In fact, certain features of the Taj's architectural conception become explicable only when the monument is interpreted as an allegory of Paradise and the Divine Throne . . . [T]he calligrapher Amanat Khan undoubtedly played an important role, since it was probably he who devised the inscriptional program" (30).

56   **"In the Islamic lands"**: Bloom, x. See also *Hand Papermaking*, 27, no. 2 (Winter 2012), for an entire issue dedicated to Islamic papermaking, including "Paper in the Islamic Lands," a detailed overview by Jonathan Bloom, 66–67.

57   **edicts that outlawed all printing**: Bloom, 219–22.

57   **King Roger II of Sicily**: *Encyclopaedia Britannica*, 11th edition, 725.

58   **Alfonso X of Castile**: See Robert I. Burns, S.J., "The Paper Revolution in Europe: Crusader Valencia's Paper Industry—A Technological and Behavioral Breakthrough," *The Pacific Historical Review* 50, no. 1 (Feb. 1981): 1–30.

58   **spread of papermaking**: For a pertinent consideration of the impact the borrowing of technology has on various cultures, see Margaret T. Hodgen, "Glass and Paper: An Historical Study of Acculturation," *Southwestern Journal of Anthropology* 1, no. 4 (Winter 1945): 466–97.

58   **Xàtiva**: See Burns, "The Paper Revolution in Europe."

59   **Canson & Montgolfier**: Though not quite as old as Montgolfier, Canson nonetheless enjoys a pedigree that can be traced to 1557, and one of the mills it uses today to make a variety of high-quality products was built in 1492, as home to Arches, another famous line of French papers.

60   **"sworn a holy oath"**: See "A Fourteenth-Century Business History," *The Business History Review* (Harvard University) 39, no. 2 (Summer 1965), 261–64 [author not attributed], 70.

61   **gelatin sizing**: See Gesa Kolbe, "Gelatin in Historical Paper Production and as Inhibiting Agent for Iron-Gall Ink Corrosion on Paper," *Restaurator: International Journal for the Preservation of Library and Archival Material* (2004), 26–39; and Barrett.

62   **"unforeseen consequences"**: Lynn White Jr., "Technology Assessment from the Stance of a Medieval Historian," *The American Historical Review* 79, no. 1 (Feb. 1974): 1–13.

63   **A plague that swept through**: Hodgen, "Glass and Paper."

63   **"no person or persons whatsoever"**: From James Thomas Law, ed., *The Ecclesiastical Statutes at Large, Extracted from the Great Body of the Statue Law, and Arranged Under Special Heads,* vol. 1 (1847).

64   **"made of the filthy linen rags"**: Thomas Dekker and George Wilkins, *Jests to Make You Merry,* 1607, quoted in Joshua Calhoun, "The Word Made Flax: Cheap Bibles, Textual Corruption, and the Poetics of Paper," *Papers of the Modern Language Association* (PMLA) (2011), 327–44.

64   **"breeches he weares"**: In Abraham Cowley, *The Guardian,* Act 1, Scene 5.

65   **"Rags are yet King!"**: Hofmann, 10.

65   *chiffoniers*: Henry Barnard, *Our Country's Wealth and Influence* (Hartford, CT: L. Stebbins, 1882), 178.

65   **"If it is to be of the best quality"**: R. R. Bowker, "Great American Industries: A Sheet of Paper," *Harper's New Monthly Magazine,* July 1887 (vol. 75, no. 445), 118–19.

65   **eighteenth-century account**: Jacob Christian Schäffer, *Versuche und Muster, Ohne Alle Lumpen Oder Doch Mit Einem Geringen Zusatze Derselben, Papier Zu Machen* (Regensburg: [Zenkel], 1765–71), 6 vols.

68   **"stoppage of a number of paper-mills"**: All quotes from Koops. The first attempt to

make paper from straw, according to Joel Munsell, was made in Germany in 1756, during a scarcity of rags, but the product was inferior, and the undertaking failed.

69 **wallpaper:** For three superb histories, see Ackerman, Entwistle, and Greysmith.

69 **"and the same principle holds":** Hunter, *History and Technique,* 345.

69 **John Bidwell:** *Fine Papers at the Oxford University Press: A Descriptive Catalogue, with Sample Pieces of Each of the Papers* (Lower Marston Farm, UK: The Whittington Press, 1998). See also: John Bidwell, *American Paper Mills, 1690–1832: A Directory of the Paper Trade with Notes on Products, Watermarks, Distribution Methods and Manufacturing Techniques* (Hanover, NH: University Press of New England and the American Antiquarian Society, 2013).

## 4. RAGS TO RICHES

74 **continent's first English-language printing press:** Spain introduced printing and papermaking to North America a full century before the English colonists. The first printer in the New World was Giovanni Paoli, an Italian who took the name Juan Pablos when he set up shop in what is today Mexico City in 1539 as the representative of Juan Cromberger of Seville, the son of a German immigrant and owner of the leading printing firm in Spain. In that year, Pablos published under Cromberger's name the first printed book in the New World, *Doctrina Christiana en la Lengua Mexicana e Castellana* ("Christian Doctrine in the Mexican and Castilian Language"); no copies are known to survive. The New York Public Library includes among its holdings a small quarto printed by Pablos for Cromberger in 1543–4, a religious text known by the short form of its title, *Doctrina Breve.* Pablos acquired full ownership of the shop in 1548, and printed a number of materials under his own name until his death in 1560. According to Dard Hunter (*History & Technique,* 479) the continent's first paper mill was established between 1575–1580 at Culhuacán (now a part of Mexico City), but very little is known about its operation. For an excellent overview of Spanish printing in the Americas prior to 1600, see Antonio Rodríguez-Buckingham, "Change and the Printing Press in Sixteenth-Century America," in *Agent of Change: Print Culture Studies After Elizabeth L. Eisenstein,* edited by Sabrina Alcorn Baron, Eric N. Lindquist, and Eleanor F. Shevlin (Amherst, MA: University of Massachusetts Press, 2007), 216–37 (chap. 10). See also: Edwin Wolfe 2nd, "The Origins of Early American Printing Shops," *The Quarterly Journal of the Library of Congress,* vol. 35, no. 3 (July 1978), 198–209; Luis Weckmann, *The Medieval Heritage of Mexico* (New York: Fordham University Press, 1992), 512–14; Dorothy Penn, "The Oldest American Book," *Hispania,* vol. 22, no. 3 (Oct. 1939), 303–6.

74 **Bay Psalm Book:** There are eleven copies of the Bay Psalm Book; two from the collection of the colonial bibliophile Thomas Prince (1687–1758) were deposited in the Boston Public Library in 1866 by the Old South Church, the owners. On Dec. 2, 2012, members of the congregation voted to sell one of the copies at auction; see Jess Bidgood, "Historic Boston Church's Decision to Sell Rare Psalmbook Divides Congregation," *New York Times,* Dec. 23, 2012. The following April, Sotheby's announced it would sell the book in New York on Nov. 26, 2013. Pre-sale estimates ranged from $15 million to $30 million, either of which would establish a record for the most money ever sent on a printed book. As I first reported in *A Gentle Madness* (138–42), a proposal by the church leadership in 1991 to sell one of the books was rejected by the full membership; the estimated value then was $1.5 to $4 million. For more on the production of the book, see George Parker Winship, *The Cambridge Press 1638–1692* (Philadelphia: University of Pennsylvania Press, 1945).

74 **"fellow laborers in the great work":** Isaiah Thomas, *The History of Printing in North America,* 38.

74 **John Eliot:** See biographical entry in *Dictionary of National Biography.* On the making of the Eliot Indian Bible, see Winship, *The Cambridge Press.* See also Gray Grif-

fin, "A Discovery of Seventeenth-Century Printing Types in Harvard Yard," *Harvard University Library Bulletin* XXX, no. 2 (April 1982), 229–31. The Philadelphia autodidact and bibliophile James Logan—the man who wrote to a London bookseller that "books are my disease" (Basbanes, *A Gentle Madness,* 129–35)—is said to have been probably the only contemporary Englishman on either side of the Atlantic other than Eliot who could read the book in the original. Most of the Indian Bibles printed were destroyed in a fire, and as a result, surviving first-issue copies are uncommonly rare.

75 **a Nipmuc tribesman:** The founding charter of Harvard College included a requirement that the institution educate Native Americans alongside the Puritan settlers. One Wampanoag graduate, Caleb Cheeshahteaumuck, was the subject of *Caleb's Crossing,* a novel by the Pulitzer Prize–winning author Geraldine Brooks (New York: Viking, 2011).

75 **"Those who lov'd Reading":** Benjamin Franklin, *Franklin: Writings* (New York: Library of America, 1987), 1379.

76 ***Publick Occurrences:*** See Lyman Horace Weeks, Edwin Monroe Bacon, eds., *An Historical Digest of the Provincial Press* (Boston: The Society for Americana, 1783), vol. 1, 24–32 [includes facsimile]. Benjamin Harris returned to England in 1694 or '95, was arrested again on charges of "printing false news," and is said to have spent his final days as a quack purveyor of "Angelical Pills" and other patent medicines. See *Dictionary of National Biography.* In 2008, the sole surviving copy of his *Publick Occurrences* was exhibited at the Newseum, in Washington, D.C.

76 ***Boston News-Letter:*** Number 775, dated "From Monday Feb. 16 to Monday Feb. 23, 1719," quoted in Robert E. Lee, *Blackbeard the Pirate* (Winston-Salem, NC: John F. Blair, 1974), 226, and in Clarence Brigham, *Paul Revere's Engravings* (Worcester, MA: American Antiquarian Society, 1954).

76 **William Bradford:** See *Dictionary of National Biography.*

77 **"been of 1900":** Weeks, *History of Paper-Manufacturing,* 15.

77 **William Rittenhouse:** See Green, *The Rittenhouse Mill.*

78 **"greenbacks":** The nickname "greenbacks" was a response to the green ink used by the American Bank Note Company to print the bills. By 1775, the Willcox mill was the exclusive producer of paper for the continental government, and when the Revolution broke out, its output was regarded as crucial in the War for Independence. In a memoir published in 1897, Joseph Willcox wrote that Thomas Willcox, his grandfather, "manufactured the paper for Dr. Franklin," who, he added, "was a frequent visitor to the mill."

78 **his common-law wife:** Franklin, *Franklin: Writings,* 1381–82.

79 **"There seems no reason":** Green and Stallybrass, 40–41. See also James N. Green, "Benjamin Franklin, Printer" (chap. 2), in Talbott, 55–90.

79 **"prohibit all other persons":** William Bradford, quoted in Weeks, *History of Paper-Manufacturing,* 16.

79 **the Stamp Act:** 5 George III, c. 12. "An Act for Granting and Applying Certain Stamp Duties, and Other Duties, in the British Colonies and Plantations in America, Towards Further Defraying the Expences of Defending, Protecting, and Securing the Same; and for Amending Such Parts of the Several Acts of Parliament Relating to the Trade and Revenues of the Said Colonies and Plantations, as Direct the Manner of Determining and Recovering the Penalties and Forfeitures Therein Mentioned."

79 **England's national debt:** Figures from Morgan and Morgan, *Stamp Act,* 21. The Stamp Act was careful to include mention of parchment and vellum in clause after clause, but since the use of cured animal skins was relatively minuscule in the recording of public documents, the focus and intent of the bill was overwhelmingly on paper. The credit for coming up with such an innovative approach is generally ascribed to one Henry McCulloh, a London speculator who owned 100,000 acres in North Carolina, and based on a duty introduced in England in 1694, following

a Dutch model. See David Lee Russell, *The American Revolution in the Southern Colonies* (Jefferson, NC: McFarland & Company, 2000), 27; and Robert W. Ramsey, *Carolina Cradle: Settlement of the Northwest Carolina Frontier, 1747–1762* (Chapel Hill: University of North Carolina Press, 1984), 93.

81 **stamps would be impressed:** See Adolph Koeppel and John Boynton Kaiser, *New Discovery from British Archives on the 1765 Tax Stamps for America* (Boyertown, PA: American Revenue Association, 1962), and Alvin Rabushka, *Taxation in Colonial America* (Princeton, NJ: Princeton University Press, 2008), 754–55. Preserved among the papers of John Hughes, the designated tax agent for Philadelphia, and now in the collections of the Historical Society of Pennsylvania (Hughes Papers B-116), is a guide for royal agents issued in anticipation of the Stamp Act: *Instructions to be Observed by Each Distributer* [sic] *of Stamped Parchment and Paper, etc. in America, and Collector of His Majesty's Duties Arising Thereon* (London: J and R Tonson, 1765.)

82 **Once arrived in London:** Schlesinger, 69.

82 **a series of eloquent essays:** See Isaacson, 222–30; Edmund S. Morgan, *Benjamin Franklin* (New Haven, CT: Yale University Press, 2002), on Hughes, 153.

83 **"for the liberties of America":** David Ramsay, *The History of the American Revolution* (Trenton, NJ: James J. Wilson, 1811), 85; also quoted in Schlesinger, 69; and Jill Lepore, "The Day the Newspaper Died," *The New Yorker,* Jan. 26, 2009.

83 **"the newspaper war on Britain":** Schlesinger, 47.

83 **In New Haven:** For the newspaper examples cited here, see Schlesinger, 75; and Ralph Frasca, "Benjamin Franklin's Printing Network and the Stamp Act," *Pennsylvania History* 71, no. 4 (Autumn 2004): 403–19. For more on the failure of the Stamp Act, see Jack P. Greene, "A Dress of Honor: Henry McCulloh's Objections to the Stamp Act," *The Huntington Library Quarterly* 26, no. 3 (May 1963): 253–62.

84 **new mills were established:** Weeks, 35–40.

85 **Schuyler apologized:** General Philip Schuyler, quoted in Weeks, *History of Paper-Manufacturing,* 46.

85 **"to make and prepare":** Nathan Sellers, quoted in Willcox, 10.

85 **Gun Wad Bible:** For the conflicting discussions on this issue, see Rumball-Petre, 51–63; and *Proceedings of the American Antiquarian Society,* New Series, vol. 31, part I (April 31, 1921–Oct. 19, 1921), 147–61.

85 **The third edition:** The third Sower Bible was noteworthy not only for using paper made in America but for being printed with punched metal type made of Sower's own design and manufacture.

86 **"Some copies of them":** Isaiah Thomas, 84.

86 **"On our entering Philadelphia":** Richard Peters Jr., quoted in Samuel Hazard, ed., *Hazard's Register of Pennsylvania: Devoted to the Preservation of Facts and Documents, and Every Kind of Useful Information Respecting the State of Pennsylvania,* vol. 2 (Philadelphia: W. F. Geddes, 1828).

87 **Ye Olde Union Oyster House:** Isaiah Thomas's original pressroom is today a second-floor dining room.

87 **195 paper mills:** John Tebbel, *A History of Book Publishing in the United States,* vol. 1 (New York: R. R. Bowker, 1972), 67.

87 **two million pounds of rags:** For 1843, see Weeks, *History of Paper-Manufacturing,* 20; for 1857, see Munsell, 134.

87 **mummies:** See S. J. Wolfe, with Robert Singerman, *Mummies in Nineteenth Century America: Ancient Egyptians as Artifacts* (Jefferson, NC: McFarland & Co., 2009).

88 **When the Civil War broke out:** Weeks, *History of Paper-Manufacturing,* 270.

88 **"temper its opinions":** *New-Orleans Commercial Bulletin,* quoted in Susan Campion, "Wallpaper Newspapers of the American Civil War," *Journal of the American Institute for Conservation,* 34, no. 2 (Summer 1995): 132. See also James Melvin Lee, *History of American Journalism* (Boston: Houghton Mifflin, 1917), 305–7.

88 **a mill outside Manchester:** Weeks, *History of Paper-Manufacturing,* 269.

88  **brown, pink, orange:** Massey, 139–44.

89  **Vicksburg *Daily Citizen:*** See Campion, "Wallpaper Newspapers," 129–40.

89  **Mary Boykin Chesnut:** Since 1905, Mary Chesnut's diary has been issued in four separate editions, including a "restored" version prepared by C. Vann Woodward and published by Yale University Press, in 1981, as *Mary Chesnut's Civil War.* The original diaries are now in the special collections library of the University of South Carolina. For more on the publishing history, see Augusta Rohrbach, "The Diary May Be from Dixie, But the Editor Is Not: Mary Chesnut and Southern Print History," *Textual Cultures: Texts, Contexts, Interpretation* 2, no. 1 (Spring 2007): 101–18. For general shortages in the South during the Civil War, see Mary Elizabeth Massey, "The Effects of Shortages on the Confederate Homefront," in *The Arkansas Historical Quarterly* 9, no. 3 (Autumn 1950): 172–93. For more on the unpublished "receipt" book, see Frances M. Burroughs, "The Confederate Receipt Book: A Study of Food Substitution in the American Civil War," *The South Carolina Historical Magazine* 93, no. 1 (Jan. 1992): 31–50. Several reprint editions of *Confederate Receipt Book,* the compilation published in 1863 by West & Johnston of Richmond, Virginia, are now in print. See the introduction by E. Merton Coulter in the edition published by the University of Georgia Press, Athens, 1960. A full-text edition is available online at Documenting the American South (http://www.docsouth.unc.edu), maintained by the University of North Carolina.

90  **"vast majority":** *Paper Trade Journal,* March 11, 1876.

91  **"nearly every paper":** David C. Smith, "Wood Pulp and Newspapers, 1867–1900," in *The Business History Review* 38, no. 3 (Autumn 1964): 328–45, 388.

92  **Clark W. Bryan:** See profile in Charles H. Barrows, *The Poets and Poetry of Springfield in Massachusetts: From Early Times to the End of the Nineteenth Century* (Springfield, MA: Connecticut Valley Historical Society, 1907), 116.

92  **"The annual product":** Figures compiled in *Paper World,* Feb. 1880, 10.

92  **experiments undertaken with corn:** See Smith, "Wood Pulp and Newspapers," and David C. Smith, "Wood Pulp Paper Comes to the Northeast, 1865–1900," *Forest History,* April 1966, 12–25.

92  **"2,000 to 3,000 cords":** Smith, "Wood Pulp Paper Comes to the Northeast," 19.

93  **U.S. Census figures:** David C. Smith, "Wood Pulp and Newspapers," and Jack P. Oden, "Charles Holmes Herty and the Birth of the Southern Newsprint Paper Industry, 1927–1940," *Journal of Forest History* 21, no. 2 (April 1977): 76–89.

93  **"In round numbers":** Haskell, 9–10.

94  **"people of the United States":** *West Coast Hemlock Pulp: A Product of American Pulp Mills,* by Weyerhaeuser Timber Company, pulp division (Minneapolis, 1937), 32.

94  **Pacific coast:** W. Claude Adams, "History of Papermaking in the Pacific Northwest: I," *Oregon Historical Quarterly* 52, no. 19 (March 1951): 21–37.

95  **"Perhaps no other industry":** Ibid., 22.

### 5. THE SOUND OF MONEY

98  **"four reams of paper":** *Proceedings of the American Antiquarian Society,* New Series, vol. 13 (April 1901), 434. Isaiah Thomas's press, "Old Number One," is maintained at the American Antiquarian Society, in Worcester, Massachusetts, and is the oldest English common press to survive in North America. For more on early Crane history, see Pierce, and also: Peter Hopkins, "The Colonial Roots of Crane & Co., Inc.," *Hand Papermaking* 16, no. 2 (Winter 2001); and Frank Luther Mott, "The Newspaper Coverage of Lexington and Concord," *The New England Quarterly* 17, no. 4 (December 1944): 489–505.

98  **warhorses:** Clarence Brigham, *Paul Revere's Engravings,* "Paper Money," 141–63.

99  **"Our wagons arrived":** Zenas Crane, quoted in Pierce, 17.

99  **a cylinder machine:** Hunter, *Papermaking,* 547.

100  **Berkshire and Hampden counties:** See McGaw.

100  **"Paper City":** Holyoke claims the title, but in Massachusetts there are two forms of municipality: city and town. Lee, a town on the Housatonic River, was home at various points over two centuries to twenty-five commercial papermakers, and calls itself Paper Town. The last company to make paper in Lee, the Eagle Mill, operated by Schweitzer-Mauduit, closed in 2008. See http://www.papertownprojects.org/history.html.

105  **outwit potential counterfeiters:** For excellent background, see Stephen Mihm, *A Nation of Counterfeiters: Capitalists, Con Men, and the Making of the United States* (Cambridge, MA: Harvard University Press, 2007).

107  **more than ten thousand variations:** See Richard Doty, *Pictures from a Distant Country: Seeing America Through Old Paper Money* (Atlanta: Whitman Publishing Co., 2013).

107  **Jewish prisoners:** See Lawrence Malkin, *Krueger's Men: The Secret Nazi Counterfeit Plot and the Prisoners of Block 19* (New York: Little Brown, 2006). A film inspired by the incident, *The Counterfeiters,* won an Academy Award for Best Foreign Language Film in 2008. For the making of the paper itself, see Peter Bower, "Operation Bernhard: The German Forgery of British Paper Currency in World War II," in Peter Bower, ed., *The Exeter Papers: Proceedings of the British Association of Paper Historians Fifth Annual Conference, Hope Hall, University of Exeter, 23–26 September 1994; Studies in British Paper History II* (1994) (London: Plough Press, 2001), 43–64.

## 6. ONE AND DONE

116  **Kleercut:** See http://www.kleercut.net/en/theissues.

117  **"forest fiber footprint":** See http://www.kimberly-clark.com/sustainability/reporting.aspx.

117  **"In 2011":** See http://investor.kimberly-clark.com/releasedetail.cfm?ReleaseID=683471.

117  **corporate excellence:** Jim Collins, *Good to Great: Why Some Companies Make the Leap . . . And Others Don't* (New York: HarperBusiness, 2001).

117  **"huggable shares":** Heinrich and Batchelor, 206.

120  **filters for gas masks:** Ibid., 41–43.

121  **"manage" their natural rhythms:** Lara Freidenfelds, *The Modern Period: Menstruation in Twentieth-Century America* (Baltimore: Johns Hopkins University Press, 2009), 1, 32.

122  **Johnny Carson:** See Andrew H. Malcolm, "The 'Shortage' of Bathroom Tissue: A Classic Study in Rumor," *New York Times,* Feb. 3, 1974.

123  **"Careless soldiers":** Reprinted in Ernie Pyle and Orr Kelly, *Here Is Your War: Story of G.I. Joe* (Lincoln: University of Nebraska Press, 2004), 149.

123  **"The British army":** Lee B. Kennett, *G.I.: The American Soldier in World War II* (Norman: University of Oklahoma Press, 1997), 96. For Scott Paper Company, see Catherine Thérèse Earley, "The Greatest Missed Luxury," published online by the Pennsylvania Center for the Book (http://www.pabook.libraries.psu.edu), Fall 2010.

123  **"The value of modern sewage systems":** Walter T. Hughes, "A Tribute to Toilet Paper," *Reviews of Infectious Diseases* 10, no. 1 (Jan.–Feb. 1988): 218–22.

124  **"a physical barrier":** Ibid., 218.

124  **"I knew a gentleman":** Philip Dormer Stanhope Chesterfield, *The Letters of Philip Dormer Stanhope, Earl of Chesterfield,* vol. 1 (Philadelphia: J. B. Lippincott Company, 1892), 99–100, 139.

124  **Joseph C. Gayetty:** *New England Stationer and Printer,* vol. 15, 1901, 70; Seth Wheeler, U.S. Patent 117,355, issued July 25, 1871.

126  **seven billion rolls:** Other top producers are Procter & Gamble, the Cincinnati-based conglomerate best known as the maker of Ivory soap, Tide detergent, Comet cleanser, Gillette razors, and Crest toothpaste and since the 1950s a leader in tissue

products; and Georgia-Pacific, founded in 1927 as a hardwood lumber manufacturer and now a leading producer of pulp, paper, packaging, chemicals, and building materials, whose line of bathroom tissues include Angel Soft, Quilted Northern, and Soft 'n Gentle. In 1978, the R. H. Bruskin Associates market research firm named "Mr. Whipple," the P&G pitchman played by Dick "please don't squeeze the Charmin" Wilson, the third-best-known American, behind Richard Nixon and Billy Graham. In 2005, Georgia-Pacific was acquired by Koch Industries for $21 billion and became a privately held, wholly owned subsidiary; it formerly traded on the New York Stock Exchange under the symbol GP. In 2004, the last year it was required to disclose financial information publicly, the company reported net sales of $19.6 billion.

127 **softness:** Leslie Kaufman, "Mr. Whipple Left It Out: Soft Is Rough on Forests," *New York Times,* Feb. 25, 2009; Bernice Kanner, "The Soft Sell," *New York,* Sept. 27, 1981, 14–19.

### 7. FIERY CONSEQUENCES

131 **forty-two steps to twenty-six:** Max Boot, *War Made New: Technology, Warfare, and the Course of History, 1500 to Today* (New York: Gotham Books, 2006), 85.

131 **"that capricious compound":** Hawes, v.

132 **Gunpowder's earliest documented uses:** See Needham, *Science and Civilisation in China,* vol. 5, part 7; Boot, *War Made New,* 21; Hans Delbrück, *The Dawn of Modern Warfare: History of the Art of War,* vol. 4 (Lincoln: University of Nebraska Press, 1990), chap. 2. Saltpeter comes from medieval Latin *sal petrae,* for "stone salt."

133 **"twelve apostles":** In colonial America, many frontiersmen carried their gunpowder in the hollow antlers of wild animals, receptacles called powder horns.

133 **the flintlock:** Clair Blair, in Pollard, 62; and H. L. Peterson, in Pollard, 106.

133 **rifling:** For an overview on the evolution and science of ballistics, see Mark Denny, *Their Arrows Will Darken the Sky* (Baltimore: Johns Hopkins University Press, 2011).

133 **Thirty Years' War:** Motivated by the high prices for imported paper, Gustavus Adolphus is credited also with arranging, in 1612, just a year after his accession to the throne, for the establishment of Sweden's first successful paper mill, at Uppsala; another Swedish mill, at Lessebo, was built to meet the rising demand for cartridge paper, though the specialty there rapidly turned to the making of fine writing paper. See Rudin, 34–38.

134 **"cartages, with the which":** Sir John Smythe, *Certain Discourses, Written by Sir Iohn Smythe, Knight: Concerning the Formes and Effects of Diuers Sorts of Weapons, and Other Verie Important Matters Militarie, Greatlie Mistaken by Diuers of Our Men of Warre in These Daies; and Chiefly, of the Mosquet, the Caliuer and the Long-Bow; as Also, of the Great Sufficiencie, Excellencie, and Wonderful Effects of Archers: With Many Notable Examples and Other Particularities, by Him Presented to the Nobilitie of This Realme, & Published for the Benefite of This His Natiue Countrie of England* (London: Richard Johnes, 1590), facsimile Early English Books Online (EEBO).

134 **John Vernon:** John Vernon, *The Young Horse-Man, or, the Honest Plain-Dealing Cavalier Wherein Is Plainly Demonstrated, by Figures and Other-Wise, the Exercise and Discipline of the Horse, Very Usefull for All Those That Desire the Knowledge of Warlike Horse-Man-Ship* (London: Andrew Coe, 1644).

136 **"Sepoys had three advantages":** G. J. Bryant, "Asymmetric Warfare: The British Experience in Eighteenth-Century India," *The Journal of Military History* 68, no. 2 (April 2004): 434.

136 **the Minié rifle:** For description of Minié's improvements, see Hess, 24–29.

137 **"We have at Barrackport":** Major General J. B. Hearsey, quoted in G. W. Forrest, *A History of the Indian Mutiny: Reviewed and Illustrated from Original Documents* (Edinburgh, London: William Blackwood, 1904), vol. 1, 6.

137 **"cartridge must be dipped"**: *Instruction of Musketry* (London: Parker, Furnivall, and Parker Military Library, Whitehall, 1854); instructions for making paper cartridges, 26–29.

138 **"was one made on paper"**: Ogborn, *Indian Ink*, xvii. Chap. 3 is of particular interest.

138 **"riveting of the men's fetters"**: Lord Canning, quoted in Frederick Sleigh Roberts, *Forty-one Years in India: From Subaltern to Commander-in-Chief* (New York: Longmans, Green, & Co., 1914), 45.

139 **"The mighty English"**: Badahur Shah II, quoted in David, 19. See Dalrymple for biography; translations vary.

139 **summary report**: *Annual Report of the Secretary of War*, Nov. 14, 1866, 39th Congress, Second Session, 657 (Washington, DC: Government Printing Office).

140 **always severe shortages**: See Massey.

141 **"regularity of texture"**: Hawes, 34–56.

141 **"had not emerged"**: Hogg, 78.

142 **artillery crews**: See Henry J. Webb, "The Science of Gunnery in Elizabethan England," *Isis* 45, no. 1 (May 1954): 10–21.

142 **"Naval and military history"**: William Jones, "Memoir on Leaden Cartridges," *Transactions of the American Philosophical Society*, New Series, vol. 1 (1818): 137–45.

142 **"My invention"**: "Patent for Making Cartridge Paper," in *The Repertory of Patent Inventions and Other Discoveries and Improvements in Arts, Manufactures, and Agriculture*, vol. 14, Second Series (London: T & G Underwood, 1808–09), 83–85.

143 **Dickinson opened his first mill**: Evans, 12.

143 **"a fresh demand"**: Ibid., 100.

143 **Thomas Frognall Dibdin**: Ibid., 21.

144 **"If you can't send money"**: George Washington, quoted in Wagner, 21.

144 **"You ask what we need"**: General John J. "Blackjack" Pershing, quoted in Klein, 142.

145 **luxury cigarettes**: See Kluger, 12–13; Relli Shechter, "The Rise of the Egyptian Cigarette and the Transformation of the Egyptian Tobacco Market, 1850–1914," *International Journal of Middle East Studies* 35, no. 1 (Feb. 2003): 51–75.

145 **genesis story**: American Tobacco Company, *"Sold American,"* 14.

145 **makers of Zig-Zag**: With the death of Jacques Braunstein, Zig-Zag was sold to a partnership of the Groupe Bolloré and competitor JOB. In 2000, Zig-Zag became part of Republic Technologies.

148 **George Arents**: See Jerome E. Brooks, *The Library Relating to Tobacco Collected by George Arents* (New York: New York Public Library, 1944).

148 **"No one can make"**: Kluger, foreword.

148 **fire fatalities**: In 2006, there were an estimated 142,900 smoking-material fires in the United States, responsible for 780 deaths and 1,600 injuries.

149 **"suitable filament"**: In Henry Ford, *The Case Against the Little White Slaver* (Detroit, privately published, 1914).

149 **"Cigarette paper"**: Legacy Tobacco Document 103280324; http://legacy.library.ucsf.edu.

149 **guaranteed orders**: *Time*, April 8, 1940. See also du Toit.

## 8. PAPERS, PLEASE

153 **"constitutes the attempt"**: Groebner, 257.

153 **portable likenesses**: See Diana Scarisbrick, *Portrait Jewels: Opulence and Intimacy from the Medici to the Romanovs* (London: Thames & Hudson, 2011), for a general description of the practice.

154 **"Such letters"**: Ogborn, 37.

154 **"Civility and Kindness"**: *Proceedings of the American Philosophical Society*, vol. 100, no. 4 (1956), 405.

155 "**gif the said Inglismen**": *Oxford English Dictionary*, "Registrum Secreti Sigilli Regum Scotorum: 1488–1529," for passport; see also Martin Lloyd, 25.

155 **King Louis XVI:** See N. W. Sibley, Esq., "The Passport System," *Journal of Comparative Legislation and International Law* (London: Society of Comparative Legislation, 1970), 26–33; and Karl E. Meyer, "The Curious Life of the Lowly Passport," *World Policy Journal* 26, no. 1 (spring 2009): 73. Sometimes the presentation of a valid document is not enough: When I traveled to the monastic republic of Mount Athos in 1998 to visit some of the libraries there, I had with me a permit, known as a *diamonitirion,* issued at the "pilgrims' office" in the Greek city of Ourinopoulos. With that in hand, two Orthodox monks still examined every visitor walking off the ferry for evidence of an Adam's apple, a safeguard against allowing women to sneak their way into a theocratic community that has remained all-male for more than a thousand years.

156 **how-to manual:** Sheldon Charrett, *Secrets of a Back Alley ID Man: Fake ID Construction Techniques of the Underground* (Boulder: Paladin Press, 2001).

156 **Bulger alleged that the aliases:** See Shelley Murphy and Maria Cramer, "Whitey Bulger's Life in Exile," *Boston Globe,* Oct. 9, 2011, and Kevin Cullen and Shelley Murphy, *Whitey Bulger: America's Most Wanted Gangster and the Manhunt That Brought Him to Justice* (New York: W. W. Norton & Co., 2013).

156 **American passports:** William E. Lingelback, "B. Franklin, Printer—New Source Materials," *Proceedings of the American Philosophical Society*, vol. 92, no. 2; "Studies of Historical Documents in the Library of the American Philosophical Society" (May 5, 1948), 79–100. For more on Benjamin Franklin's press in France during the American Revolution, see Ellen R. Cohn, "The Printer at Passy" (chap. 7), in Talbott, 235–69.

157 **"No document confers"**: Meyer, "The Curious Life of the Lowly Passport," 71.

158 **"well-regulated police state"**: Johann Gottlieb Fichte, quoted in Groebner, 229.

159 **"I decided"**: Lovell, 24.

160 *The Man Who Never Was:* Montagu.

165 *Argo:* For more on the Tehran operation, see Mendez and Baglio and Mendez and McConnell. For a technical paper prepared for intelligence professionals, see Antonio J. Mendez, "A Classic Case of Deception: CIA Goes Hollywood," *Studies in Intelligence,* CSI Publications, Winter 1999–2000, https://www.cia.gov/library/center-for-the-study-of-intelligence/csi-publications/csi-studies/studies/winter99-00/art1.html.

170 **"a new weapon of warfare"**: Quotations in Stuart, 4–5, 47, 60, 93.

171 **"This was a new weapon"**: Field Marshal Paul von Hindenburg, *Out of My Life* (1920), quoted in Stuart, 95.

171 **"Phony War"**: As reported on Sept. 5, 1939, in *The Telegraph;* see also Philip M. Taylor, " 'If War Should Come': Preparing the Fifth Arm for Total War 1935–1939," *Journal of Contemporary History*, vol. 16, no. 1, "The Second World War: Part 1" (Jan. 1981): 27–51.

172 **"My personal view"**: Sir Arthur Harris, *Bomber Offensive* (London: Collins, 1947), 36–37.

172 **General Mark W. Clark:** Quoted in John A. Pollard, "Words Are Cheaper Than Blood," *The Public Opinion Quarterly* 9, no. 3 (Autumn 1945): 283–304.

172 **Monte Cassino:** Bytwerk.

## 9. HARD COPY

174 **"Your Red Tapist"**: Charles Dickens, "Red Tape," in *Household Words,* Feb. 15, 1851.

174 **"Alas I have failed"**: Sir Francis Bertie, quoted in Zara Steiner, "The Last Years of the Old Foreign Office, 1898–1905," *The Historical Journal* 6, no. 1 (1963): 80.

174   **"We can lick gravity"**: Wernher von Braun, quoted in *Chicago Sun Times*, July 10, 1958.

175   **"gobbledygook"**: According to the *Oxford English Dictionary*, the word was first used in 1944 by Maury Maverick, a Texas congressman, to describe "the long high-sounding words of Washington's red-tape language."

177   **"I suppose you could say"**: For one of the best contemporary pieces to appear on this incident, see Howard Kurtz, Michael Dobbs, and James V. Grimaldi, "In Rush to Air, CBS Quashed Memo Worries," *Washington Post*, Sept. 19, 2004. See also Dan Rather with Digby Diehl, *Rather Outspoken: My Life in the News* (New York: Grand Central Publishing, 2012), 32–67, 256–83. Rather's lawsuit against CBS was dismissed in 2009.

177   **Project MKULTRA**: See *U.S. Congress, Senate Select Committee to Study Governmental Operations with Respect to Intelligence Activities. Final Report.* 94th Cong., 2d sess. S. Report no. 94–755, 6 vols. (Washington, DC: GPO, 1976).

178   **"It was the practice"**: *Project MKULTRA, the CIA's Program of Research in Behavioral Modification, Joint Hearing Before the Select Committee on Intelligence and the Subcommittee on Health and Scientific Research of the Committee on Human Resources, United States Senate*, 95th Cong., 1st sess. (August 3, 1977), 9, 14.

178   **Retired Records Center**: Ibid., 5.

179   **Nuremberg Laws**: See Greg Bradsher, "The Nuremberg Laws: Archives Receives Original Nazi Documents That 'Legalized' Persecution of Jews," *Prologue Magazine* 42, no. 4 (Winter 2010); and Michael E. Ruane, "Huntington Library to Give Original Nuremberg Laws to National Archives," *Washington Post*, Aug. 25, 2010.

180   **"the most important public figure"**: William E. Leuchtenburg, in Robert H. Jackson, *That Man: An Insider's Portrait of Franklin D. Roosevelt*, ed. by John Q. Barrett (New York: Oxford University Press, 2003), vii. See also Jeffrey Hockett, "Justice Robert H. Jackson, The Supreme Court, and the Nuremberg Trial," *The Supreme Court Review* 1990 (1990): 257–99.

180   **"The case as presented"**: Robert Jackson, "Opening Address for the United States," in *Nazi Conspiracy & Aggression*, vol. I, chap. 7, Office of United States Chief of Counsel for Prosecution of Axis Criminality (Washington, DC: Government Printing Office, 1946). See also *Trial of the Major War Criminals before the International Military Tribunal, Nuremberg, 14 November 1945–1 October 1946* (Nuremberg, Germany: International Military Tribunal, Nuremberg, 1947–1949), 42 vols.; contains the day-to-day proceedings of the tribunal and documents offered in evidence by the prosecution and defense.

181   **"In only two or three instances"**: Robert H. Jackson, "The Significance of the Nuremberg Trials to the Armed Forces: Previously Unpublished Personal Observations by the Chief Counsel for the United States," *Military Affairs* 10, no. 4 (Winter 1946): 2–15.

181   **Jackson offered further insight**: Robert H. Jackson, in Whitney R. Harris, xxxv–xxxvi.

181   **"No well-rounded study"**: Telford Taylor, "The Nuremberg War Crimes Trials: An Appraisal," *Proceedings of the Academy of Political Science* 23, no. 3, "The United States and the Atlantic Community" (May 1949): 19–34. See also Erich Haberer, "History and Justice: Paradigms of the Prosecution of Nazi Crimes," *Holocaust and Genocide Studies* 19, no. 3 (Winter 2005): 487–519, to wit: "Unlike ordinary criminal cases, which rely exclusively on witnesses, incriminating objects, and forensic evidence, war crimes trials rely heavily on documentary evidence to prove the facts of the crime and ascertain the credibility of the testimonies. On the issue of evidence, therefore, the courts depend on the 'stuff' of history—that is, documents—and the historians who handle them" (490). See also Jeffrey D. Hockett, "Justice Robert H. Jackson, the Supreme Court, and the Nuremberg Trial," *The Supreme Court Review* 1990 (1990):

257–99: "Nuremberg documented Nazi aggressions, persecution, and atrocities, and illuminated the methods by which the Nazis obtained and held power; it provided 'the world's first post-mortem examination of a totalitarian regime'" (261).

181 **"surprising number of documents"**: Robert G. Storey, in Whitney R. Harris, xi–xii.

182 **cottage industry**: See Jeff Gottlieb, "Searching through Soviet Archives Chaotic as Rules Change on Whims," *Dallas Morning News,* March 26, 1993 (first published in *San Jose Mercury News*).

182 **Annals of Communism**: See Basbanes, *A World of Letters* (New Haven, CT: Yale University Press, 2008), 149–59.

183 **"We are witnessing"**: Lech Walesa, quoted in John-Thor Dahlburg, "Yeltsin Tells of Soviet Atrocities," *Los Angeles Times,* Oct. 15, 1992. See also Benjamin B. Fischer, "The Katyn Controversy: Stalin's Killing Field," *Studies in Intelligence* (Winter 2009–2010). Figures for those killed include identities of military officers, physicians, lawyers, engineers, teachers, and writers.

184 **"to the practice of diplomacy"**: Paul Heinbecker, "Keeping Secrets Too Safe," *The Globe and Mail* (Toronto), Dec. 7, 2010.

184 **"Top Secret America"**: Dana Priest and William M. Arkin, "Top Secret America," *Washington Post,* July 19, 20, 21, 2010, and Dec. 20, 2010.

185 **Pentagon Papers**: See David Rudenstine, *The Day the Presses Stopped: A History of the Pentagon Papers Case* (Berkeley/Los Angeles: University of California Press, 1996).

186 **"As far as I knew"**: Daniel Ellsberg, *Secrets* (New York: Penguin, 2003), 304.

186 **"You're to break into the place"**: Richard M. Nixon, quoted in "Tapes Show Nixon Ordering Theft of Files," *New York Times,* Nov. 22, 1996. For a reflection on their reporting of the scandal, see Carl Bernstein and Bob Woodward, "Woodward and Bernstein: 40 Years after Watergate, Nixon Was Far Worse Than We Thought," *Washington Post,* June 8, 2012.

187 **"similar to those confronting"**: Posner, 76.

188 **"preserved even now"**: Ibid., 93. See also Sickinger, 132, 189–90.

189 **Ottoman Archives**: For contrasting views on access, see Jeremy Salt, "The Narrative Gap in Ottoman Armenian History," *Middle Eastern Studies* 39, no. 1 (Jan. 2003): 19–36, and Bernard Lewis, quoted in Yücel Güçlü, "Will Untapped Ottoman Archives Reshape the Armenian Debate? Turkey, Present and Past," *Middle East Quarterly* 16, no. 2 (Spring 2009): 35–42.

191 **"The replacement of the warrior king"**: J. H. Elliott, *Imperial Spain, 1469–1716* (New York: St. Martin's Press, 1990), 161.

191 **"giant power set in motion"**: Honoré de Balzac,, *Bureaucracy,* Marco Diani, ed., Charles Foulkes, tr. (Evanston: Northwestern University Press, 1993): xii, 78.

192 **Charles Dickens**: "Red Tape," in *Household Words,* Feb. 15, 1851. Dickens continued his attack on bureaucratic paperwork in *Little Dorrit.*

192 **"mistily engaged"**: Charles Dickens, *Bleak House* (London: Bradbury & Evans, 1853), 2, 615.

193 **"being suffocated by files"**: Count Erich Kielmansegg, quoted in Stanley Corngold and Jack Greenberg, eds., *Franz Kafka: The Office Writings* (Princeton, NJ: Princeton University Press, 2009), 29–30.

193 **"the real hell is there"**: Franz Kafka, quoted in Jeremy D. Adler, *Franz Kafka: Illustrated Lives* (New York: Overlook, 2002), 46.

193 **Office for Administration Reform**: see www.kafka.be.

194 **"Whether it's a Senegalese"**: Ben Kafka, "The Demon of Writing: Paperwork, Public Safety, and the Reign of Terror," *Representations* 98 (Spring 2007): 1–24.

195 **"The prolixity"**: Ibid., 3.

195 **"when this emergency is over"**: Franklin D. Roosevelt, quoted in Steve Vogel, *The Pentagon: A History* (New York: Random House, 2007), 96–97.

196 **a determined bibliophile**: See Basbanes, *Patience & Fortitude,* 516–17.

196    **ten billion separate files:** Tara E. C. McLoughlin, "Ready Access: NARA's Federal Records Centers Offer Agencies Storage, Easy Use for 80 Billion Pages of Documents," *Prologue,* vol. 40, no. 1 (Spring 2008).

197    **"For a nation whose government":** H. G. Jones, 3.

199    **Florida voters:** See: Frank Cerabino, "Ten Years Later, Infamous 2000 Election Ballot Recount Still Defines Palm Beach County to Many," *Palm Beach Post,* Nov. 6, 2010; Abby Goodnough and Christopher Drew, "Florida to Shift Voting System with Paper Trail," *New York Times,* Feb. 2, 2007; Linda Kleindienst, "Voters in Florida Will Get a Paper Trail," *South Florida Sun-Sentinel,* April 29, 2007; Ian Urbina, "Ohio to Delay Destruction of Presidential Ballots," *New York Times,* Aug. 31, 2006; Thomas C. Tobin, "When Ballots Go Bad," *St. Petersburg Times,* Oct. 5, 2008.

## 10. METAMORPHOSIS

201    **"For a culture":** Malcolm Byrne, quoted in Douglas Heingartner, "Picking Up the Pieces," *New York Times,* July 17, 2003.

202    **the shredder:** Abbot Augustus Low of Horseshoe, New York, US Patent 929,960, issued Aug. 3, 1909.

203    **"They were working on their project":** Oliver North, quoted in David E. Rosenbaum, "Iran-Contra Hearings; North Says His Shredding Continued Despite Presence of Justice Department Aides," *New York Times,* July 10, 1987.

203    **biggest "mistake":** Dan Morgan and Walter Pincus, "Hall Testifies of Necessity 'To Go Above Written Law,'" *Washington Post,* June 10, 1987.

203    **Arthur Andersen LLP:** The convictions were later vacated by the U.S. Supreme Court on grounds that the presiding judge had issued vague instructions to the jury.

203    **Sarbanes-Oxley Act:** See Douglas Heingartner, "Back Together Again," *New York Times,* July 17, 2003.

204    **"horror files":** Stephen Kinzer, "East Germans Face Their Accusers," *New York Times,* April 12, 1992.

205    **the ePuzzler:** See Andrew Curry, "Piecing Together the Dark Legacy of East Germany's Secret Police," *Wired,* Jan. 18, 2008; Kate Connolly, " 'Puzzlers' Reassemble Shredded Stasi Files, Bit by Bit," *Los Angeles Times,* Nov. 1, 2009; Chris Bowlby, "Stasi Files: The World's Biggest Jigsaw Puzzle," *BBC News Magazine,* Sept. 13, 2012. See also http://www.ipk.fraunhofer.de/en/pr.

207    **"With more secrets":** James Bamford, *Body of Secrets: Anatomy of the Ultra-Secret National Security Agency* (New York: Doubleday, 2001), 516.

207    **"When they get down to work":** Kahn, 724–25. This continued reliance on paper in sophisticated workplaces is by no means unique to National Security Agency code breakers, as Abigail J. Sellen, a cognitive psychologist, and Richard H. R. Harper, a social scientist, assert in *The Myth of the Paperless Office* (Cambridge, MA: MIT Press, 2002), a scholarly study that demonstrates how paper has persisted in such high-tech workplaces as air-traffic control rooms and how paper was "found to play an important role in what might best be described as thinking and planning activities, and in the organization of reports" (63). For a further discussion of their findings, see Malcolm Gladwell, "The Social Life of Paper," *The New Yorker,* March 25, 2002, 92–96.

209    **Zhang Yin:** See David Barboza, "Blazing a Paper Trail in China: A Self-Made Billionaire Wrote Her Ticket on Recycled Cardboard," *New York Times,* Jan. 16, 2007.

210    **Marcal Manufacturing LLC:** In July 2009, Randall Suliga was appointed president and chief operating officer of National Golden Tissue, a start-up manufacturer of recycled paper products based in Hagerstown, Maryland.

211    **"He looked at New York City":** Joan Verdon, "No Pulp Fiction: Color This Company Green: Turning Waste Paper into New Products at Marcal," *The Record* (Bergen County, NJ), May 19, 2002.

## II. FACE VALUE

215 **not worth the paper:** There are variants of the expression, one that uses *written* as the verb, another *printed*.

216 **"So the printing presses ran":** Adam Smith, 58.

217 **using reichsmarks to wallpaper:** For more on creative uses of Weimar banknotes, see John Willett, *The Weimar Years* (London: Thames & Hudson, 1984).

217 **five hundred quintillion:** Niall Ferguson, 105. See also William Guttman, *The Great Inflation: Germany 1919* (London: Gordon & Cremonesi, 1976), 23. The relative scarcity today of Weimar notes is such that the prominent manuscript dealer Kenneth Rendell keeps a formidable stash of them under protective glass in one of the displays he has assembled in his private museum of World War II artifacts and documents, in Natick, Massachusetts.

217 **"a waggon load of money":** George Washington to John Jay, April 23, 1779, in *The Writings of George Washington from the Original Manuscripts* (Washington, DC: Government Printing Office, 1936), vol. 14, 435–37. For an excellent overview of currency in the American colonies and the early republic, see O. Glenn Saxon, "Commodity and Paper Dollars 1619–1792," *The Analysts Journal* 9, no. 2 (May 1953): 35–40.

218 **"The price of toilet paper":** Michael Wines, "How Bad Is Inflation in Zimbabwe?," *New York Times,* May 2, 2006.

218 **"but Robert Mugabe's misrule":** Sebastien Berger, "Zimbabwe to Cut Ten Zeros from Banknotes in Fight Against Inflation," *The Telegraph* (London), July 30, 2008.

220 *Beijing Evening News:* For a commentary on the 1.2-million-circulation newspaper, including its sale by street vendors to scrap merchants, see Michael Meyer, *The Last Days of Old Beijing: Life in the Vanishing Backstreets of a City* (New York: Bloomsbury, 2008), 82–87.

220 **commitments known as IOUs:** During a critical cash crisis in 2009, the state of California issued to taxpayers, vendors, and local governments what it called "registered warrants" in lieu of checks—government-sanctioned IOUs that the state treasurer called "an embarrassment."

220 **International Star Registry:** See http://www.starregistry.com.

220 **"You could call it a fraud":** Swarthmore College astronomer Wulff Heintz, quoted in Frederic Golden and Philip Faflic, "Stellar Idea or Cosmic Scam?," *Time,* Jan. 11, 1982. See also Patrick Di Justo, "Buy a Star, But It's Not Yours," *Wired,* Dec. 26, 2001.

222 **"He fooled me":** Charles Hamilton, quoted in Robert Lindsey, "Dealer in Mormon Fraud Called a Master Forger," *New York Times,* Feb. 11, 1987. For more on Hofmann, see Nicolas Barker, "The Forger of Printed Documents," in Robin Myers and Michael Harris, eds., *Fakes & Frauds* (Winchester, UK: St. Paul's Bibliographies, 1989), 109–23.

223 **Hofmann admitted:** For excerpts from the interview with Mark Hofmann, see Gilreath, 230–367; see also Lindsey, *A Gathering of Saints,* 369.

223 **Whistler:** Otto H. Bacher, *With Whistler in Venice* (New York: Century, 1909), 128–29.

224 **"a very advanced and sophisticated":** Greg Rohan, president of Heritage Auction Galleries, quoted in "Art Collector Pays $2.3M for $1,000 Bill from 1890," *USA Today,* Dec. 12, 2006.

224 **T206 Honus Wagner:** See Dave Jamieson, *Mint Condition: How Baseball Cards Became an American Obsession* (New York: Atlantic Monthly Press, 2010); Josh Wilker, *Cardboard Gods: An All-American Tale Told Through Baseball Cards* (New York: Seven Footer Press, 2010).

225 **"small stamped detached labels":** Sir Rowland Hill and George Kirkbeck Norman Hill, *The Life of Sir Rowland Hill and the History of Penny Postage,* vol. 1 (London: Thomas de la Rue Co., 1880), 346–47.

225 **the comic book:** See Michael Cavna, "Batman, Superman Comic Books Set Records for Sale Price," *Washington Post,* Feb. 27, 2010; Associated Press, "Superman's Debut

1938 Comic Sells for a Record $1.5 million," *Daily News* (New York), March 30, 2010; Andy Lewis, "Nicolas Cage's Superman Comic Nets Record $2.1 Million at Auction," *Hollywood Reporter,* Nov. 30, 2011.

226 **Bruce Kovner:** See Daniel J. Wakin, "Juilliard Receives Music Manuscript Collection," *New York Times,* March 1, 2006; James R. Oestreich, "For Sale: Beethoven's Scribbles on the Ninth," *New York Times,* April 7, 2003; Maev Kennedy, "Beethoven's Ninth Manuscript Could Fetch £3m," *The Guardian* (London), April 8, 2003. Kovner directed that the archive not bear his name, and that it be called the Juilliard Manuscript Collection. See http://www.juilliardmanuscriptcollection.org for a complete catalog of the holdings.

226 **A speech Abraham Lincoln delivered:** Christie's sale 2263, Lot 51, Feb. 12, 2009; price realized, $3.4 million.

226 **letter written by George Washington:** Christie's sale 2227, Lot 257, Dec. 4, 2009. See Michael E. Ruane, "1787 Washington Letter Sells for $3.2 Million," *Washington Post,* Dec. 5, 2009.

226 **Casanova:** In November 2011, the Bibliothèque Nationale mounted a three-month exhibition of the diary. See Elaine Sciolino, "Saluting a Serial Seducer and His Steamy Tell-All," *New York Times,* Nov. 28, 2011. Catalog of the exhibit: Chantal Thomas and Marie-Laure Prévost with Corinne Le Bitouzé and Frédéric Manfrin, *Casanova, La Passion de la Liberté* (Paris: Bibliothèque Nationale de France/Seuil, 2011).

227 **Raphael:** Christie's sale 7782, Lot 43, London, December 8, 2009. See Adam Gabbatt, "Rembrandt and Raphael Works Sell for Record £49m," *The Guardian* (London), Dec. 9, 2009. For full provenance and description, see Christie's Sale Catalog 7782, *Old Master & 19th Century Paintings, Drawings & Watercolours Evening Sale,* London, Dec. 8, 2009, Lot. 43. Four years later, another Raphael drawing on paper, "Head of a Young Apostle" (c. 1519–20), sold for £29.7 million ($47.8 million) at a sale in London, leading one observer to calculate that the purchase price worked out to £200,000 per square inch. See Sotheby's sale catalogue *Old Master & British Paintings Evening Sale Including Three Renaissance Masterworks from Chatsworth* (L12036), Dec. 5, 2012, Lot 52.

227 **specially formulated paper:** See Reese V. Jenkins, *Images and Enterprise: Technology and the American Photographic Industry 1839–1925* (Baltimore: Johns Hopkins University Press, 1975); Kit Funderburk, *History of the Papermills at Kodak Park* (Rochester, NY: privately printed, 2006), which incorporates accounts of papermaking at Eastman Kodak Co., written by John M. Shepherd in 1919, Gerould T. Lane in 1932 and 1946, and Wesley W. Bills in 1976; and Kit Funderburk, *Kodak Fiber Based Black and White Papers* (Rochester, NY: privately printed, 2007).

227 **Edward Steichen's:** Roger Tooth, "At $2.9m, Pond-Moonlight Becomes World's Most Expensive Photograph," *The Guardian,* Feb. 14, 2006.

227 **John Grossman:** See http://www.johngrossmancollection.com; also http://www.winterthur.org.

230 **"I'm sure if an American institution":** Tom Kelly, "Rare Copy of the U.S. Declaration of Independence Found Gathering Dust in Britain's National Archive," *Daily Mail,* July 2, 2009.

231 **"This is an incredibly exciting find":** *The Guardian,* July 2, 2009.

231 **"the urgency which prevailed":** Goff, 10.

232 **"this holy bond of our union":** Thomas Jefferson, letter to Dr. John Mease; Sept. 26, 1825, in Paul Leicester Ford, ed. *The Writings of Thomas Jefferson,* vol. 10 (New York: G. P. Putnam's, 1899), 346; see also Julian P. Boyd, "The Declaration of Independence: The Mystery of the Lost Original," *The Pennsylvania Magazine of History and Biography,* vol. 100, no. 4 (Oct. 1976): 438–67.257.

232 **antiquarian book and document collecting:** See http://www.museumofworldwarii.com. For a selective catalog of Rendell's holdings, with many facsimile reproductions, see Kenneth W. Rendell, *World War II: Saving the Reality, A Collector's Vault* (Atlanta: Whitman Publishing Co., 2009). The late A. S. W. Rosenbach of Phila-

delphia, by acclamation the outstanding bookseller of the twentieth century, also converted his private book-and-manuscript collection into a library and museum. See Basbanes, *A Gentle Madness,* chap. 4, and http://www.rosenbach.org.

## 12. ON PAPER

234 **"I am willing even":** Jeremy Belknap, quoted in *Collections of the Massachusetts Historical Society,* vol. 2, 5th series (Boston: Massachusetts Historical Society, 1877), 178.

234 **"readers will find":** Alexis de Tocqueville, *Tocqueville: Democracy in America* (New York: Library of America, 2004), 849.

234 **"American Plutarch":** Noah Webster, quoted in Sidney Kaplan, "The History of New-Hampshire: Jeremy Belknap as Literary Craftsman," in *The William and Mary Quarterly,* 3rd Series, vol. 21, no. 1 (Jan. 1964): 19.

235 **"not to lie waiting":** Jeremy Belknap to Ebenezer Hazard, Aug. 21, 1795, American Historical Association, *Writings on American History,* vol. 1 (Washington, DC: Smithsonian Institution Press, 1913), 258.

235 **"the fullest account":** Stephen T. Riley, "Manuscripts in the Massachusetts Historical Society," *Proceedings of the Massachusetts Historical Society,* 3rd Series, vol. 92 (1980): 100–116.

239 **"This set of texts":** Richard S. Dunn, "John Winthrop Writes His Journal," *The William and Mary Quarterly,* 3rd Series, vol. 41, no. 2 (April 1984): 186–212.

239 **adventure to the New World:** Ibid., 190.

240 **"Of its kind, the collection":** L. H. Butterfield, "The Papers of the Adams Family: Some Account of Their History," *Proceedings of the Massachusetts Historical Society,* 3rd Series, vol. 71 (Oct. 1953–May 1957): 328–56.

241 **"like the race of a man":** John Quincy Adams, journal entry, March 25, 1844, in Charles Francis Adams, ed., *Memoirs of John Quincy Adams,* vol. 11 (Philadelphia: J. B. Lippincott, 1876), 542.

245 **Folger Shakespeare Library:** Toward the end of her life, Emily Jordan Folger said that the original plan of the library itself was to serve as an architectural equivalent of the First Folio. See Owen and Lazzuri.

246 **"according to the true original copies":** In his will, Shakespeare left memorial gifts for Heminge and Condell—evidence, some have suggested, that he had entrusted publication of his plays to them.

246 **Paul G. Allen:** Christie's sale 9878, Lot 100, New York, October, 8–9, 2001, "The Library of Abel E. Berland." See also Peter W. M. Blayney, *The First Folio of Shakespeare* (Washington, DC: Folger Shakespeare Library, 1991).

247 **Abel E. Berland:** See Basbanes, *Patience & Fortitude,* 155–62.

247 **"The True Text of Shakespeare":** Owen and Lazzuri, 51.

247 **Stephen Enniss:** In April 2013, the University of Texas at Austin announced the appointment of Enniss to succeed Thomas F. Staley as director of the Harry Ransom Center (formerly known as the Humanities Research Center). The Ransom Center maintains what is arguably the preeminent repository in the world of twentieth-century literary and cultural artifacts from the United States and Europe, with collections that include 42 million manuscripts, one million rare books, five million photographs, and 100,000 works of art. For more on Harry Ransom and the explosive growth of the HRC collections in the 1960s and '70s, see Basbanes, *A Gentle Madness,* "Instant Ivy" (chap. 9).

248 **Emory University:** The Raymond Danowski Poetry Library, 75,000 volumes, acquired in 2004; see http://marbl.library.emory.edu/collection-overview/raymond-danowski-poetry-library.

249 **J. Franklin Mowery:** Also an accomplished fine-book binder, Mowery's work was featured in 1982 in a one-man exhibition at the Metropolitan Museum of Art, in New York, and he remains at the Folger as the library's rare-binding specialist.

249   **most likely from Normandy:** Blayney, 5.

250   *Trevelyon Miscellany:* The many problems the conservation team faced on this project were detailed in the introduction to a reduced facsimile edition the Folger Library published in 2007 to observe the seventy-fifth anniversary of its founding.

250   **sheets of decaying paper are split:** See Basbanes, *Splendor of Letters,* 262–65.

## 13. THINGS UNKNOWN

255   **"Of all forms of expression":** Marks, 2.

257   **"Yet how alive":** Adrian Sarle, "Leonardo da Vinci: Experience, Experiment and Design," *The Guardian,* Sept. 14, 2004. For an exhibition of Leonardo's anatomical drawings in the Queen's Gallery, Buckingham Palace, in 2012, see Clayton and Philo.

257   **"No one covered":** Kemp, *Experience, Experiment and Design,* 2–3.

258   **the "key" to grasping:** Bambach, 5.

258   **cartoons:** Ibid., 109.

259   **Codex Leicester:** When owned by the Armand Hammer Museum of Art and Culture Center, UCLA, the manuscript was known as Codex Hammer, but has since been renamed Codex Leicester by the current owner, Bill Gates, who bought it on Nov. 11, 1994, for $30,802,500, at Christie's. See *The Leonardo da Vinci Codex Hammer* (New York: Christie, Manson & Woods, Inc., 1994) for full description of the manuscript. For my account of the sale, see *A Gentle Madness,* 227–28.

259   **prolific with paper:** Bambach, 116.

260   **"never ceased drawing":** Giovani Vasari, *The Lives of the Most Excellent Painters, Sculptors, and Architects,* trans. by Gaston du C. de Vere, ed. by Philip Jacks (New York: Modern Library/Random House, 2006), 229.

260   **"No one was ever more inventive":** Kemp, *Experience, Experiment and Design,* 97.

260   **"one of the greatest visualizers":** Kemp, in Gary M. Radke, ed., *Leonardo da Vinci and the Art of Sculpture* (Atlanta: High Museum of Art, 2009), 63.

262   **"theory machines":** Kemp, *Experience, Experiment and Design,* 117.

265   **"is a universal phenomenon":** Iro Tembeck, "The Written Language of Dance or Preserving Dance on Paper," *SubStance,* no. 33/34 (1982): 66–83.

265   **"Dance has been called":** Ann Hutchinson Guest, "Dance Notation," in *Perspecta* 26 (1990): 203–14. Not until 1952 was a choreographed work—the dance sequences from *Kiss Me Kate,* by Hanya Holm—accepted for copyright protection in the United States, made possible then by the introduction of the Laban system.

269   **"conversation books":** See Alan Tyson, "Conversations with Beethoven," *The Musical Times* 111, no. 1523 (Jan. 1970): 25–28.

270   **"He was never to be seen":** Ignaz von Seyfried, quoted in Barry Cooper, *Beethoven and the Creative Process* (Oxford, UK: Oxford University Press, 1992), 7.

270   **professional copyists:** See Alan Tyson, "Notes on Five of Beethoven's Copyists," *Journal of the American Musicological Society* 23, no. 3 (Autumn 1970): 439–71.

271   **Thomas Edison National Historical Park:** TENHP is one of three National Park Service properties with substantial collections of manuscripts and archives; others include the home of the poet Henry Wadsworth Longfellow, in Cambridge, Massachusetts, and the house of master garden architect Frederick Law Olmsted, in the Boston suburb of Brookline.

274   **the Edison Papers:** See Kathleen McAuliffe, "The Undiscovered World of Thomas Edison," *The Atlantic,* December 1995.

## 14. THE DRAWING BOARD

277   **"I cannot so well set it forth":** Guido da Vigevano, *Texaurus Regis Francie* (1335); quoted in Eugene S. Ferguson.

277   **"Nor did he rest until":** Giovani Vasari, *The Lives of the Most Excellent Painters,*

*Sculptors, and Architects,* trans. by Gaston du C. de Vere, ed. by Philip Jacks (New York: Modern Library/Random House, 2006), 113.

277 **"Now regard this pure":** Frank Lloyd Wright, *An Autobiography* (Petaluma, CA: Pomegranate Publishers, 1943), 156.

277 **"The Creator created paper":** Alvar Aalto, *Sketches* (Cambridge, MA: MIT Press, 1978), 104.

277 **"Do not disturb my circles":** Archimedes, in Livy (Titus Livius), *The History of Rome* (XXV, 31). In *An Introduction to Mathematics* (London: Williams & Norgate, 1911), Alfred North Whitehead cited the murder of Archimedes as "symbolical of a world-change of the first magnitude: the Greeks, with their love of abstract science, were superseded in the leadership of the European world by the practical Romans," and added this: "The Romans were a great race, but they were cursed with the sterility which waits upon practicality. They did not improve upon the knowledge of their forefathers, and all their advances were confined to the minor technical details of engineering. They were not dreamers enough to arrive at new points of view, which could give a more fundamental control over the forces of nature. No Roman lost his life because he was absorbed in the contemplation of a mathematical diagram" (40–41).

279 **"a pretty large compass":** "Alexander," in A. L. Clough, ed., *Plutarch's Lives: The Translation Called Dryden's,* vol. 4 (Boston: Little Brown, 1863), 192.

279 **Jacques Carrey:** For reproductions of the sketches and a history of their making, see Theodore Robert Bowie, *The Carrey Drawings of the Parthenon Marbles* (Bloomington: Indiana University Press, 1971). For an examination of procedures likely used to build the temple, see Manolis Korres, *The Stones of the Parthenon* (Los Angeles: J. Paul Getty Museum, 2000).

280 **Sir William Dugdale:** See *Dictionary of National Biography.*

280 **"often and earnestly incited":** Full facsimile of William Dugdale, *The History of St. Pauls Cathedral in London from Its Foundation Untill These Times Extracted out of Originall Charters, Records, Leiger Books, and Other Manuscripts: Beautified with Sundry Prospects of the Church, Figures of Tombes and Monuments* (London: Thomas Warren, 1658), available on Early English Books Online (EEBO).

282 **"paper revolution":** See Gerbino and Johnston, 31–44.

282 **"resolved not by erasing":** Ibid., 24.

282 **Baghdad:** See Amenn Ghazarian and Robert Ousterhout, "A Muqarnas Drawing from Thirteenth-Century Armenia and the Use of Architectural Drawings During the Middle Ages," *Muqarnas: An Annual on the Visual Culture of the Islamic World* 18 (2001): 141–54.

283 **"Before a thing is made":** Eugene S. Ferguson, 3.

284 **the Great Exhibition:** The Crystal Palace was also the first major installation of public toilets; during the run of the exhibition, 827,280 visitors paid one penny to use them.

285 **Filippo Brunelleschi:** See Prager and Scaglia; and Ross King, *Brunelleschi's Dome: How a Renaissance Genius Reinvented Architecture* (New York: Walker & Co., 2000).

286 **"capture fleeting ideas on paper":** Eugene S. Ferguson, 96–97.

286 **"show designers how their ideas":** Ibid., 5. The phrase "mind's eye" has been invoked often over the centuries, most famously by Shakespeare, when Hamlet cites it as the location for where he had just seen the ghost of his murdered father.

289 **"The drawings are intricate":** Doron Swade, *The Difference Engine: Charles Babbage and the Quest to Build the First Computer* (New York: Viking, 2000), 221–51; above quotes, 227 and 238. See also Anthony Hyman, *Charles Babbage: Pioneer of the Computer* (Princeton, NJ: Princeton University Press, 1982).

289 **"When each process":** Charles Babbage, *On the Economy of Machinery and Manufactures,* 3rd ed., vol. 2 (London: Carey & Lea, 1833), 174–75.

291 **the blueprint:** See Jeffrey S. Murray, "Blueprinting in the History of Cartography,"

*The Cartographic Journal* 46, no. 3 (Aug. 2009): 257–61; and Mike Ware, *Cyanotype: The History, Science and Art of Photographic Printing in Prussian Blue* (London: Science Museum and National Museum of Photography, Film & Television, 1999).

291 **"We despise the French"**: An unnamed engineer on von Braun's team, speaking immediately after the war, quoted by Neufeld, 258.

292 **"These documents were"**: Dr. Dieter K. Huzel, quoted in Frederick I. Ordway III and Mitchell R. Sharpe, *The Rocket Team* (New York: Crowell, 1979), 261; see also Gardner Soule, "History's Wildest Game of Hide and Seek," *Popular Science,* Dec. 1962, 67–69. The original mineshaft papers were returned to Germany in 1959 and are now split between Deutsches Museum, Munich, and the Bundesarchiv/ Militärarchiv, Freiburg. A collection on microfilm is held by the National Air and Space Museum Archives, at the Steven F. Udvar-Hazy Center, in Chantilly, Virginia (Neufeld, 333). The program to relocate the rocket scientists to the United States was fraught with complications. The 118 scientists finally chosen were represented by a stack of carefully paper-clipped documents, giving the top-secret undertaking the code name Operation Paperclip. In an e-mail exchange with me, Michael Neufeld, curator of the early rocketry collection for the National Air and Space Museum and author of *The Rocket and the Reich,* stressed that "paper alone was not sufficient" to the American space program and that the "technology transfer involved in German rocket technology was greatly aided by having people from the program who could make the documents understandable, plus technology in the form of concrete objects. The naïve view of blueprints is often the expectation that you could simply convert them into devices. In reality, you need help to translate that kind of information into useful information, especially in another linguistic and engineering culture."

293 **surreptitious introduction of technology**: See David J. Jeremy, "Damming the Flood: British Government Efforts to Check the Outflow of Technicians and Machinery, 1780–1843," *The Business History Review* 51, no. 1 (Spring 1977): 1–34.

293 **Francis Cabot Lowell**: See Robert F. Dalzell Jr., *Enterprising Elite: The Boston Associates and the World They Made* (Cambridge, MA: Harvard University Press, 1987), notably chap. 1, "Yankee Abroad: Francis Cabot Lowell in Scotland." See also Robert B. Gordon and Patrick M. Malone, *The Texture of Industry: An Archaeological View of the Industrialization of North America* (New York: Oxford University Press, 1997).

293 **"fully acquainted"**: Charles C. P. Moody, *Biographical Sketches of the Moody Family* (Boston, S. G. Drake, 1847), 145–57. See also John N. Ingham, *Biographical Dictionary of American Business Leaders,* vol. 2 (Westport, CT: Greenwood Publishing Co., 1983), 951–53.

295 **Charles Dickens**: For more on his visit to Lowell, see Charles Dickens, *American Notes for General Circulation,* vol. 1 (London: Chapman & Hall, 1842), 145–65.

295 **Locks and Canals**: See Nathan Appleton, *Introduction of the Power Loom and Origin of Lowell* (Lowell, MA: B. H. Penhallow, 1858).

296 **James B. Francis**: See Patrick M. Malone, *Waterpower in Lowell: Engineering and Industry in Nineteenth-Century America* (Baltimore: Johns Hopkins University Press, 2009); and Theodore Steinberg, *Nature Incorporated: Industrialization and the Waters of New England* (Amherst: University of Massachusetts Press, 1991).

296 **Whatman paper**: See Balston; for the paper's use specifically by J. M. W. Turner (1775–1851), see Bower, *Turner's Papers* and *Turner's Later Papers.* Benjamin Franklin's purchase of Whatman paper during the war with England is detailed by Ellen R. Cohn in Talbott, 254–55.

## 15. SLEIGHT OF HAND

298 **"In the days before the cabaret"**: Harry Houdini, *Houdini's Paper Magic: The Whole Art of Performing with Paper, Including Paper Tearing, Paper Folding, and Paper Puzzles* (New York: E. P. Dutton, 1922), 117.

298   **"One of my dreams"**: Akira Yoshizawa, quoted in Engel, 36.

298   **"Anything is possible"**: Robert J. Lang, e-mail to author, Oct. 23, 2011. The general
      context of our running exchange on origami included a brief discussion of the pro-
      posal made in 2008 by a professor at Tokyo University's Department of Aeronautics
      and Astronautics to make a number of paper airplanes, and release them from an
      American Space Shuttle while in orbit with the hope one might survive reentry and
      return to earth intact. The idea was seriously considered, but never attempted. I
      asked Lang, a laser physicist with extensive expertise in aeronautics, what he thought
      of the idea. "It's a neat concept," he replied. "The idea is sound: if you make some-
      thing small and light enough, then upon reentry, the compression heating is low
      enough that the object can survive." For more on the science that supported the
      proposal, see Anna Davison, "Origami Spaceplane Aims for Space Station Descent,"
      *New Scientist,* Jan. 21, 2008. On Feb. 26, 2012, and much closer to earth, a paper air-
      plane was thrown a world-record-setting 226 feet and 10 inches by Joe Ayoob, a for-
      mer college quarterback who had logged more than 1,700 passing yards in one season
      while playing football for the University of California, Berkeley. See John Letzing,
      "Paper Plane Champ Watches His Record Fly, Fly Away," *Wall Street Journal,* May
      17, 2012. On Feb. 24, 2013, the Walt Disney Animation Studios' *Paperman* won an
      Academy Award for best animated short film. The six-minute romance employed as
      a narrative device the flight of paper airplanes through the concrete canyons of New
      York City.

299   **Claire Van Vliet:** See Ruth Fine, *The Janus Press, Fifty Years: Catalogue Raisonné for
      1991–2005, Indexes for 1955–2005* (Burlington: University of Vermont Libraries, 2006).

299   **Walter Hamady:** See Walter Hamady, *Papermaking by Hand: A Book of Suspicions*
      (Perry Township, Dane County, WI: Perishable Press, 1982).

300   **"A leaf of a book":** Nicholson Baker, 157. For more on what Baker called his "library
      activism," see Basbanes, *Patience & Fortitude,* 392–402, and *Splendor of Letters,*
      224–28.

301   **"Try to make something":** Hannes Beckmann, "Formative Years," in Eckhard
      Neumann, ed., *Bauhaus and Bauhaus People* (New York: Van Nostrand Reinhold,
      1970), 196.

302   **"If a sick person":** Eleanor Coerr, *Sadako and the Thousand Paper Cranes* (New York:
      G. P. Putnam's Sons, 1977), 36. Recent editions include illustrated directions for
      making paper cranes.

302   **Michael G. LaFosse:** See http://www.origamido.com.

303   **Akira Yoshizawa:** For a profile of the master folder, see Engel, 33–40.

307   **Robert J. Lang:** Susan Orlean, "The Origami Lab: Why a Physicist Dropped Every-
      thing for Paper Folding," *The New Yorker,* Feb. 19, 2007; Beth Jensen, "Into the Fold:
      Physicist Robert Lang Has Taken the Ancient Art of Origami to New Dimensions,"
      *Smithsonian,* June 2007. For his website, see: http://www.langorigami.com.

312   **Erik Demaine:** See http://erikdemaine.org.

### 16.  IN THE MOLD

317   **"The machine age":** Hunter, *My Life with Paper,* 3.

317   **"Had the choice of place":** Ibid.

319   **"I saw for the first time":** Ibid., 51–52.

319   **Jew's Creek:** The waterway got its name from having been the site where Luis Moses
      Gomez (1660–1740), a Sephardic Jewish immigrant from Spain, established a fur
      trading post in 1714. The blockhouse he built of fieldstone is operated today as
      Gomez Mill House, a museum, and is recognized by the National Register of His-
      toric Places as being the oldest Jewish dwelling still standing in North America. See
      www.gomez.org.

319   **"I used no tools":** Letter from Dard Hunter to Ruel Pardee Tolman at the Smithso-

nian Institution, Sept. 17, 1921, quoted in Helena E. Wright, "Dard Hunter at the Smithsonian," *Printing History,* 28, Journal of the American Printing History Association, vol. 14, no. 2 (1992).

320    **"stands as a symbol":** Will Ransom, *Private Presses and Their Books* (New York: Philip C. Duschness, 1929), 113.

320    **"I would not go through all this again":** Dard Hunter, quoted in Cathleen Baker, *By His Own Labor,* 139. The few Old Lyme sheets that remained were later used as one-page inserts in his 1958 memoir, *My Life with Paper.*

321    **Henry Morris:** See Howell J. Heaney and Henry Morris, *Thirty Years of Bird & Bull: A Bibliography, 1958–1988* (Newtown, PA: Bird & Bull Press, 1988); Sidney E. Berger and Henry Morris, *Forty-four Years of Bird & Bull: A Bibliography, 1958–2002* (Newtown, PA: Bird & Bull Press, 2002).

322    **Ellen Shaffer:** See Basbanes, *A Gentle Madness,* 455–57.

327    **Tatyana Grosman:** See Calvin Tomkins, "The Art World: Tatyana Grosman," *The New Yorker,* Aug. 9, 1982, 82; and Riva Castleman, *Tatyana Grosman: A Scrapbook* (Bay Shore, NY: Universal Limited Art Editions, 2008). See also http://www.ulae .com.

327    **June Wayne:** See Garo Z. Antreasian and Clinton Adams, *The Tamarind Book of Lithography: Art & Techniques* (Los Angeles: Tamarind Lithography Workshop, 1971); and Marjorie Devon, Bill Lagattuta, and Rodney Hamon, *Tamarind Techniques for Fine Art Lithography* (New York: Harry N. Abrams, 2009). See also http://tamarind .unm.edu.

## 17. AT THE CROSSROADS

333    **240,000 jobs lost:** In 2000, according to the Pulp and Paper Products Council (PPPC), based in Montreal, there were 604,700 workers employed in the production of pulp and paper in the United States, 96,909 in Canada; by 2010, those figures were 396,818 and 60,638, respectively, accounting for reductions in the workforces of 207,882 (34 percent) and 36,273 (37 percent), respectively. U.S. figures: Bureau of Labor Statistics. Canada figures: Statistics Canada (StatCan).

334    **Verso Paper:** For more on Verso and its role in helping to rejuvenate Maine's paper industry, see Henry Garfield, "Rolling with the Changes," *Maine Ahead,* January 2011.

336    **"not just survive":** Christopher Power, "Six Score and Two Years Ago," *Forbes,* March 10, 1986.

337    **"abundant native energy":** J. G. Gibson, *History of York County, Pennsylvania* (1886), quoted in Lipper, 37. For the full family chronology and relationships, see Lipper.

344    **Yale University Press:** See Basbanes, *World of Letters.*

346    **total holdings:** Association of American Libraries (ARL) annual compilations of holdings, acquisitions, and staffing. See http://www.arl.org/stats/annualsurveys/ arlstats.

348    **"a huge library like this":** See *Report of the Task Force on University Libraries: Harvard University November 2009.* A complete list of the university's seventy-three libraries is included in an appendix. Full text: http://www.provost.harvard.edu/reports/ Library_Task_Force_Report.pdf.

348    **Archibald Cary Coolidge:** Quotations by Coolidge and Kittredge are in Basbanes, *Patience & Fortitude,* 475–76.

349    **"Books belong to economics":** Jennifer Geenstein Altmann, "Books Reveal Volumes About Times Past," *Princeton Weekly Bulletin,* March 28, 2005.

350    **"an open, distributed network":** John Palfrey, "Building a Digital Public Library of America," *Library Journal,* Nov. 26, 2012; Robert Darnton, "The National Digital Library Is Launched," *New York Review of Books,* April 25, 2013.

## 18. ELEGY IN FRAGMENTS

353 **"Au fond, le papier"**: Jacques Derrida, in an interview with Marc Guillaume and Daniel Bougnoux, «Le Papier ou moi, vous savez . . . (nouvelles spéculations sur un luxe des pauvres)», *Les Cahiers de Médiologie*, no. 4, 1997 (Paris, Gallimard). See full text at http://www.jacquesderrida.com.ar/frances/papier.htm.

353 **office paper**: According to the Deposit Trust & Clearing Corporation (DTCC), which provides custody and asset servicing for more than 3.6 million securities issues from the United States and 121 other countries valued at $36.5 trillion in 2013, the cost to replace $16 billion of paper stock certificates destroyed in the collapse of the World Trade Center towers came to about $300 million. Almost all security transactions are now recorded electronically, though the agency still maintains custody of archival paper certificates in several locations, about 1.3 million of which were severely damaged in flooding at its 55 Water St. headquarters in Lower Manhattan during Hurricane Sandy in October 2012. See Nina Mehta, "Stock, Bond Certificates Held by DTCC Damaged by Sandy Flood," Bloomberg News (www.bloomberg.com /news/), Nov. 15, 2012, and www.dtcc.com.

354 **"poetic, imagistic, and simple"**: Caryn James, "Television's Special Day of Pain and Comfort," *New York Times,* Sept. 6, 2002.

354 **"the ground itself"**: David Horrigan, "A Sea of Paper," *Law Technology News,* Oct. 2001. In the same issue, see Monica Bay, "Fiat Lux," for the reflections of his photographer.

355 **Susan Meiselas**: See http://www.susanmeiselas.com.

356 **New York State Museum**: See http://www.nysm.nysed.gov.

360 **Mickey Kross**: See Maria Janchenko, "Ground Hero," *The Globe and Mail,* Sept. 7, 2002.

360 **Pablo Ortiz**: See Kevin Flynn, "Fresh Glimpse in 9/11 Files of the Struggle for Survival," *New York Times,* Aug. 29, 2003.

361 **"It was difficult to conceive"**: John Johnson, "9/11 Items Head to Museum," *Cincinnati Enquirer,* Dec. 29, 2009. On May 6, 2013, just three weeks after two pressure-cooker bombs exploded at the finish line of the Boston Marathon killing three people and injuring 260 others—and with rain in the forecast—a team of archivists hastily gathered thousands of makeshift tributes left in Copley Square by people from around the world, and moved them to a municipal archives facility where they were to be catalogued, photographed, and shelved in acid-free folders and boxes. "While the memorial is a testament to the city's strength," Evan Allen and Andrew Ryan wrote that day in the *Boston Globe,* "it is also largely composed of paper."

### EPILOGUE

367 **United Airlines Flight 175**: See chap. 9 in *The 9/11 Commission Report: Final Report of the National Commission on Terrorist Attacks upon the United States* (Washington, DC: Executive Agency Publications, 2004); full text available at http://www.gpo.gov . See also "Flight Path Study: United Airlines Flight 175," National Transportation Safety Board, Feb. 19, 2002.

368 **Ron DiFrancesco**: See Andrew Duffy, "Tower of Pain for Canadian Who Survived 9/11: Last Man Out of the South Tower Feels Guilty About His Survival," *The Gazette* (Montreal), June 5, 2004 (first published in the *Ottawa Citizen,* June 4, 2005).

368 **Brian Clark**: See Dennis Cauchon, "Four Survived by Ignoring Words of Advice," *USA Today,* Dec. 18, 2001; Eric Lipton, "Accounts from the South Tower," *New York Times,* May 26, 2002.

369 ***Stamford Advocate***: See John Breunig, "Father's Note Changes Family's 9/11 Account," *Stamford Advocate,* Sept. 10, 2012.

# Bibliography

Ackerman, Phyllis. *Wallpaper: Its History, Design, and Use.* New York: Tudor Publishing Co., 1923.

Adams, Clinton. *American Lithographers, 1900–1960: The Artists and Their Printers.* Albuquerque: University of New Mexico Press, 1983.

Allen, Gerald, and Richard Oliver. *Architectural Drawings: The Art and the Process.* New York: Whitney Library of Design, 1981.

Ambrosini, Maria Luisa, with Mary Willis. *The Secret Archives of the Vatican.* Boston: Little Brown, 1969.

American Tobacco Company. *"Sold American": The First Fifty Years.* New York: The American Tobacco Company, 1954.

Andés, Louis E. *The Treatment of Paper for Special Purposes.* Trans. from German by Charles Salter. London: Scott, Greenwood & Son, 1907.

Baker, Cathleen A. *By His Own Labor: The Biography of Dard Hunter.* New Castle, DE: Oak Knoll Press, 2000.

———. *From the Hand to the Machine: Nineteenth-Century American Paper and Mediums: Technologies, Materials, and Conservation.* Ann Arbor, MI: The Legacy Press, 2010.

Baker, Nicholson. *Double Fold: Libraries and the Assault on Paper.* New York: Random House, 2001.

Baldassari, Anne. *Picasso: Working on Paper.* London: Merrell Publishers Ltd., 2000.

Balston, John. *The Whatmans and Wove Paper: Its Invention and Development in the West: Research into the Origins of Wove Paper and of Genuine Loom-Woven Wire-Cloth.* West Farleigh, Kent, UK: J. N. Balston, 1998 [privately printed].

Bambach, Carmen C., ed. *Leonardo da Vinci, Master Draftsman.* New York: The Metropolitan Museum of Art; New Haven and London: Yale University Press, 2003.

Barkan, Leonard. *Michelangelo: A Life on Paper.* Princeton and Oxford: Princeton University Press, 2010.

Barrett, Timothy. *Japanese Papermaking: Traditions, Tools, and Techniques.* With an appendix on alternative fibers by Winifred Lutz. New York: Weatherhill, 1983.

Basbanes, Nicholas A. *A Gentle Madness: Bibliophiles, Bibliomanes, and the Eternal Passion for Books.* New York: Henry Holt, 1995.

———. *A Splendor of Letters: The Permanence of Books in an Impermanent World.* New York: HarperCollins, 2003.

———. *A World of Letters: Yale University Press, 1908–2008.* New Haven, CT: Yale University Press, 2008.

————. *Patience & Fortitude: A Roving Chronicle of Book People, Book Places, and Book Culture.* New York: HarperCollins, 2001.

Baynes, Ken, and Francis Pugh. *The Art of the Engineer.* Woodstock, NY: The Overlook Press, 1981.

Bender, John, and Michael Marrinan. *The Culture of Diagram.* Stanford, CA: Stanford University Press, 2010.

Bennison, Amira K. *The Great Caliphs: The Golden Age of the 'Abbasid Empire.* New Haven, CT, and London: Yale University Press, 2009.

Benson, Richard. *The Printed Picture.* New York: Museum of Modern Art, 2008.

Billeter, Jean François. *The Chinese Art of Writing.* New York: Rizzoli International Publications, 1990.

Bliss, Douglas Percy. *A History of Wood Engraving.* London: Spring Books, 1964. First published 1928.

Bloom, Jonathan M. *Paper before Print: The History and Impact of Paper in the Islamic World.* New Haven, CT: Yale University Press, 2001.

Blum, André. *On the Origin of Paper.* Trans. from French by Harry Miller Lydenberg. New York: R. R. Bowker, 1934.

Bower, Peter. *Turner's Later Papers: A Study of the Manufacture, Selection and Use of His Drawing Papers 1820–1851.* London: Tate Gallery Publishing, 1999.

————. *Turner's Papers: A Study of the Manufacture, Selection and Use of His Drawing Papers, 1787–1820.* London: Tate Gallery Publishing, 1990.

Bozeman, Barry. *Bureaucracy and Red Tape.* Upper Saddle River, NJ: Prentice-Hall, 2000.

Brothers, Cammy. *Michelangelo, Drawing, and the Invention of Architecture.* New Haven, CT, and London: Yale University Press, 2008.

Browning, B. L. [Bertie Lee]. *Analysis of Paper.* New York: Marcel Dekker Inc., 1977.

Buisson, Dominique. *The Art of Japanese Paper: Masks, Lanterns, Kites, Dolls, Origami.* Trans. from French by Elizabeth MacDonald. Paris: Éditions Pierre Terrail, 1992.

Bytwerk, Randall L. Introduction in *Paper War: Nazi Propaganda in One Battle, on a Single Day, Cassino, Italy, May 11, 1944.* No author given. West New York, NJ: Mark Batty Publisher, 2005.

Carter, Thomas Francis. *The Invention of Printing in China and Its Spread Westward.* New York: Columbia University Press, 1931. First published 1925.

Churchill, W. A. *Watermarks in Paper in Holland, England, France, etc. in the XVII and XVIII Centuries and Their Interconnection.* Amsterdam: Menno Hertzberger & Co., 1935.

Clapperton, R. H. *Paper: An Historical Account of Its Making by Hand from Its Earliest Times Down to the Present Day.* Oxford, U.K.: Oxford University Press, 1934.

————. *Modern Paper-Making.* 3rd ed. Oxford, U.K.: Basil Blackwell, 1952.

————. *The Paper-Making Machine: Its Invention, Evolution and Development.* Oxford: Pergamon Press, 1967.

Clayton, Martin, and Ron Philo. *Leonardo da Vinci, Anatomist.* [London:] Royal Collection Publications, 2012.

Dalrymple, William. *The Last Mughal: The Fall of a Dynasty, Delhi, 1857.* New York: Alfred A. Knopf, 2007.

Darnton, Robert. *The Case for Books: Past, Present, and Future.* New York: PublicAffairs Press, 2009.

David, Saul. *The Indian Mutiny.* New York: Viking Press, 2002.

Davies, Glyn. *History of Money: From Ancient Times to the Present Day.* Cardiff, UK: University of Wales Press, 2002.

Décultot, Elisabeth, ed., with Gabriele Bickendorf and Valentin Kockel. *Musées de Papier: L'Antiquité en Livres, 1600–1800.* Paris: Gourcuff Gradenigo/Musée du Louvre, 2010.

Dodge, Charles Richard. *A Descriptive Catalogue of Useful Fiber Plants of the World, Including the Structural and Economic Classifications of Fibers.* Washington, DC: Government Printing Office, 1897.

Dugan, Frances L. S., and Jacqueline P. Bull, eds. *Bluegrass Craftsman: Being the Remi-*

*niscences of Ebenezer Hiram Stedman Papermaker 1808–1885.* Frankfort, KY: Frankfort Heritage Press, 2006.

du Toit, Brian M. *Ecusta and the Legacy of Harry H. Straus.* Baltimore: PublishAmerica, 2007.

Engel, Peter. *Folding Universe: Origami from Angelfish to Zen.* New York: Vintage Press, 1989.

Entwistle, E. A. *The Book of Wallpaper: A History and an Appreciation.* London: Arthur Barker, 1954.

Evans, Joan. *The Endless Webb: John Dickinson & Co., Ltd. 1804–1954.* Westport, CT: Greenwood Publishing Co., 1978. Reprint of 1955 edition published by Jonathan Cape, Ltd., London.

Farnsworth, Donald. *A Guide to Japanese Papermaking.* Oakland, CA: Magnolia Editions, 1997.

Ferguson, Eugene S. *Engineering and the Mind's Eye.* Cambridge, MA: MIT Press, 1992.

Ferguson, Niall. *The Ascent of Money: A Financial History of the World.* New York: Penguin, 2008.

Field, Dorothy. *Paper and Threshold: The Paradox of Spiritual Connection in Asian Cultures.* Ann Arbor, MI: The Legacy Press, 2007.

Fox, Celina. *The Arts of Industry in the Age of Enlightenment.* New Haven, CT, and London: Yale University Press, 2010.

Freely, John. *Aladdin's Lamp: How Greek Science Came to Europe through the Islamic World.* New York: Alfred A. Knopf, 2009.

Gardner, Howard. *Creating Minds: An Anatomy of Creativity Seen through the Lives of Freud, Einstein, Picasso, Stravinsky, Eliot, Graham, and Gandhi.* New York: Basic Books, 1993.

Gerbino, Anthony, and Stephen Johnston. *Compass and Rule: Architecture as Mathematical Practice in England.* New Haven, CT, and London: Yale University Press, 2009.

Gillispie, Charles Coulston. *The Montgolfier Brothers and the Invention of Aviation.* Princeton, NJ: Princeton University Press, 1983.

Gilreath, James, ed. *The Judgment of Experts: Essays and Documents about the Investigation of the Forging of the "Oath of a Freeman."* Worcester, MA: American Antiquarian Society, 1991.

Gipson, Lawrence Henry. *The Coming of the Revolution: 1763–1775.* New York: Harper & Row, 1962.

Glaser, Lynn. *America on Paper: The First Hundred Years.* Philadelphia: Associated Antiquaries, 1989.

Glassner, Jean-Jacques. *The Invention of Cuneiform: Writing in Sumer.* Trans. and ed. by Zainab Bahrani and Marc Van De Mieroop. Baltimore: The Johns Hopkins University Press, 2003.

Goff, Frederick R. *The John Dunlap Broadside: The First Printing of the Declaration of Independence.* Washington, DC: Library of Congress, 1976.

Green, James N. *The Rittenhouse Mill and the Beginnings of Papermaking in America.* Philadelphia: Library Company of Philadelphia and Friends of Historic Rittenhouse Town, 1990.

Green, James N., and Peter Stallybrass. *Benjamin Franklin: Writer and Printer.* New Castle, DE: Oak Knoll Press; London: British Library, 2006.

Greysmith, Brenda. *Wallpaper.* London: Studio Vista/Casell & Collier Macmillan, 1976.

Griffin, Russell B., and Arthur D. Little. *The Chemistry of Paper-Making: Together with the Principles of General Chemistry; A Handbook for the Student and Manufacturer.* New York: Howard Lockwood & Co., 1894.

Groebner, Valentin. *Who Are You? Identification, Deception, and Surveillance in Early Modern Europe.* Trans. from German by Mark Kyburz and John Peck. New York: Zone Books, 2007.

Haggith, Mandy. *Paper Trails: From Trees to Trash—The True Cost of Paper.* London: Virgin Books/Random House, 2008.

Handcock, Percy S. P. *Mesopotamian Archaeology.* London: Macmillan and Co. Ltd. and Philip Lee Warner, 1912.

Harris, Theresa Fairbanks, and Scott Wilcox. *Papermaking and the Art of Watercolor in Eighteenth-Century Britain: Paul Sandby and the Whatman Paper Mill.* Essays and contributions by Stephen Daniels, Michael Fuller, and Maureen Green. New Haven, CT: Yale Center for British Art; London: Yale University Press, 2006.

Harris, Whitney R. *Tyranny on Trial: The Trial of the Major German War Criminals at the End of World War II at Nuremberg, Germany, 1945–1946,* rev. ed. Dallas: Southern Methodist University Press, 1999.

Haskell, W. E. *News Print: The Origin of Paper Making and the Manufacturing of News Print.* New York: International Paper Company, 1921.

Hawes, Arthur B. *Rifle Ammunition: Being Notes on the Manufactures Connected Therewith, as Conducted in the Royal Arsenal, Woolwich.* London: W. O. Mitchell, 1859. Reprinted by Thomas Publications, Gettysburg, PA, 2004.

Heinrich, Thomas, and Bob Batchelor. *Kotex, Kleenex, Huggies: Kimberly-Clark and the Consumer Revolution in American Business.* Columbus: The Ohio State University Press, 2004.

Helfand, Jessica. *Scrapbooks: An American History.* New Haven, CT: Yale University Press, 2008.

Henderson, Kathryn. *On Line and On Paper: Visual Representations, Visual Culture, and Computer Graphics in Design Engineering.* Cambridge, MA, and London: MIT Press, 1999.

Herring, Richard. *Paper and Paper Making, Ancient and Modern,* 3rd ed. London: Longman, Green, Longman, Roberts & Green, 1863.

Hess, Earl J. *The Rifle Musket in Civil War Combat: Reality and Myth.* Lawrence: University Press of Kansas, 2008.

Hibbert, Christopher. *The Great Mutiny: India 1857.* New York: The Viking Press, 1978.

Hidy, Ralph H., Frank Ernest Hill, and Allan Nevins. *Timber and Men: The Weyerhaeuser Story.* New York: Macmillan, 1963.

Hills, Richard L. *Papermaking in Britain 1488–1988.* London and Atlantic Highlands, NJ: The Athlone Press, 1988.

Hoffman, Adina, and Peter Cole. *Sacred Trash: The Lost and Found World of the Cairo Geniza.* New York: Shocken, 2011.

Hofmann, Carl. *A Practical Treatise on the Manufacture of Paper in All Its Branches.* Philadelphia: Henry Carey Baird, 1873.

Hogg, Oliver Frederick Gillilan. *The Royal Arsenal: Its Background, Origin, and Subsequent History.* 2 vols. London: Oxford University Press, 1963.

Holcomb, Melanie, ed. *Pen and Parchment: Drawing in the Middle Ages.* New York/New Haven, CT: Metropolitan Museum of Art; London: Yale University Press, 2009.

Hughes, Sukey. *Washi: The World of Japanese Paper.* Tokyo and New York: Kodansha International, 1978.

Hull, Matthew S. *Government of Paper: The Materiality of Bureaucracy in Urban Pakistan.* Berkeley and Los Angeles: University of California Press, 2012.

Hunter, Dard. *My Life with Paper: An Autobiography.* New York: Alfred A. Knopf, 1958.

———. *Papermaking in Pioneer America.* Philadelphia: University of Pennsylvania Press, 1952.

———. *Papermaking: The History and Technique of an Ancient Craft,* 2nd ed., rev. and enlarged. New York: Alfred A. Knopf, 1947. First published 1944.

———. *Papermaking through Eighteen Centuries.* New York: William Edwin Rudge, 1930.

Isaacson, Walter. *Benjamin Franklin: An American Life.* New York: Simon & Schuster, 2003.

Jackson, Paul. *The Encyclopedia of Origami and Papercraft Techniques.* Philadelphia: Running Press, 1991.

Jamieson, Dave. *Mint Condition: How Baseball Cards Became an American Obsession.* New York: Atlantic Monthly Press, 2010.

Jay, Robert. *The Trade Card in Nineteenth-Century America.* Columbia: University of Missouri Press, 1987.

Johnson, Douglas, Alan Tyson, and Robert Winter. *The Beethoven Sketchbooks: History, Reconstruction, Inventory.* Berkeley and Los Angeles: University of California Press, 1985.

John-Steiner, Vera. *Notebooks of the Mind: Explorations of Thinking.* Albuquerque: University of New Mexico Press, 1985.

Jones, H. G. *The Records of a Nation: Their Management, Preservation, and Use.* New York: Atheneum, 1969.

Kahn, David. *The Code-Breakers: The Comprehensive History of Secret Communication from Ancient Times to the Internet,* rev. and updated. New York: Scribner, 1996. First published 1967.

Kafka, Ben. *The Demon of Writing: Powers and Failures of Paperwork.* New York: Zone Books, 2012.

Karabacek, Joseph von. *Arab Paper.* Trans. by Don Baker and Suzy Dittmar, additional notes by Don Baker. London: Archetype Publications, 2001.

Kaufman, Herbert. *Red Tape: Its Origins, Uses and Abuses.* Washington, DC: The Brookings Institution, 1977.

Kemp, Martin. *Leonardo.* Oxford and New York: Oxford University Press, 2004.

———. *Leonardo da Vinci: Experience, Experiment and Design.* Princeton, NJ: Princeton University Press, 2006.

———. *Leonardo da Vinci: The Marvellous Works of Nature and Man.* Cambridge, MA: Harvard University Press, 1981.

Klein, Richard. *Cigarettes Are Sublime.* Durham, NC: Duke University Press, 1993.

Kluger, Richard. *Ashes to Ashes: America's Hundred-Year Cigarette War, the Public Health, and Unabashed Triumph of Philip Morris.* New York: Alfred A. Knopf, 1996.

Kobayashi, Makoto. *Echizen Washi: The History and Technique of the Ancient Japanese Craft of Papermaking with Stories of Great Handmade Paper Makers.* Fukui-ken, Japan: Imadate Cultural Association, 1981.

Koops, Matthias. *Historical Account of the Substances Which Have Been Used to Describe Events and to Convey Ideas, from the Earliest Date, to the Invention of Paper.* London: T. Burton, 1800.

Koretsky, Elaine. *Killing Green: An Account of Hand Papermaking in China.* Ann Arbor, MI: Legacy Press, 2009.

Kostof, Spiro. *A History of Architecture.* Ed. Greg Castillo, illustrations by Richard Tobias. New York and Oxford: Oxford University Press, 1995.

Krill, John. *English Artists' Paper: Renaissance to Regency.* London: Trefoil Publications Ltd., 1987.

Labarre, E. J. *Dictionary and Encyclopaedia of Paper and Paper-Making with Equivalents of the Technical Terms in French, German, Dutch, Italian, Spanish and Swedish.* London and Toronto: Oxford University Press, 1952.

Laird, Mark, and Alicia Weisberg-Roberts. *Mrs. Delaney and Her Circle.* New Haven, CT: Yale University Press, 2009.

Lancaster, F. W. *Toward Paperless Information Systems.* New York: Academic Press, 1978.

Lehmann-Haupt, Hellmut, with Lawrence C. Wroth and Rollo G. Silver. *The Book in America: A History of the Making and Selling of Books in the United States,* 2nd ed., rev. and enlarged. New York: R. R. Bowker, 1951.

Lindsey, Robert. *A Gathering of Saints: A True Story of Money, Murder, and Deceit.* New York: Simon & Schuster, 1988.

Lipper, Mark. *Paper, People, Progress: The Story of the P. H. Glatfelter Company of Spring Grove, Pennsylvania.* Englewood Cliffs, NJ: Prentice-Hall, 1980.

Lloyd, Martin. *The Passport: The History of Man's Most Travelled Document.* Stroud, Gloucestershire, UK: Sutton Publishing Ltd., 2003.

Lloyd, Seton. *Foundations in the Dust: The Story of Mesopotamian Exploration,* rev. and enlarged. New York: Thames and Hudson, 1980.

Lovell, Stanley P. *Of Spies & Stratagems.* Englewood Cliffs, NJ: Prentice-Hall, 1963.

Macfarlane, Alan, and Gerry Martin. *Glass: A World History.* Chicago: University of Chicago Press, 2002.

Maddox, H. A. *Paper: Its History, Sources, and Manufacture.* London: Sir Isaac Pitman & Sons Ltd., [1916].

Malkin, Lawrence. *Krueger's Men: The Secret Nazi Counterfeit Plot and the Prisoners of Block 19.* New York: Little, Brown, 2006.

Marks, Leo. *Between Silk and Cyanide: A Codemaker's War, 1941–1945.* New York: The Free Press, 1998.

Massey, Mary Elizabeth. *Ersatz in the Confederacy: Shortages and Substitutes on the Southern Homefront.* Columbia: University of South Carolina Press, 1952.

Mayor, A. Hyatt. *Prints and People: A Social History of Printed Pictures.* New York: Metropolitan Museum of Art, 1971.

McGaw, Judith A. *Most Wonderful Machine: Mechanization and Social Change in Berkshire Paper Making, 1801–1885.* Princeton, NJ: Princeton University Press, 1987.

McWilliams, Mary, and David J. Roxburgh. *Traces of the Calligrapher: Islamic Calligraphy in Practice, c. 1600–1900.* Houston: The Museum of Fine Arts, 2007.

Mendez, Antonio J., and Matt Baglio. *Argo: How the CIA and Hollywood Pulled Off the Most Audacious Rescue in History.* New York: Viking Penguin, 2012.

Mendez, Antonio J., with Malcolm McConnell. *The Master of Disguise: My Secret Life in the CIA.* New York: William Morrow, 1999.

Mihm, Stephen. *A Nation of Counterfeiters: Capitalists, Con Men, and the Making of the United States.* Cambridge, MA: Harvard University Press, 2007.

Mikesh, Robert C. *Japan's World War II Balloon Bomb Attacks on North America.* Washington, DC: Smithsonian Institution Press, 1973.

Montagu, Ewen. *The Man Who Never Was: World War II's Boldest Counterintelligence Operation.* Annapolis, MD: Naval Institute Press, 2001. First published 1953 by Oxford University Press, New York.

Morgan, Edmund S., and Helen M. Morgan. *The Stamp Act: Prologue to Revolution.* Chapel Hill: University of North Carolina Press, 1953. Published for the Institute of Early American History and Culture, Williamsburg, VA.

Munsell, Joel. *Chronology of the Origin and Progress of Paper and Paper-Making,* 5th ed., with additions. Albany, NY: J. Munsell, 1876.

Myers, Robin, and Michael Harris, eds. *Fakes and Frauds: Varieties of Deception in Print and Manuscript.* Winchester, UK: St. Paul's Bibliographies; New Castle, DE: Oak Knoll Press, 1989.

Narita, Kiyofusa. *Japanese Paper-Making.* Tokyo: Hokuseido Press, 1954.

Needham, Joseph, with Ho Ping-Yü, Lu Gwei-Djen, and Wang Ling. *Science and Civilisation in China.* Vol. 5, part 7: *Military Technology; The Gunpowder Epic.* Cambridge, UK: Cambridge University Press, 1986.

———. *Science and Civilisation in China.* Vol. 5, part 1: *Paper and Printing.* By Tsien Tsuen-Hsuin. Cambridge, UK: Cambridge University Press, 1985.

Neufeld, Michael J. *The Rocket and the Reich: Peenemünde and the Coming of the Ballistic Missile Era.* Cambridge, MA: Harvard University Press, 1995.

Ogborn, Miles. *Indian Ink: Script and Print in the Making of the English East India Company.* Chicago: University of Chicago Press, 2008.

Oswald, John Clyde. *Printing in the Americas.* New York: Gregg Publishing Co., 1937.

*The Paper Maker.* Wilmington, DE: Hercules Powder Co., 1932–1970.

Parkinson, Richard, and Stephen Quirke. *Papyrus.* London: British Museum Press, 1995.

Pauly, Roger. *Firearms: The Life Story of a Technology.* Westport, CT: Greenwood Press, 2004.

Pedersen, Johannes. *The Arabic Book.* Trans. from Danish by Geoffrey French, ed. with introduction by Robert Hillenbrand. Princeton, NJ: Princeton University Press, 1984.

Pettegree, Andrew. *The Book in the Renaissance*. New Haven, CT, and London: Yale University Press, 2010.

Pierce, Wadsworth R. *The First 175 Years of Crane Papermaking*. [Dalton, MA]: Crane, [1977].

Pollard, Hugh B. C. *Pollard's History of Firearms*. Ed. Claude Blair. Feltham, UK: Country Life Books, 1983.

Polo, Marco. *The Travels of Marco Polo*. Trans. with an introduction by Ronald Latham. New York: Abaris Books, 1982.

Posner, Ernst. *Archives in the Ancient World*. Cambridge, MA: Harvard University Press, 1972.

Prager, Frank D., and Gustina Scaglia. *Brunelleschi: Studies of His Technology and Inventions*. Mineola, NY: Dover Publications. First published 1970 by MIT Press, Cambridge, MA.

Price, Lois Olcott. *Line, Shade, and Shadow: The Fabrication and Preservation of Architectural Drawings*. New Castle, DE: Oak Knoll Press; Winterthur, DE: Winterthur Museum & Country Estate, 2010.

Proudfoot, W. B. *The Origin of Stencil Duplicating*. London: Hutchinson & Co., 1972.

Radkau, Joachim. *Wood: A History*. Trans. from German by Patrick Camiller. Cambridge, UK: Polity Press, 2012.

Rendell, Kenneth W. *Forging History: The Detection of Fake Letters and Documents*. Norman: University of Oklahoma Press, 1994.

Roseman, Will. *The Strathmore Century: The 100th Anniversary Issue of the Strathmorean*. Westfield, MA: Strathmore Paper, 1992.

Rosenband, Leonard N. *Papermaking in Eighteenth-Century France: Management, Labor, and Revolution at the Montgolfier Mill, 1761–1805*. Baltimore: The Johns Hopkins University Press, 2000.

Rudin, Max. *Making Paper: A Look into the History of an Ancient Craft*. Trans. from Swedish by Robert G. Tanner. Vällingby, Sweden: Rudins, 1990.

Rumball-Petre, Edwin A. R. *America's First Bibles: With a Census of 555 Extant Bibles*. Portland, ME: The Southworth-Anthoensen Press, 1940.

Schaaf, Larry J. *Out of the Shadows: Herschel, Talbot, and the Invention of Photography*. New Haven and London: Yale University Press, 1992.

Schlesinger, Arthur M. *Prelude to Independence: The Newspaper War on Britain 1764–1776*. New York: Alfred A. Knopf, 1958.

Schlosser, Leonard B., ed. *Paper in Printing History: A Celebration of Milestones in the Graphic Arts*. Designed by Bradbury Thompson. New York: Lindenmeyr Paper Corp., 1981.

Schreyer, Alice. *East-West: Hand Papermaking Traditions and Innovations*. Newark: University of Delaware Library, 1998.

Schweidler, Max. *The Restoration of Engravings, Drawings, Books, and Other Works on Paper*. Translated from German and ed. by Roy Perkinson. Los Angeles: The Getty Conservation Institute, 2006.

Sellen, Abigail J., and Richard H. Harper. *The Myth of the Paperless Office*. Cambridge, MA: MIT Press, 2002.

Sickinger, James P. *Public Records and Archives in Classical Athens*. Chapel Hill: The University of North Carolina Press, 1999.

Sider, David. *The Library of the Villa dei Papiri at Herculaneum*. Los Angeles: Getty Publications, 2005.

Smith, Adam [George J. W. Goodman]. *Paper Money*. New York: Summit Books, 1981.

Soteriou, Alexandra. *Gift of Conquerors: Hand Papermaking in India*. Middletown, NJ: Grantha Corporation; Ahmedabad, India: Mapin Publishing Pvt. Ltd., 1999.

Spector, Robert, and William W. Wicks. *Shared Values: A History of Kimberly-Clark*. Lyme, CT: Greenwich Publishing Group, 1997.

Spicer, A. Dykes. *The Paper Trade: A Descriptive and Historical Survey of the Paper Trade from the Commencement of the Nineteenth Century*. London: Methuen, 1907.

Standish, David. *The Art of Money: The History and Design of Paper Currency from Around the World*. San Francisco: Chronicle Books, 2000.

Staubach, Suzanne. *Clay: The History and Evolution of Humankind's Relationship with Earth's Most Primal Element*. New York: Berkley Books, 2005.

Stuart, Sir Campbell, K.B.E. *Secrets of Crewe House: The Story of a Famous Campaign*. London: Hodder and Stoughton, 1920.

Swasy, Alecia. *Soap Opera: The Inside Story of Procter & Gamble*. New York: Times Books, 1993.

Talbott, Page, ed. *Benjamin Franklin: In Search of a Better World*. New Haven, CT, and London: Yale University Press, 2005.

Taylor, Philip M. *Munitions of the Mind: War Propaganda from the Ancient World to the Nuclear Age*. Willingborough, Northamptonshire, UK: Patrick Stephens Ltd., 1990.

Thomas, Isaiah. *The History of Printing in America, with a Biography of Printers,* 2nd ed. 2 vols. New York: Burt Franklin, 1874.

Thomas, James E., and Dean S. Thomas. *A Handbook of Civil War Bullets and Cartridges*. Gettysburg, PA: Thomas Publications, 1996.

Thomas, P. D. G. *British Politics and the Stamp Act Crisis: The First Phase of the American Revolution, 1763–1767*. Oxford, U.K.: Oxford University Press, 1975.

Thompson, Claudia G. *Recycled Papers: The Essential Guide*. Cambridge, MA: The MIT Press, 1992.

Tsuen-Hsuin, Tsien. *Written on Bamboo and Silk: The Beginnings of Chinese Books and Inscriptions*. Chicago: The University of Chicago Press, 1962.

Tyrrell, Arthur. *Basics of Reprography*. London: Focal Press, 1972.

Van Kampen, Kimberly, and Paul Saenger, eds. *The Bible as Book: The First Printed Editions*. New Castle, DE: Oak Knoll Press; London: The British Library, 1999.

Von Hagen, Victor Wolfgang. *The Aztec and Maya Papermakers*. New York: J. J. Augustin, 1944.

Voss, Julia. *Darwin's Pictures: Views of Evolutionary Theory, 1837–1874*. New Haven, CT, and London: Yale University Press, 2010.

Wagner, Susan. *Cigarette Country: Tobacco in American History and Politics*. New York: Praeger Publishers, 1971.

Weeks, Lyman Horace. *A History of Paper-Manufacturing in the United States, 1690–1916*. New York: The Lockwood Trade Journal Company, 1916.

White, Lynn, Jr. *Medieval Technology and Social Change*. Oxford, UK: Oxford University Press, 1967.

Whitfield, Roderick, Susan Whitfield, and Neville Agnew. *Cave Temples of Mogao: Art and History on the Silk Road*. Los Angeles: The Getty Conservation Institute and the J. Paul Getty Museum, 2000.

Wilkinson, Norman B. *Papermaking in America*. Greenville, DE: The Hagley Museum, 1875.

Willcox, Joseph. *The Willcox Paper Mill (Ivy Mills): 1729–1866*. Philadelphia: American Catholic Historical Society, 1897.

Williams, Owen, and Caryn Lazzuri, eds. *Foliomania! Stories Behind Shakespeare's Most Important Book*. Washington, DC: Folger Shakespeare Library, 2011.

Wiswall, Clarence A., with Eleanor Boit Crafts. *One Hundred Years of Paper Making: A History of the Industry on the Charles River at Newton Lower Falls, Massachusetts*. Reading, MA: Reading Chronicle Press, 1938.

Wood, Frances, and Mark Bernard. *The Diamond Sutra: The Story of the World's Earliest Dated Printed Book*. London: The British Library, 2010.

Wroth, Lawrence C. *The Colonial Printer*. New York: The Grolier Club, 1931.

Zhang, Wei. *The Four Treasures: Inside the Scholar's Studio*. San Francisco: Long River Press, 2004.

# Index

Page numbers in *italics* refer to illustrations.